THE TOURIST BUSINESS

THE TOURIST BUSINESS

DONALD E. LUNDBERG, PH. D.
Chairman, Department of
Hotel and Restaurant Management
School of Business Administration
California State Polytechnic University, Pomona

SECOND EDITION

Jule Wilkinson, Editor

CAHNERS BOOKS
A Division of Cahners Publishing Company, Inc.
89 Franklin Street, Boston, Mass. 02110
Publishers of Institutions/Volume Feeding Magazine

ISBN 0-8436-0579-0 (Cloth)
ISBN 0-8436-0592-8 (Paper)

Library of Congress Catalog Card No. 77-161432

Printed in the United States of America

TABLE OF CONTENTS

ILLUSTRATIONS, CHARTS, MAPS

TABLES

ACKNOWLEDGEMENTS

I am deeply indebted to a number of people for their help in making suggestions and providing materials for the book. Dr. Edward M. Barnet, Professor Louis J. Crampon, and Dr. Charles Metelka of the School of Travel Industry Management at the University of Hawaii were especially helpful in allowing me to sit in on some of their lectures, in discussing some of the points made and in referring me to source materials. Professor Crampon was an active critic. Other persons among many who provided materials or ideas include Arthur Averbook of the Ministry of Tourism, the Bahamas; Eric Greene, of Harris, Kerr, Forster and Co.; Thomas Sandor and R. W. Lee of Peat, Marwick and Mitchell; C. P. Austin, Director of Visitor Services, U. S. Travel Service; Arnold C. Rigby of Arnold Tours; Sanford I. Gadient and Mark Cockrell of Pacific Area Management Consultants; Warren Dillon of the Department of Commerce and Industry of the Commonwealth of Massachusetts, and Bulent I. Kastarlak, travel consultant.

In writing the revision of this book a number of people were especially kind and helpful, including William B. Tabler, Richard L. Erb, and William E. Gilbert. Information on trendlines which will affect the hospitality industry was drawn from symposia lead by Arnold Brown, Edith Weiner, Walter Matthews, George P. Hinckley and Gemma Baker. A number of officers of State Tourist Departments were generous with time and information concerning developments in state tourism offices and the growth of state operated tourist facilities. Of course, no book such as this could be written without drawing upon the ideas and research of a number of people.

Special thanks go to those secretaries par excellence, Helen, Nancy, Yuki and Ruth.

Errors and omissions, of course, are my own responsibility which hopefully will be corrected in future editions.

Donald E. Lundberg

THE TOURIST BUSINESS

INTRODUCTION

The economic and social importance of travel and tourism is only now becoming recognized, and well it might. Considered to be the largest single item in international trade, travel and tourism represents a world wide activity valued in excess of $100 billion. Estimates of its economic importance vary widely because of the unreliability and lack of traveler statistics and expenditures. Definitions of travelers and tourists also vary widely and each year the travel picture changes markedly.

A 1971 estimate for world travel expenditures exceeded $124 billion broken down as follows:[1]

$12.12 billion from international tourists
7.2 billion for international transport
48.00 billion for domestic tourism
57.00 billion for domestic transportation
Total $124.32 billion

Expenditures for travel within the U. S. (domestic travel) totaled $61[2] billion and a large scale study of U. S. tourism projected that figure to reach $127 billion by 1980. The same study found that 2.3 million persons were employed in this country in tourism related enterprises.[3]

Travel and tourism can be defined to include the hospitality field—hotels, motels, resorts, restaurants, rental cars and camping. It can be extended to those businesses which serve travelers and vacationers—sporting goods, gasoline stations, vacation photography. Even suntan lotion, sun glasses, and sport clothes. The chart on page 2 suggests some of these aspects of travel and tourism. Destination development including marinas, condominiums, parks and shops is a giant business in itself. (The statistics are for the U. S. only).

Considering its dimension, the student almost immediately recognizes that comprehension of the dynamics of the burgeoning tourist business requires an inter-disciplinary approach. It becomes clear that an understanding of tourism depends on relating to it pertinent developments in economics, business, ecology, government, law, psychology, sociology and even anthropology. Because tourism is so responsive to a variety of developments, statistics must be constantly re-evaluated and updated.

An understanding of the development and promotion of tourist areas involves feasibility studies, analysis of economic and sociological impacts, financing, marketing and promotion. Governments play a large part in these activities.

The travel modes—especially the airplane, automobile and railroad—are aspects of tourism.

In the 1960's, the broad field of travel increasingly became integrated by individual companies. Today, one company may own travel agencies, an airline, hotels, tour service and rent-a-cars. Resort development nowadays is usually a part of land development. What, a few years ago, were individual fields of endeavor are now seen as one.

The unifying theme running through much of leisure-time activity is travel. People move from their residences to a destination and back again. The purpose of the trip may be pleasure, necessity or business. En route, travelers are accommodated in motels, on ships, railroads, at campsites and in other facilities. The travel mode, usually the auto, bus, plane, train or ship, is part of the travel experience. At the destination, the traveler is housed, fed, toured, educated, entertained. The unifying concept of the

[1]Henry O. Barbour. *Tourism and the Advent of International Hotel-keeping.* (Statler Lectures, University of Massachusetts, 1971).
[2]U. S. Travel Service, 1974.
[3]National Tourism Resources Commission; 1973, Washington, D. C., 1973.

THE SCOPE OF THE TOURIST BUSINESS

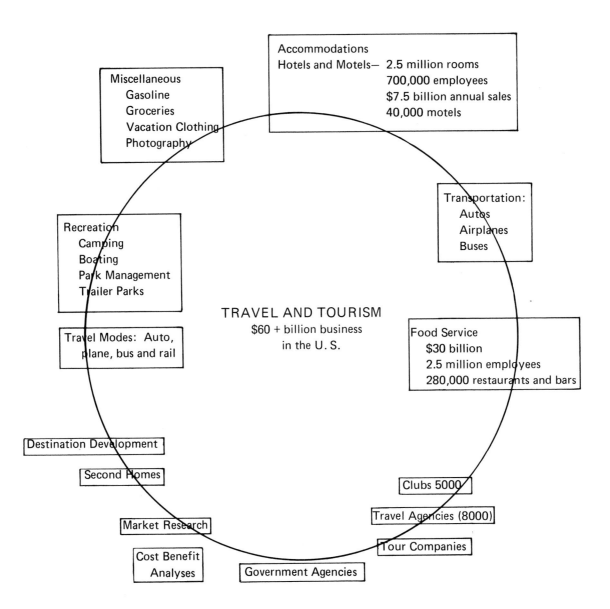

Accommodations
Hotels and Motels— 2.5 million rooms
700,000 employees
$7.5 billion annual sales
40,000 motels

Miscellaneous
Gasoline
Groceries
Vacation Clothing
Photography

Transportation:
Autos
Airplanes
Buses

Recreation
Camping
Boating
Park Management
Trailer Parks

Travel Modes: Auto,
plane, bus and rail

TRAVEL AND TOURISM
$60 + billion business
in the U. S.

Food Service
$30 billion
2.5 million employees
280,000 restaurants and bars

Destination Development

Second Homes

Clubs 5000

Travel Agencies (8000)

Market Research

Tour Companies

Cost Benefit
Analyses

Government Agencies

experience is travel. The people who offer products and services to facilitate this travel are in the travel business. They are, in part, travel managers.

International travel exceeds the $20 billion mark as a desirable "invisible and smokeless export." According to the International Union of Official Travel Organizations (IUOTO), there were 200 million international tourist arrivals in 1972. Some $24 billion was expended by these travelers between countries.[1]

Travel is the largest "export item" for a number of countries, including the United Kingdom, Spain, Italy, Mexico and Ireland.

Income from tourism must be viewed against income from other exports to see the relative importance of tourism to a destination. It will be repeated in this book that tourist statistics are more suggestive than real, in that methodology and definition play such a large part in determining the figures that are collected on tourism. The chart below shows tourism receipts in millions of U. S. dollars for ten leading destination nations for the year 1970. The chart also shows the number of millions of dollars spent by each government concerned in promoting tourism.[2]

Country	Tourism Receipts*	Gov't. Tourism Promotion*
U. S. A.	$1,770.0	$1.4
Italy	1,476.0	3.0
Spain	1,179.0	3.0
France	954.0	3.8
Canada	920.0	5.2
Germany	911.0	1.7
Austria	687.0	1.7
U. K.	678.0	7.2
Switzerland	592.0	2.7
Netherlands	342.0	1.5

Source: U. S. Travel Service

*in millions of U. S. dollars

INTERNATIONAL TOURIST RECEIPTS 1971-1972[1]
in millions of U. S. dollars

Region [2]	1972 [3] estimated
Africa [4]	560
Americas [5]	5,600
Europe	16,200
Middle East	370
Pacific and East Asia	1,280
South Asia	180
World total	U.S.$24.2

Rounded figures

Notes:

(1) At current (i.e. non-deflated) prices.

(2) The six regions are delineated according to the membership of the respective IUOTO Regional Commissions, as at January 1973 with the addition of South Africa.

(3) *Provisional* estimates in millions of U. S. dollars made by the IUOTO Secretariat General, Geneva, and based on the 9-month statistical returns of the world's national tourist offices.

(4) The figures for Africa constitute a new series.

(5) A change in the basis of recording travel payments of Canadian nationals and visitors to Canada has made accurate comparison of 1971 with 1972 difficult. The 1972 figure is, therefore, an estimate incorporating a large error component.

The figures above are impressive but for the North American must be compared with domestic travel expenditures for perspective. Eight states in the U. S. each have reported tourist expenditures in excess of $1 billion for a given year.[3] California and Florida tourism offices each report tourism expenditures of about $5 billion a year in their states.

Islands like Bermuda, The Virgin Islands, and the Bahamas depend almost en-

[1]IUOTO, *Technical Bulletin* (Geneva, Switzerland: Feb., 1973). (The IUOTO was established in 1934 to represent national tourist offices and promote world travel. It has consultative status to the United Nations. Headquarters are at Montbrillant, Geneva.)

[2]U. S. Travel Service, *Service World International,* August, 1971.

[3]Business Research Division, *Travel Trends in the United States and Canada.* (Boulder: University of Colorado, 1973).

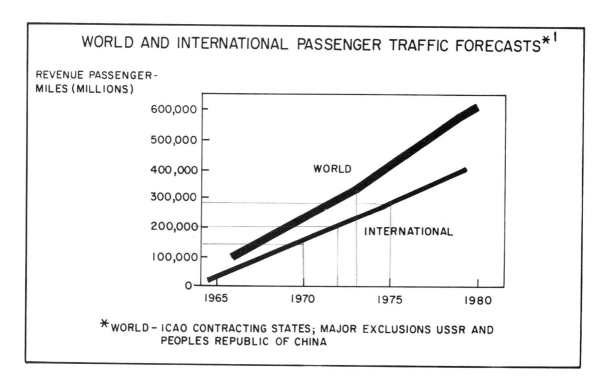

WORLD AND INTERNATIONAL PASSENGER TRAFFIC FORECASTS*[1]

REVENUE PASSENGER-
MILES (MILLIONS)

*WORLD – ICAO CONTRACTING STATES; MAJOR EXCLUSIONS USSR AND
PEOPLES REPUBLIC OF CHINA

tirely on tourism for their income. The Bahamas take in $250 million a year from tourists, more than $1300 for each resident. Per capita income from tourism in Bermuda and the Bahamas exceeds $1200 a year. This is a larger amount than total per capita income in any Latin-American country. Per capita income for the U. S. Virgin Islands, mostly from tourism, reaches almost $3000. Many of the less developed nations look to international tourism as the major means of balancing trade deficits and stimulating their economies.

Tourism may represent a relatively small percent of the total economic activity of a country or area yet be of major importance to the economy. Tourism in Switzerland, for example, accounts for only 8.4 percent of the total Swiss national income. Income from foreign tourists in 1970 was 3.125 billion francs. This "invisible export," however, covered up to 85 percent of the deficit experienced by the country in its trade balance, the difference between imports and exports.[2]

Tourism is growing rapidly throughout the world and at almost double the rate of world income growth. During the past 20 years, while world exports showed an annual growth rate of 7.7 percent, world tourism grew at a 12 percent average rate, or tenfold.

According to the Lockheed Aircraft Corporation, world scheduled air traffic as reported by the International Civil Aviation Organization (excludes USSR and the Republic of China), will increase at an average annual rate of 10.6 percent between 1970 and 1980. Non-scheduled passenger traffic will grow at an annual rate of 15 percent during the same period.[3] One big reason: only about 3 percent of the world's population has ever traveled by plane. The graph above shows the world and international passenger traffic forecast, as made by Lockheed, projected to the year 1980.

The Boeing Company predicts a threefold increase in North Atlantic travel between 1970 and 1980.[4] One of the slower rates of growth will be U. S. domestic trav-

[1]*Service World International,* May, 1968.
[2]Swiss National Tourist Office, 1971 (Report).
[3]George N. Sarames, "World Air Demand: 1950-1980," *Journal of Travel and Research* (Spring, 1973).
[4]The Boeing Company, *The North American Travel Market in a New Decade* (Renton, Wash.: The Boeing Company, 1971).

el, for the very good reason that the base is so high initially.

Disposable income, income left after personal taxes, is a key to travel growth. Disposable per capita income in the U. S. in 1963 was $2138; by 1971, it had increased to $3595. The median family income in the U. S. had increased to $10,285 by 1971. Factors such as education, age and lifestyle affect travel but the number one consideration remains whether or not people have the wherewithal to travel if they so desire.

Travel Before Modern Times

Travel, as we know it today, is distinctly a twentieth century phenomenon. More precisely, travel in this country has been largely shaped by the automobile; international travel by the jet plane.

To be sure, travel for trade and for religious purposes dates back to antiquity. Caravans moved through the middle East and the early Phoenicians "toured" the Mediterranean as traders. War forced travel upon soldier and noncombatant alike. Nomads moved about in search of pasture for their animals. Gypsies moved from habit and as a means of finding jobs.

Certainly, there were pleasure travelers before 1800, but not many. The ancient Romans, both the rich and government officials, could travel throughout the empire on good roads. By employing relays of horses, distances of 100 miles or more a day could be covered on the main roads.

Romans traveled to Egypt and Greece, to baths, shrines and seaside resorts.[1] Testimony to their vacation habits are the excavated towns of Herculaneum and Pompeii, buried for centuries by lava, hot mud and volcanic ash from the eruption of nearby Mt. Vesuvius. Tabernas, snack bars and restaurants still stand partly intact for the tourist of today to view.

Roman tourists were interested in history and religion, making the rounds of Greek temples, trekking to where Alexander the Great slept, Socrates lived, where Ajax committed suicide, where Achilles was buried. Romans, believe it or not, visited Egypt to see the Pyramids, the Sphinx and the Valley of the Kings as do modern tourists. Tourist attractions there were too. Up in the hills some priests had taught their sacred crocodiles to come when called and on command to open their jaws and show their teeth to the crowd.[2] The tourists then also griped about the inns and the guides and scratched their names on statues.

During the Medieval Period travel came almost to a standstill. Travel, coming from the word travail, was indeed burdensome, unpredictably dangerous and demanding. Most of society was bound to the soil, immobile, parochial. Travel for pleasure was inconceivable for most.

Religious travel there was. Religious persuasion has motivated millions to travel— Moslems to Mecca, Christians to Jerusalem and Rome, other millions to lesser shrines. Chaucer's Canterbury Tales concern travel to the Cathedral of Canterbury in the 14th century. Fear and guilt have motivated much of such travel but the sense of excitement and adventure, the desire to break out of the routines of life color the religious feelings with the mundane.

With the Renaissance, a few prestigious universities developed and "education for travel" was introduced, largely by the British. A few scholars went off to Oxford, Paris, Salamanca or Bologna. Travel for education became the "in-thing" beginning in the 16th century. The young aristocracy as well as members of the rising middle class took to the continent to round out their education, and perhaps sin a little. What, by 1670, was known as the Grand Tour was no light undertaking, sometimes lasting up to three years. Its snob appeal must have been great.

Travel for health became important about the same time. At first, only those with bona fide illness went to the spas, named after a small Belgian village, to drink or bathe in the horrible smelling waters. By the 1750's, taking the waters (really, in many cases, to "dry out") became a social necessity.

---

[1] Lickorish and Kershaw, *Travel Trade* (London: Practical Press, 1958) p. 21 and "A Short History of Tourism," *Travel and Tourism Encyclopedia* (London: Travel World, 1959) p. 29.
[2] Lionel Casson, "After 2000 Years Tours Have Changed but Tourists Have Not," *Smithsonian,* Washington, D. C., Sept., 1971.

Tunbridge Wells in Kent (not far from London) gained importance in the 1660's. Charles II transferred his court there from time to time.

In the reign of Queen Anne, ladies and gentlemen were carried to the bath in sedan chairs and with the greatest of decorum immersed themselves in the healing (?) waters.[1]

Entertainment was added and dozens of watering spots became, in effect, resort hotels. Bath in England, Baden Baden in Germany, Baden in Austria, Baines-les-Bains in France, Lucca in Italy, Karlsbad and Marienbad in Bohemia, and dozens of other springs were fashionable in the 18th and 19th centuries. In the United States, White Sulphur Springs, French Lick Springs and Saratoga Springs were resorts of renown, built around the idea of drinking or bathing in mineral waters for their alleged medical benefit. Packaged laxatives are more convenient today.

The spas are not dead; they live on in Russia today and in Europe. Nowhere is the "health vacation" more widely practiced or taken more seriously than in the Soviet Union. There are special spas for heart conditions, others for tuberculosis, but most are designed to resuscitate the work-weary. Upon the recommendation of a doctor, the worker is assigned to a resort where he embarks upon a therapeutic program of mineral baths, mud packs, daily walks and body building. Switzerland, Germany and France have a number of spas. Switzerland, for example, has 109 spa hotels and high altitude sanitoria with almost 10,000 beds.

An indication of how fashions in vacationing can quickly change came early, even before the word "tourist" was coined. About 1750, the English spas lost their favored position when sea water suddenly became popular and "medicinal." Scarborough and Margate changed into seaside resorts. At first, the sick came to be healed; pleasure seekers followed. Brighton, a small fishing village in England, in 1760 became the most famous of them all. How and why? Simple. Where the elite go, the mass-class market follows.

The Duke of Gloucester came to Brighton in 1765. Later in 1783, the Prince of Wales began his famous Pavilion, a Chinese pleasure house, there. By 1800, Brighton was the most fashionable resort in Europe.

Today, the Prince's Pavilion is open to the public, but few royalty or other elite are to be seen. They have long since deserted Brighton for other, more exclusive spots. Vacationing at the seashore in Britain, however, was a well-established custom, so much so that, by 1963, three-quarters of the 31-million holidays taken within Britain were spent at the seaside.

Travel, as we know it today, could not have developed without a middle class and without relatively inexpensive transportation. The industrial revolution in Britain and the U. S. made possible the development of a large middle class; the railroad brought rapid, relatively cheap transportation. Outings, excursions by rail and boat, could be taken by hundreds of thousands in the U. S. and Europe. The summer resort became an American institution in the late 19th and early 20th century. Switzerland was "discovered" by the English, before 1860, later by the Germans. According to reliable estimates, there were more hotel beds and as many visitors to Switzerland just prior to World War I as there are now.[2]

The automobile in the first few decades of the 20th century changed our society, giving it a mobility never before dreamed of. Then the airplane—the most glamorous mode of transportation of all—came into its own in the fifties.

Tourists were first recognized by that name in England in the 19th century. Today, tourists are defined as "people traveling for pleasure or business, and staying away from home at least overnight."[3]

---

[1]James Laver, *The Age of Illusion* (New York: David McKay Co., 1972) pp. 48-49.
[2]Swiss Embassy release.
[3]Tourists are defined differently by various researchers. Convention-goers are sometimes included, sometimes not. An example of differences in definition: studies for the State of Florida restrict the term "tourist" to persons from out of state and those who are staying overnight for purposes of recreation or vacationing; a 1970 study of tourism in Massachusetts defined the "tourist" as any person on a pleasure, business or vacation trip traveling outside of his normal commuting radius. A Bureau of Labor Statistics definition described a "tourist" as being an overnighter, an out-of-state person who is traveling for purposes of recreation or vacationing. It precludes the person traveling for business or conventioning.

The 19th century dictionary defines tourists as "people who travel for the pleasure of traveling, out of curiosity, and because they have nothing better to do," and even "for the joy of boasting about it afterwards."[1] The term "tourist," the Oxford English Dictionary tells us, was used as early as 1800; "tourism" as a word appeared in 1811.

Tourists as Defined Today

The United Nations gives a much broader definition of tourism, one adopted from the International Union of Official Travel Organizations (IUOTO). The United Nations' definition adds an array of travelers to those traveling for fun: persons traveling for business, family, mission or meeting purposes.[2]

Tourists, according to IUOTO, are temporary visitors staying at least 24 hours in a country visited, when the purpose of the journey can be classified under one of the following headings:

A. Leisure (recreation, holiday, health, study, religion and sport).

B. Business, family, mission, meetings.

Travelers staying less than twenty-four hours, according to IUOTO, are "excursionists."[3]

In this book, we are mainly concerned with persons traveling for purposes of pleasure. According to Blaine Cooke, Senior Vice-President—Marketing, Trans-World Airlines, pleasure travel is the growth sector of the travel market. In 1970, pleasure travel accounted for 75 percent of international travel and about 50 percent of domestic travel in this country. The percentage is almost certain to increase.[4] A 1971 study of 224 hotels with a total of 63,000 rooms outside the U. S. showed about half of all their guests to be tourists.[5]

The term "tourist" has a number of connotations, not all of them favorable. Tourist class accommodations are the least costly on regularly scheduled ships and airplanes. The term "tourist" is often used disparagingly. The sophisticated traveler often resents being taken for a tourist, someone he may think of as a gawking, often unmannered bumpkin.

To avoid the term, tourist, other terms are brought into use: "traveler," "visitor" and "guest" being common. Hawaii has no tourist bureau, rather it has the Hawaii Visitors Bureau. Travelers become "guests" in hotels, "patrons" when in restaurants.

Probably most tourists don't mind being identified as tourists. Otherwise, how can we explain the ubiquitous camera hanging over the shoulder, the dark sunglasses and the unabashed craning of the necks to see everything. Experienced travelers would probably rather not be taken as tourists. They are the ones who want to blend with the population, to eat the native foods, to experience the native pleasures and, perhaps, some of the pain as well.

Tourist Camouflage

Richard Bissell, writing in Venture Magazine,[6] offers advice on camouflage. In East Africa, he said, "Make like a missionary, wear white robes and dash about on a motorbike doing good works." In France, he recommends parting your hair in the middle, wearing a pinchback suit, and carrying a trumpet or trombone. Another ploy in France, recommended by Bissell, is to wear a blue serge suit with peak lapels and pointy shoes, and grow a toothbrush mustache. Everybody will know you are French, probably a banker, especially if your blue serge is turning green in places and the elbows are shining like a mirror.

When in Greece, says Bissell, try to look and act like Anthony Quinn. If you are traveling with your wife, she should be very earthy, dressed in black and needing a shave. Both of you should talk very loud and alternate between hilarity and retrospective gloom. In Hawaii, there is no way to avoid being a tourist because everybody looks like one, even the natives.

---

[1] Gilbert Sigaux, "The History of Tourism," The *Dictionaire Universal du XIXe,* Siecle of 1876. (Geneva, Switzerland: Edito Service Ltd.).

[2] *The United Nations Conference on International Travel and Tourism,* 1963.

[3] *Ibid.*

[4] Blaine Cooke, "Travel in the 70's—The Luxury Market," *Operations Bulletin,* American Hotel and Motel Assn., New York, Dec., 1970.

[5] *Worldwide Operating Statistics of the Hotel Industry, 1972,* (New York: Horwath and Horwath International, 1972).

[6] *Venture Magazine,* Sept., 1969-Jan., 1970, p. 11.

Presumably there are also statements one should not make on returning from a trip, if you are really well-traveled and don't want to be considered a tourist.[1]

"It's a wonderful place to visit but I couldn't possibly live there."

"But everybody knows they are the worst drivers in Europe."

"You mean they don't still roast a baby whale stuffed with swordfish in the village square on the eve of St. Frideswid—it was the big event of the year there when I was a boy."

"You can buy six lobsters, two bottles of brandy, a thousand cigarettes, and have a hand-tailored silk suit run up overnight, for less than a hundred zlotys, which is roughly 16¢ in American money."

"You're supposed to catch dysentery there. It immunizes you against jungle rot."

"Those men in Rome! They really make you feel like a woman."

Identifying the Tourist

Identifying the tourist is not as easy as might be thought. He constitutes a relatively small percentage of the world's population. The overseas travelers from the United States constitute less than three percent of the population. Of the 3.5 billion persons inhabiting the globe, cross off most of the 800 million residing in China, the 520 million in India and most of the millions in Africa.

George Newman of Pan American World Airways defines the potential foreign travel market succinctly: ". . . subtract 30 percent for the very old, the very young, the sick and the poor who will always be with us. Another 15 percent might be classified as 'hard core non-travelers,' leaving 55 percent." A Newsweek Travel and Vacation Study found that about 12 percent of U. S. adults over 18 years of age had never had a vacation lasting one week.[2]

Taken as a group, a major characteristic of the North American is his mobility, his desire to move, to go and go. The urge to travel—to travel anywhere is endemic, even funny. Russell Baker writing in the New York Times nicely satirizes this compulsion to go.[3]

"It doesn t matter where you go, but it is better if you go a long distance. It is particularly good if you go but don't know where you're going. Guitar players will write songs about you and there will be a general feeling in the country that you are a poet.

"Young people should go at least three times in the summer and once during each of the other three seasons, preferably in Volkswagen buses with curtains on the windows, in airplanes or by hitchhiking.

"Singles should go in sports cars. So should couples who are living together but not married, unless they wear jeans or overalls, in which case they should go in Volkswagen buses with curtains on the windows.

"Married people with children should go in station wagons.

"Businessmen and politicians should go in airplanes and never check their luggage.

"Cowards should go in trains and ships.

"People who like to feel cuddled deep in the center of a great cone of noise should go on motorcycles, and wear sunglasses.

"Rich people who start drinking before lunch and have skin that looks as if it might be on loan from an alligator suitcase should go in their private boats.

"Presidents of the United States should go in personal four-engine jets, yachts, helicopters, limousines and golf carts. When they get there, they should issue a press release."

Throughout history, travel has been a class phenomenon. Personal economics control travel expenditures to a great extent. If a person has limited means, he can spend only a small amount of his resources, if any of it, for travel and vacation. As income increases, the individual obviously can spend more of it for travel, if he wishes. Prior to the modern period, travel was pretty much limited to the elite, the nomad and to the warrior. Today, travel, to a large extent, reflects income and educational level, but also age, race, occupation, place of residence and a particular way of life.

---

[1]"Remarks About Holidays I Never Want to Hear Again," *The New York Times,* Sept. 20, 1969 and *New Statesman,* Oct. 11, 1970.
[2]Sindlinger and Co., *Newsweek Travel and Vacation Study, Table 1.* (Norwood, Pa., 1971).
[3]*The New York Times,* Sept. 2, 1973.

For a specific travel destination a tourist is someone who has the wherewithal and the inclination to go to that destination. The tourist market for that place may be a very thin slice of the total population. The market may be centered in a few major cities or even within a fairly small radius of a destination.

The market for Cape Cod, Mass., for example, is largely centered within a 500-mile driving radius of the Cape. The winter market for Miami Beach is largely centered in Metropolitan New York City. The two states which produce the largest number of tourists for the State of Hawaii are California and New York State. The big market for Las Vegas is California. Major problems for tourist promoters are (1) determining the markets for particular destinations and (2) transforming nontourists into tourists for those destinations.

Most travel is domestic travel, that taking place within a country. The IUOTO estimates that 75 to 80 percent of all tourist expenditures are made within the traveler's own country. These figures vary widely, 94 percent for the U. S.; 70 percent for the United Kingdom, 46 percent for Italy, 44 percent for Switzerland.[1]

Except for some of the more developed countries, statistics concerning domestic tourist travel are not widely available. As an approach to the amount of tourism travel, Professor Wilfred Owen has developed an index of "passenger mobility."

The index is an average of the following: passenger miles per capita, passenger cars per capita, rail lines per 100 square miles, rail lines per 10,000 population, surfaced highways per 100 square miles, and surfaced highways per 10,000 population.[2] The index is based on 100, France being the normative country.

For the majority of developing countries, the index ranges below 25, going as low as 2 in Ethiopia. United States and Canada have an index of close to 150. The table below shows the range of passenger mobility in selected countries as of 1961.

The index is an indication of mobility within the country and shows the degree to which passenger transportation has been developed. Since passenger transportation is a predominant component of tourism, the in-

TABLE I—INDEX OF PASSENGER MOBILITY OF SELECTED COUNTRIES 1961[3]

(Index of France = 100)

DEVELOPING COUNTRIES

2-5	5-10	10-15	15-20	Over 20
Ethiopia	U. A. R.	Peru	Algeria	Ceylon (22)
Nigeria	Ghana	Paraguay	Malaya	Mexico (23)
Iran	Burma	India	Brazil	Chile (36)
	Philippines		Bolivia	
	Syria			
	Thailand			
	Ecuador			
	Colombia			
	Indonesia			
	Pakistan			

DEVELOPED COUNTRIES

40-60	60-80	90-100	Over 100
Japan	Netherlands	France (100)	U. S. A. (147)
Italy	Norway	U.K.	Canada (149)
	Finland	West Germany	
	Austria		

---

[1] IUOTO, *World Travel,* Dec., 1969-Jan., 1970.
[2] Wilfred Owen, *Strategy for Mobility,* (Washington, D. C.: Brookings Institute, 1964) p. 14.
[3] *Ibid.*

dex gives an idea of the degree of development of tourism in a particular country.

Travel Within the U. S.

Travel within the United States, domestic travel, has become a consuming interest, almost doubling in the period 1967-1972. According to the 1972 Census of Transportation conducted by the Bureau of Census, about 114 million people or approximately 55 percent of all civilians in the country took at least one trip of at least 100 miles away from home and returned. The Bureau of Census uses the term "Person-Trip" as meaning one person on one trip. If three persons from the same household take a trip together, it is counted as three person-trips. The average traveler, the person who took at least one trip of 100 miles or more during the year, was away about 15.6 nights and traveled a rather amazing total of 3239 miles on these trips. What is even more amazing is that between 1967 and 1972 the number of trips increased by 82 percent. Little wonder that the nation experienced a national gasoline crisis in 1974.

That North Americans are go-go types has been observed by visitors for some time. Alexis de Toqueville, a perceptive French observer of America in the 1830's, declared that movement had become a "historical task" for Americans.[1] A little later, in 1847, a South American statesman, D. F. Sarmiento opined that "If God were suddenly to call the world to judgment, He would surprise two-thirds of the American population on the road like ants."[2] If driving an auto is outdoor recreation, it is America's favorite such pastime. The American Automobile Association estimated that in 1971 110 million Americans junketed 280 billion highway miles in holiday travel alone.

The urge to travel is not unique to Americans; however, to some it seems a national passion. As expressed by Walt Whitman

"I know my life is nearly spent
Because my want to go is went."[3]

More recently John Steinbeck elucidated the urge in a conversation in *Travels With Charley: In Search of America:*

"Lord! I wish I could go."
"Don't you like it here?"
"Sure. It's all right, but I wish I could go."

"You don't even know where you're going."
"I don't care. I'd like to go anywhere."[4]

Because of the go-go urge New Hampshire has been labeled a glorified boarding house; Hawaii and Florida, hotel aggregates. The weekend skiers have been said to have saved Vermont from going back to the Indians. The Plains Indians had a culture based on riding on the horse. Californians ride in an automobile over a matrix of freeways. Newcomers are as baffled and startled by these freeways as white rats in a complex maze. The urge to movement gone mad.

Something like 30 million Americans change residence each year. Some professions—hotel management and university teaching as examples—almost demand several moves in the course of a career.

The major source of travel data—and probably the most reliable—is that collected by the U. S. Bureau of Census every five years. This data sometimes differs widely from statistics collected by State and Regional Governments. One reason for the differences springs from the variation in definitions used; another difference comes from the kind of sampling and methodology employed.

Based on the 1972 census, the profiles of travel are shown on page 11.

About 85 percent of the travel in the United States was done in the automobile, that instrument which has more than replaced the horse in the affection of mankind and has, in some cases, become an obsession. About 12 percent of the total travel was done in an airplane, a 93 percent increase in the five-year period 1967-1972. Bus travel declined in importance to about 2 percent of total travel while less than .5 percent was done by train.

Surprising to a number of people interested in travel, more travel was undertaken to visit friends and relatives than for any other reason, 38.4 percent of the total. Business and convention trips accounted

[1]George W. Pierson, *The Moving American,* New York: Alfred A. Knopf, 1973).
[2]*Ibid.*
[3]*Ibid.*
[4]*Ibid.*

Profiles of Travel by Trip Characteristics: 1972
(Based upon 458.5 million person-trips)

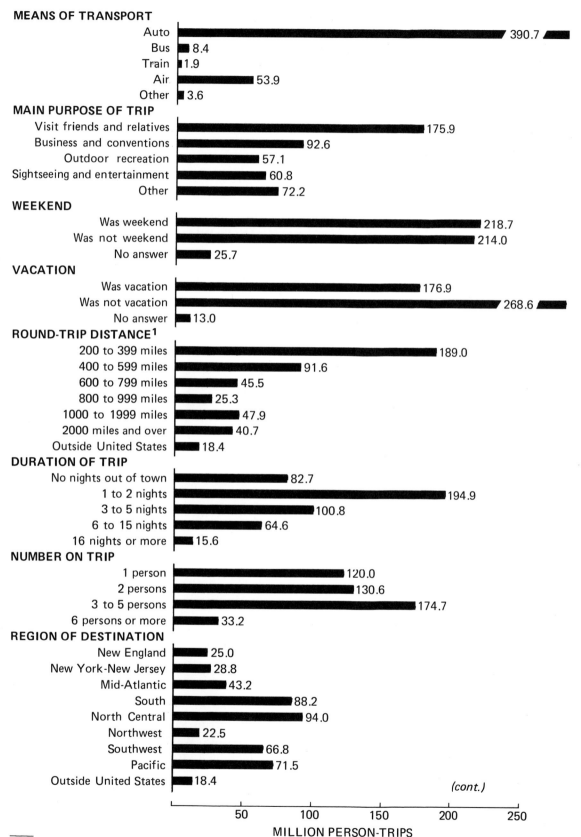

MEANS OF TRANSPORT
- Auto — 390.7
- Bus — 8.4
- Train — 1.9
- Air — 53.9
- Other — 3.6

MAIN PURPOSE OF TRIP
- Visit friends and relatives — 175.9
- Business and conventions — 92.6
- Outdoor recreation — 57.1
- Sightseeing and entertainment — 60.8
- Other — 72.2

WEEKEND
- Was weekend — 218.7
- Was not weekend — 214.0
- No answer — 25.7

VACATION
- Was vacation — 176.9
- Was not vacation — 268.6
- No answer — 13.0

ROUND-TRIP DISTANCE[1]
- 200 to 399 miles — 189.0
- 400 to 599 miles — 91.6
- 600 to 799 miles — 45.5
- 800 to 999 miles — 25.3
- 1000 to 1999 miles — 47.9
- 2000 miles and over — 40.7
- Outside United States — 18.4

DURATION OF TRIP
- No nights out of town — 82.7
- 1 to 2 nights — 194.9
- 3 to 5 nights — 100.8
- 6 to 15 nights — 64.6
- 16 nights or more — 15.6

NUMBER ON TRIP
- 1 person — 120.0
- 2 persons — 130.6
- 3 to 5 persons — 174.7
- 6 persons or more — 33.2

REGION OF DESTINATION
- New England — 25.0
- New York-New Jersey — 28.8
- Mid-Atlantic — 43.2
- South — 88.2
- North Central — 94.0
- Northwest — 22.5
- Southwest — 66.8
- Pacific — 71.5
- Outside United States — 18.4

(cont.)

50   100   150   200   250
MILLION PERSON-TRIPS

[1]Round-trip distance is route miles and includes circuitry. Miles do not include any portion of trips with destinations outside the United States.

Profiles of Travel by Trip Characteristics: 1972 *(cont.)*

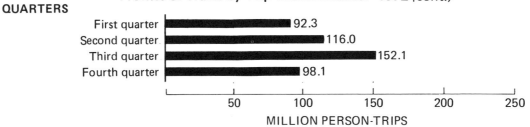

QUARTERS

Source: *National Travel Survey, 1972 Census of Transportation,* Bureau of the Census.

TABLE II—ESTIMATED TRAVEL VOLUME AND TRAVEL INTENSITY[1] INDEX FOR LEADING STANDARD METROPOLITAN STATISTICAL AREAS: 1967

Standard Metropolitan Statistical Area		Millions of Person-trips To SMSA	Travel Intensity Index[a]
Rank	Name		
1	New York.	8.2	0.7
2	Los Angeles.	6.1	0.9
3	Chicago	6.1	0.9
4	Philadelphia.	3.5	0.9
5	Detroit.	2.9	0.7
6	Boston.	3.0	0.9
7	San Francisco-Oakland.	4.2	1.4
8	Washington, D.C..	4.9	1.8
9	Pittsburgh.	2.1	0.9
10	St. Louis.	2.2	1.0
11	Cleveland.	2.3	1.1
12	Baltimore.	1.3	0.7
13	Newark, N.J.	1.3	0.7
14	Houston.	1.9	1.1
15	Minneapolis-St. Paul	2.8	1.8
16	Dallas	2.1	1.5
17	Cincinnati.	1.1	0.8
18	Milwaukee.	1.7	1.3
19	Patterson-Clifton-Passaic..	0.8	0.6
20	Buffalo.	1.1	0.8

[a]Travel Intensity Index is the average number of person-trips to an area per person living in the area. For example, in New York where the population was about 11.6 million, there were about 8.2 million person-trips to that SMSA, making a "travel intensity index" of 0.7 person-trips.

_____

[1]Donald E. Church, "Measuring Travel Volume and Characteristics," *Travel Research Bulletin,* Winter 1970-71.

TOTAL PASSENGERS DEPARTED FROM THE UNITED STATES, BY SEA AND AIR, TO FOREIGN COUNTRIES, 1946-1968

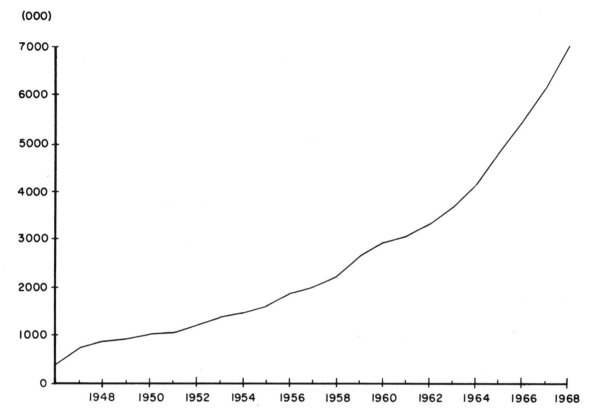

SOURCE: UNITED STATES DEPARTMENT OF JUSTICE, IMMIGRATION AND NATURALIZATION SERVICE

Travel volume to the various states and intensity indexes are seen in this table:

TABLE III—ESTIMATED TRAVEL VOLUME AND TRAVEL

Travel Region[a] State	Volume of Travel		Travel Intensity Indexes[b]	
	Person-trips to destinations in state (millions)	Person-nights spent in state (millions)	Person-trip index	Person-nights index
Yankee				
Maine	3.5	17.1	3.9	19.0
New Hampshire	2.8	12.6	4.0	18.0
Vermont	1.8	9.7	4.5	24.3
New York	19.9	90.0	1.1	5.0
Massachusetts	7.1	34.5	1.3	6.4
Connecticut	3.5	16.2	1.2	5.6
New Jersey	9.6	45.2	1.4	6.5
Rhode Island	1.5	6.8	1.7	7.6
Total	49.7	232.1	1.4	6.4
Dixie Land				
North Carolina	9.3	46.2	1.8	9.1
South Carolina	4.9	19.4	1.9	7.5
Kentucky	5.9	22.0	1.8	6.9
Tennessee	5.3	23.2	1.4	6.0
Georgia	6.5	33.2	1.4	7.4
Florida	12.6	119.8	2.1	20.0
Alabama	4.7	20.7	1.3	5.9
Mississippi	3.7	13.4	1.6	5.8
Louisiana	5.4	19.1	1.5	5.2
Arkansas	4.0	15.0	2.0	7.5
Total	62.3	332.0	1.7	9.0
Mid-America				
Ohio	12.8	43.4	1.2	4.1
Michigan	16.5	62.1	1.9	7.2
Indiana	8.1	31.5	1.6	6.3
Illinois	11.9	48.0	1.1	4.4
Wisconsin	11.2	41.4	2.7	9.9
Minnesota	12.6	47.7	3.5	13.3
Iowa	4.5	19.4	1.6	6.9
Missouri	10.8	40.1	2.3	8.7
Total	88.5	333.6	1.8	6.6

[a]Travel Region is the region adopted by DATA for travel analysis; it differs from the customary census region and division classification.

[b]Travel Intensity Indexes are the average number of person-trips to an area and person-nights spent in an area per person living in the area.

INTENSITY INDEXES FOR LEADING STATES: 1967[1]

Travel Region[a] State	Volume of Travel		Travel Intensity Indexes[b]	
	Person-trips to destinations in state (millions)	*Person-nights spent in state (millions)*	*Person-trip index*	*Person-nights index*
George Washington				
Pennsylvania	16.2	61.5	1.4	5.3
Maryland	4.2	19.5	1.1	5.3
Delaware	1.0	4.8	2.0	9.6
District of Columbia	3.4	11.7	4.3	14.6
Virginia	7.5	31.7	1.7	7.0
West Virginia	3.5	11.4	1.9	6.3
Total	35.8	140.6	1.6	6.1
Frontier West				
Montana	1.9	8.9	2.7	12.7
Wyoming	1.2	8.5	4.0	28.3
North Dakota	1.6	7.8	2.7	13.0
South Dakota	1.4	6.8	2.0	9.7
Nebraska	2.2	8.5	1.6	6.1
Kansas	3.5	13.3	1.5	5.8
Colorado	3.8	21.1	1.9	10.6
Utah	1.9	9.5	1.9	9.5
Oklahoma	4.8	17.7	1.9	7.1
New Mexico	2.4	12.9	2.4	12.9
Texas	21.8	82.7	2.0	7.6
Total	46.5	197.7	2.0	8.4
Far West				
Washington	9.4	36.6	2.9	11.4
Oregon	6.3	27.3	3.2	13.7
Idaho	1.6	7.8	2.3	11.1
Nevada	3.4	15.4	8.5	38.5
California	36.4	164.8	1.9	8.7
Arizona	4.7	31.0	2.9	8.6
Alaska	.8	4.2	2.7	14.0
Total	62.6	287.1	2.3	10.6

[a]*Ibid.*
[b]*Ibid.*
[1]Donald E. Church, "Measuring Travel Volume and Characteristics," *Travel Resources Bulletin* (University of Colorado, Winter 1970-71).

for about 20 percent of the total and increased by almost 100 percent during the 1967-1972 period. Nearly 29 percent of person-trips for business and conventions were made by air while 68 percent were made by automobile.

Sight-seeing and entertainment were responsible for 13.3 percent of the personal trips taken in 1972. Outdoor recreation person-trips also almost doubled during that period, trips—as might be guessed—taken almost exclusively by automobile. The usual such trip involved traveling between 200 and 400 miles and a one- or two-night stay away from home. Families in the middle income group were the big travelers: 59 percent of all person-trips being taken by members of households with incomes of more than $10,000 a year. Families with incomes of $15,000 a year accounted for about half the air travel and business trips.

Travel and travel-related businesses are of major importance to the huge metropolitan centers of the world. It is estimated that close to 25 million visitors, probably 40 percent on pleasure trips, visit the three largest cities—New York City, London and Tokyo. Some 180,000 persons fly in and out of these cities each day. Hotel rooms in the three cities total more than 170,000.

New York City's visitor industry is the largest in the world. During 1970, it was estimated that more than 16 million tourists and convention delegates came there and spent more than $1.25 billion (it should be emphasized that such statistics are only estimates).

As might be expected, Canadians and Mexicans comprise the major groups of visitors to the U. S. In 1972, Canada was the origin of 67 percent of our foreign visitors; Mexico the origin of 11 percent of the total. Of the $3.2 billion in tourist receipts from abroad, Canadians expended 29 percent of that total, Mexicans, 19 percent. By comparison, other foreign visitors were relatively few in number. Japan and the United Kingdom each provided 3 percent of the some 12.8 million visitors to the U. S. for 1972.

The pie charts below summarize foreign travel to the U. S. in 1972:

Six countries—Canada, Mexico, Japan, United Kingdom, West Germany and France —accounted for 87 percent of all U. S. arrivals in 1972 and for 74 percent of the spending by visitors to the U. S.

Some 8.6 million visitors from Canada stayed 24 hours or more and spent $922 million here. (This figure excludes the day-trippers, mostly shoppers from Canada.)

FOREIGN TRAVEL TO THE UNITED STATES—1972

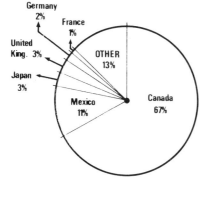

ARRIVALS
Total = 12,884,801

RECEIPTS
Total = $3.206 billion

6 COUNTRIES SPECIFIED ACCOUNT FOR:

87% OF TOTAL ARRIVALS
62% OF TOTAL RECEIPTS
(74% IF TRANSPORTATION RECEIPTS ARE EXCLUDED)

Source: *Cornell Hotel Quarterly,* February, 1974.

Mexican visitors spent an average of $415 in the U. S. for a total of $615 million.

Tourist $ for United States

It was expected that total visitors to the U. S. would increase to 14 million in 1973 and that they would leave $3.65 billion here as a result.

Even so, U. S. citizens spending on foreign travel for 1973 would climb to $6.8 billion, leaving a "travel deficit" of $3.45 billion. There is some concern about the travel deficit developed as a result of this travel abroad by U. S. citizens. This sort of deficit can be expected in the developed nations. Seven of the twelve major tourist-originating countries showed a deficit of some sort, including Canada, The Netherlands, Belgium-Luxemburg, Sweden and Japan. Germany has a deficit of over $2 billion, approximately that of the U. S.

The figures listed on page 19 from *Service World International,* show tourist expenditures and number of tourists going abroad for 13 of the major tourist generating countries in 1969.

The great volume of international travel takes place within the developed nations of Europe and North America, and between these nations. Americans travel more and spend more money in travel than do the citizens of any other nation.

The table below, taken from the Report of the National Tourism Resources Review Commission shows the twelve major tourist receiving nations in 1971.

It is interesting to see that Spain ranks just after the U. S. in tourism receipts. Little Austria probably experiences the greatest economic impact from tourism, about $171 received each year for each resident in the country.

TABLE IV—THE TWELVE MAJOR TOURIST RECEIVING COUNTRIES: 1971

	Country	Receipts (US$)*	% World Receipts	$ Receipts Per Capita
1.	United States	2,457,000	12.3	11.87
2.	Spain	2,063,000	10.4	60.44
3.	Italy	1,882,000	9.4	34.28
4.	Mexico	1,583,000	8.0	31.14
5.	Germany	1,534,000	7.7	24.71
6.	France	1,451,000	7.3	28.31
7.	Canada	1,272,000	6.4	58.92
8.	Austria	1,271.000	6.4	170.74
9.	United Kingdom	1,195,000	6.0	21.51
10.	Switzerland	875,000	4.4	138.67
11.	Netherlands	674,000	3.4	51.10
12.	Denmark	387,000	1.9	78.02
	Total of twelve leaders	16,644,000	83.6	—
	All other countries	3,256,000	16.4	—
	World Total	19,900,000	100.00	—

*Excludes transoceanic fare receipts.

Source: Organization of Economic Cooperation and Development, International Monetary Fund, International Union of Official Travel Organizations.

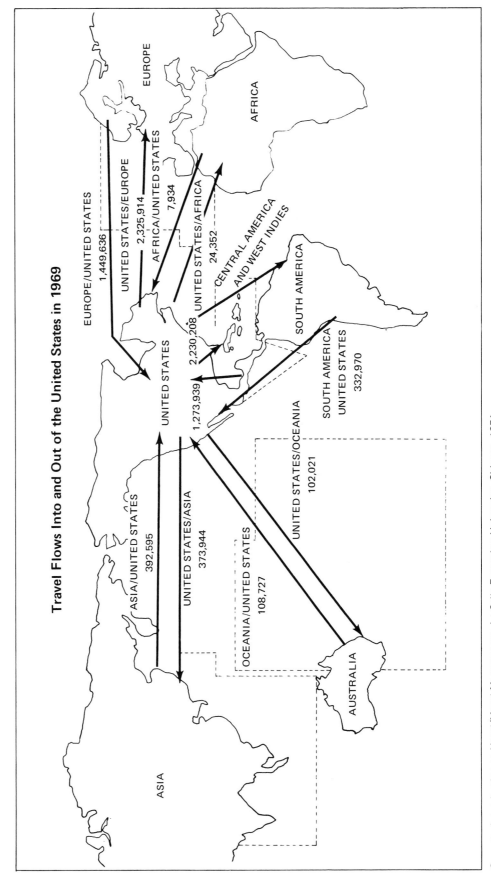

Travel Flows Into and Out of the United States in 1969

EUROPE

AFRICA

EUROPE/UNITED STATES
1,449,636

UNITED STATES/EUROPE
2,325,914

AFRICA/UNITED STATES
7,934

UNITED STATES/AFRICA
24,352

CENTRAL AMERICA
AND WEST INDIES

2,230,208

UNITED STATES

1,273,939

SOUTH AMERICA

SOUTH AMERICA
UNITED STATES
332,970

ASIA/UNITED STATES
392,595

UNITED STATES/ASIA
373,944

UNITED STATES/OCEANIA
102,021

OCEANIA/UNITED STATES
108,727

AUSTRALIA

ASIA

Source: Introduction to Hotel/Motel Management, La Salle Extension University, Chicago, 1971.

WORLD TOURISM LEAGUE[1]

		Tourist Expenditure for 1969 (in $ million)	Number of tourists going abroad 1969 (million)
(1)	United States	4,372	20.1
(2)	West Germany	1,962	14.0
(3)	Canada	1,189	9.0
(4)	France	1,006	5.7
(5)	Great Britain	1,175 (1970)	5.7
(6)	Netherlands	540	3.4
(7)	Italy	493	3.0
(8)	Belgium	454	2.5
(9)	Sweden	365	1.8
(10)	Austria	295	1.8
(11)	Switzerland	265	1.4
(12)	Japan	241	0.5
(13)	Spain	86	0.8

The map on page 20 expresses in a general way the major flows of tourists to and within Europe. It is seen that, in 1970, the United Kingdom attracted some 4.9 million tourists, 1.6 million of them coming from the U. S. Within Europe, Italy attracts the most tourists, about 10.4 million each year, most of these coming from France and Northern Europe. France, too, attracts a large number of tourists, about 12 million each year and little Switzerland attracts more than 6 million tourists a year. Spain and Portugal are emphasizing tourism as a means of economic development and this effort is reflected in the fact that Spain attracts 9.5 million tourists a year while tourism in Portugal exceeds the 1 million mark.

It is relatively easy and inexpensive for Europeans to cross national borders, which partly accounts for the sizable tourist travel to Italy, France and Spain. Within Europe, W. Germany and the United Kingdom supply large numbers of tourists for the other nations.

Americans are said to be the most traveled and the biggest spenders among all tourists. In 1970, about 21.9 million U. S. citizens departed for countries abroad; 6.1 million of them for overseas countries. The dominance of the U. S. traveler is seen in the fact that even in Japan over half the foreign visitors (207,000) were U. S. citizens. A rather amazing fact: of the $17 billion estimated as being spent in international travel in 1970, some $5 billion of the total was spent by U. S. travelers.

Major destinations for U. S. travelers to Europe in 1969 were:[2]

United Kingdom	944,000
	(1.3 million in 1971)
Germany	712,000
Italy	632,000
France	580,000
Switzerland	554,000
Netherlands	397,000

The Germans spent $79 million in 1971; Britain, $67 million; France, $48 million.

Per capita travel in Europe is high. A much larger percentage of West Germans, Danes and Swedes than U. S. citizens travel abroad. In 1970, about 20 million West Germans traveled outside of Germany and 1.6 million Swedes left their countries for travel abroad.

The propensity to travel abroad varies widely. The Dutch, Germans and Scandinavians may take as many as half of their holidays abroad. The French are relative stay-at-homes. Only about 14 percent of the holidays taken by the French are taken abroad. Tour companies in Denmark, Germany, the Netherlands and elsewhere have made it possible for thousands of Northern Europeans to vacation in Spain and Morocco relatively cheaply. The tour companies own their own planes, load them to capacity, and fly the passengers to their own hotels or to hotels that have been rented en bloc for the group.

Growth of Travel and Tourism

The future of travel and tourism in the U. S. will be shaped by several factors already evident.

(1) Increasing discretionary time
(2) Greater disposable income
(3) Higher educational level

---

[1]The estimates come from *Service World International*, Nov., 1970.
[2]Official U. S. figures.

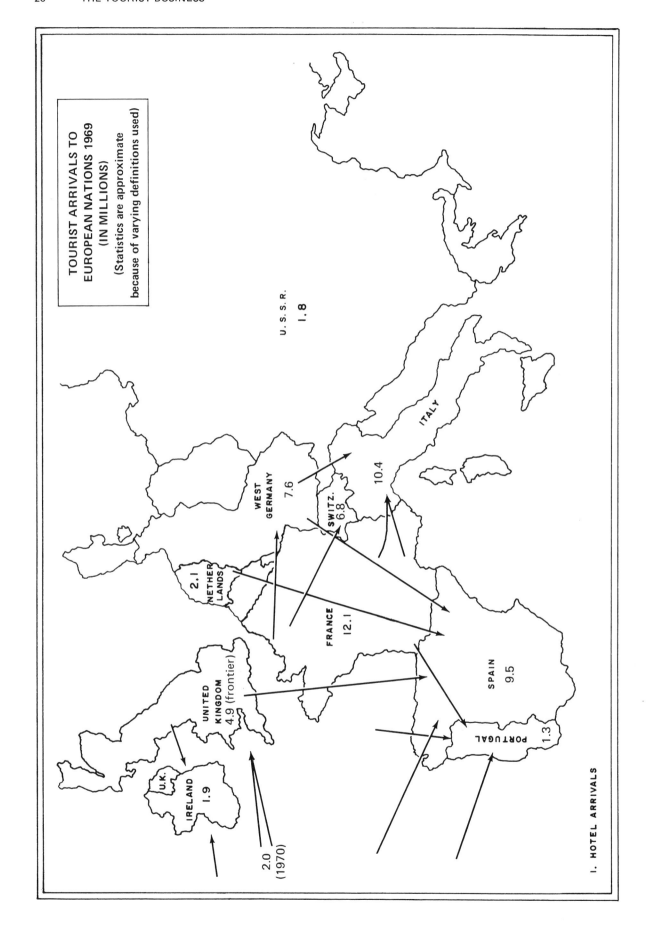

TOURIST ARRIVALS TO
EUROPEAN NATIONS 1969
(IN MILLIONS)
(Statistics are approximate
because of varying definitions used)

U. S. S. R.
1.8

ITALY
10.4

WEST
GERMANY
7.6

SWITZ.
6.8

NETHER-
LANDS
2.1

FRANCE
12.1

UNITED
KINGDOM
4.9 (frontier)

U.K.

IRELAND
1.9

2.0
(1970)

SPAIN
9.5

PORTUGAL
1.3

I. HOTEL ARRIVALS

(4) Larger percentage of young adults

(5) Changing life styles which include travel as an important part of living.

Despite the impressive travel statistics, tourist travel is now largely limited to a small number of countries, the rich ones in Western Europe and North America. Further, it is restricted to a very small proportion of the total population of these areas. Only .35 of 1 percent of the world population left their homeland to travel to another country in 1968. Of domestic travel done in the USA, for example, 20 percent of the travelers accounted for 80 percent of the trips.

The Pan American chart on page 23 is a projection of international travel for pleasure through the turn of the century. The implications are awesome. In 1970, only three percent of the U. S. residents took pleasure trips overseas. That figure is forecast to increase sevenfold by the year 2000. What is significant for the future of tourism is not the impressive numbers of tourists now traveling but the massive numbers of those who are not. Within the U. S., 32 percent of adults living in households with incomes of $10,000 a year and more have never flown in a plane.[1] If sizable proportions of populations begin to travel to the same extent that the well-traveled groups now do, tourism in many parts of the world will eclipse manufacturing and agriculture.

The observer at a busy airport in the U. S. may feel that just about everybody is moving around by air. Not so. A 1971 study found that 35 percent of all U. S. consumers (about 48 million people) said that they had never used air travel at all. Of those that hadn't flown, 30 percent said they had no reason to fly and 21 percent said they were afraid to fly. About 13 million persons, according to the survey, said they could not afford to fly, or that it was too expensive.[2] The implications of this latter statement are enormous. As disposable income increases or as the cost of air travel is reduced compared to other costs, more people will be getting on and off planes in the future. Growth is predicted for domestic air travel at between 8 and 12 percent a year. In times of economic recession, the growth curve flattens.

The growth of international travel will largely depend, as it has in the past, upon disposable income and political stability. Population growth is only an incidental factor, since the world already has 3.5 billion people only a small percentage of whom travel very far. Growth in travel will increase as greater numbers of the world's population increase their educational level and gain more leisure time. Even when these factors are equalized among the different groups, some groups will travel much more than others, as a result of differing life styles and cultures.

Of course, no one can predict the future, but a number of people are trying to identify underlying forces in our society that will have impact on the hospitality business, and especially travel and tourism. Among the factors which have significant implication for travel and tourism are the following:[3]

1. Early retirement. Social values and union pressures are forcing the retirement age down in the U. S. This trend, if continued, will result in hundreds of thousands of people who are relatively still young, vigorous, and with enough discretionary income to travel and vacation if so inclined.

2. The growth of government security programs. Changing social values toward security indicate that people are more ready to accept government security plans for themselves which relieves them of the need to save for the future, "Carpe diem," or the tendency to live for today, is enhanced. More money is available for spending on travel and vacationing.

3. A reduction in the values placed on material ownership. Fewer homes are being bought. Status from large automobile ownership is not as great as in the past. The younger generation

[1]Elayn K. Bernay, "Emerging Life Styles and Their Effect on the Travel Market," *(Proceedings First Annual Conference,* The Travel Research Assn., 1970).
[2]Albert E. Sindlinger, *Sindlinger's Air Travel Demand Study,* (presentation for the Eastern Council for Travel Research, Dec. 7, 1971).
[3]Arnold Brown and Edith Weiner, *Symposia for the Study of 21st Century Hospitality,* (University of Massachusetts: Life Insurance Institute, 1973) (abstracted).

is not as impressed with material possessions as were past generations. Again there is more money available for doing as one pleases, including travel and vacation.

4. Decline in physical labor. The U. S. has arrived at a point where less than 50 percent of the work force is engaged in actual physical labor. Attention to health programs encourages people to engage in camping out, cycling, hiking and the like, activities which involve travel.

5. A shorter work week. The work week has declined sharply since the turn of the century, from 50 to 60 hours to in some cases less than 35 hours. There are more long weekends available because of holidays. Some businesses arrange for "the flexible work week," a plan by which people arrange their own number of hours and their schedule. These trends permit more travel and tourism.

6. Greater affluence. Personal income continues to increase and the purchasing power of the family increases despite the rise in the cost of several necessities. Once people have sated themselves on such things as TV's, automobiles, and clothes they are likely to turn to travel and tourism as a means of gratification.

7. Greater mobility of the population. The rapid growth in mobile homes and statistics concerning the number of times a family moves in a lifetime indicate greater mobility of the population generally with concomitant travel involved.

8. Growth of employee benefits. Statistics show that employee benefits may constitute as much as 30 percent of the payroll and are likely to increase. Union pressures may shift from wages to benefits to such things as more vacation time and even to travel benefits such as are available in some European countries.

9. Smaller families. The U. S. birth rate per family is the lowest in history—2.03 children per family. Although the population will continue

to grow, the smaller family unit will have greater discretionary income and more freedom to purchase travel and entertainment.

10. Improved transportation technology and relative decrease in cost. Mass transportation is likely to increase with attendant lower cost per mile as compared with auto and air travel. It is likely that government subsidy of mass transportation will increase which reduces cost to the traveler and increases the propensity to travel.

11. Increases in longevity—breakthroughs in the understanding of the aging process are likely. The chronic killers such as heart disease and cancer will probably be solved permitting people to live longer with greater vigor. Such people will have the time and, hopefully, the money to travel.

12. Growth of multi-national companies. Supra national companies with production and sales units around the world increase the need for business travel. Some of these companies, such as ITT and Gulf Western, are already deeply involved in the travel picture. The multi-national companies search for sources of cheap raw materials, move them to areas where they can be processed cheaply and then to markets which will produce the greatest profits. All of this results in increased business travel.

Other factors for optimism in tourism growth in the U. S. include:

1. Rising incomes in other parts of the world. Japan and West Germany are prime examples of nations which now produce per capita incomes large enough for masses of people to afford travel to the U. S. More upper income families in such places as Mexico, the Bahamas, and Puerto Rico will probably come to this country in larger numbers.

2. The fact that more wives are working, more families living in apartments means greater discretionary time as well as discretionary income.

3. The quantum jump in rapid communications—TV via satellite, for example—may stimulate curiosity about far-away places and encourage travel.

PARTICIPATION IN AND FREQUENCY OF TRAVEL

A GROWTH MODEL FOR INTERNATIONAL PLEASURE TRAVEL BY U.S. RESIDENTS						
	1950	1960	1970	1980	1990	2000
PERCENT OF POPULATION TRAVELING	0.3	1.1	3.0	7.0	13.3	22.5
AVERAGE ANNUAL FREQUENCY	0.3	0.4	0.5	0.6	0.8	1.0
TRIPS AS A PERCENT OF POPULATION	0.1	0.5	1.6	4.6	10.9	22.5

4. Travel as a status leisure time activity. Travel has always been a prestige conversation piece and could increase as the value of material possessions declines.

5. Higher education as a stimulus to travel. Travel abroad is highly correlated with advanced education. As millions attend colleges and universities, the curiosity and psychological set for travel will probably increase.

Social Implications of Tourism

Tourism has vast economic implications but its social implications may be even more profound. It can have significant cultural importance, as is seen in the restorations at Williamsburg, Sturbridge Village, Old Deerfield Village and numerous other historical re-creations. It stimulates interest in the past, in architecture and in the arts, as people travel to music festivals and to visit historic centers here and abroad.

Tourism can add to the esthetic qualities of life, for example, through dramatic resort design, landscaping of parks and the preservation of natural beauty. Tourism has vast implications for the health of a people as is seen by the fact that several European countries mandate minimum vacations for all workers. It can be a vehicle for international understanding by bringing diverse peoples face-to-face. Tourism also has political overtones since it affects world trade and nearly everyone in a destination area.

Tourism can also blight an area and much concern is being shown in planning for tourism so as to achieve a desirable life quality in the environment. It has sociological implications in that as a destination area moves into tourism, the style of life of the residents changes radically.

Rather than promoting all-out tourism, leaders in many destination areas want to know what the effects of tourism will be on their present society. How, for example, will tourism affect the value systems and social structure of Western Samoa or Fiji? What kind of tourism, mass or class, or a mixture of both, is best for an area? At what rate can tourism expand in an area without causing sharp social tensions or ecological imbalance?

Nations suffering a dollar gap in their trade with the rest of the world are much concerned over a surplus or deficit of tourist dollars coming into or leaving their country. When it is realized that per capita income for many developing countries is less than $500 a year, it is easy to see why many governments look to tourism for economic salvation. Islands, such as St. Lucia and Grenada in the Caribbean, for example, have per capita incomes of less than $300. Since they are situated near the United States, the development of tourism could quickly double such income.

What are the effects of tourism on an area? Will workers need to be invited in to man the new tourist facilities? If so, how will they be housed and educated? How will these workers adapt to the present society? What benefits, what costs, does tourism bring to an area? What investments and facilities will be needed to prime the pump of tourism? How much money should be spent in advertising and promotion? Tourism can be a boon to many an area, but its growth must be directed and controlled. Without planning and controls, the benefits of tourism may go to a relative few while leaving the mass of residents of the area excluded and resentful.

Freeport, Grand Bahama Island, where much of the tourist business in the Bahamas is centered. As recently as 1960, Grand Bahama was almost completely undeveloped. Special tax concessions, gambling privileges and the right to import expatriate workers all help to account for the rapid development of the island.

THE COMPONENTS OF TOURISM

Tourism is the business of the transport, care, feeding and entertainment of the tourist; its components are many and diverse. It is a vast, complex industry which can be thought of as beginning with the millions of dollars that are spent on advertising and promotion to interest someone in traveling. Once interested, the prospective traveler may then get in touch with a travel agent, although a travel agent may or may not be involved in the actual arrangements. Most travelers make their own travel plans and arrangements.

For some destination areas, more than 90 percent of the bookings are done through agents. Agents handle almost all tour and cruise business. If a travel agent is consulted, he will arrange for parts or for all of the travel, and often for accommodations and sight-seeing at the destination area as well. The arrangements may be included as part of a total package or the trip can be assembled piece by piece. The traveler may go independently or as a part of a tour.

At this stage, the carrier becomes involved in transporting the traveler to a destination. At the destination, the tourist wants much more than a sunny beach, a room and his meals. He may want to be edified, tantalized and excited. He may want to be entertained or to gamble. Both body and ego may need massage.

Some tourists need rest; others want anything but rest. Tourists coming to Honolulu, for example, are likely to take a trip to the neighboring islands, but only for a maximum of three days. After that, the great silence becomes boring.

Most destination areas have a variety of attractions which include shopping, sightseeing and the opportunity to acquire the prestige tan—signal evidence that the tourist has been vacationing.

Some segments of the tourist business are obvious: the travel agent, airline, hotel and restaurant. Others are not. Which segments of tourism loom largest in economic importance varies with the destination or region. Resort hotels are the major part of tourism at many destinations. For an entire State, tourism may be seen most prominently in restaurant and bar sales. In Massachusetts, for example, tourism (as defined by the U. S. Dept. of Labor) is evidenced in sales in these kinds of establishments and in this order of importance:

> Eating and drinking establishments
> Hotels and motels
> Trailer parks and camps
> Sports and miscellaneous amusements
> Laundries and dry cleaning establishments
> Gasoline service stations
> Retail trade in souvenirs and gifts
> Rooming and boarding houses
> Motion pictures
> Theatrical productions

What about all of the secondary businesses fed by purchases made by the tourist: film purchases, long-distance phone calls, clothes purchases before and during the trip, suntan lotion, sun glasses—the list goes on and on.

The parameters of tourism are not all well identified; the boundaries of tourism are at points permeable, spilling over into businesses not ordinarily thought of as tourism. As a discipline to be studied, tourism is cross-sectional. As noted in the introduction to this book, economics, business, ecology, geography, government and law are much a part of tourism. The psychologist, the sociologist, yes, and the anthropologist, also can contribute to an understanding of the tourist and the business of tourism. Of all subjects, it is one of the most interdisciplinary.

The development of a tourist area—feasibility studies, financing and control—constitutes one of the more complex and interesting aspects of tourism. Analysis of the economic impact of tourism in an area is a major dimension of tourism.

Government agencies involved in planning and promoting tourism may be considered part of the broad tourism picture. Such agencies spend millions of dollars each year to attract travelers to the areas they represent.

Tourist Accommodations

The range and variety of accommodations that are part of tourist facilities are extensive. The young hiker is delighted to have a place to spread his sleeping bag and have access to cold running water in a youth hostel, for which he will pay two dollars or less a day. According to the American Automobile Assn., 4200 hostels were operating in 1970. Located in 47 countries, overnight fees at hostels ranged from $.40 to $1.25 abroad; $1.50 to $2.00 in the United States and Canada. The non-profit Youth Hostel Associations had nearly two million members.

The traveling salesman may be pleased with a minimum motel accommodation at $8.00 or less a day. The traveler with his family will find a Holiday Inn with its swimming pool and moderately priced restaurant highly satisfactory at $24.00 a day. A vacationer may be pleased to spend $56.00 a day at the George V in Paris. Or if he wants complete isolation and luxury, the rate is $120.00 per day double at Little Dix Bay on the Island of Virgin Gorda in the Virgin Islands.

The acme in facilities and services is found at the handful of luxury health spas which charge as much as $1500 a week for a suite. Food cost for the operator is low. The guest gets to eat less while being manicured, pedicured and given lessons in such esoteric subjects as body control and yoga. One guest at the Golden Door, near San Diego, figured that it cost her $375 for each pound she lost.[1] U. S. Industries operates 100 spas; Holiday Universal has 17. Each is a publicly-held corporation.

Campers are not forgotten. More than 17,000 campground and recreational area parks are listed for the U. S. and Canada,

nearly 8000 are privately owned.[2] About 7700 developed campgrounds and picnic grounds, capable of accommodating 490,000 people, are available in National forests.[3] State and Federal parks offer thousands more. In addition to campsites in dozens of the Federal and state parks and forests, private campgrounds are opening all over the U. S., now totalling more than 430,000 individual campsites. Kampground of America (KOA), a franchise campground company patterned after Holiday Inns, has more than 500 campgrounds under its banner. A subsidiary, Ranch Kampgrounds of America, has one ranch at Chinwater, Wyoming with no less than 75,000 acres. Holiday Inns and Gulf Oil have joined in the campout franchise business.[4] Camping takes on some of the features of a resort at some sites; the camper can rent air conditioners, electric heaters and even television.

Inventory of Hotel Rooms

Tourist destinations imply hotels, and lots of them. New York City, not usually thought of as a resort, is a mecca for business and fun. It inventories 117,000 guest rooms, the largest concentration in the world. Miami Beach has over 36,000 guest rooms. Las Vegas and Hawaii have about 30,000 each. Puerto Rico has about 9000. The total for guest rooms in the United States in 1969 was about 2.5 million, half of them in hotels, the other half in motels. Gross sales of the entire innkeeping industry in the United States in 1969 was about $7.6 billion.

Service World International estimates the number of guest rooms in the world at between 10 and 18 million, depending upon whether pensions are included. Total world sales is estimated by the same source at $27 billion annually. Various countries state their tourist accommodations differently so that statistics cannot be compared except by approximation. The table on the facing page, developed by *Service World Interna-*

[1]*The Wall Street Journal,* April, 1970.
[2]Paul J. C. Friedlander, "Into the Great Outdoors," *The New York Times,* June 6, 1971, p. 67.
[3]U. S. Dept. of Agriculture Forest Service, *National Forest Vacations,* 1968.
[4]*Time Magazine,* July 6, 1970.

TABLE V—NUMBER OF BEDS IN HOTELS OF THE WORLD[1]

U. S. A.	2,386,000	Norway	89,000
Italy	1,332,000	Portugal	78,000
Germany	847,000	Japan (European Style)	60,000
United Kingdom	773,000	Denmark	55,000
France	761,000	Ireland	53,000
Spain	668,000	Mexico	44,000
Austria	495,000	Finland	33,000
Canada	266,000	Bulgaria	29,000
Switzerland	256,000	Yugoslavia	23,000
Yugoslavia	176,000	Singapore	22,000
Turkey	166,000	USSR	18,000
Netherlands	131,000	Luxemburg	16,000
Greece	118,000	Brazil	16,000
Belgium	102,000	Argentina	13,000
Sweden	95,000	East Germany	12,000

tional, is an approximation of the number of hotel beds in the various countries listed.

Perhaps a better indication of the extent of the hotel business in a country is the number of staff employed in hotels and restaurants, as noted in the following OECD figures: United Kingdom, 543,000; West Germany, 420,000; Austria, 87,000; Italy, 309,000.

Totals for those employed in hotels in other countries: Yugoslavia, 126,000; Switzerland, 74,500; Japan, 40,000; Norway, 33,000; Portugal, 23,000; Ireland, 16,000. The lodging business in the United States employs more than 733,000 people.[2] The total restaurant business, including institutional foodservices, is manned by about 3.3 million people.[3]

Another aspect of tourism, especially important to the hotel sector, is the conven-

tion business. Increasingly, conventions are being held at resort destinations and many hotels depend upon convention sales, at least in part, and in some cases almost exclusively. The Loew's chain reported that half of its national sales volume comes from conventions and meetings.

The New York Hilton and the Americana, in New York City, were designed and built as convention properties. The New York Hilton gets 40 percent of its annual volume from conventions and business meetings. The Shoreham Hotel, in Washington,

[1]*Service World International.*
[2]U. S. Bureau of the Census, *Statistical Abstract of the U. S.,* (Washington, D. C.: Government Printing Office, 1967), p. 782.
[3]National Restaurant Assn., *Washington Report,* Aug. 18, 1969.

D. C., receives 67 percent of its business from conventions. In Chicago, The Sherman House gets 70 percent of its dollar volume from the same source.

San Juan, Miami Beach, Las Vegas, Honolulu and numerous other destination areas are seeing convention customers increase each year. According to *Sales Meetings Magazine,* there were more than 35,000 association conventions in 1968, with attendance numbering more than 12 million persons. Twenty-nine thousand of the conventions were state or regional meetings; 6300 were international and national in character.[1]

The periodical, *World Convention Dates,* published monthly, announces over 28,000 conventions, conferences, banquets, expositions and trade shows each year.[2]

One reason for the increasing attendance at such meetings is the tax status accorded business travel. If a meeting can be justified as a business expense, it is tax deductible. Many companies are sending employees to meetings at company expense. Airlines, to make bringing wives along easy, offer special rates. From 60 to 75 percent of convention goers are accompanied by wives.

Chicago, New York City, Miami Beach, San Francisco, Atlantic City, Washington, D. C., Los Angeles and Las Vegas are the big convention centers. Many other areas are moving rapidly into the convention business.

Convention Hotels Near Airports

There is an increasing tendency to hold meetings near airports, a growing practice at O'Hare Airport in Chicago. Numerous hotels with convention facilities have been built in the area of airports.

An airport hotel was first built in the U. S. in 1929, the 37-room Oakland Municipal Airport Inn. It had been preceded by a 200-room aerodrome hotel at Croyden Airport in England and by a hotel at Templehof Airport in Berlin.

A survey conducted by *Hospitality Magazine* found that there were some 36,000 guest rooms operated by chains that depended upon airports for their business.[3] Most of the newer properties include facilities for handling group business. The occupancy rate for airport hotels is considerably higher than that found in the hotel business generally and runs into the 80's and 90's. Some of the reasons are obvious: The air traveler saves time and avoids the cost of limousine or cab fare. (Airport hotels usually provide complimentary limousines or mini-bus service to and from the hotel.)

A vacation begins for some travelers at an airport hotel. The O'Hareport Hotel and Convention Center, a 500-room facility, gives a surprisingly large number of scuba-diving lessons to persons flying to the Caribbean. The customer doesn't have to waste time learning while on the vacation site.

Future Convention Changes

Closed-circuit TV linking 21 major cities in the U. S. may change the nature of convention business in this country. In 1970, General Electric formed a permanent closed-circuit color television system which was installed in special hotel meeting rooms. Time on the network will be sold largely to major U. S. corporations having nationwide sales and distribution systems. Instead of sales personnel traveling to a central resort or city for a sales meeting, they go to the nearest city included in the network. Time on the network is sold in blocks of one hour, at the rate of $35,000 for use of the entire configuration. The network was planned initially to include 35 cities.

It is quite natural for the airlines to be interested in hotel ownership. Hotel space can be sold at the same time as the airline ticket, booked via the airline reservation system. Some destination areas lack first-class hotel accommodations and if no one else is interested, the airlines may, by default, construct and operate them. If the airline is already operating a good hotel at a particular destination, it may have a better chance of being assigned a route to that area by the Civil Aeronautics Board. The airlines have become major factors in the

---

[1]Urban Land Institute, Washington, D. C. *Land: Recreation and Leisure,* 1970, p. 37.
[2]*World Convention Dates,* Hendrickson Pub. Co., New York City.
[3]"Hotels at the Sky," *Hospitality Magazine,* July, 1970.

hotel business; one business complements the other.

The international carriers are especially interested in hotel chains. In 1946, Pan American World Airways established Intercontinental Hotels Corporation as a subsidiary and began operating and participating in ownership of hotels in Latin America and Cuba. In 1948, the Hilton Company began its first overseas operations at the Caribe Hilton in Puerto Rico. International hotel-keeping is dominated by Americans, principally by four large companies: Hilton International; Intercontinental Hotels; Holiday Inns and Western International Hotels.

Hotel Chain Expansion

Hilton International announced in 1970 that by the mid 70's they will have 100 hotels abroad, nearly all of which will be managed under contract. Intercontinental will double its room capacity to close to 30,000 rooms. Holiday Inn expects to have 1200 inns under franchise or owned outside the United States.

As of 1970, nine American companies operated more than 230 hotels or motor inns overseas; another 160 were under construction or in the planning stage. ITT-Sheraton Hotels have a number of hotels outside the United States and are planning many more. Western International Hotels (owned by United Airlines) operates some 19 hotels in Mexico and is affiliated with 21 others. Western International Hotels also has four properties in Central America, 11 in Venezuela, and one in Ecuador. Other hotel chains which are operating abroad include Sonesta, Knott Hotels, TraveLodge, Loew's, Rockresorts and Howard Johnson's.

Eastern Airlines owns Rockresorts.* American Airlines has hotels and motor inns in the United States, Mexico and Korea. Braniff International has a hotel in Lima, Peru and is expected to build throughout South America. Continental Airlines is moving into Samoa and the Micronesian Islands.

European airlines are also busy developing hotel interests. BOAC has hotels in such little-known places as Georgetown, Guyana, Kenya and Bahrain. KLM Royal Dutch Airline owns a hotel in Amsterdam and has a minority interest in several others in the Netherlands, Pakistan, Aruba and Curacao. Quantas, Australia's international airline, owns the Winthrop Hotel in Sydney.

To meet the critical shortage of moderately-priced modern hotels in capital cities catering to the 747 group package tour market, several European airlines have banded together under the aegis of European Hotel Corporation Services, Ltd. (EHC). Seventy-five percent of the capital of the company is owned by BEA, BOAC, Alitalia, Swissair, Lufthansa. The remaining 25 percent of the capital is being put up by banks in the United Kingdom, France, Italy, Germany and Switzerland. Basic room rates for the chain will be $7.50 to $10.00, single; $11 to $15, double. The kitchens will be designed around total convenience food and limited menu operations. Self-service will be the order of the day with launderettes and carry-your-own luggage. Plans include developing hotels in about 20 cities before 1975.

Airlines Building Hotels

The airlines may well dominate most aspects of the travel business in the years to come. The traveler wants convenience, speed and economy in travel. For long distance travel, the airlines have no competition. The airlines have access to huge amounts of capital which enables them to expand rapidly in the ownership of resort hotels. They have the personnel and organization to market and sell travel packages of all kinds.

If the traveler is offered a convenient way to purchase a complete package of travel services—transport to the airport, air transportation, transport from the airport at the resort destination to the resort, resort accommodation and entertainment—he will probably buy it, especially if it is offered on credit. The airlines are in a position to do this. It remains for the airlines to purchase or create rent-a-car systems or for the airlines to be merged into even larger conglomerates, within such organizations as ITT, RCA, U. S. Steel and Alcoa.

---

*The Rockefellers are major stockholders in both Eastern Airlines and Rockresorts.

American Hegemony in World Travel

American emphasis on business management techniques, international promotion and advertising and the use of vast networks of computerized reservation systems have helped to bring American hegemony in world travel. The role of international hotelier, once held by the Swiss, has shifted to Americans. This position is likely to be strengthened by the rapid movement of several American airlines into hotel business around the world.

In the free world, the airlines of the U. S. A. are by far the largest international carrier. In 1966, Pan American and TWA together carried 14.8 million international passengers as compared with Britain's British European Airlines which carried 4.1 million passengers and Air France which carried 3.6 million. In 1968, Pan American had 144 jets in operation; TWA had 173. Air France in the same year had 76 such planes; BOAC, 44 and Lufthansa, 43.[1]

According to the Transport Association of America, U. S. carriers did 55.8 percent of the overseas air traffic in 1968; with the remainder handled by other carriers. In 1968, income to U. S. carriers from overseas passengers was $7.07 billion; for other carriers, $6.34 billion.[2]

Airplane manufacture is dominated by such American companies as Boeing, Douglas and Lockheed, companies that gained their expertise developing military planes during World War II.

Travel Conglomerates

The travel-accommodations-entertainment business is being integrated and controlled by conglomerate companies. As mentioned, nearly every major airline is in the hotel business. Some airlines have gone much further in their activities and have covered most of the areas of travel.

Canadian Pacific, for example, controls an airline, 36 hotels, more than 100 restaurants, rail lines, ship lines as well as local transportation. It is also in the wholesale travel and tour business, often providing tours to its own operations. Further, it is in the world travel and referral business. It has its own traveler's checks, credit card and world communication system.

Several of the large conglomerates, originally not a part of the travel business, have moved into the tourist business through massive purchases of existing chains. Nestle's, a Swiss conglomerate, owns the large table service restaurant chain of Stouffer's. ITT, originally a telephone and communications company, owns Sheraton Hotels.

The major oil companies are fast getting into aspects of travel other than selling gasoline. Esso (Europe) built a number of hotels and motels, most of them on the highways between the Baltic and the Mediterranean. Gulf Oil is affiliated with Holiday Inns, the largest of all accommodation enterprises the world has known.

Quite logically, the major food manufacturers, Pillsbury, Campbell Soup, General Mills and General Foods, are rapidly expanding into the restaurant business.

National Governments and Tourism

Government leaders around the world are likely to think of tourism as a necessary or desirable source of income for their countries. Tourism stimulates investment, provides a means of earning foreign exchange and is a source of employment. (Not as well understood is the fact that tourism brings social change, changes in attitudes, expectations and personal habits. It may radically change the life style of a remote area, introducing unexpected tensions and environmental erosion.)

National tourist promotion became important in the early part of the century. The Swiss Federal Railways set up offices in Paris, New York, Berlin, Cairo and Venice in 1903. The Swiss National Tourist Office was formed later, in 1917. A National Tourist Office for France dates from 1910. In 1924, the International Union of Official Organisations for Tourist Propaganda was set up and a congress held at the Hague in 1925. Delegates from national tourist offices of 14 European countries attended.[3]

In 1934, an International Union of Na-

---

[1] "What Makes the Going Great at Pan Am," *Business Week,* Feb. 17, 1968.
[2] *Cornell Hotel and Restaurant Administration Quarterly,* Feb., 1970, p. 7.
[3] Lickorish and Kershaw, *The Travel Trade,* (London: Practical Press, 1958), p. 44.

tional Tourist Propaganda Organisations was formed, only to be interrupted by World War II. Following the war, the name was changed to the International Union of Official Travel Organizations. Today, more than a hundred countries are members and the organization acts in a consultative capacity to the United Nations.

National tourist offices have several responsibilities, among them are the following:

To promote and advertise the country to attract more tourists.

To promote legislation for and regulation of the tourist industry.

To plan and coordinate various sectors of the industry.

To operate nationalized sections of the travel industry or certain state-owned sections of it.

Nearly every country of any size has a national tourist office. In some countries, the national tourism office is a part of the central machinery of government through which the government operates directly in the tourism sector. In Spain and Portugal, for example, the national tourist offices have financed and operate a number of hotels and restaurants. In the socialistic countries, everything, including spas, restaurants and hotels, is owned and operated by the state. Even the beach equipment and ski equipment is state owned and rented.

In some countries, tourism ranks as a full ministry and, in some of these, its minister enjoys cabinet rank. The activities of the national tourism office are, in some countries, financed in part by means of a direct tax on tourists. Such a tax tends to create resentment on the part of the tourist, even though it may be nominal as compared to his total expenditure. Such a tax is tantamount to double taxation since the tourist is already contributing to the tax revenues of the country via his purchases in that country.

Nearly all tourist offices in other countries are more directly related to government policy than is the United States Travel Service. In Great Britain, for example, the government directly or indirectly controls tourist effort. BOAC and BEA, the national airlines, are government-owned. BOAC owns hotels in Ceylon, South America and in London. It also has numerous restaurants and is a wholesale travel and tour operator. Until recently it owned Thos. Cook, which, in turn is affiliated with Wagon-Lits, which operates over 1000 sleeping and dining cars in Europe.

Outside of the U. S., travel conglomerates owned by government have been the rule. Nearly all of the railroads and large airlines of the world outside of the United States are government owned. Probably all of them are government subsidized, if judged by normal accounting procedures. The ownership and control may be direct, as in the case of most of the developing countries where government-owned national airlines are a losing proposition but are kept going for reasons of national prestige. In the United Kingdom, almost all public transportation is owned or indirectly controlled by the government.

The Canadian National Company, which operates Air Canada, a number of restaurants, rail lines, ship lines and offers credit cards, is government owned. Quantas, the Australian Airline, is government owned and is entering the hotel business. Japanese Airlines is owned by the Japanese government. It is affiliated with the government-owned Japanese Travel Bureau, which controls rail lines, ship lines and tour operations located in 300 cities. The Greek government owns Xeni, the Greek tourist bureau, which has 65 hotels and numerous restaurants together with travel bureaus. That the airlines of the U. S. have been profitable and dominate international travel in the free world says something about private versus government enterprise.

Government Controlled Tourism

As mentioned, in socialistic countries travel is completely owned and controlled by the government. The In-Tourist-Aeroflot travel conglomerate, owned by the Soviet Union, bills itself as the largest carrier in the world and has 40,000 rooms for foreigners. It is, perhaps, the most comprehensive travel agency in the world: no tourists may travel in Russia except via In-Tourist. Orbus of Poland owns the national air line, the rail service and 17 hotels plus being a full travel agency.

The Rumanian National Tourist runs airports, Black Sea resorts, river boats, local sight-seeing festivals and all of the restaurants in the country. In the socialist nations, tourism may be conducted at a loss in order to attract foreign currency. The Yugoslavian National Tourist Bureau has pegged tourist prices at a lower-than-cost level, with the result that tourism is booming. The Bureau operates all airports, airlines, hotels and motels, railroads and shipping. Interhotel Interflug of East Germany controls the airports, all new hotels, the restaurants on the Autobahn, travel bureaus and the railroads.

In New Zealand, the government's tourist arm, Tourist Hotel Corporation of New Zealand, operates the major hotels, the airlines, railroad, shipping lines and the tourist agency business.

In France, the tourist office takes responsibility for providing low cost holiday facilities for the working classes. Camps are subsidized and farmers with large and antiquated buildings have been encouraged to borrow money at nominal rates of interest to convert part of their buildings for rentals to industrial workers.

Where tourism is already fairly advanced in capitalistic countries, the national tourism office may have semi-autonomous status and act more as a catalytic agent than as a regulatory body. Concern for tourism as an industry by the U. S. government came only in the late 50's as the Federal government cast about for ways of reducing the disparity between the dollar outflow and inflow. In 1970, Americans were estimated to have spent almost $5 billion abroad, compared to $2.352 billion spent by foreigners visiting the United States.[1] The Johnson Administration advocated setting limits on expenditures by Americans abroad, as the United Kingdom had done with its citizens when traveling outside the country. Limiting tourist expenditures was not acceptable politically; instead, an effort was made to balance the dollar gap by encouraging travel to America.

Several national tourist offices have sizable budgets for promotion. In 1970, for example, some of the larger promotion budgets were:[2]

United Kingdom	$4.8 million
Greece	4.6 million
Bahamas	5.0 million
Canada	5.9 million
Italy	3.2 million

In that year, the U.S.T.S. had $2.3 million in its promotion budget.

Most of the larger nations publish directories of accommodations in their countries and most maintain offices in the major cities of the world, especially New York and London.

The United States Travel Service

The International Travel Act of June 29, 1961 established the United States Travel Service (U.S.T.S) as part of the Department of Commerce. The Act gave the U.S.T.S. authority to advertise and promote travel to the United States and to facilitate that travel wherever possible. Its principal purpose is to increase the number of travelers to the United States. The 1970 budget was $4.5 million; budgets for 1971 and 1972 were for $15 million each year.

The organization of the U.S.T.S. includes the seven foreign offices where promotion activities are carried on. Both the Director and Deputy Director are political appointees. The Director has the rank of Assistant Secretary of Commerce. Other employees are civil servants. Interestingly, the offices in foreign capitals were at first maintained on choice locations on the ground floor level. Large numbers of the curious, most of whom had little intention of traveling to the U. S., came in to chat with the attractive service representatives. It was found to be more effective to remove the office from the street level and work completely with groups or with people whose business it is to sell travel services.

Through an arrangement with TraveLodge International, any foreign visitor to the U. S. can call tollfree the TraveLodge Reservations Center in Kansas City where travel questions will be answered in French, German, Spanish or Japanese. The Service

---

[1] *The Wall Street Journal,* Apr. 9, 1970.
[2] Organization for Economic Cooperation and Development, *Tourism in OECD Member Countries, 1970.* (Paris, 1970).

also sponsors travel promotion sales meetings around the world. Presidents and chairmen of boards of American companies engaged in tourism are paired with competitors in foreign countries. Rent-a-car executives from the U. S. discuss car renting with executives of foreign rental car companies. Similarly, hotel, busline, tourist agency and convention bureau officers confer on problems with their counterparts abroad.

The U.S.T.S. has been highly successful considering the size of its budget which is small as compared with those of some other nations. It has rightly concentrated its efforts on the countries that have in the past produced the most tourists to the United States.

Within the United States, the U.S.T.S. has encouraged low cost travel and reduced rates for foreigners. It has actively encouraged hotels to provide multi-lingual services for travelers. Hotels are asked to employ persons on the front desk, at the switchboard and in the restaurants who can speak Spanish, French, Japanese or German.

State and Territorial Travel Offices

Every state in the Union maintains a travel office. Some are a part of the State Highway Department, some a branch of a Department of Industry, Commerce or Economics. A few are part of a Department of Parks and Recreation. Several are separate departments or offices which report directly to the governor of the state.

Puerto Rico has an active department as part of the Puerto Rico Economic Development Administration. The Virgin Islands, American Samoa, Guam, the Ryuku Islands and the Trust Territory of Pacific Islands also maintain tourism offices. A list of the State and Territorial Travel Information offices in the USA is available.

Tourist Attractions

Tourist attractions—by definition anything that attracts tourists, and they can be just about anything—are an important part of tourism. Tourist attractions take many forms, seemingly limited only by the imagination. The Smithsonian Institution in Washington, D. C. with its educational appeal attracts 12 million visitors each year,

is more popular than Disneyland in Anaheim, California.

Natural beauty as represented by the Grand Canyon, Yellowstone National Park, the Swiss Alps or an erupting volcano are tourist attractions, over which man has relatively little control. South Florida has a number of natural springs—Silver Springs, Weekiwatchee and Cypress Gardens—which are well exploited. Marinelands can be developed almost anywhere and are popular in Ohio, Florida, Southern California and Hawaii. Dog and horse race tracks, or any kind of a contest on which bets can be placed, have a broad appeal.

Museums and zoos are natural tourist attractions as are historic ruins and restorations, if properly developed and promoted. Nearly every Caribbean Island has an old fort. Hawaii is fortunate in having a number of remnants of old Hawaii—temples, cities of refuge, residences of former royalty.

A great appeal of the United Kingdom and much of Europe is the presence of hundreds of palaces and castles, cathedrals and monuments.

In 1971, nearly 34 million visitors, about 16 percent from overseas, trooped through Britain's historic properties. The Tower of London quite naturally led the list of attractions with more than 2.5 million visitors. The Marquis of Bath has added free-roaming lions to the appeal of his Elizabethan home and attracts hundreds of thousands. Another nobleman attracts visitors with an antique car collection. Several of the ducal homes—Blenheim Palace, Belvoir Castle, Alnwick Castle, Arundel Castle and Chatsworth—attract hundreds of thousands of people. Britain is replete with historic homes, beautiful gardens, and is a mecca for Anglophiles who think of Stratford-upon-Avon as a literary mecca.

Scotsmen from around the world romantically cling to the idea of the clan. Some hundred thousand visitors, many of them of the Campbell clan visit their chief's residence, Inverary Castle in Argyle. An equal number of Murray clansmen come to Blair Castle in Perthshire, Scotland to get a glimpse of the Duke of Athol and his little private army, the only one permitted in Britain. A tourist can spend weeks traipsing from one stately home to another, each wrapped in history and romance. For those who wish to see it that way, Britain can be viewed as a "complete museum" country.

Even these must be promoted to be successful. The Duke of Bedford has turned showman and added a number of attractions to Woburn Abbey to attract tourists.

Age adds interest—old ships, old mines, old locomotives. Age may bring a pleasant patina to everything, except people. A large number of tourist attractions call forth the history of the area, allowing the tourist to step back in time and to experience symbolically previous periods, minus the inconveniences and frustrations of the period.

The Irish Tourist Board does a magnificent job of carrying tourists back several hundred years, to the days before the arrival of the English in Ireland. Three castles of the period, near Shannon Airport, have been restored and trips are arranged to the castles for an immersion in history. A medieval banquet includes the coarse bread of the time and mead (actually hard cider with honey). A pageant accompanies the banquet, a performance with costumed players and singers conveys an impression of Irish history that cannot be gained by reading books. Historical commentaries add to remarks made by tour guides. Taped commentaries, including historical remarks, are a part of the tour bus and ferry rides in Hong Kong.

The well-traveled tourist today responds to the tourist attraction which offers more than pure entertainment and is eager to savor the flavor of an area and its past. Costuming and artifacts, if authentic, add depth to an attraction. A tourist attraction which is only partly done or poorly done may attract one-time visitors but not repeat customers. Gift shops, if well done, can be visual displays rather than tourist traps. Gifts on sale should at least partly reflect the area.

Four-Way Development

Harrison A. Price, president of Economics Research Associates, a company which has done considerable research in planning tourist attractions, believes that a tourist attraction can be developed in four ways:

1. By capitalizing on a natural physical amenity: lake, mountain, gorge, etc.
2. By capitalizing on a location.
3. By capitalizing on a reputation.
4. By creating something out of nothing.

Most destination attractions in this country, he believes, are those that have capitalized on natural physical assets. Lake Tahoe, in northern California, is an example. Developers at Lake Tahoe complemented the beauties of a crystal-blue lake, mountains and high elevation scenery with golf courses, marinas, ski facilities, overnight accommodations, restaurants, night clubs, retail shops and service establishments.

Beauty and Culture Combined

An example of combining natural beauty with cultural interest is the Tanglewood Music Festival. Held each summer in Berkshire County, Mass., it attracts 200,000 people who come to listen to the Boston Symphony Orchestra and enjoy the Berkshire Mountains. Some 120,000 stay in the area at least 2½ days and spend $30 a day. The Festival accounts for $9 million in income to the area.[1]

The second most frequent method used to create a tourist destination is to capitalize on a location that has the latent potential for capturing the traveler who is enroute to another destination. Gatlinburg, Tenn., lying at the entrance to Great Smoky Mountains National Park, is one successful example. The Park draws some 6 million visitors a year. Gatlinburg, says Price, was a natural site for motels, restaurants and retail stores. The town has 157 motels, 5 hotels, 57 restaurants and 56 craft and hobby shops to make it an attractive stopping-off place for visitors to the park. (Some commentators refer to the commercial part of Gatlinburg as a good example of lack of planning.)

Capitalizing on the reputation of a place takes the form of devising events and facilities that are in keeping with an already established reputation. Olvera Street in Los

---

[1]Mass. Dept. of Commerce and Development, *Commerce Digest,* (Boston, Apr., 1971).

Angeles is known as the Mexican-American community. Pageants and festivals add to its appeal.

The old whaling port of Lahaina on Maui in Hawaii, by building on its unique history, developed as a tourist attraction. Milwaukee has taken advantage of its German traditions to develop a major festival in the spirit of the Oktoberfest of Munich. The festival drew over a million people in 1970.

Seattle had created a reputation for its World's Fair of 1962. By keeping the Monorail, Space Needle Restaurant and Fun Forest amusement complex, a continuing attraction has been developed. Similarly, the recreation island of LaRonde, which was part of Montreal's Expo, remains an attraction.

Because of our nostalgia for things past, many old ships have been preserved for their historic and educational value. A replica of the Mayflower docked at Plymouth, Mass. attracts thousands of visitors each year. Lord Nelson's flagship is a similar attraction in Portsmouth, England. The U.S.S. Constitution in Boston Harbor attracts thousands. Other thousands tour Honolulu's Pearl Harbor, scene of the debacle of December 7, 1941.

The Queen Mary, famous formerly as a Cunard Liner, attracts many more visitors as a museum and hotel than it ever did as a passenger carrying vessel. The luxury ship is now docked in Long Beach, California harbor where, at a cost of $52 million, it has become a major tourist attraction.

Like many business ventures, the Queen Mary's development as a tourist attraction ran into economic problems. Although the ship, which cost $28 million in 1936, was bought by the city of Long Beach for only $3.5 million from the Cunard Steamship Company, the cost of converting it to a marine museum and a convention center soared beyond all projections. A State Labor Commission ruling that building trades unions should work on the project rather than maritime union workers increased the cost of labor by $6.6 million. A permanent mooring site cost $7.9 million. Land fill for additional parking at the site cost another $2 million. Total cost of adding hotels, restaurants and shops may reach $160 million.[1]

The "biggest" anything may create interest—the Empire State Building in New York City, the Eiffel Tower, the highest mountain, the longest tunnel. People also go underground for fun. Some 165 caves in the U. S. are open to the public with guides provided.

Religious shrines, cathedrals and monasteries often take on tourist appeal.

Some of the more successful tourist attractions contrive to evoke or amplify the character of the area. Sea Life Park on the Island of Oahu is built alongside the ocean and contains a living reef. To insure the injection of new exhibits, 12 percent of the annual profits are allocated to the Oceanic Institute, a research organization which develops information and ideas which can be used in the Park.

The Educational Tourist Attraction

What is attractive to a tourist, of course, depends upon a number of factors, not the least being the age, educational level, curiosity and general background of the tourist. The dimensions of scale and variety add appeal, as witness the tremendous popularity of expositions and fairs which are large and offer a variety of entertainment and educational features.

World expositions are tremendous tourist attractions. The first international exposition was London's Crystal Palace Exhibition in 1851. Century 21, held in Seattle in 1962, attracted 9.64 million persons. The New York World's Fair, 1965, attracted about 26 million. Montreal's Expo '67 attracted slightly more than 50 million. Expo '70, Osaka attracted 64.2 million persons and made a $30 million profit.[2]

Harrison A. Price, the tourism researcher, points out that the modern American, first and foremost, wants to be amused, entertained, instructed and enlightened. Mr. Price recommends placing increased emphasis on educational-cultural attractions such

[1]*The Wall Street Journal*, Feb. 9, 1971, p. 34.
[2]Arthur D. Little, Inc., *Attendance Visitor Spending and Economic Impact of the U. S. Bi-Centennial, World Exposition, 1969*, (unpublished) and *The Wall Street Journal*, Sept. 14, 1970.

as music festivals, and historical sights. More and more, he says, people feel the need to justify their travel by including what might be called *purposiveness* in their travel planning.

Another consideration in planning a tourist attraction, says Price, is that the attraction must reflect the fact that mass leisure, along with mass higher education, has brought a significant rise in mass taste and expectation. The old family-owned thrill park or roadside cave and reptile show have only a small place in today's travel environment.

The tourist attraction must have scale and depth, "critical mass." The old time amusement park has changed to a theme park attracting visitors from long distances. Even Santa Barbara's Children's Park is not large enough to attract people from 80 miles away. The zoo would have to increase its size and scope of facilities to be able to do that. San Diego Zoo and Gardens, however, brings people from hundreds of miles. Disneyland, Anaheim led the way. Walt Disney World in Florida is the best known. Six Flags over Texas in Dallas opened in 1961; Six Flags over Georgia, 1967; Six Flags over the Midwest, 1971. Opryland was built in

Nashville, Tenn. in 1972 at a cost of $30 million. Hershey Foods is building a Chocolate World. The open zoo is another new attraction—Longleat, Woburn Abbey in England; Jungle Habitat in West Milford, N. J. are examples.[1]

Colonial Williamsburg, Inc.

Colonial Williamsburg, financed by John D. Rockefeller, Jr. is the best example of a historical restoration in the U. S. Restoration is still going on and will continue for years to come. Numerous buildings have been completely restored, including several taverns, the Palace of the Royal Governors, the House of Burgesses, shops and private residences, the old Powder Magazine, the courthouse, printing office and the church.

In 1932, the first exhibition building was opened and official attendance was 4047. The 1969 attendance reached 880,889.

The economic impact of the Williamsburg restoration has been sizable. What had been a sleepy little Virginia town now has over 2500 guest rooms, 40 restaurants and 37 gas stations. The restaurants served

[1]*The Wall Street Journal,* July 2, 1972.

Left: The Governor's Palace at Colonial Williamsburg. The Restoration of Colonial Williamsburg was begun in the early 1930's and today is one of the most comprehensive restoration projects anywhere. While Colonial Williamsburg was not built primarily as a tourist attraction, it has become an extremely popular attraction which combines history, education, and entertainment.

Facing page: The Restoration of a Milliner's Shop, part of Colonial Williamsburg. The shelves are stocked with wares of the 18th Century: night shirts, wig accessories, ruffles and snuff boxes.

The Capitol Building in Colonial Williamsburg—
The House of Burgesses, right, America's first
representative legislative assembly met here. It
also housed the Governor's Council and the
High Court.

The Public Gaol of Colonial Williamsburg, below,
an authentic part of the restoration which has
obvious tourist appeal.

over 2 million meals during 1969. Colonial Williamsburg, Inc. had a 1969 payroll in excess of $9 million and over 1.5 million visitors. The average visitor stayed 2.5 days and spent $20 per day. Gross tourism income for the city of Williamsburg is estimated at $45 million a year. A similar amount probably is generated by the visitor within the state of Virginia as he goes to and from Williamsburg.

Colonial Williamsburg's motto is "That the future may learn from the past."

Parks and Forests as Tourist Attractions

In the United States, the largest tourist attractions in land area are the State and National Parks. Nearly 47,000 sq. mi. of "outdoor museums" are contained in the nation's 35 National Parks. The National Park Service, part of the U. S. Dept. of Interior, counted 200 million visitor-days for its national recreational and historical areas in 1971. It has 71,800 full time personnel and a budget of $225 million. Since 1950, the average annual percentage increase has been about 20 percent. In 1969, attendance at the top ten of the areas administered by the National Park Service was as follows:

Blue Ridge Parkway	11,865,100
Natchez Trace Parkway	10,451,000
Colonial National Historical Park	8,470,100
Great Smoky Mountains National Park	6,331,100
Lake Mead National Recreation Area	5,614,900
George Washington Memorial Parkway	4,361,900
Cape Cod National Seashore	4,031,300
Lincoln Memorial	3,874,500
Gettysburg National Cemetery	3,279,100
Grand Teton National Park	3,134,400

As might be expected, eight of the top ten areas of the National Park system, in terms of attracting visitors, are east of the Mississippi River, drawing upon the heavily populated areas of the East for visitors.[1]

The National Park Service is an illustration of Government and private enterprise working together to produce and operate tourist facilities. Numerous hotel, motel and cabin accommodations have been built in the National Parks by concessionaires, private persons or companies using their capital. All plans and specifications for new construction must be approved in advance by the Park Service. The government controls accommodations and other rates charged to visitors, including food prices. Advertising and items that can be sold are also government controlled. Standards covering public health sanitation, visitor comfort, and convenience are under government supervision. The concessionaire must be in sympathy with the ideals and objectives of the park service. Concessionaire operations are controlled to the extent that wages, hours, conditions of employment, safety and sanitation standards must be met.

The concessionaire is given certain assurances. Once granted a contract to build and operate, he may receive an operational contract for up to 30 years. The arrangement, in some people's eyes, is the best of two worlds, the government insuring that facilities are available for the public and the concessionaire motivated by a desire for profit. In many state tourist facilities, however, the state builds and operates the facilities.[2]

Federally operated recreational areas include the national forests, parks, wildlife refuges, wilderness areas, seashores, recreation areas, historic monuments, historic landmarks, historic sites, grasslands, canoe areas, wild and scenic rivers and recreation trails. The best known of the recreation trails are the Appalachian Trail in the East and the Pacific Crest Trail in the West.

The Forest Service supervises 6000 camp grounds, 1664 picnic grounds, 14 hotels and lodges, 296 swimming sites, 726 boating areas, 200 winter sport and skiing centers, 421 major observation sites and 31 visitor centers. In 1970, some 170 million or more visitor-days of use were anticipated in the areas supervised by the Service. The Forest Service, a part of the U. S. Dept. of Agriculture, has jurisdiction over 154 national forests which cover a total of 187 million acres.[3] More than 400 resorts operate on National Forest land, most are owned and operated by concessionaires.

The State of Kentucky has an elaborate resort system operated by the state. Eight

[1] Business Research Division, *Travel Trends in the United States and Canada*, University of Colorado, 1970, p. 4.
[2] Thomas F. Flynn, Jr., "The Management of Concessions and Other Services in National Parks in the United States," *Trends in Parks and Recreation*, Oct., 1969.
[3] *The New York Times*, June 4, 1970.

state "resort parks" are open year round, offering package plan vacations which can be charged on Bank-Americard or any Inter-Bank credit card. Reservations can be made tollfree from within the state and from adjoining states. The facilities are among the most modern and attractive in the country.

Sixteen state resort parks have been established which offer hotel rooms, motel rooms and various sizes of cottages. Some of the facilities offer rental cars and rental houseboats, golf, ski lifts, regattas and planned recreation programs. One park has constructed trails for mini-biking. The state has involved itself in social tourism by offering facilities for its own state residents as well as by attracting visitors from out of state to bolster the economy.

Several other states are also engaged in operating tourist facilities of various kinds in state parks.

Classification of Tourist Attractions

Tourist attractions have been classified in various ways. Bulent Kastarlak divides them into site attractions and event attractions.[1] Beauty contests, centennials, wine festivals, flower shows and the like could be classified as event attractions. The Grand Canyon, the Statue of Liberty, or the U.S.S. Massachusetts, anchored at Fall River, Mass., are examples of site attractions.

Conceivably, a tourist attraction can be created almost anywhere that can be reached by the tourist. The U.S.S. Massachusetts, mentioned earlier, is an example of an attraction created at will and not necessarily related to tourist travel patterns. The battleship is berthed at Fall River, Mass., an area which was not known as a tourist area until the attraction was introduced.

In 1965, the battleship was released by the Navy to a non-profit educational corporation. Original cost of bringing the ship to Fall River was about $100,000. Refurbishing cost another $10,000, plus considerable free labor contributed by local people. Since the time the battleship was opened for visitors, some 200,000 people a year have toured the ship. About $2.6 million has been generated by the ship into the regional economy annually and the area's economy has improved appreciably as a result.

Old Sturbridge Village, another "created" tourist attraction in Massachusetts, is one more example of how tourism can be developed. Gross revenue from visitors to the Village each year exceeds $2.3 million.

Another way of classifying tourist attractions is to divide them into those which are local or regional in character as compared with those which are national or international in appeal.

Some tourist attractions are built around a unifying concept or theme. Disneyland is a good example of how an idea, largely drawn from fiction, can be transformed into reality. The theme in this case was the world of fantasy.

The wide range of what can be identified as tourist attractions is seen in the Kastarlak study covering tourism in Massachusetts. Over 5000 tourist attractions were identified in Massachusetts alone.

Condominiums are very much a part of the hotel world and will increase in importance with time. From the Latin and French, "condominium" means joint domain, or joint ownership; the condominium owner actually has full ownership of a unit in a complex, usually sharing in the cost of taxes and maintenance of jointly used facilities and services including cost of security, upkeep of grounds, roads and recreation facilities such as tennis courts, parks and marinas.

Condominium Resorts

The concept is said to have originated in southern Europe and come to the continental U. S. via Puerto Rico. In 1958, the Puerto Rican government approved condominium ownership and obtained Federal Housing Authority approval for mortgage loans to owners in 1959. The concept has spread to the U. S. Virgins, Florida, Hawaii, California, Colorado and to other states. In 1973, there were more than 500 resort condominiums completed or in some stage of planning in the U. S. and the Caribbean.[2]

[1]Bulent Kastarlak, *Tourism Potential and Planning for Growth at the State Level,* Division of Tourism, Mass., 1970.
[2]"Resort Hotel Condominiums, Guidelines for Resort Development," *Cornell Hotel and Restaurant Administration Quarterly,* May, 1973.

The condominium, an apartment or individual dwelling unit, is owned by an individual but the management and services for the unit are part of a pooled effort. Services and jointly owned recreational facilities are usually managed by an independent company. The company will often contract to rent the condominium when it is not being used by the owner.

Condominiums have special appeal because of tax advantages, property appreciation in recent years, and the fact that the condominium is cared for in the owner s absence. (The literal meaning of "condominium" is "joint dominion;" Roman law provided for independent ownership of the same property by two or more owners, its meaning today. Each owner can sell his share, apartment or other dwelling unit, independently of the other owners.)

The condominium idea has spread to include the trailer park. The trailer traveler buys a pad at a park of his choice and uses the pad for his trailer when he desires. The pad has water, utilities, sewage connections. Heated pools and recreation centers may be owned in common. The park manager rents the site in the owner's absence, if the owner wishes, to help defray its cost.

Gulf Oil has a 49 percent interest in Venture Out in America, Inc., which, in 1970, owned seven condominium resort centers: three in Florida, Lake Tansi and Gatlinburg in Tennessee, and Mesa and Woodland in Colorado.

For those who like to travel by trailer, there is a drive-camp overnight plan operated by Avis, the car rental firm. Under the plan, the traveler flies to a starting point and rents a car. Instead of staying at a hotel or motel, he stops at one of the Kampgrounds of America (KOA) where he sojourns in a rental trailer.

The financial aspects of the condominium are discussed in Chapter 8.

Sports Generate Tourism

Much of the sporting life is an aspect of tourism involving travel, resort living and the development of huge leisure-time complexes. *U. S. News and World Report* estimates that 10 million Americans are avid water skiers. Some 12 million people in this country play golf regularly at about 10,000 courses; about 9 million play tennis. Snow is growing in popularity. More than 600,000 snowmobiles were sold in the fiscal year, 1971-72, as reported by the Snowmobile Assn.

Growing Numbers of Skiers

Snow skiers—4 million strong—pour almost $1 billion into the economy. The number of skiers in the USA grows at an estimated 20 percent annually, calling for more ski lodges, more tows and a great array of ski clothing and equipment. With man-made snow, skiing is possible anywhere the temperature will remain below freezing for a reasonable period of time. Ski lodges exist as far south as the Great Smoky Mountains in Tennessee. Skiing is also growing by leaps and bounds in places other than the traditional ski areas in France, Switzerland and Scandinavia. Northern England and Scotland have a number of ski resorts.

Japan has taken to skiing with fervor and dedication. About 8 million Japanese spend $4 billion a year on skis, parkas, lodging and transportation to and from ski areas. Honshu, Japan's main island, has about 400 ski resorts. Japan's National Railroads put on about 50,000 special ski trains. A "normal" weekend at Ueno Station in Tokyo finds 30,000 skiers crowding pell mell on to trains which pull out of the platform every four minutes.

Crowds at some of the slopes are so great that waits for ski lifts may drag on as long as 50 minutes. As one wag put it, "In Japan you ski on people." A third of the accidents are caused by skiers running into each other.[1]

Mobile and second homes are also factors in tourism. Prefabricated houses—alpine style cottages and the like, are sprouting on lakesites at costs between $5000 to $40,000. It is relatively easy to tow a mobile home from one area to another. Thousands of mobile homes are permanently parked as second homes in Florida, Arizona and other warm-winter states. More than 6.5 million people in the United States in 1970 lived in mobile homes; by the end of

---

[1]*The Wall Street Journal,* Apr. 9, 1970.

Club Mediterranee Martinique
View from the solarium of the restaurant and theater complex,
plus some residential blocks.

The port with the club's 60-foot yacht "Paisano" tied up.
Round building with the hat is the "Cafe Du Port" which also
houses the nightclub discotheque. Buildings on the other side
of the harbor contain guest rooms. The two small white build-
ings nearest the wharf house the sailing and diving schools.

1980, that number is predicted to reach 13.5 million. One reason for the rapid growth in the mobile home market is that they can be financed like a car—come fully equipped with appliances.[1]

Vacation Clubs

The vacation club on a large scale is a means of bringing like-minded persons together for vacations, presumably at reduced cost to the vacationer. France has set the pace in vacation clubs; the first, the Touring Club of France, dating back to 1890, today has 600,000 members. At first, it concentrated on offering hiking, motorbikes and automobile tours. It now organizes cruises and trips to the seashore and mountains. Another French vacation club, Tourism and Labor, has 190,000 members. The European Tourism Club, another French vacation club, has 150,000 members.

Club Mediterranee is the largest of the travel clubs in this country. It offers a vacation plan and facilities which are especially appealing to the young and sportsminded. In 1970, some 226,000 people vacationed in its 17 ski, 35 summer and 8 all-year villages. American Express is a major stockholder in the club.

The first Mediterranee village, one established on the island of Majorca, in 1950, was a back-to-nature facility, with sleeping bags, and members taking turns to help cook and wash dishes. The original concept was that people wanted a vacation environment radically different than that in which they live their daily lives. Informality was the village feature—no telephones, radios or newspapers.

Sports equipment and instruction are part of the all-inclusive price which includes sailing, water skiing, scuba diving, and spear fishing at the warm-water resorts. Ski instruction is included as part of the rate at the 17 ski resorts maintained by the club. Riding, yoga, judo and fencing instruction are offered at some of the villages.

French cookery, with unlimited wine service, characterizes the cuisine. A no-cash economy—only drinks at the bar and personal purchases are paid for, and these by beads which are worn around the neck. No tipping is allowed. Rather than employees,

there are "gentile organisateurs," literally "pleasing organizers," so-called working members who mix freely with the guests. As such, these working members do not conflict with local labor laws, or with laws excluding expatriate employees.

Club villages are of two styles: "Hotel Villages" and "Traditional Villages." The hotel villages resemble the usual hotel or resort while the traditional villages provide thatched huts with minimal furnishings, no electric current and no plumbing.

In 1966, the Club became a publicly owned company and launched its Western Hemisphere operation with headquarters in New York City. In 1971, the Club numbered 32,000 American and Canadian members and had Western Hemisphere villages in Guadalupe and Martinique in the Caribbean, Moorea near the island of Tahiti, and Acapulco, Mexico. By 1973 there were 57 "villages" in 18 countries. Beds numbered about 40,000.

To vacation at any of the Club resorts, membership in the Club is required but membership is open to all and can be arranged through any American Express office or travel agent. Club Mediterranee appeals to the younger person who wants togetherness, casualness and a free-form lifestyle, with emphasis on activity.

Travel Savings Clubs are a recent development based on the idea of prepaid vacations. Membership is usually on a three-year basis with a specified amount of money (usually $25-$35) paid in each month. Members then are eligible to choose between several alternative vacation trips. The first of these, Club Internationale, organized in 1966 and now a subsidiary of Diner's Club/Fugazy Travel, has been so successful that a number of other similar clubs have been formed.

In 1973, Club Internationale had arranged travel for some 50,000 members, operating in more than 50 cities in the U. S. The Club negotiates leases with hotels, guaranteeing a certain minimum number of guests during the year for which a specified rate structure is given by the hotel. One of

---

[1]Donald S. Jones, *The Honolulu Advertiser*, Apr. 23, 1970.

the features of the club is the planning of people-to-people programs, receptions by local dignitaries and parties offering social interchange with local groups.

Some travel clubs own their own aircraft, the oldest (started in 1962) being the Emerald Shillelagh Chowder & Marching Society, Inc. of Fairfax, Virginia. The Shillelagh Club runs about 40 trips a year featuring a different destination in the snow country, the Caribbean, or Mexico throughout the winter; and Europe, Alaska, Canada and cooler points in the United States through the summer.[1] Members pay an initiation fee plus annual dues of $60 for a single membership. Sky Roamers Limited, with groups in New York, Boston and Philadelphia has a membership exceeding 3500. As of 1972, 26 travel clubs were licensed by the Federal Aviation Administration to operate their own planes. Voyager 1000, an Indianapolis-based travel club, has six planes including a Boeing 720 medium-range jet, 25 full-time pilots and navigators, more than 30,000 members.[2]

Largest of all the travel clubs is the American Automobile Assn., with some 8 million Master members in the United States. Founded in 1902, it has some 870 affiliated clubs and branches in the U. S. and Canada as well as contract agents in the nearly 100 countries and affiliation with other motor clubs throughout the world. Total revenue from dues, premiums on insurance, commissions and other fees reaches $1 billion a year. While the emphasis is on automobile travel, the various AAA offices maintain complete travel agency services, arranging for plane, cruise ship, train and hotel reservations, selling travelers checks, travel insurance, foreign car rental, sales of foreign cars and shipment of automobiles. They also arrange for international driver's licenses. Millions of trips within the U. S. have been carefully planned by marked roadmaps, showing the traveler the most scenic or most efficient routes between origin and destination. A major service of AAA is the auto breakdown insurance which is available. Some 23,000 garages in the U. S. are under contract to AAA to give priority service to their members.

The World Wide Travel segment of AAA, with some 500 offices, generates more than $250 million in travel sales a year ranking it at or near the top in travel sales in the world.

AAA is a curious combination of nonprofit service and for-profit business. Most of the profits, if they may be called that, come from the sale of tires, batteries and insurance. The central offices near Washington, D. C. employ about 1000 persons.

Incentive Travel

Using all-expense trips as incentives, particularly for salesmen, has become a big business in itself. Trans-International Airlines, a charter airline, estimated that American companies spent $525 million in 1973 in providing free trips to top salesmen and other income producers. The same company estimated that some 8000 companies utilize some kind of incentive travel. Sperry and Hutchison Company, best known for its S & H Green Stamps, has more than 100 people in its incentive travel section. In 1972, S & H arranged for 8200 Ford Motor people to go to the Canary Islands. In 1973, about 9800 Ford Motor employees went to Caracas, Venezuela, courtesy of the Ford Motor Company for their sales efforts. As long as tax laws are what they are, incentive travel will probably continue to grow. Prizes in the form of travel are considered a business expense to the company offering them. For the employee who wins the travel prize, it is a completely free trip. He pays no tax on it—it is better than money.

Promoters of incentive travel say that offering travel as a prize or inducement to perform appeals to almost everyone. A color TV, automobile or boat was once highly valued but is less so since the contestants are likely already to own them. Travel with its multitude of destinations offers almost unlimited possibilities.

The use of credit cards for travel and vacationing is another means of facilitating travel and, in many cases, increasing expenditures. It has been found that people who

---

[1]Business Research Division, *Travel Trends in the United States and Canada,* University of Colorado in cooperation with The Travel Research Assn., Boulder, 1971, p. 36.
[2]*The New York Times,* Feb. 15, 1972.

have credit cards tend to spend more in hotels, restaurants and in travel than if they did not use the cards. With a credit card (or several of them), the traveler may go almost any place in the world, even Russia, with little or no cash.

Of course, someone pays for arranging all of this. American Express and Diners Club, among the largest of the credit card companies, sell the card to the holder. The hotel, restaurant or other merchant who accepts the card in payment also pays the credit card company a percentage of the purchase price, whatever it may be. The percentage varies from about 1 percent in the case of airlines and other big users to over 7 percent in the case of a restaurant that wants cash payments immediately for a bill that it renders to the credit card company.

Master Card issues cards at no cost to the holder and charges the lowest percentage, usually 2 to 4 percent to the merchant. New England Bankard Association, for example, has set a 2 percent rate on Master Card accounts for all hotels, motels, and restaurants in Massachusetts. The banks participating in the plan make their profit on the fact that most users overdraw their balances in the bank whereupon they are charged at the rate of 1½ percent a month for the money they, in effect, have borrowed from the bank.

Credit cards have been issued by the millions. Nearly every major hotel chain has issued its own credit card at one time or another. Most will accept the major credit cards in payment of a bill. Credit cards are one more means of making travel easier and more attractive to the traveler.

Tourism as an Abstraction

In this chapter only the major and more obvious components of tourism have been cataloged. Tourism is an abstraction, a unifying concept used for convenience and simplification. The list of what comprises tourism could go on and on. Travel and vacationing touch the lives of nearly everyone in industrialized society. The producer of sun glasses, the maker of sun tan lotion, the manufacturer of skis and sport clothes has an interest in tourism only slightly less than the hotel manager or the airplane pilot. The filling station operator or the supermarket manager may derive a large part of his sales from tourists. Even the bookseller is affected by tourism: aside from the numerous travel books, some of the bestsellers—Hotel and Airport—concern travel and tourism.

The other chapters in this book will detail some of the more central aspects of tourism. The broad ramifications of the tourism concept can only be suggested.

The Careenage area of downtown Bridgetown, Barbados, is a ready-made tourist attraction. Here, vessels are careened (turned on their sides) to clean hulls.

THE TRAVEL MODES

Tourism is inseparable from and dependent upon travel. The means of travel, the travel modes as they are technically called, change and as they do they have an immediate impact on tourism, the numbers of travelers and the travel experience. Technological change in travel has widespread implications for much of social life.

Tourism implies pleasurable travel be it by land, sea or air. Since recorded history, ship travel could be fairly comfortable for the wealthy, but it awaited the development of the railroad in the 1830's to make travel comfortable for the masses and cheap enough to be within their reach.

By the 1920's, the automobile and the bus began usurping the position of the railroad as the leading tourist carrier. The auto has since become the predominant mode of transportation for tourism.

The airplane, an infant in the 1920's, soared upward as a favored travel mode for long-distance travel following World War II, and especially after 1959 when the commercial jets were introduced. Shipboard travel, relatively slow and expensive, has been relegated at this point to the role of passenger cruising. In 1969, the percentage of travel in the United States by each mode was as follows:[1]

Mode	Percentage
Automobile	86.8
Air	9.8
Bus	2.3
Rail	1.1
Water	.3

Change in travel technology has been dramatic since World War II. Airplane technology developed during the war was brought to the commercial airliner soon after the war, the U. S. leading the way. In 1950, 286,226 American tourists went to Europe; more than 2.9 million went in 1971. In 1952, the Superliner United States won the Blue Ribbon for the fastest transatlantic time—the ship is now in mothballs and nearly all of the transatlantic liners have been diverted elsewhere or similarly retired.

The railroad, the automobile and the airplane have added mobility and glamor to the American way of life. The power, the sound, the speed represented, first, by the railroad, then the auto and now the airplane stir the emotions and evoke a sense of awe. Half the fun of getting there may well be the travel experience itself. The sense of movement over space, pride of ownership of an automobile, the cloud perspective from an airplane provide thrills for what may be an otherwise prosaic life. From as early as the 1830's, the railroad contributed special significance to the American way of life and to the many who were engaged in railroading, it was a respected and pleasurable occupation. Particular trains were personalized and given names, the Green Devil, The Rocky Mountain Rocket, The Royal Blue and the ultimate in American passenger trains was named the Twentieth Century Limited. A visiting French economist, Michel Chevalier, summed it up, "The American has a perfect passion for railroads."[2]

Later, the automobile became the preferred possession and means of transport. The owner might live in a shack and give little thought to personal grooming but the chrome-plated automobile was displayed and given loving care. The automobile has become a part of the American way of life as has no other artifact in history. People crowd automobile shows and each year a model change has been cause for national discussion. General Motors has become the largest company in the world, with operating revenues exceeding that of several size-

[1]Transportation Assn. of America, *Annual Report,* Washington, D. C., 1970.
[2]*The New York Times,* May 1, 1971, p. 34.

able countries.

The railroad began to recede in popular imagination and use during the depression of the 1930's. Yet thousands queued up to view the nation's first streamliner, the Burlington Pioneer Zephyr in 1934.

Then the airlines began stealing the travel show and as each larger and faster plane appeared, it became the subject of interest for the traveler, especially those who were affluent.

As the modes of transportation change and costs are reduced, the effects on tourism are almost immediate. This chapter traces the development of the principal modes of travel and the effect each had made on tourism.

As already noted, the vehicle that transports the tourist is today only one facet of the travel mode. Many of the major transportation companies, especially the airlines, are also hotel and resort operators. In Canada and the United Kingdom, the major railroads own and operate hotels and restaurants. The airlines sell tours. A major busline in this country is owned by Holiday Inns.

The travel chart on the facing page shows the changing popularity of the three modes of public transportation: the railroads, the airlines and the buses.

By 1916, the number of miles of railroad track in the United States had reached its maximum and began to decline. Looking around the country, especially in the East and South, you will see the remains of old railroad lines, no longer in use.

World War II put extreme demands upon the railroads. By the 1920's, bus routes were already operating. The private automobile began siphoning off much of the passenger travel on the railroads. The depression years of the 30's did little to increase the number of passengers using the railroads, even though the new streamliners introduced in the mid-30's were well received.

World War II brought a tremendous surge in the number of passengers using the railroads, but they seldom traveled for pleasure. Old passenger cars were brought out of retirement and the trains had a field day hauling passengers as well as freight. Traffic soared to a record 95.6 billion passenger

miles. At the close of the war, passenger service held for awhile but by 1950 slipped to 31.8 billion passenger miles. Since then the curve is down, down, down. Recent legislation, described later, may reverse the curve.

Intercity travel by bus presents a fairly flat curve from 1951 into the present time.

As of now, the glamor girl of passenger travel is the airlines. Starting in the late 30's, the curve has continued to rise. By 1956, the airline curve and the railroad passenger curve had crossed; each was carrying the same number of passengers. The airline curve continues up. In 1929, some 20,000 intercity trains operated in the U. S.; the number dropped to about 1500 in 1960; to about 185 in 1971.

The Railroad Changes Travel, Vacationing

The major lubricants of travel are economy, speed and convenience. The railroad, developed in the 1830's, offered cheap transportation and rapid travel as compared to the horse and ship. Later, as tracks were laid across North America and Europe, the railroad station became a central part of nearly every community, offering convenience to the traveler. Hotels and restaurants were built around the depot.

Great complexes of hotels and restaurants grew up around the railroad station, prime examples being those in New York City around Grand Central Station and the Pennsylvania Station. Thousands of hotel rooms surround and sit upon Grand Central Station. The Pennsylvania Statler, the largest hotel when it was built in 1919, was financed by the Pennsylvania Railroad and joined to the Pennsylvania Station by an underground walkway. Nearly every sizable town in North America and England had at least one hotel adjacent to the depot. (Sometimes the hotel guest thought the train was coming through his room.)

The flesh-and-blood horse, the primary mode of travel before the 1830's, was no match for the iron-horse in cost per passenger mile or in speed of travel. The success of the railroad was immediate and pervasive. By 1835, more than 200 railroad charters had been granted in 11 states and more than 1000 miles of track were in use. The B & O

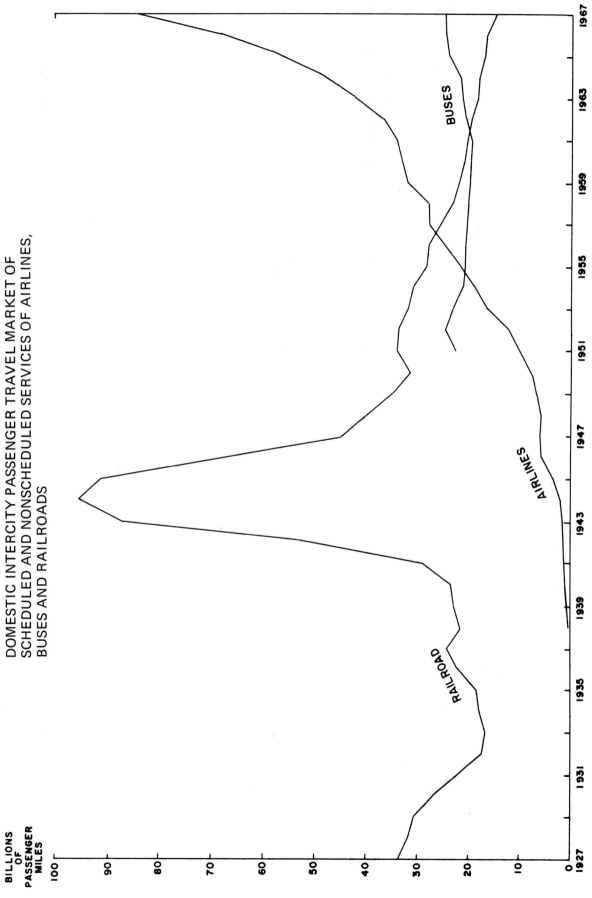

DOMESTIC INTERCITY PASSENGER TRAVEL MARKET OF
SCHEDULED AND NONSCHEDULED SERVICES OF AIRLINES,
BUSES AND RAILROADS

BILLIONS
OF
PASSENGER
MILES

100
90
80
70
60
50
40
30
20
10
0

BUSES

AIRLINES

RAILROAD

1927   1931   1935   1939   1943   1947   1951   1955   1959   1963   1967

SOURCE: HISTORICAL STATISTICS OF THE U.S. AND CIVIL AERONAUTICS BOARD

railroad announced they had sold 97,000 tickets to passengers.

By 1842, some 20 million people were using the railroads in Britain. The reason: reduced cost, increased speed. In the coaching days of 1837, the average Englishman traveled 13 miles per year at nine miles per hour. His cost was five cents a mile. Fifty years later, the cost of travel by train was reduced to 1.25 cents per mile, with the trains traveling at a speed of 25 to 30 miles an hour (express trains at that time averaged 42 m.p.h.).[1]

The railroads set the pattern for mobility and permitted intercourse between the distant parts of the country. Railroading soon became the largest business after agriculture. At the end of the nineteenth century, 59 percent more capital was invested in railroads than all manufacturing enterprises combined.[2] Railroads were the vehicle for the "take-off" of our modern economy. Without them, Western expansion would have been delayed for decades.

THE RAILROAD

With the coming of the railroad to this country, the tranquility of stage and canal travel vanished. The steam and noise of the locomotive roared across America, to become a symbol of America's energy and restlessness.

Railroad words came into our vocabulary: whistle stop, highballing, gandy dancer, jerkwater town, tank town, cowcatcher. The railroad depot became a permanent part of the national architecture, from a little sod depot in the prairie village to the magnificent Grand Central Station and Pennsylvania Station in New York City.

It is the English who are credited with starting modern tourism and it was they who first used a locomotive to transport passengers, between Stockton and Darlington, a ten-mile railway. Oddly enough, the railway operated for five years before anyone thought to offer passage to people. A railroad between Liverpool and Manchester, completed in 1830, cut the stage time between the two cities by three-fourths and the fare by two-thirds. Its success was assured.

The first railroad in the United States, in 1831, pulled two "pleasure-cars" with about 100 invited guests between Charleston and Hamburg, S. C. Suitably enough for such a momentous occasion, one of the cars carried a detachment of military who loaded and fired a field piece, loaned for the event.

Travel has its dangers, as was learned a few months later, when the fireman of the locomotive, bothered by the rush of steam escaping from the safety valve, sat on the lever controlling it. The boiler burst and was thrown a distance of 25 feet. When a new engine arrived, the railroad officials took no chance of injury to the passengers. The first car behind the locomotive was piled high with baled cotton. The second car carried a Negro brass band.

To stageline operators and canal boat owners, the railroads might seem chimerical but owners of stage and canal transportation took no chances; they opposed the railroads from the start. The storm of protest against railroads was so great in Massachusetts that the proposers of the Boston and Lowell Railroad employed no less a person than Daniel Webster to plead their cause. The railroads, said Webster, far from being wild and fanciful, might in the forseeable future extend 50 and 100 miles from Beacon Hill in Boston.[3]

The effect of the railroad on other means of transportation was almost immediate. Within five years after the railroads came into being, traffic on the canals began to decline. By the beginning of the 1840's, it was apparent that the canal boat and the stagecoach were no longer competitive. In 1910, trains carried 95 percent of the intercity travelers in America.

---

[1] "Rail Transport," *Travel and Tourism Encyclopedia* (London: Travel World, 1959), p. 297.
[2] Michael Peters, *International Tourism* (London: Hutchinson, 1969), p. 2.
[3] Beebe and Clegg, *Hear the Train Blow* (New York: Grossett and Dunlap, 1952).

The table below shows the amazing increase in railroad mileage in the United States between 1830 and 1916, when the miles of track reached a peak.[1]

1830	23
1840	2,808
1850	5,021
1860	30,626
1870	52,922
1880	93,267
1890	163,597
1900	193,346
1916	254,037
1919	217,563

By 1971, miles of track had been reduced to about 206,000. According to knowledgeable observers, as much as half of this may be ripped up and carted off before 1980.

In Europe, the railroad had no less an impact on other means of travel and the re-ordering of people's lives. Between 1830 and 1850, in England and in the principal European countries, 12,000 miles of railway were built.

Trains Put Resorts Within Reach

In the United States, resorts and seaside areas which were some distance from population centers were now made accessible by train. The train also made it possible, for those with the means to escape from the winter, to travel to Florida, Arizona and California.

Mountain resorts were the first to feel the impact of tourist travel by rail. The mountains had long been used as a summer retreat from the heat, even though travel by carriage was tiring and time-consuming. The railroad made many mountain areas convenient to the population centers of the East Coast. Tourists in deer-stalker hats and pork-pie bonnets, in the early 1870's, rode the open platform of the New Haven Railroad to the White Mountains of New Hampshire. One of the thrills was the ascent of Mt. Washington by cogwheel railroad.

From Boston, railroads radiated to Cape Cod, as well as the White Mountains and the coast of Maine. The Boston and Maine Railroad carried tourists to Concord, N. H. where they changed cars to the Northern New Hampshire Railroad, and then traveled on north to Franklin, Enfield, Franconia and West Lebanon. The trip was slow.

The cream of society in the 1870's and 80's traveled to Saratoga Springs. During the racing season, late in the summer, the Rensselaer and Saratoga Railroad ran 10 to 12 trains a day to America's most celebrated spa. The Saratoga Trunk became a symbol of travel, appearing at Pinehurst, Bretton Woods and Martha's Vineyard. Saratoga offered cures and carousing, gambling and high style.

Railroad Companies Built Hotels

In the 1880's and 1890's, resorting became fashionable up and down the East Coast and reached into Florida. Numbers of white sprawling resorts were built in New England, in the mountains and at the sea coast. A few still operate. Wentworth-by-the-Sea, near Portsmouth, N. H. and the New Ocean House at Swampscott, Mass. survive because they are close to population centers and cater to group business.

Railroads enabled people to go places hitherto beyond their means and endurance. Railroad companies built hotels in Europe, Canada and the United States. The Canadian Pacific and the Canadian National Railroads still operate a sizable number of hotels and resorts. The Union Pacific built the Glacier Park Hotels and Sun Valley.

In the 1890's, the flight to the sun was well underway. Henry M. Flagler, who had been treasurer of Standard Oil, and had managed to sequester some $50 million, came to St. Augustine on a second honeymoon and was so enchanted with Florida that he decided to make it into a grand resort area.

Resorts and railroads went together. For each mile of railroad that Flagler built, he was given acres of land by the state of Florida. As the railroad traveled down Florida, hotels were built along the way, two at St. Augustine, the Ormond at Ormond Beach, the Royal Poinciana and the Breakers at Palm Beach and the Royal Palm at

---

[1]*American Railroads* (Chicago: Stover, 1961), p. 224

Miami. The Florida East Coast Railway transported millionaires and would-be-millionaires to Florida during the winter season. Later, Flagler pushed the railroad all the way to Key West.

On the West Coast of Florida another Henry, Henry Plant, who made his millions in railroads, pushed a railroad down the West Coast of Florida to Tampa and built a series of resort hotels.

Riding in one's private railroad car to Florida was the apogee of luxury. Dozens of private cars were parked at some of the resorts on both the East and the West Coast of Florida during the height of the winter season at the turn of the century and on into the twenties.

Today only a few of the famous resorts are left of the dozens that operated at the turn of the century: The Homestead at Hot Springs, Va. and The Greenbrier in W. Va. The Greenbrier, owned by the Chesapeake and Ohio Railroad which has invested over $25 million in the resort, is now a grand convention property. It is lavish to say the least, with 650 rooms, no two identical in decor.

With a few exceptions, mountain resorts in the eastern U. S. have not been profitable in recent years. This has not always been the case. Before air conditioning and airplane travel, spending the summer or part of it in the cool mountains was the social thing to do and a pleasant way to escape the heat of the city. By 1890, the mountain resorts were the center of the summer social season, and presented a way of life unique for both the guests and the operator, an aspect of Americana overlooked by history books. The White Mountains of N. H. had some 60 resort hotels with more than 11,000 guest rooms. By 1959, the number of guest rooms had dropped to about half as many and as of today the number is considerably less.

The railroads made travel possible for the masses. The elite were not forgotten and never have been. Special arrangements and luxury cars were available to the rich. A few of the best known trains had barbershops and manicurists.

Some of the cars contained paintings, bathrooms, libraries, ottomans and arm chairs upholstered in red and gold brocade.

One of the great pleasures of rail travel in earlier times was the excellent food and service found on many of the long-distance trains. At first, the trains carried no dining cars. In 1868, the Chicago and Alton introduced the "Delmonico" diner into service. Ten years later, dining cars ran on all mainline railroads. Many of the dining cars were generously stocked with Burgundies and Bordeaux, hocks, champagnes and Madeiras. Krug's private choice, a champagne, was widely listed as a refreshment on dining car breakfast menus.

Railroad Dining Service

The menus offered by some of the dining cars were elaborate, including oysters, turtle, trout, mutton, buffalo tongue, chicken, turkey, beef, pheasant larded with truffles, pate de foie gras, sweetbreads, antelope, woodcock, prairie chicken, snipe and a dozen or so desserts.

As one writer put it who traveled from Chicago to Omaha in 1872, "It is now the custom to charge a dollar per meal on these cars; and as the cooking is admirable, the service excellent and the food various and abundant, this is not too much. You may have your choice in the wilderness, eating, at the rate of twenty-two miles an hour, off buffalo, elk, antelope, beefsteak, mutton chops and grouse. Breakfast wines are claret and sauterne; champagne wines, Heidsick and Krug."[1]

George Pullman, in 1863, built the "Pullman Car" which attracted so much publicity that Mrs. Abraham Lincoln insisted on riding in it as part of the funeral train for President Lincoln. Mrs. Lincoln was not deterred by the fact that the Chicago and Alton Railroad had to add two feet to the clearance of every bridge, depot and platform along its entire right of way to accommodate the special car.

The Fred Harvey Company (now owned by AmFac, a Hawaiian-based conglomerate), got its start in 1875 when Fred Harvey, an Englishman, secured verbal permission to

[1] Beebe and Clegg, *Hear the Train Blow* (New York: Grossett and Dunlap, 1952).

open a railroad restaurant on the Santa Fe line in Topeka, Kan. Soon after that, in Florence, Kan., he employed a chef from the Palmer House in Chicago at a salary of $5000 which was $2500 more than anyone else in the county made, including the banker.

Harvey did everything in equally impressive style. The silver was from England, Irish linens were used on the tables; menus offered imported turtle from Mexico and the best imported wine. By 1901, when Harvey died, the system he founded included 15 hotels, 47 restaurants and 15 dining cars.

The economics of feeding passengers on the train sets meals as a cost which must be charged against the overall revenue of the train. Dining cars are additional pieces of rolling stock which cost money to maintain and operate. The revenue from them never covers the expense. As one railroad commissary manager put it, "If I stood at the door and paid everyone fifty cents not to come in, we might break even." (By cutting out the dining car.)

The Baltimore and Ohio has substituted a snack bar coach for the usual diner. Revenues rose 30 percent. It is the only meal service on the B & O which operates in the black. The coach passengers of today apparently represent a hamburger market.

Start of Railroad Losses

By the late 1930's, the American Railroads were already losing passenger service, even though in 1939 over 18,000 passenger trains operated and carried 450 million passengers. The gleaming streamliners that had been introduced at the time of the World's Fair in Chicago, in 1934, were popular. During the peak season, Atlantic Coast Line's Florida Special, ran six sections featuring hostesses and an Hawaiian Band.

Competition proved desirable for the general public in that the automobile and bus forced the railroads, in the second half of the 1930's, to put on all-coach streamliners. Coast-to-coast coach trains with reclining seats were given many of the frills of the deluxe trains and some of the standard pullmans were made available at only 25 percent more than coach fare.

The first-class traveler, by 1939, did not have a butler's car, a special coach for domestics, on the train (as was carried by the Bar Harbor Express), but the 20th Century Limited gave everyone the red-carpet treatment. A real red carpet, nearly a quarter of a mile long, was laid out for the departure in Chicago and New York. It was known as a drinking train, but otherwise quite sedate. In Europe, the Germans hurtled "The Flying Hamburger" between Hamburg and Berlin at 80 m.p.h. The British, proud of their "Coronation Scot," sent it on tour of the United States.[1]

Recent Developments

Passenger service on the railroads is a mixed bag. In Japan, the high speed Tokaido Line has been a resounding success, running at an average speed of 103 miles per hour. Tokaido trains carried more than 55 million passengers in 1968. The Soviet Union is working on 125-mile per hour trains for the Moscow-Leningrad Corridor. Italy and Germany have plans for high speed super expresses. For the relatively short runs through highly congested areas, the super trains have promise, especially if stack-ups over the airports, such as at Boston, New York and Washington, continue.

While several of the foreign passenger train systems in Europe and in Japan, are looked on with envy by North American tourists, the tourists don't realize the cost to the government involved. Japanese railroads lose $1 million a day. "Many of the overseas systems are operated partly as make-work projects and are featherbedded to an extent that would shock even a U. S. unionist."[2]

The cost of nationalizing U. S. railroads, says *Time Magazine,* would be staggering; $60 billion just to buy them. One can imagine the cost of government operation which would immediately take on even greater bureaucracy and politics.

Britain, first to develop the railroad, nationalized its train service in 1947, following World War II. British Rail, the Brit-

---

[1]K. C. Tessendorf, "On Land and Sea, Part II," *Travel Marketing,* Sept. 29, 1969.
[2]*Time Magazine,* July 6, 1970, p. 59.

ish nationalized rail service, operates 33 hotels and 77 ships. Employees number 339,000. British Rails Inter-City runs well over 1600 trains a day over 9375 miles of track.[1]

By pruning out branch lines, total trackage was reduced from 20,000 to 12,000 miles. British Rail has lost money continuously since 1952 ($353.8 million in 1968). Losses of over $1.5 billion were piled up in the period 1963-67. By subsidizing commuter lines, a paper profit of $36 million was shown in 1969.

Service is improving; only 40 percent of the trains ran late in 1969 (even though the longest runs seldom exceed 250 miles). A new 150-mile an hour train is under development.[2]

New High-Speed Trains

A demonstration train service, initiated formally in October, 1970 between New York City and Washington, D. C., was partially financed by the terms of the High Speed Ground Transportation Act of 1965. The "Metroliners" make the New York to Washington trip in about three hours. Average speed is 75 miles per hour and, as the roadbeds are improved, speeds are expected to increase to over 100 miles per hour.

The train has proved popular. Airliner-style meals and beverages are served in the train's parlor cars at popular prices. Snack-bar cars for the coach passengers feature hot or cold sandwiches and beverages which can be eaten at a stand-up counter. A mobile phone system allows passengers to make or receive calls while en route. Hostesses aboard act much like airline stewardesses in assisting travelers.

Eventually there will be 22 trains a day between New York and Philadelphia, with departures every half hour during most of the day and every hour to Washington, D. C. All seats are reserved.[3]

The government is also subsidizing a New York to Boston "Turbo-Train", powered by gas-turbine engines produced by United Aircraft, and operated by a subsidiary of Penn Central Railroad. By 1970, one train was making a daily round trip with space for 144 riders. The trip took 3 hours and 40 minutes each way. By eliminating grade cross-

ings and improving the track, the time for the trip was expected to be reduced.[4]

Trains which run on a cushion of air are being developed cooperatively by Grumman Aircraft Engineering Corp. and General Electric. Speeds with the new type train are predicted to reach 250 to 300 miles per hour.

Hitachi, a Japanese company, announced, in 1970 that it is developing a magnetic system in which, instead of flotation by compressed air, repelling magnets are used to lift the train from the tracks. The result is said to be an operation which is comparatively silent and is capable of creating speeds up to 310 miles per hour.

The train, where it is fast, clean and convenient, in some areas can partially replace its arch rival, the automobile. For long distances, the train is no match for the plane in cost, convenience or time. Travel by rail in Europe is relatively cheap, fast and highly popular. Tourists can purchase for $140 a Eurailpass which entitles them to unlimited first-class travel through 13 countries of Europe for one month. For a small additional charge, the traveler can buy sleeping accommodations at a much less expensive rate than a hotel room. Because of the short distances involved in the United Kingdom and much of Europe, train travel for many trips has time and cost advantages over other modes of travel. In time, similar conditions may prevail within the vast megalopolises building up on the East and West Coasts of the United States.

More Pleasure for Travelers

The railroads could do much to increase the convenience and pleasure of travel. One railroad offers fashion shows, hair styling and wine-tasting parties. Another has installed telephones and mini-skirted hostesses. Armchair TV sets, stereo sound systems and movies, as offered by the airlines, could also be made available to rail-

---

[1]"New Facilities, Services on Foreign Railroads," *The Travel Agent,* Apr. 22, 1971, p. 8.
[2]Graham Turner, *Business in Britain* (London: Eyre and Spottiswoode, 1969), p. 183.
[3]*The Wall Street Journal*, Aug. 19, 1970.
[4]*The Wall Street Journal*, Oct. 13, 1970.

The United Aircraft Turbo Train is in service between New York and Boston as part of the U. S. Dept. of Transportation's Northeast Corridor high-speed ground transportation demonstration project. Train is powered by gas turbine engines and has a pendulous banking suspension system which enables it to round curves with passenger comfort and safety at speeds 30 to 40 percent faster than regular trains. The train has been operated at a speed of 170 miles an hour, hits more than 100 miles an hour in operational service on some stretches of the Penn Central's track.

On another high speed new train, the Metroliner, running from New York to Washington, D. C. at left, woman in Metro-club car enjoys full course hot meal while businessman in background utilizes high speed travel time to work. Below, a coach passenger en route to Boston uses Touch Tone phone booth to talk to his office. Phones in club car are also available for incoming and outgoing calls.

road passengers for an additional charge.

What happened to the passenger service between Chicago and New York is representative of what has happened to much of railroad passenger service around the United States. The once-plush upholstery on the Broadway, Ltd., erstwhile crack express train between Chicago and New York, is threadbare. The beds in the sleeping cars have been in use so long that they sag in the middle. The people who ride the train do it out of nostalgia or fear of air travel and are in no great hurry. The food is still excellent, however, and the dining car well appointed.

The trip is scheduled for 16 hours, 40 minutes—contrasted with the roughly 2 hours of a jet airliner flight. One-way coach fare in 1970 was $46.50; fare that included a tiny roomette with a convertible cot was $90.61. Jet coach fare was $44. In 1970, the Penn Central Railroad requested permission from the Interstate Commerce Commission to discontinue the train because, in 1969, it had slipped into the red and lost $102,932.[1]

In 1967, the railroad earnings had been dropping for more than 30 years. Though their accounting methods are seriously questioned, railroads complained that they had been losing $485 million a year on passenger traffic. Trains now account for less than two percent of all intercity traffic.

In the highly congested population corridors of this country, the railroad may indeed stage a comeback. Congress is concerned about providing less expensive transportation, reducing congestion on the highways and cutting back on the pollution caused by other modes of transportation (the electric train is a "clean" form of transportation). The Federal government, faced with the fact that there might be a complete collapse of rail passenger service, gave attention to the possibilities of subsidizing money-losing passenger trains and also supporting and maintaining new rail equipment.

AMTRAK

In 1971, the National Railroad Passenger Corporation began operation as a semipublic corporation to operate inter-city passenger trains, defined by the Interstate Commerce Commission as trains that run 75 miles or more. It is a move to semi-nationalize American railroads. The Corporation is directed by a 15-man board, eight selected by the President of the United States, three by the railroads, and four by private, preferred-stock holders.

The corporation, known as AMTRAK, seeks to eliminate most of the unprofitable runs and to improve the ones which are authorized. The national train system will be coordinated and fares set without ICC or State regulatory approval. Better equipment will include sleepers and dining cars.[2]

Decline in Trains

In 1971, there were 366 non-commuter passenger trains running in the United States (as compared with 20,000 in 1920). Under the new system, about 185 passenger trains are in operation. Presumably, these will be operated more efficiently and provide better service to the rider.[3] The better passenger cars will be taken from the runs that have been cut and put into service on the remaining scheduled trains.

American Airlines has been given a contract to design for AMTRAK a reservation and ticket-issuing system similar to their own Sabre communication and computer system (which was patterned after the Air Force's early warning communications network). A central reservation and time table information service is proposed which can be reached by dialing a toll-free number anywhere in the country.[4]

As happened many years ago in this country, the railroads in Europe are now being dieselized and electrified. Even though most of the railroads are nationally owned and subsidized, total mileage and the number of passengers is dropping off.[5]

[1] *The Wall Street Journal,* Mar. 10, 1970.
[2] *The Wall Street Journal,* Nov. 3, 1970.
[3] *The New York Times,* May 1, 1971, p. 34.
[4] "Change of Pace for America's Railroads," *The New York Times,* Mar. 7, 1971, p. 47.
[5] *European Conference of Ministers of Transport Fourteenth Annual Report,* Paris, 1968.

TRAVEL BY SHIP

Until the 1950's, nearly all overseas travel was necessarily done aboard a vessel of some type. Immigration, business and war were the principal reasons for undertaking water travel until about the 1830's; however, some ocean travel in the ancient world could be considered pleasure travel. How about Antony's trips from Rome to Egypt to visit Cleopatra?

The first regular steamship service on the North Atlantic was begun by the "Great Western." On its first east-bound journey in 1838, it carried 68 passengers from New York to England. Four years later, Samuel Cunard, a Canadian, formed the famous Cunard Steamship Co. In the same year, the Peninsular and Oriental Co., the well-known British firm, was formed.

The practice of complimenting travel and accommodations started early. In 1844, the P & O invited William Makepeace Thackeray, the well-known British writer, to cruise the Mediterranean. In return, he wrote a book praising the pleasures of sea travel. (Travel writers have been taking similar trips ever since.)

The number of Americans traveling abroad rose from 8000 to 26,000 during the period 1840 to 1860.

Travel overseas for pleasure dates from the 1860's. What was probably the first ocean cruise for "tourists" was the voyage of the Quaker City to the Mediterranean and the Holy Land in 1867. Sixty passengers, including Mark Twain, who recorded the journey in *Innocents Abroad,* paid $1200 each for the trip.[1]

Americans traveling to Europe increased from 52,812 in 1882 to 120,477 in 1900. By 1914, shipping lines, such as Cunard, Canadian Pacific, Holland-American and others, were operating luxury services to Europe. World War I stopped pleasure travel almost completely as the ships were outfitted to carry troops.

After the war, the number of Americans touring to Europe climbed sharply, to reach a peak in 1929. In that year 511,814 persons traveled the Atlantic eastbound, 743,618 westbound, the highest ever.[2] During the depression years of the 30's, the kinds of overseas travelers shifted to include large numbers of immigrants, who were returning for a visit to "the old country," as well as teachers and students. Teachers got an off-season reduction in fare of 20 percent, and there was the possibility of signing on as a crew member.

The Cruise Ship Gains Importance

By 1932, the depression was in full swing and the shipping companies, such as Cunard and the P & O, turned to cruising as a means of keeping their ships occupied. Fares were low because of the depression. Among the cruises most popular were the 7- and 14-day cruises scheduled through the Mediterranean and the Baltic.[3]

The Furness Line operated 6-day cruises to Bermuda starting at $65. The Normandy, pride of the French Line, cruised to Rio; Matson's Lurline and Matsonia made the Hawaii trip available for about $250 round trip first class, $160 for cabin class.[4] By the end of the depression, cruising had become a well established means of vacationing.

Steamboat excursions up and down the Hudson were popular as early as the 1850's. Coastal cruising along the East Coast was in effect until the 30's. In 1937, the famous Fall River Line expired, displaced by the auto and bus.

World War II again stopped pleasure travel overseas, as all shipping was used for the war effort.

The S.S.* Lurline, a former Matson Line ship, has a story typical of many a United States passenger ship. The ship was built in 1932 and did a good business until World War II when it was used as a troop transport. With the coming of the jets, it was idled but when the original Lurline was

[1]Lickorish and Kershaw, *The Travel Trade* (London: Practical Press, Ltd., 1958), p. 35.
[2]"ASTA at 40: A Few Signs of Wear But Still Vigorous," *The Travel Agent,* Apr. 19, 1971, p. 30.
[3]*International Travel,* Jan. 26, 1970, Sydney, Australia.
[4]K. C. Tessendorf, "On Land and Sea, Part II," *Travel Marketing,* Sept. 29, 1969.
*"SS" stands for steamship, a designation still used even though the ship is driven by diesel engines. MS is motor ship; MV, motor vessel. Other initials include QSS (quadruple screw steamship), RMS (Royal mail ship), TS (turbine ship), TV, (turbine vessel) and NS (nuclear ship).

knocked out of service because of an engine failure, the last turbine was placed in service after rechristening. In 1957, it was renovated so that some 800 people could be accommodated. It became a one-class ship, although there are some 13 different rates available, depending upon the size and location of the stateroom.

A crew of 400 was needed to keep the ship in operation. The passenger-to-crew ratio was about 2 to 1, a little smaller than the usual hotel and considerably smaller than a first-class resort. In 1970 the Lurline was sold to the Chandris Company, credited with introducing the air/ship fly-and-cruise in 1960.

In many ways, the passenger ship is a floating hotel, more precisely a floating resort, in that the guest must be roomed, fed and entertained. Because he has no options about "leaving the resort," the guest is likely to become more critical as the cruise continues. As one ship sales manager put it, "The first week out the passengers are busy overeating; the rest of the cruise they are busy complaining about the food."

Foodservice on Board Ship

Passengers usually have little real basis for complaint about food on passenger ships. The ship lines, recognizing the importance of meals in a "closed" environment, usually spend a great deal of time, thought and money on providing the best in food and service. Quite naturally, Americans prefer American-type food. The breakfast menu for the Lurline (on the facing page) is an example of the lavishness and expensiveness of a passenger ship menu. Its culinary tradition was the same as the dining car on the railroad and the American plan resort hotel.

How many menus in commercial restaurants or even the usual fine hotel include tripe, sole and cod on the breakfast menu? Shades of Diamond Jim Brady. The other meals were equally lavish, including appetizers, soups, fish, entrees, roasts, vegetables, salads, desserts, cheese and beverages.

What do guests do on a cruise ship beside eat, sleep, talk and drink? The Lurline carried 13 social hosts and hostesses who engineered all sorts of fun and games for the passengers. A number of the games cen-

tered around chance, indicating a deep-seated desire in many people to contest for and win something. Horse racing with miniature play horses, bingo and a daily pool on the ship's mileage were provided. Horse racing was made even more realistic by showing films of actual horse races and permitting passengers to bet on the outcome.

Legalized gambling including slot machines was proscribed by the Federal Government in 1952. The shipping lines hope that the ban on shipboard gambling will be rescinded. No doubt, legalized gambling would divert thousands of tourists from Reno, Las Vegas and the Bahamas, as short cruises out of Los Angeles, San Francisco and East Coast cities would be offered.

Interdicting gambling on U. S. ships has been one more boon for foreign flags. The Queen Elizabeth 2 reluctantly added a casino in the late 60's, then had to double its size in 1972.

By the 60's, the passenger ships had largely lost out to the airlines as the choice of long-distance travelers who were concerned with either speed or economy. In 1969, transatlantic ship passengers numbered 258,478. In the same year, close to 6 million passengers crossed the North Atlantic by air.[1] The passenger ship remained for those with time and money, for those who were in no hurry to get anywhere and could afford to go there with a degree of luxury, or much luxury. The S.S. France and the S.S. Queen Mary 2 are the last of the great Atlantic luxury vessels. The Queen Mary 2 is indeed a luxury ship with berthing for 1700 passengers, 900 crew.

New ships especially designed for the cruise market are being built. Unlike the old ocean liners, the new ones provide ocean views for nearly every cabin, enough dining seats for everyone to eat at one time, more luxury such as original art in each cabin, public rooms with wide picture windows instead of portholes. A German ship offers complimentary liquor at all times.

The cruise market is growing at a 10 percent yearly rate. Cruises are announced several months in advance of departure. Most of the cruises are to tropical or sub-

[1]*The New York Times,* Jan. 9, 1971, p. 44.

Good Morning - - -

BREAKFAST

S S L U R L I N E   SATURDAY, MARCH 14, 1970

EGGS

Poached on Toast   Boiled   Fried with Ham or Bacon

Scrambled with Chipped Beef, Asparagus Tips, Shrimps or Plain

Omelet with Mushrooms, Green Onions, Confiture or Plain

Shirred with Canadian Bacon or Plain

MEATS

Breakfast Bacon   Grilled Canadian Bacon

Grilled Little Pork Sausages   Cured Farmer Ham

Stewed Honey Comb Tripe, Creole

POTATOES

Hashed Brown   Saratoga Chips

SWEET ROLLS...TOAST

Assorted Sweet Rolls   Almond Slice

Roman Meal or Griddle Cakes with Honey or Maple Syrup

Buttered, Cinnamon, Milk, Dry or Whole Wheat Toast

Butter Horns and Snails   Coffee Cake   Corn Muffins

JAMS...JELLIES

Guava Jelly   Plum Jam   Peach Jam   Grape Jelly

Orange Marmalade   Grape Jam   Blackberry Jam

BEVERAGES

Chocolate   Buttermilk

Orange Pekoe   Coffee   Milk   Cocoa

Ovaltine

Complete Breakfast—$4.00

FRUITS

Stewed Santa Clara Prunes in Syrup   Green Apple Sauce

Fresh Hawaiian Pineapple   Baked Oregon Apple

Sliced Banana in Cream   Chilled Half Grapefruit

Fresh Island Papaya   Frosted Strawberries in Syrup

Iced Apple, Grapefruit or Tomato Juice

HOT AND COLD CEREALS

Rolled Oats   Pep   Puffed Wheat   Cream of Wheat

Wheaties   Puffed Rice   Corn Flakes   Shredded Wheat

FISH

Rex Sole, Saute Meuniere, Parsley Potatoes

Boiled Alaska Cod, Fines Herbes

tropical waters, to such places as Hawaii, the Orient, the Caribbean and the Mediterranean. A number of cruises are also scheduled for Alaska. Around-the-world cruises run as high as $8000 in cost per person, or about $100 a day on the Swedish American Lines. The rule of thumb is "the longer the trip, the older—and richer—the passengers."

Cruise Market Delineated

The traditional, long cruise market comprises people in the age group of 50 and up, retired or semi-retired, leading some wits to liken the cruise ship to a floating retirement home. Ship lines prefer to call them floating resorts. The P&O Lines say they have 15,000 resort beds. The passengers enjoy the cruise as a cruise, not as a means of transportation. They are in no hurry to get anywhere.

Shorter cruises attract those in younger age groups and the entertainment aboard ship is changed, accordingly, to provide more of a night club atmosphere.

By the 1970's, winter sailings across the Atlantic had stopped. The cruises from New York City south proved unpopular because of the cold and heavy weather experienced out of New York and down the coast of the United States during the winter. Several ships were directed south for winter cruises in the Caribbean and elsewhere.

Some of the cruises are combination air-ship tours, for which arrangements are made for the travelers to fly to Port Everglades in Florida or San Juan, there to pick up a cruise for several days. At the end of the cruise, they return home by air. In 1970, the Port of Miami handled 569,000 cruise passengers, double the number for 1968. Much of the increase was attributed to the fly-cruise business.[1]

Some 3600 cruises, carrying 1.5 million passengers, sailed from East Coast ports during the 1966-70 period. Los Angeles became the home port for several lines, mostly foreign, cruising to Mexico, the Caribbean and Alaska. In 1970, the P&O scheduled 36 cruises from Australia through the Pacific, and 39 from Southampton to the Mediterranean and European ports. No doubt, cruise ships will be positioned in the tropical waters of the Pacific as part of air-and-sea vacation cruises.

Ships of the future will be designed for flexibility. Shipline executives say they will cater to convention groups as well as to traditional markets, to younger people during high-density summer cruising as well as the older, more affluent market for the rest of the year.

United States' shipping, including passenger ships, operates under the burden of the highest operating costs in the world. The liabilities begin with the cost of the vessel, which may run as much as four times that of a ship built in Japan and elsewhere. Wages and salaries to officers and crew of United States vessels continue upward because of union pressures. As a result, nearly all of the passenger ships operating in 1970 were subsidized in one way or another by the Federal government. Rationale for subsidization is that the hulls would be needed for defense in case of a national emergency.

Nearly all cruising is done under other than the U. S. flag. In 1972 only two U. S. ships, the S.S. Mariposa and the S.S. Monterey, sailing from San Francisco, were left. The proud S.S. United States, built to emulate the France and the Queen Elizabeth 2, was in mothballs in Norfolk. Nations with lower labor costs are increasing their cruise fleets. Greek, Italian, British, German, Dutch, Swedish and Norwegian ships were being built to carry American vacationers.

Hydrofoils and Hovercrafts

Now, over-the-water transport has been introduced that can be considered a part of the vacation business. Lifting the hull of a vessel out of the water reduces drag and makes higher speed possible. Hovercrafts (lifted by propeller-induced pressure) operate between Portsmouth and the Isle of Wight in England and between Dover and Boulogne on the English Channel. The hovercraft between Dover and Boulogne travels on a cushion of air eight feet above water at 75 m.p.h. A giant craft, it carries 30 cars and 254 passengers.[2]

[1]*Ibid*, Dec. 13, 1970.
[2]"New Facilities, Services on Foreign Railroads," *The Travel Agent* (Apr. 22, 1971), p. 10.

Hydrofoils (lifted by foil action through the water) are an exciting and relatively fast over-water transport. One Swiss firm has sold some 100 hydrofoils which are operating satisfactorily in such places as Sweden and between some of the Virgin Islands. The 35-minute hydrofoil service between Copenhagen, Denmark and Malmo, Sweden is available as part of the Eurailpass. Several 28-passenger hydrofoils traveling at 34.5 m.p.h. operate between Miami and Fort Lauderdale. Hydrofoils operate between Marbella, Spain and Tangier, Morocco, and between Naples and Capri. A number of others are operating successfully in relatively calm waters. Attempts to operate hydrofoils between Cape Cod, Martha's Vineyard and Nantucket have not proved satisfactory.

In open sea, the larger the vessel, generally, the smoother the ride. Inter-island ferries planned for Hawaii will be over 400 feet in length, long enough to ride across the swells in Hawaiian waters, minimizing pitch and roll.

THE AUTOMOBILE

The automobile is by all odds the principal mode of transportation in this country. Some 85 percent of vacation travel in the United States is done riding on four rubber tires, very likely in the family car. According to the American Automobile Assn., 110 million Americans traveled upwards of 250 billion miles on vacation or pleasure trips in 1970. These motorists spent about $34.5 billion of the total $38 billion which was spent on domestic travel.

The auto changed the American way of life, added a new dimension to life, especially in the leisure area. It released and created the urge to travel in millions of people. It has also become a kind of monster, polluting the air, taking thousands of lives each year, and adding to congestion. In the downtown business district of Detroit, for example, 62 percent of all land is devoted to the automobile in the form of roads, parking lots and garages.

Like many good things, the automobile came to the classes before it reached the masses.[1] In 1895, there were in the United States about 300 horseless carriages of one kind or another—gasoline buggies, electric and steam cars. In 1914, there were some 2 million in the country. By the 1930's, the total had risen to over 25 million.* Even during the depression years of the 30's, about two-thirds of the families in the country had automobiles.

Henry Ford and good roads helped make the automobile the symbol of American life it is today. Ford produced his Model T in 1908. Six years later, he applied the assembly line technique of mass production to cars. By 1916, he was selling half a million cars a year. The figure increased to 2 million in 1923 and by 1927 to 15 million cars. Price elasticity for autos was highly apparent. The price for the Model T started at $825; by 1925, it had been reduced to $260.

The Model T allowed the skilled worker in town or city to live miles from his job and to drive his family out into the country in the evenings and on weekends. It emancipated the farmer and allowed many grain farmers in the Midwest to take off for California or Florida for the winter. The automobile led to the motel and the tourist camp, then later to the motor hotel and the highway restaurant.

At first, roads were the biggest obstacle to making the automobile popular. In 1900, there were but 150 miles of paved roads in the United States. Prior to World War I, at least nine out of ten car owners in the Northern States "put up" their cars in the winter and went back to horse or steam transportation.

Road Building Freely Supported

Congress, in 1916, passed an act matching state appropriations for new roads dollar-for-dollar. When, by 1925, more than

---

[1]Samuel Eliot Morison, *The Oxford History of the American People* (New York: Oxford University Press, 1965).
*The Department of Transportation reports about 108 million automobiles and trucks on the highways in 1970, a figure expected to increase 8 million vehicles a year for the next 20 years. Then try to find a parking space.

half of the families in the North either owned a car, or were about to buy one on the installment plan, appropriations for hard top roads began to pour freely from the state legislatures.[1]   Road building continued even during the depression years of the 1930's.   The automobile had achieved a rank in value ahead of home ownership, far above the telephone, the electric light and even the bathtub.

Freeways and turnpikes spurred automobile travel, the first being the Pennsylvania Turnpike built in 1940. World War II brought road building to a halt. In 1954, the Federal Government began paying 90 percent of the cost of roads approved by the Secretary of the Interior. The Interstate Highway System was begun. In 1970, 30,000 miles were completed.

Between 1976 and 1978, the motorist will be able to drive coast to coast without hitting a traffic light or stop sign. (Many observers wonder if the driver will see anything except concrete and cars.) The Interstate Highway, 42,500 miles of it, will link 90 percent of our cities with populations of 50,000 or more and will carry 20 percent of the nation's traffic.

Some see the automobile as the noisy polluter of the environment, gobbling up great spaces for roads and parking, breaking up the family and breaking down morals. Without question, it has made the Americans the most mobile people in history and given them options and choices not otherwise possible.

The automobile has proved to be the most dangerous instrument in the hands of man, at least in the hands of the American man. Since 1900, some 1.7 million people have been killed in automobiles, many more than have been killed in all of the wars in which the United States has engaged. Even with better roads and safer cars, about 50,000 Americans die in auto accidents each year.

For the average person not living in a congested downtown area, the automobile is the most convenient and rapid form of transportation for short and medium distances. At first it was limited to 35 miles per hour, the speed of the fastest horse. Speed limits have been raised on highways until most turnpike and throughway speed limits are 65 miles per hour, and a few higher. The current maximum speed for an average driver is considered by automotive engineers and designers to be about 70-80 miles per hour with today's cars. According to some engineers, by 1975, the safe and comfortable limit on the best highways may go higher although whether these speeds will be permitted will depend on the availability of gasoline.

The automobile is not cheap as compared with bus, rail and air. The usual American car costs 8 to 15 cents per mile to operate (when all costs are considered), whereas plane, rail and bus fares range from about 3 to 7 cents per mile. The automobile is less expensive per person if it carries several passengers.

Convenience counts, however, and Americans are more than ready to pay for it. Europeans are fast acquiring the automotive way of life.

INTERCITY BUS TRAVEL

In 1968, some 375 million persons took intercity bus trips, well over double the number of people who flew on domestic airlines. Put another way, this means that every man, woman and child in the United States took an average of nearly two intercity bus trips that year.[2]

It is known that few people choose the bus in traveling for business purposes. Just how much bus travel can be considered pleasure travel is not known but 13½ percent of the miles of regular-route intercity and local-suburban service was run by charter and special service buses.[3] Much of the special service was for pleasure.

The major reasons for selecting bus travel over other modes of travel are convenience and economy. Bus service is available in virtually every town of 1000 population

[1]Samuel Eliot Morison, *The Oxford History of the American People* (New York: Oxford University Press, 1965).
[2]National Assn. of Motorbus Owners, *Bus Facts*, 1968, 35th Ed. (Washington, D. C., 1969), p. 5.
[3]*Ibid*, p. 11.

or more, and a passenger station or ticket agent for bus service is at hand in each of these communities. Most people do not choose bus travel for long trips, although there are a few "aficianados" who are thrilled by sitting in a bus hour after hour, even day after day.

Travel by bus is the cheapest of all travel for short trips in most sections of the United States. In many communities, it is the only public transportation available. When the Interstate Highway System is completed, bus travel will be even faster and more convenient for many trips. Sight-seeing buses and tour buses are widely used in almost every tourist destination, especially in the United Kingdom and the rest of Europe. The Gray Line sight-seeing buses, frequently encountered in U. S. cities, are franchised by Gray Line Sight-Seeing Companies Associated, 1 Rockefeller Plaza, New York City.

Travel by bus for pleasure purposes varies widely within the United States and around the world. The convenience and economy of bus transportation between some destinations highly favors the bus over other modes, including the private automobile. For example, there is regular bus service between most sizable communities in New England and New York City. It is often easier for the traveler to ride the bus than to drive his own automobile into the city, and less expensive when the cost of parking is considered. Travel time by air from Bradley Airport near Hartford to New York City is only 23 minutes but the time to get to the airport, to wait for the plane, the possible delay in landing at the New York airport and the time to get from the airport into the city may total as long as the time required to travel by bus from communities such as Amherst or Northampton, Mass. Total travel cost by bus is less than half that by air in this instance.

Early History

It started back in 1900, when a bus was used to carry sight-seeing passengers around Prospect Park in Brooklyn, New York. By 1905, buses rumbled along Manhattan's Fifth Avenue. Travel by intercity bus was hampered by the absence of good roads. As late as 1921, there were only 84,000 miles of surfaced highway in the United States, a total which rose to 302,000 miles in 1940 and 489,000 miles in 1960.[1]

The early bus operators were usually small businessmen who improvised their own buses. Earl Wickman, of Hibbing, Minn. was an example of the early bus operator. In 1914, he used a seven-passenger motor truck Hupmobile for a bus. Loads of fifteen to twenty passengers were not unusual. It was a utilitarian arrangement, an example of American enterprise devised to meet a specific need. Wickman carried his neighbors to work in Alice, four miles away, for a fare of fifteen cents per passenger each way. Later, in 1928, it was Wickman who organized the Greyhound Company, now the largest, privately owned bus company in the world.

By 1928, through buses were scheduled from Los Angeles to New York City. The 3433 mile trip took 5 days and 14 hours. The passengers slept as best they could sitting up. The cross-country trip was, and still is, something in the nature of a marathon, a challenge to the passenger.

Travel Time Reduced

As roads and buses improved, travel time dropped. A trans-continental trip before World War II required about 90 hours of sitting. Just waiting for the agent to make out such a ticket was time-consuming. A ticket 18 feet long was required for one 15,391 mile trip in 1939.

With better roads and better buses, travel time decreased. The bus trip from New York to Chicago took 28 hours in 1947, 17 hours in 1962, 16 hours in 1966. When compared with the travel time of 1½ hours by plane, however, it is easy to see why the time-conscious traveler on a long trip chooses air over other modes of transportation.

With time, buses were improved in power and in comfort for the passenger. In the early days, passengers on some pioneer lines were furnished lap robes and hot bricks during sub-zero weather, but it was not long before heating and air conditioning systems

---

[1]National Assn. of Motorbus Owners, *Development of Intercity Bus Transportation* (Washington, D. C., 1962).

were introduced. Sleeping arrangements were added as early as 1928 on the bus which did the overnight run between London and Liverpool. Later, pullman-like accommodations were made available on buses between San Francisco and Los Angeles. Sleeping arrangements have not proved popular.

In some buses, stewards and stewardesses were installed. Restroom facilities are installed in many buses, particularly those in express service over long routes. Diesel power is almost universally used in this country. Large picture windows provide maximum vision for passengers, and can be pushed out completely if emergency exits are needed. As of 1970, buses are limited to a width of 96 inches, the maximum allowable on the Interstate Highway System.

In the minds of many travelers, safety of travel is paramount, and influences their choice of travel mode. The railroads have generally been considered a safe, or the safest, means of travel. The National Association of Motorbus Owners states that "intercity bus passengers are far safer than automobile riders and generally at least as safe as passengers on the railroads and domestic airlines."[1] The Association, quoting the National Safety Council, reported that in 1967-68, the fatality rate was .08 deaths per 100 million passenger miles.

Travel Safety

In 1968, deaths and accidents involving class I intercity buses (those carriers who do $1 million or more per year in sales) resulted in 19 passenger fatalities in 1967. The railroad rate for 1967 was .12, the airlines .20. The automobile, of course, is a national disaster area: According to the National Safety Council, 70,400 people were killed in automobile accidents in 1968, a rate of 2.44 per 100 million passenger miles. Using these figures then, the bus is the safest mode of transportation available to the general public, at least the general public of the United States, and those who ride the class I bus lines.

A curious note on bus safety comes from Japan. According to a United Press release, a sizable bus company operating in Japan has drastically reduced bus accidents

by applying a psychological theory developed in Europe in the early part of the century. According to this theory, man passes through bio-rhythm cycles and if the bus driver is made aware of his own cycle, it will reduce his number of accidents.

The male feeling of physical fitness, says the theory, passes from low to high and back to low in 23-day cycles. The male ego goes through an emotional cycle of 28 days and a cycle of intellectual activity that lasts 33 days. In the Nagahama City area, the company operates 52 buses which have traveled 1.5 million miles without a single accident since the bio-rhythm program was introduced. Perhaps the attention given safety, as a result of the program, was as beneficial as awareness of the theory itself.[2]

The Greyhound System

Greyhound believes its customers are a no-frill, economy-minded market. No food or hostesses appear on their buses. Greyhound (and Trailways) offers a $99 ticket good for unlimited rides during a 21-day period. One Australian couple logged 18,000 miles on Greyhound Lines using the $99 tickets.[3]

Greyhound operates more than 5700 buses over 100,000 miles of routes in almost every part of this country and Canada. Their buses roll more than one million miles each day. Greyhound is a travel conglomerate, a sizable amount of its revenue coming from restaurant sales, institutional food-service contract feeding, leasing of jet aircraft, Greyhound Rent-A-Car, sales of money orders, van line moving, computer services and insurance.

Continental Trailways, second largest of the bus companies, is a part of Holiday Inns. Continental Trailways offers a "five-star luxury service" featuring hostesses, lounges and foodservice on a few of its routes. The male passengers may find an electric razor in the restroom and mothers

[1]National Assn. of Motorbus Owners, *Bus Facts,* 35th Ed. (Washington, D. C., 1969), p. 15.
[2]Shota Ushio, "Bus Safety, Thanks to Psychology," *The Sunday Star-Bulletin and Advertiser,* Honolulu, Apr. 5, 1970.
[3]James P. Gannon, "The Bus Set," *Passenger Transportation* (Michigan State University, 1958), p. 275.

traveling with their babies are provided with bottle warmers.

Rise and Leveling Off of Demand

Bus service caught on quickly in the United States, especially because the 1930's were depression years and the bus was the cheapest mode of transportation available. By 1936, motor buses were carrying over three billion passengers. With the war, every available means of transport was pushed to capacity and the figure tripled, then climbed to a peak in 1949. (See the chart on page 47.) The war showed that at maximum demand the practical load factor was about 80 percent. During the 50's, the bus lost its momentum and total number of passengers declined.[1] In 1972 World Airways and Greyhound Lines reached an agreement by which they sell each other to promote low cost charter packages to the U. S., Europe and the Far East.[2]

Depending upon the part of the country, the bus traveler is likely to be either an older person or a younger person. In some parts of the country, economy is the principal reason for choosing the bus; in other parts, convenience. The usual intercity bus trip is not long, about 80 miles.

In recent years, the curve of bus travel has been fairly flat, the number of people choosing the bus as a mode of transportation has remained about the same. In the period, 1960-1970, about ten billion intercity passenger miles were logged each year, the total fluctuating year by year around the ten billion figure because of world fairs in New York and Montreal and because of a prolonged airline strike in 1966.[3]

AIR TRANSPORTATION

The airplane has made possible the tremendous surge in long-distance travel. Air travel dominates commercial carrier traffic for all trips of over 300 miles. In 1950, 1,094,000 passengers traveled by air between the United States and foreign countries. By 1969, the figure had grown to 83 million.[4] Aeroflot is the largest airline (83 million passengers in 1971). United Air Lines is second with 26 million passengers in 1971. Aeroflot planes are used to sow seed and lay down insecticides on the plains of Kazakh which are virgin lands; they also make emergency medical flights there. Aerial photographs taken from Aeroflot planes help ships find paths through ice-bound passages.[5]

According to the International Air Transport Association, air transport around the world grows at a rate of about 15 percent a year.[6] Between 1959 and 1969, air traffic growth in the U. S. averaged 13 percent a year.[7] The free world has 115 airlines, excluding the substantial air systems of Russia and Communist China.

Compared to travel by any other means, air travel over long distances is the epitome of economy and speed. The traveler usually rides comfortably and safely, enjoying food and beverages and often a movie or stereo enroute. The vast expanses of land and ocean have been shrunk by the jet. No mode of transportation contains the intrinsic excitement of the airplane. Its growing speed, size and luxury are a constant marvel. The fact that man can lift himself above the earth and move at the speed of sound, and faster, is hard to believe. That such transport is available to the average person in the developed world for his pleasure and convenience is even more incredible.

As cost of a mode of travel drops, use increases. Until 1968, the cost of air travel dropped over the years as seen in the chart on p. 64. In 1959, the air traveler's average cost per mile was 5.96¢. It dropped to 5.59¢ by 1968.[8] The 1969 figure was 5.88¢ per mile. In 1971, the rate was up to 6.91¢.[9] Costs, and consequently air fares,

---

[1]*Statistical Abstract of the U. S.,* 1969.
[2]*Travel Trade,* Dec. 11, 1972.
[3]Gerald Traitman, Address before the Cleveland Society of Security Analysts, The Greyhound Corp., 1969.
[4]Air Transport Assn. of America, *1970 Air Transport Facts and Figures* (Washington, D. C.), 1971, p. 5.
[5]*The Wall Street Journal,* Sept. 19, 1972.
[6]*The Wall Street Journal,* Oct. 5, 1970, p. 1.
[7]Air Transport Assn. of America, *1970 Air Transport Facts and Figures* (Washington, D. C.), p. 17.
[8]*Ibid.*
[9]"Changes Ahead in Air Fares," *U. S. News and World Report,* Jan. 22, 1973.

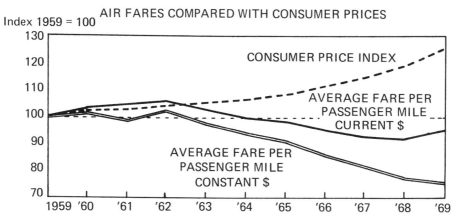

SOURCE: *AIR TRANSPORT FACTS AND FIGURES,* AIR TRANSPORT ASSOCIATION OF AMERICA, 1971.

are likely to continue up. In 1970, American Airlines lost more than $150 million and the Civil Aeronautics Board raised to 12 percent the guidelines for reasonable return on airline investments.

Blaine Cooke, TWA Vice-President of Marketing, said recently the average round trip to Europe in 1970 cost $329.70, 37 percent less than in 1960. However, Cooke also believes the direction of cost has changed and in the future will move in only one direction and "that direction is up."[1]

A vivid example of the drop in long distance fares has been the reduction in fares between the West Coast and Hawaii. As new and faster equipment has become available, fares have come down but more recently are increasing.

Year	Type of Plane	One-Way Cost
1936	Martin-China Clipper	$360
1946	DC-4	195
1949	DC-6	160
1953	DC-7	175
1959	B-707	116
1970	B-747	100
1973	B-747	113

The average round trip flight to Europe in 1970 cost $329.70, 37 percent less than in 1960.[2]

As pointed out by the Air Transport Association of America, while airline fares remained relatively stable during the 1960-70 decade, hotel and restaurant prices rose sharply. One survey of hotel prices in 24 major cities around the world showed that the average price of a room rose 44 percent between 1963 and 1968. Restaurant meals

in the same cities increased 34 percent.[3] In other words, the air fare has become a smaller part of the total vacation expense package, a factor which might encourage longer-distance travel in vacationing.

Because of its cost, its speed, and the rising affluence of the population of much of the world, air travel the world over has been growing. In 1967, the world's scheduled airlines carried 235 million passengers. The Lockheed California Company and the Boeing Company in 1966 both forecasted a growth rate in the free world passenger air travel of 13.7 percent a year.[4] In 1970, some 300 billion passenger miles were flown by the world's airlines.

Domestic air travel will continue to grow, but at a declining rate: 12 percent in the 70's, 10 percent in the 80's, and 8 percent in the 90's.[5] The U. S. airline industry is an oligopoly in that eleven domestic airlines plus Pan American received almost 90 percent of the air fares in 1968. Only five carriers received 70 percent of the revenue. Unlike good oligopolists, the contenders are highly competitive, refusing to divide up air routes even though to do so would mean increased profits for all. The growth of flight for international travel de-

---

[1]Blaine Cooke, "Travel in the 70's—The Luxury Market," *OPERATIONS Bulletin,* American Hotel and Motel Assn., Dec., 1970.
[2]Blaine Cooke, TWA-2nd Conference, p. 70.
[3]Air Transport Assn. of America, *1970 Air Transport Facts and Figures* (Washington, D. C.: 1971), p. 17.
[4]*Air Traffic Demand,* Lockheed California Company, Nov. 1966, and *International Air Traffic Forecast,* Boeing Company, Jan., 1966.
[5]John A. Summerfield, Pan American World Airways, Address, Urban Land Institute, Honolulu, 1970.

pends on the economic development of the world. The Russians and Japanese in 1985 will be traveling in numbers equivalent to Americans today. If affluence arrives for large numbers of people, international tourism will leap forward.

The air traveler, of course, varies widely around the world. In some remote areas, the travelers include pigs and chickens, as well as men, women and children. American Airlines identifies its United States passenger as being typically a businessman between the ages of 35 and 50 years. He is likely to be married with two or more children between the ages of 2 and 15. Well educated, he is articulate and well read. As an executive or junior executive, his earnings place him in the upper middle or higher income brackets.

Americans traveling to Europe divide about 50-50 between those going for business and those who are traveling purely for pleasure. To other parts of the world, about 70 percent of the American travelers are going because of business, or say they are, the other 30 percent traveling for pleasure.

Pleasure is coming to the fore. By 1980, says a Boeing Aircraft forecast, 70 percent of total air travel will be leisure-oriented, only 30 percent will be for business. The airplane has opened new and exotic vacation vistas, bringing once-remote areas to within a few hours flying time. Not so long ago, vacation travel was largely restricted to about a 250-mile radius of the vacationer's home. Today, the jet puts nearly any spot in the world within the range of a two-week vacation.

Many New Yorkers think nothing of hopping a plane for the Virgin Islands or to Paris for a weekend.

Domination of world air travel by the U. S. is seen in the chart on p. 79. Almost 40 percent of the total world air travel is done within the U. S. while another 13 percent of the total air travel is carried out over the North Atlantic. The "total revenue passengers transported one mile in revenue service" adds up to a staggering 351.7 billion in 1972.[1]

The airplane was first flown in 1903 at a village in North Carolina giving it, Kitty Hawk, a touch of immortality. In World War I, the airplane was important as a mo-

bile observation post. After the war, thousands in America traveled out to their local airports to see stunt flyers and perhaps to take the $1 ride over the town. The airplane soon began to be seen as a means of public transport. The first international commercial flight was offered between London and Paris in 1919. Some countries—among them Germany and France—subsidized airlines in the 1920's. The British Government began subsidizing air companies in 1921, and daily service was scheduled between London and Paris. Total route miles over the world grew from 9700 in 1920 to 156,800 in 1930.[2]

First U. S. Passenger Station

The first international air passenger station in the United States was a little field in Key West which Pan American World Airways used in 1927 for flights to Havana and back. The Federal Health and Customs Immigration officials came to the station when notified of the arrival or departure of a plane.

As a regular means of reliable transportation, air travel in the United States was rather slow in developing. The first regularly scheduled passenger service, between Boston and New York, started in 1927 but the age of the modern air liner did not begin until 1932 when Douglas Aircraft sold Trans-World Airlines two dozen, two-engined DC-2's, capable of carrying a pay load of 12 passengers at 150 m.p.h.

The Boeing-247, with retractable landing gear and cowled, air-cooled engines, was another step forward. In 1933, United Airlines flying the 247 carried 10 passengers on a then-astounding and somewhat grueling 19½-hour flight from coast to coast.[3] Douglas, in 1936, produced the DC-3 which became the "Model T" of the industry. It carried 21 passengers and sold at about $100,000. Almost 11,000 of these fast durable planes were built.

Stewardesses, originally nurses, began flying with United Airlines in 1930. Eastern Airlines insisted on stewards well into

[1]*Dimensions of Airline Growth,* Boeing Commercial Airplane Co., Renton, Wash., 1974.
[2]Lickorish and Kershaw, *The Travel Trade* (London: Practical Press, Ltd., 1958), p. 39.
[3]"Card: An Ace for an Airline," *Dupont Magazine* (Jan.-Feb., 1971), p. 10.

the 1940's. Since about 1970, stewards are again being hired and some airlines place them in charge of all baggage handling and in-flight service. By 1970, there were more than 50,000 stewardesses around the world. Most are young and attractive. The airlines insist on it. Overweight stewardesses are suspended. In Yugoslavia it is different. Some of the hostesses fly while obviously pregnant. More power to the people. In the U. S., age limits for stewardesses have been lifted and senior women may receive as much as $15,000 a year.

By 1939, Pan Am had scheduled a regular transatlantic flight using a seaplane, the Dixie-Clipper. It stopped in the Azores, at Lisbon and Marseilles. Cost for the trip was $375 each way. Transpacific service, using the Martin M-130 flying boat, began the same year. The flight left San Francisco, stopped at Hawaii, Midway, Wake, Guam, then on to Manila.

A year later the Boeing-207's, "Stratoliners," commercial planes with pressurized cabins, carrying 40 passengers at some four miles above the ground, rolled down the runways.

During World War II every available plane was pressed into service to carry the load generated by war. Plane seats were difficult to buy. Every passenger was given a priority number and found he could be "bumped" by someone else with a higher priority anywhere the plane stopped. The war familiarized thousands of servicemen with air travel. Thousands of pilots were trained, airports built, advances in aircraft design made. Between 1941 and 1957, the number of U. S. airports tripled. The number of passengers carried rose from 3.5 million to 48.5 million.

Quantum Jumps in Design, Repercussions

Each advance in the design of a mode of travel has produced repercussions throughout the travel industry. An advance in design in a mode increases its competitive advantage and moves it ahead in the great game of travel. The railroad replaced the horse. The automobile and the bus largely replaced the railroad for passenger travel. For long-distance travel, the airplane supersedes all other modes. In the airlines, speed has doubled about every 20 years. The supersonic cruises about 1400 miles per hour. The next step may be hypersonic or rocket travel.

By 1970, the airlines, having experienced two major transitions, were experiencing a third, and anticipating a fourth. Dramatic advances in equipment were part of the reason behind the changes. In 1947, the then Douglas Aircraft Company ushered in a new era of air travel by introducing the four engine, propeller-driven DC-6, capable of flying 4000 miles, nonstop and at a speed of 320 m.p.h. These aircraft could carry up to 89 passengers and proved to be highly durable. One of them flew 57,000 hours, or the equivalent of 6½ years in the air.[1]

Their long-range capability made transcontinental and transatlantic flights possible. A sharp increase in air travel was one result. By 1955, the number of Americans flying the Atlantic exceeded those traveling by ship and five years later the airplane carried three-fourths of the total transatlantic passenger traffic.

The second revolution was brought on by the introduction of the jets, the Boeing 707 and the DC-8, in 1958-59, the shift from piston-driven aircraft, flying at a little over 300 m.p.h., to jet propelled aircraft, flying slightly over 600 m.p.h. and carrying over 100 passengers. Flight time was halved; pay load dramatically increased. The effect was to increase the efficiency of the aircraft by more than 100 percent.

The shiftover from propeller to jet came relatively fast. At the beginning of 1960, about 20 percent of the total passenger service in this country was performed by jet, another 14 percent by turbo-prop. By 1970, virtually all but a tiny fraction of commercial traffic was powered by pure jet aircraft.[2]

The number of seats in commercial planes increased regularly, year after year. The average seating capacity on transatlantic flights went from 54 in 1954, to 74 in 1959, to 144 in 1966.

---

[1]Michael Peters, *International Tourism* (London: Hutchinson, 1969), p. 72.
[2]Air Transport Assn. of America, *1970 Air Transport Facts and Figures* (Washington, D. C., 1971), p. 16.

The figures for representative American planes show the shift from smaller to larger planes since 1947; DC-6 (89 passengers) to DC-8 (129 passengers) to stretched DC-8 (196 passengers) to Boeing 707 (155 passengers) to Boeing 747 (360 and over, depending upon seating configuration.)

Pan American World Airways, pioneer of several changes in air travel, inaugurated the Boeing 747 on the transatlantic flight from New York to London, February 1970, and soon after scheduled it on the New York to San Juan run. A 747 flight was started between Los Angeles and Honolulu in March.

The statistics of the plane are staggering: 232 feet long (nearly 100 feet longer than the 707); 196 feet wing-tip-to-wing-tip; 710,000 lbs. maximum gross weight at take-off. The tail section of the plane is five stories tall. The Federal Aviation Administration has certified the plane to carry up to 490 passengers. Most of the airlines configure the plane so that 35 to 60 passengers are seated first class, the remainder in economy.

Each plane costs between $20 and $23 million (depending upon spare parts and extras ordered), as compared with about $9 million for a Boeing 707.[1] Cruising speed is 625 m.p.h. The 747's are said to be safer and to give a smoother ride because their huge size makes them react less to air turbulence.

The introduction of the Boeing 747 will probably have results equal to the two previous revolutions in vehicle design. In effect, possible payload is tripled. The cost of the plane is about 2½ times that of a Boeing 707 but large economies in operation are said to be possible.

The Boeing Company states that a 40 percent load factor is the break-even point on the Boeing 747. If the plane is configured to carry 360, the break-even point would be 144 passengers. If the plane were full, 216 passengers would represent pure profit. Profit per flight could exceed $20,000. Little wonder that, in 1970, the airlines scrambled to put the 747 into operation. American Airlines paid Pan Am $10 million for 15 months use of a single 747.

The 747's can be especially profitable on the high density long runs. When all of the 747's are in service for Pan Am, they will take 88 percent of its San Juan traffic, 65 percent of the carrier's Atlantic passenger volume, 84 percent of Tokyo traffic and 55 percent of passengers to Hawaii.

Up to 80 percent of passengers riding the 747 for the first time are thrilled by its size and the features that make for an entertaining and comfortable flight. Trans World Airlines allows the passenger a choice of sections within the plane, depending upon his preference in movies—"general," "mature," or no movie at all. Some airlines install up to six large movie screens and offer ten channels of individual audio controls. The big person gets a break, as the seats are two inches wider than on the 707. On the 747's used by TWA, each seat has a built-in pneumatic lumbar control. The passenger can inflate or deflate a back cushion to suit his own spinal curvature (TWA found that 35 people out of 100 have back trouble when sitting in one spot too long).

Speedy Foodservice

On the big planes, the ratio of flight attendants to passengers remains the same as on the Boeing 707, about 1 to every 25 passengers. Foodservice is speeded by the use of modules, similar to cargo modules, which are snapped in place in the aircraft on a lower level. The galley modules contain pre-prepared foods which are heated in flight by convection and microwave ovens, located adjacent to the module storage area. Elevators raise the food to the passenger deck when ready.

A new job category, flight service supervisor, has been established. This person, whose job title varies with the airline, is in charge of all the flight service personnel on a plane, luggage handling and service to passengers generally. The job differs from the flight attendant's also in that it is a management (non-union) job.

The 747 passenger jet is expected to revolutionize the air cargo trade—especially over long hauls—since it carries as much cargo in its belly as any predecessor jet freighter does in the entire plane.

By 1972 other large craft were flying. The Douglas DC-10, a little slower and a

---

[1]*The Wall Street Journal*, Oct. 5, 1970.

little smaller, has a cruising speed of 600 miles per hour. The Lockheed 1011 is a little larger than the DC-10 and has a cruising speed of 500 m.p.h. Both are three-engined. Fuselages are almost 20 feet in diameter and are designed to carry 270 to 345. The airbuses are able to land in smaller airports that cannot handle the Jumbo 747. Cost per plane is $14 to $15 million.[1] Several airlines including American and Eastern are shifting over to these planes since they are more economical to operate and can land and take off at the usual airfield since they require less distance for landing and take-off.

A consortium of English, German, French and Dutch aircraft manufacturers are building another airbus, the A-300B. It will seat up to 280 passengers and fly at speeds up to 660 m.p.h. for distances up to 1400 miles. Cost is said to be over $12 million each.[2]

Airbuses Could Cut Number of Flights

Since the airbuses double the number of passengers that can be carried in a commercial jet plane, their use can theoretically reduce the number of flights needed, at least for a time. Crises had been reached at some of the major air terminals, such as New York's Kennedy, O'Hare in Chicago and the Atlanta airport. Traffic volume at O'Hare, busiest of all airports, reached 2400 a day in 1970. So many planes were scheduled that bad weather or other difficulties caused hours-long delays in take-off and landing. Each airbus can replace two of the previous jets and theoretically reduce the number of flights, if not by 100 percent, at least by a large percentage. In 1970, each of a number of 747 flights did replace two 707 flights. This should reduce traffic congestion at the major airports measurably. FAA has set quotas on flights at Kennedy, Newark, O'Hare and Washington National Airport.

Whether or not the number of planes flying in the air will be reduced is a matter for conjecture. Longer intervals are required between landings and take-offs because of greater turbulence created by the large planes. Pan American, which will have 33 of the large planes in service in 1971, is

disposing of about 30 of its line fleet of 155 smaller jets, about an even exchange in number of planes.

A major problem for the airlines has been the fact that equipment technology has changed too rapidly. New generations of planes have been produced faster than can be absorbed by the industry. Nevertheless, the airlines have had to re-equip themselves with each new advance in plane size and speed. Each conversion from one size and type of plane to the next costs many millions of dollars to accomplish. For example, Pan American World Airways lost $28.9 million in 1969; $48.4 in 1970 and $45.5 in 1971. Much of the losses are attributed to the purchase of the B-747, their introduction into service and the fact that passenger growth did not take place as forecasted.

Because of competition, the airlines have been forced to buy the bigger and better planes as they appear on the scene, regardless of business economics. Once a conversion has been made from one type of plane to another, profits shoot up. As a new design becomes available, the airlines are then forced to convert to it. Several years are required to stabilize earnings with the new design. Then another design appears and the process is repeated. Accompanying the problems of change-over in planes is the pressure of rising wages and salaries.

As conversion from piston to jet took place (1959-1961), air fares, which had been declining, rose, reflecting the need for financing the conversion. Once the conversion was made, the airlines enjoyed a halcyon period with rising profits and sales.

In 1967, the world's scheduled airlines earned $12.5 billion gross revenue with an 8.5 percent operating profit. Then towards the end of the 60's, heavy scheduling of flights reduced the load factor of U. S. planes to a little over 50 percent, and several of the major airlines began losing money in large amounts. Scheduled airlines of the U. S. lost more than $200 million in 1970; made $30 million in 1971 and made $230 million in 1972: a 5 percent return on in-

[1]*The New York Times,* July 18, 1970.
[2]*The Wall Street Journal,* Sept. 16, 1970.
[3]*The Wall Street Journal,* Feb. 16, 1973, p. 5.

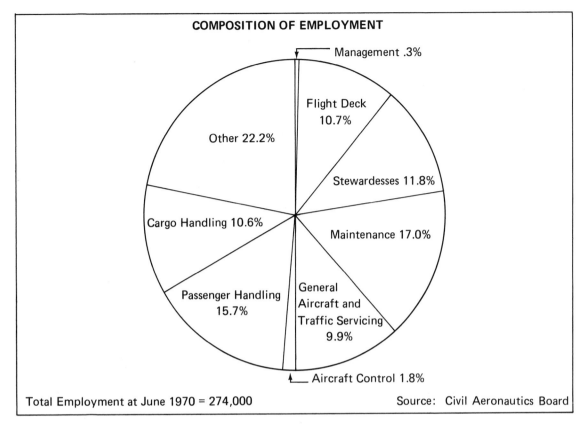

COMPOSITION OF EMPLOYMENT

Management .3%

Flight Deck 10.7%

Stewardesses 11.8%

Maintenance 17.0%

General Aircraft and Traffic Servicing 9.9%

Aircraft Control 1.8%

Passenger Handling 15.7%

Cargo Handling 10.6%

Other 22.2%

Total Employment at June 1970 = 274,000   Source: Civil Aeronautics Board

vestment; CAB allows 12 percent.[3] Pan American lost $28.9 million in 1969; $48.4 million in 1970 and $45.5 million in 1971.[1] The Civil Aeronautics Board began permitting fare increases.

Beginning in 1970, with the introduction of the B-747's, another financial squeeze developed, comparable to what happened in the early 1960's when the transition from piston to jet-propelled planes took place. The acquisition of the bigger planes and the associated equipment needed to service them will cost the airlines an unprecedented $10 billion in the period 1970 to 1973.[2] Of this total cost, $8.3 billion will be for the planes; $1.7 billion will be for the necessary ground equipment.[3] Faulty traffic forecasting tied to the purchase of 747's almost spelled disaster for some airlines, especially Pan American.

Wages for U. S. airline employees jumped from an average of $6686 in 1960 to $10,652 in 1970; employment increased from 167,000 to 311,922.[4] Pilots flying scheduled planes for U. S. airlines are grossly overpaid, as compared with other pilots around the world and as compared with other jobs of comparable qualifications and responsibility. Pilots flying United Airlines 747 jumbo jets receive $57,000 annually, flying no more than 75 hours a month.[5] Stewardesses with years of seniority receive as much as $15,000 a year. Most airline employees also receive extensive flight privileges at reduced or minimal cost.

Only One-Fourth Ride Planes

It is interesting to note that less than one-fourth of the personnel that work for airlines actually ride in the planes—the flight deck and flight attendants. The chart above shows the breakdown of employment of the eleven major trunklines and Pan American Airways, a total of 274,000 personnel. The "Flight Deck" personnel comprised about 11 percent of the total, stewardesses about 12 percent, management less than 1 percent. Average salary in 1970 for the

[1]*Ibid,* March 31, 1972.
[2]Air Transport Assn. of America, *1970 Air Transport Facts and Figures* (Washington, D. C., 1971), p. 5.
[3]*The Wall Street Journal,* Oct. 5, 1970.
[4]Air Transport Assn. of America, *1970 Air Transport Facts and Figures* (Washington, D. C., 1971), p. 45.
[5]*The Wall Street Journal,* Aug. 24, 1970.

rank and file employees, excluding management and flight deck personnel, was $9710. Average salary for management was $37,707 while that for flight deck personnel was $26,488 as reported by the Civil Aeronautics Board.

Some airline administrators were not reluctant at all to add to the costs. David Lewis, president of Delta Airlines, in 1971 had a seven-year contract calling for a base salary of $180,000 a year with lifetime retirement of $50,000 a year. If he had been fired in 1972, he would have received $100,000 a year for five years and retirement pay of $16,000. If he is demoted from chief executive officer, he continues at the rate of $180,000 until 1977, then shifts to $50,000 a year. George Keck, who was dismissed as president of United Airlines in 1970, received payments starting at $100,000 in 1971 and was scheduled for further payments for several years. Charles C. Tillinghast, Jr., chairman of TWA, was paid $100,000 a year in 1971 and will receive $30,000 a year for life if he retires. Harding L. Lawrence, chief executive officer of Braniff Airlines, is scheduled to receive $220,000 a year until June, 1980. He has a contract by which, in case of merger or other consolidation with another carrier, his pay will be adjusted to a basic minimum of $250,000 a year until 1975 and $300,000 a year until 1980. For ten years after that he will receive a consultant's fee of $80,000 a year. If he dies before 1980, Braniff must pay his estate $1,000,000.[1]   George A. Spater, chairman of American Airlines, received $150,000 a year in 1971. TWA Vice President for Marketing, Blaine Cooke's salary exceeds $100,000.

Effects of Over-Scheduling, Rising Costs

In 1969, the load factor fell to 50 percent, (from 53 percent in 1968), the lowest in air history in this country since 1937, when it was 49.1 percent. Since the break-even point for most airlines is thought to be about 47 percent, profit margins for many airlines were low or nonexistent. The average rate of return was 3.7 percent, far below the Civil Aeronautics Board guideline of 12.5 percent. In 1970, traffic which CAB had forecast to grow at 6 percent, down

from an annual rate of 17 percent between 1963 and 1968, only increased about 2 percent.[2]   In 1970, scheduled U. S. airlines were reported to have lost $180 million.

Load Factor Break-Even

The load-factor break-even point on a plane is similar to the occupancy break-even point in a hotel/motel. It varies with the flight; long distance flights usually require fewer seats filled to break even. On some flights the break-even point may be as low as 30, on others 50. Overall load factor break-even points vary with the airlines—may be in the high 40's or low 50's. It is said that a point increase in load factor can raise net income for a carrier by 10 percent.[3]

Part of the profit squeeze was due to over-scheduling, many airlines scheduling flights with well below a 50 percent load factor. Growth for 1968 was forecast at 14 percent. Actual growth was 9 percent. Economies were necessary. An example was a savings of $450,000 made by TWA on import duties merely by switching to domestic china from a fancy German pattern which had been in use for its first-class passengers. United Airlines said it saved $250,000 annually by cutting out macadamia nuts on most flights.[4] Other costs that affect profits include landing fees; there is a $1618 landing fee for a 747 at Heathrow airport in England.

Blaine Cooke, Vice President Marketing, TWA, suggests charging for meals and for full cost of movies, perhaps even for reserved seats. "Only on cruise ships and at Salvation Army Missions can you get free meals."[5]   Movies cost TWA $4 million, meals $50 million a year.

In 1963, President Kennedy proposed building America's first supersonic transport (SST) with speeds up to 1800 m.p.h. (A supersonic plane flies faster than Mach 1, the speed of sound). His decision followed those made by Britain and France to build

[1]"Corporate Heartbalm," The New York Times, July 4, 1971.
[2]The Wall Street Journal, Nov. 16, 1970.
[3]TWA-2nd Conference, p. 113.
[4]Ibid.
[5]Blaine Cooke, TWA-2nd Annual Conference Proceedings, 1971, p. 63.

a similar aircraft which would travel 1450 m.p.h.[1] By 1971, two supersonics, the Russian TU-144 and the British-French Concorde, had been test flown at twice the speed of sound.

Supersonics Shorten Time

This new generation of planes would put New York and London less than three hours apart. No point on the globe will be more than eight hours away for tomorrow's tourist: the world itself will be girdled in 106 hours.[2] Because of the sonic boom created by such speeds, overland flights in the USA would be restricted to speeds less than the speed of sound.

The economics of the supersonics are not clear. Their payload will be smaller but since they fly more than twice as fast as the present jets they presumably can make more trips in the course of a 24-hour period. Cost of a Concorde, with spare parts, is close to $60 million; yet it will seat only about 108 passengers.

In 1971, the American Congress voted to cut developmental spending on the American version of the supersonic plane. Concern over ecological disturbances which might be brought on by the plane were a factor but there were economic factors as well. One aviation economist declared that the introduction of an SST would reduce overall travel by raising the cost of travel.[3] Mr. Ferguson, writing in the *Wall Street Journal,* pointed out that air travel is highly sensitive to fares charged. An average reduction of about 15 percent in fares beginning in 1964 was followed by a 40 percent increase in travel. Another study he reported indicated that for each 1 percent change in fares there has tended to be a 2 percent change in travel.

Ferguson's thesis was that if the government placed pressure on airlines to make SST fares about the same as that of other aircraft, travelers would presumably choose to fly on the SST. The whole rate structure would be increased which would reduce the total amount of travel. Operational costs. he said, would also be higher and he quoted the British Aircraft Corporation as announcing that the Concorde's expected seat-mile cost would be 36 percent higher than that

of the Boeing 747. He also pointed out that the supersonics would not be able to fly non-stop over the long distances which many people expect. His recommendation: allow the SST to develop in due course as technological advances in various areas and changes in air transport markets (1) reduce the cost and uncertainties now associated with it or (2) produce other developments that obviate the "need" for the SST.

The Russian-built TU 144 was readied for service in 1971.[4] Cruising at 1560 m.p.h. at 65,000 feet, it flew faster than the French/English Concorde which has a cruising speed of 1458 m.p.h. at 50,000 to 60,000 feet. The Russians contend that their TU 144 can replace three conventional jets. Even though they will cost about $25 million (without spare parts), say the Russians, the TU 144's will be cheaper to buy and operate than the three conventional jets. (The Russians, it is contended, will sell their plane below cost.)

The Supersonics will undoubtedly be used for long distance flights over water or sparsely populated land. We can expect another shift in airports to accommodate them. New regional-international airports will probably be built just as jet ports replaced propellor-plane ports in several places in the sixties.

Short Take-Off and Landing

While the jets get the publicity, the STOLs, "short take-off and landing" planes, may be just as important for short flights of the future. Requiring only 2000 ft. runways, as compared with the 10,000 feet needed for a jet, the STOLs can make travel between cities close to each other much more convenient. The Hypersonics are, in effect, rocket ships.

It takes as long to go from downtown New York to downtown Washington in 1973 as it did in 1950. The flight with a 500 m.p.h. jet takes only minutes—but total travel time to and from airports plus run-

[1]Everett Clark, "Up in the Clouds with the SST," *Saturday Review,* Jan. 6, 1968, p. 47.
[2]*The Big Picture,* 1966-67, Patterson, pp. 23-24.
[3]"Why the SST Is Not Good Business," *The Wall Street Journal,* March 23, 1971.
[4]*The Wall Street Journal,* May 14, 1971, pp. 1 and 17.

way waiting time effectively removes the pleasure of such travel. The STOLs are scheduled to land and take off from downtown areas. Even though present STOLs fly only about 150 m.p.h., the planned "metroflights" will cut total travel time and hopefully relieve pressures on existing airports in Boston, New York, Newark, Philadelphia and Washington, St. Louis, Houston and Los Angeles. Tokyo and cities in Europe have plans for downtown metroports.[1]

The economic importance of STOLs is more vividly seen in the light of the tremendous cost of airport development. Some 16,000 to 20,000 acres of land are needed for the development of a modern jet airport, land which is usually very costly. The STOLs, requiring relatively small strips of land, may be able to use such places as the dock areas of downtown Manhattan. STOL service is scheduled to begin between the East River near Wall Street in New York City and downtown Philadelphia in 1973. The 20-passenger De Haviland Twin Otter on floats will be used.

VTOLS are Vertical Take-Off and Landing Planes, which means the plane can elevate itself vertically and land perpendicular to the earth like a helicopter.

The pay-off for a particular mode of transportation comes in the number of passengers that can be carried in a given period of time and the cost per passenger. When one jet plane can carry more passengers than the Queen Elizabeth 2, a passenger train or bus over the same travel distance, the profit is considerable. The key to understanding this statement is that the jet makes several trips in the same period of time required by the other forms of transportation. A jet carrying 300 people theoretically could make 12 or more trips across the Atlantic in the same time required for the Queen Elizabeth 2 to make one trip.

It must be pointed out that costs per passenger mile vary considerably. Short flights eat gasoline and time in take off, climbing, descending and landing. Fuel economies are possible at high altitudes. Cost per mile may be half as much on a long flight as compared with a short one.

In a Boeing study, the estimate is made that one 300-passenger SST will be as pro-

ductive as four 707's, and will be about 75 percent more productive than the 747.[2]

Charter Planes, Commuter Airlines, Air Taxis, Air Tours

The traveler in a hurry who wants special service can charter a plane, fly on a commuter airline, or take an air taxi service from almost any population center to another within the United States and certain foreign countries. For small groups, it is often less expensive to charter a plane, fly to a particular destination, and return, than it is to use commercial air service. As many corporations consider the travel time of their executives as part of the cost of the particular project requiring the travel, they have found it feasible to have their own private aircraft. Many of these aircraft are jets costing in excess of $1 million. The larger corporate jets have worldwide capability and you will see many of these aircraft, operated by large American corporations, at foreign airports throughout the world.

Air tours have been established in some destination areas; for example, the Cook Mountains of New Zealand and the State of Hawaii. For the tourist who wants a comprehensive topographical and geographical understanding of an area, the air tour is the quickest means of getting it. Smaller planes can fly into remote valleys and around mountains and seashores inaccessible by other means. The actual visual experience of flying over an active volcano cannot be duplicated by reading or in films.

Hawaiian Air Tour Service, operating within the eight islands of Hawaii, is perhaps the oldest air tour service today. The HATS operation illustrates the need for special expertise and tight management. The company, largely owned by one person, Hans Mueller, was started in 1953. Mueller, who had come to Hawaii as a military transport pilot, started the company with a total capital outlay of approximately $200. The first purchase was a war surplus plane. The fabric-covered Cessna T-50, nicknamed the Bamboo Bomber, carried only six passengers. It was soon necessary to buy two oth-

[1]"A Revolution In Air Travel: Let's Fly Downtown," *Parade,* Apr. 19, 1970.
[2]*AAA Traveletter,* Washington, D. C., Apr., 1970.

er such Cessnas, one for flying duty and one from which to get spare parts.

The economics of an air tour service are marginal. HATS maintenance is performed by part-time aircraft mechanics employed from nearby Hickam Air Force Base. The majority of HATS pilots are retired military air transport service aircraft commanders, who have retired to live in the Honolulu area. Careful maintenance permits the use of used aircraft.

Approximately 80 percent of the 15,000 passengers who took the HATS tour in 1969 were sold by retail travel agents, wholesale travel agents and scheduled airlines. A 10 percent commission is paid on the transportation portion of the tour, and commissions on the land arrangements vary from 10 percent, based upon the sales volume the particular agent produces for HATS. The balance of passengers were sold by the company from their own sales office. In conjunction with major airlines, travel agents are offered familiarization tours.

Testimony to the rewards of the trip are the increasing numbers who take the trip and the growing numbers who repeat it. One repeat customer was a lady 93 years of age.

Control of Rates and Fares

Rates and fares for airline services are controlled within this country by the Civil Aeronautics Board; outside of the United States rates and fares are controlled by international agreement, working through the International Air Transport Association. The predecessor organization to IATA was the International Air Traffic Association formed in 1919, an association of six airline companies. In 1945, the organization took its present form and, in 1946, it was decided that the IATA Traffic Conferences should determine fares and rates for international travel. In 1970, IATA included 105 members.

Any airline certified by a government eligible to join the United Nations can join IATA which has administrative offices in Montreal and branch offices in New York, Paris, London and Singapore. International fares are agreed upon by the member airlines working through the IATA Traffic Conferences. Fare formulas, to be adopted,

must receive unanimous approval by the passenger conferences.

Since much of international travel is interline, a great many credit and debit balances between airlines must be cleared. This is also done by IATA in London, working through the Bank of England. The International Civil Aviation Organization, an association of governments, works with IATA and operates as a specialized agency of the United Nations. Both organizations have as a common purpose the promotion of civil aviation on a worldwide scale, promoting safety in civil aviation, reducing red tape and ironing out legal problems concerned with commercial flying.

Elasticity of Demand

As fares are reduced, does the number of passengers increase? Is the demand for air travel elastic?

Much—perhaps most—of business travel is inelastic. If there is economic necessity, the businessman takes the trip with little regard for cost. Of course, if air fares rise excessively even the businessman will consider alternate means of travel. He is continually balancing the cost of his time with the cost of air fare and may shift to auto if the distance to travel is not too long, or to bus or train. This has happened in a number of cases in travel between New York City and Washington, D C., where the Metroliner has become the choice of numerous travelers.

Pleasure travel is more likely to have elastic demand. Cost looms much larger in the travel decision when the expense comes directly out of the traveler's pocket.

A cost-benefit study of the visitor industry in Hawaii was specific. By use of time-series analysis, it was found that a 10 percent reduction in air fare increases the number of visitors to Hawaii by about 15 percent. The same fare reduction increases the house count in the Hawaiian hotels by about 9 percent. The length of stay would rise by about 3 percent.[1]

Evidence for price elasticity in air travel was found in a *Business Week* survey of 4000 charter passengers who crossed the

[1]"The Visitor Industry in Hawaii's Economy: A Cost-Benefit Analysis," Mathematica, 1970, pp. 27-29; pp. 187-203.

TABLE VI—LONG-TERM COEFFICIENTS OF INCOME ELASTICITY[1]
OF FOREIGN TRAVEL DEMAND

	Coefficient of Income Elasticity of Demand for Foreign Travel	
Country	IUOTO (Period 1956-65) (Based on GNP)	OECD (Period 1960-69) (Based on Private Consumption Expenditure)
France	3.2	2.5
Netherlands	2.6	1.7
Italy	2.2	1.7
Sweden	1.9	—*
Denmark	1.9	—*
Germany	1.8	1.6
UK	1.6	1.5
USA	1.5	1.1
Canada	1.4	1.2
Belgium	1.3	2.0
Switzerland	1.3	—*
Japan	—*	1.5

*Not studied

Atlantic in 1971. Of them, 74 percent said "no" to the question, "Would you have made the trip if the cheap charter fare had not been available?" Price sensitivity, of course, varies with the market. Some 26 percent of the respondents in the *Business Week* survey said they would have taken the flight on a scheduled airline if the charter were not available. The majority of students probably would not travel abroad unless inexpensive fares were available. Some 8000 members of the British Universities' North American Club, passengers who flew from England to North America in 1970, were polled. Eighty-one percent said they would not have gone without the inexpensive fare.[2] Surveys by Overseas National Airways and by World Airways (both nonscheduled airlines, to be sure) found similar results.[3]

A 1967 study by the International Union of Official Travel Organizations (IUOTO) and a 1970 study conducted by the Organization for Economic Cooperation and Development (OECD) found essentially the same results as regards the marginal propensity to spend on foreign travel related to gross national product or private consumption. The table above shows the results of the two studies in terms of relationships between income and amount of foreign travel.

For example, with every unit increase in Gross National Product the average French citizen spent 3.2 in additional units on foreign travel. For each unit increase in the French private consumption expenditure, 2.5 units were spent on foreign travel. In other words, as a Frenchman's income increased, his expenditure for foreign travel increased even more.

Supplemental Versus Scheduled Airlines

Congress passed legislation, in 1962, permitting the development of airlines which supplemented the scheduled services, but were not held to definite, scheduled flights. By 1970, there were ten member lines in the National Air Carrier Association (NACA) that operated more than 65 jet planes. Their military and commerical charter business brought in an estimated $370 million in 1969. Revenues quadrupled from 1963 to 1969. In 1968, profits were $17.5 million, but in 1969 they suffered a net loss of $3 to $5 million.[4]

[1]*The Tourism Gap: Can It Be Bridged,* Laventhol, Krekstein, Horwath and Horwath (Philadelphia: 1973), p. 38.

[2]*Ibid,* p. 45.

[3]"Charting the Charter Phenomenon," Vincent R. Duffey. Paper presented to The Travel Research Assn., 1972.

[4]*The New York Times,* Aug. 9, 1970, p. 45.

By the late 60's, the scheduled airlines were receiving a large amount of unwanted competition from the "supplementals." On some routes the competition was rough indeed. In 1969, chartered flights carried 68 percent of the West Coast-to-Europe passengers; one-quarter of the almost eight million transatlantic passengers flew charter. About half flew on supplemental airlines; the balance on jets chartered for single trips by the scheduled lines.[1] The supplementals insist that they do not divert traffic from scheduled airlines but are tapping new markets, ones the scheduled airlines have missed because of cost. The scheduled airlines believe otherwise.

The principal reason for the huge traffic of the supplementals is their low-cost fares, about half that of the economy rate of the scheduled airlines. Supplementals can offer lower fares because they can operate at close to a 100 percent load factor, as compared with the load factor of the scheduled airlines which is in the 50 percent range.

The measurement of the demand for travel is complex and raises highly abstract questions. At what difference in price will a traveler choose one mode over another? How important is the factor of comfort? Of convenience?

How much will a traveler pay to save an hour of waiting in an airline terminal, or to save 15 minutes of waiting on a cold day for a bus to arrive?

The answers vary with the individual, his level of patience, his disposable income, his available time at the moment. How highly does he value convenience and comfort? How tired will he be when he must travel that extra hour?

Cost is a factor for nearly everyone: the millionaire out of habit; the working man because of necessity.

A number of attempts to quantify and make models for predicting travel demand have been made. They are theoretical and highly statistical in nature.[2]

Scheduled airlines have higher overhead costs. Salaries paid to their personnel are usually higher and the flag carriers try to maintain a policy of stabilizing fare rates so that profits on some routes compensate for losses on others. Even so, in a bad year supplementals suffer along with the scheduled airlines. Several have gone out of business.

According to the scheduled carriers, the supplemental airlines are price-butting spoilers who skim the cream off the overseas travel business. Supplementals do their major business during the summer, the profitable period for the scheduled lines. From another viewpoint, the supplementals are gallant and socially-useful competitors who jumped the international air cartels to provide the public with low cost bulk transportation. From a government viewpoint, supplementals are valuable for standby airlift capacity in case of war. Charters serve a useful function in transporting the huge summer travel, especially across the Atlantic. In 1972, about one passenger in three flew the Atlantic by charter plane.[3]

According to CAB regulations, supplementals may engage in three types of charter:

Single entity: An entire plane load is purchased, as when large companies take salesmen on trips.

Affinity group: An organization contracts for the plane with costs prorated among the members taking the trip. Membership in the group must pre-date the trip by at least six months.

Inclusive Tour Charters: Travel agents contract for the space, then sell complete travel package tours to individual customers.

The CAB can impose civil penalties against the airlines of up to $1000 for each unauthorized passenger carried.

To combat the supplementals, the scheduled carriers fought back with "bulk tour" rates. In December, 1968, an agreement negotiated at Caracas by IATA proposed bulk tour rates competitive with the supplementals. Interestingly, IATA-approved bargain rates are only available on those routes where supplementals have carved out a significant market.

Major factors in the development of an area are its accessibility and convenience, and the cost of the travel to the area. Of

---

[1]*Ibid.*
[2]Richard E. Quandt, The Demand for Travel: Theory and Measurement (Lexington, Mass.: D. C. Heath, 1970)
[3]*Travel Trade,* June 5, 1972, p. 55.

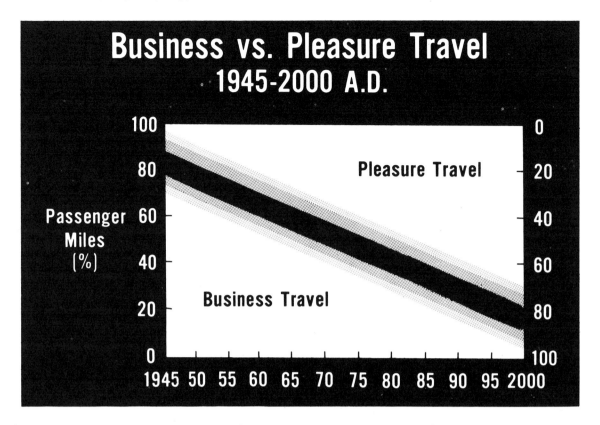

course, the area has to have something to attract the potential visitor. The development of many tourist areas depends upon the number of airlines which serve them. Generally speaking, the more airlines serving an area, the greater the competition and the more promotion and advertising done for the area by the competing lines.

Airline fares also greatly influence the number of travelers to an area. The lower the fare, the greater the number of people who will consider traveling to the area. Today, 95 percent of overseas travel is by airlines, of which 80 percent is at the economy fare rate.

Elasticity of demand for business travel is probably much less than for pleasure travel. Business enterprises are apt to think of business travel as a necessity, though even they will begin to curtail such travel if they feel that the price of travel has increased inordinately. Pleasure travel seems to be highly sensitive to costs. In the graph above it is seen that pleasure travel is increasing rapidly as compared with travel for business purposes. The McDonnell-Douglas Com-

pany, source of the graph, projects that business travel will constitute 80 percent of all travel by the year 2000. This would suggest that much of the marketing of travel will be divided into two parts; that aimed at the business traveler, and another very large section at the pleasure traveler. The pleasure traveler will likely be offered economy travel via special rates for groups and for off-peak periods, as is being done now.

Skyjacking as an Air Travel Problem

Skyjacking, the commandeering of a plane by force or threat, reached epidemic proportions in 1968 to 1972. By the end of 1971, over 335 skyjackings had taken place world wide; 75 percent occurring between 1969 and 1971. The airlines were beset by the public, the government, and the skyjacker.[1] By 1972, the Federal government acted massively to eliminate skyjackings by screening every passenger who boarded a plane. In 1973, every passenger

[1]Elizabeth Rich, *Flying Scared* (New York: Stein and Day, 1972).

who boarded a plane was subject to personal scrutiny, his person and luggage searched for weapons of any kind. Hundreds of weapons were seized and numerous arrests made.

Skyjacking originated for political reasons when in 1930 a group of Peruvian rebels commandeered a Pan American Ford Tri-motor and forced the pilot to land at Arequipa where a revolution was in progress. Numerous planes were seized by people in communist countries and flown to the so-called Free World from that period to the present. The first skyjacking of a U. S. plane occurred in 1954. Between then and 1972, there were 159 skyjackings of U. S. planes.[1] When Fidel Castro seized political control of Cuba in 1959, a number of Cubans seized planes and flew them to the United States where the government seized at least nine of them and sold them to satisfy American business claims against property nationalized by the Castro government.

During the 1960's most of the planes skyjacked over U. S. territory were forced to fly to Cuba. As a result of the publicity given to the skyjackings, a number of unbalanced individuals took over planes for purposes of extortion. Several million dollars was extracted from the airlines by such means. Skyjackers usually directed the planes to Havana where the planes were detained a few hours and then allowed to return to the U. S. Cost and inconvenience of the hi-jacking was considerable. Palestinian terrorists also skyjacked and, in several instances, destroyed planes.

In 1970, skyjacking took a new turn when Arabs began using skyjacking as a means of forcing political concessions from various governments. A Boeing 747, owned by Pan American World Airways, was hijacked and blown up in Cairo. The value of the plane was close to $25 million. In September 1970, three more planes were forced to fly to Jordan where a number of hostages were held and the planes, owned by TWA, Swissair and BOAC, were blown up. Insurance coverage for the four planes totaled $48 million.

To counteract skyjacking, governments and airlines immediately began instituting careful searches, looking for persons representing the "typical profile" of a hi-jacker. The profile is made of those traits which have been found to characterize skyjackers in the past. Among other behavioral characteristics, would-by skyjackers usually buy a one-way ticket, quite logically, and are

U. S. "Skymarshalls," trained armed guards provided by the FBI and military, began riding overseas commercial flights in an attempt to thwart further hi-jacking.

Since 1972, when comprehensive search measures have been instituted for all passengers boarding an airplane in the U. S., skyjackings have been almost eliminated (at least for the time being) in the U. S. A major deterrent to skyjacking took place on February 5, 1973 when a memorandum of understanding was reached between U. S. and Cuban governments. Skyjackers arriving in Cuba would be tried for the offense punishable by the most severe penalty—or the hijacker would be returned to the U. S. However, political asylum would be given those who steal transport for strictly political reasons without alternatives for leaving a country. Both nations agreed to punish anyone using their territory to organize attacks against the other. The U. S. agreed to apply immigration laws strictly which would reduce the number of Cubans coming to the U. S.

The Ethiopian government airlines handle skyjackers in a manner designed to discourage anyone from even contemplating such a venture. Guards aboard an Ethiopian airliner dispensed summary punishment to two hi-jackers by strapping them down in seats in the first-class section, where there were no passengers, wrapping towels around their shoulders, and quietly cutting their throats.

Problems of Growth in Air Travel

With air fares holding relatively steady. education and affluence on the increase around much of the world, projections of air travel are a little dizzying, even frightening. According to IATA, world scheduled

---

[1] *The Wall Street Journal,* June 6, 1972.

passenger service is expected to continue its 12 percent a year growth rate from 1970 to 1980. Pressures on airports and air control systems will continue.

Ground transportation problems to and from airports are certain to enlarge. In 1970, ground time took 30 percent of the total time required for city-center to city-center travel between London and New York. The supersonics could drastically shorten air time. The ratio of ground to air time will increase to the point where it may take as much time to get to and from an international airport at each end of the trip as for the trip itself. Air traffic congestion may force a return to ground transportation in the Washington, D. C.-Boston corridor, and elsewhere around the world in congested areas.

The air traveler who has "stacked up" over New York or Chicago or other cities is almost as concerned with airport congestion as he is with auto traffic congestion and air pollution. As one commentator put it, "Go to any airport in the world on any Sunday in the summer. If you call that fun, you're a heavy drinker."[1]

The traveler, once he is ensconced in a plane, may be royally treated with hot towels, champagne and a meal which may cost the airlines as much as $10 to $15 per person on an international flight. Getting to and from the plane is something else again. Once he gets off the plane, he may become a part of the jostling herd, struggling to get his luggage and fighting the machinations of the cab driver. At Kennedy Airport, for example, New York cabbies employ a number of ruses to avoid taking any but the long distance fares. The international traveler is often confronted with long lines waiting to be processed through immigration and customs; and he faces this at a time when he's already feeling let down at the end of a long flight.

To combat these more than inconveniences, airports are being changed and rapid transit systems to mid-cities from airports installed. At Hong Kong's Kai Tak Airport, immigration procedures will take place aboard the aircraft; TWA's Flight Wing One at JFK International will have its own private customs to move overseas passengers.

Customs inspections for persons traveling from the Bahamas take place in the Bahamas, not at the destination. In several airports, moving sidewalks have been installed within the terminals to reduce the blocks of walking formerly required.

Rapid transit systems are being set up between Amsterdam and its airport so that railroad travel time is cut from 30 minutes to 10 minutes. At Frankfurt, a below-level railroad and bus station system will cut travel to and from the city to 10 minutes. Plans are being made for a high speed railroad between Kennedy Airport and mid-town Manhattan.

Around the larger airports, such as O'Hare in Chicago and the Los Angeles International Airport, vast complexes of rooms, convention facilities, restaurants, and shops have been built, making, in effect, an airport city or omniport. The traveler need not leave the airport area except for sight-seeing.

The Future of Air Travel?

Nearly everyone assumes that air travel will increase. The rate of growth and its ultimate magnitude have been the subject of a number of studies, none of which, of course, can predict the future with clarity. George Newman, of Pan American World Airways, points out that, in the past, forecasts of international travel growth have erred on the side of conservatism.[2] Nearly all long-term forecasts project a high growth rate for the first half of the period which they cover (usually ten years), followed by a slower growth rate.

Mr. Newman is more optimistic. According to his studies, a 10 percent increase in income by 1000 upper middle-income families in the 1980's will produce 27 additional foreign trips. He estimates that, on the average, a 1 percent increase in income triggers a 2.2 percent increase in the number of international pleasure trips. The necessities and semi-necessities for the middle

[1]F. W. Weisser, "TWA," *Service World International,* New York, May, 1970.
[2]George Newman, "Saturation in Travel—Facts and Fantasies." Paper presented at New York Travel Research Assn. meeting, Nov. 17, 1970.

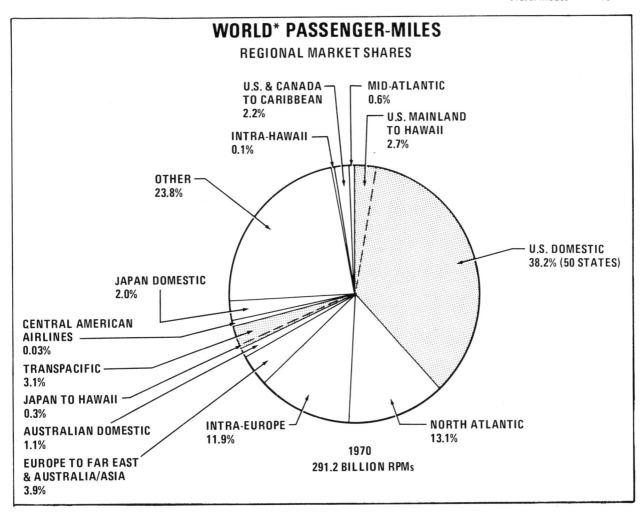

WORLD* PASSENGER-MILES
REGIONAL MARKET SHARES

U.S. & CANADA
TO CARIBBEAN
2.2%

MID-ATLANTIC
0.6%

INTRA-HAWAII
0.1%

U.S. MAINLAND
TO HAWAII
2.7%

OTHER
23.8%

U.S. DOMESTIC
38.2% (50 STATES)

JAPAN DOMESTIC
2.0%

CENTRAL AMERICAN
AIRLINES
0.03%

TRANSPACIFIC
3.1%

JAPAN TO HAWAII
0.3%

AUSTRALIAN DOMESTIC
1.1%

EUROPE TO FAR EAST
& AUSTRALIA/ASIA
3.9%

INTRA-EUROPE
11.9%

NORTH ATLANTIC
13.1%

1970
291.2 BILLION RPMs

income families have already been met; added income can be spent for travel.

The big growth in foreign travel will come from middle and low-income families who are moving into higher brackets and acquire the travel habits of their new income group, and also from students. The potential market, according to Newman, is about 55 percent of the entire population. (As stated previously, he subtracts 30 percent for the very old, the very young, the sick and the poor, and another 15 percent as "hard core, non-travelers.")

According to Hershel B. Sarbin, publisher of *Travel Weekly,* only 30 percent of the United States adult population had ever taken a trip by air in 1960. By 1969, that number had increased to 45 percent.[1] Put in other terms, in 1960, the air market in the U. S. was 54 million persons; in 1970,

the market was 95 million. The population of the U. S. in 1980 will increase to 230 million with 140 million air travelers. Using a modest growth rate of 10 percent, U. S. domestic air travel will increase 260 percent in the 1970-1980 decades.

Population growth, higher education, "internationalism," status seeking, social pressures, more disposable income, more and longer vacations will all increase travel of all kinds. Recessions, political instability, congestion, higher costs will tend to force travel down. On balance, and over a period of time, barring world destruction, business and pleasure travel, especially by air, is almost certain to increase dramatically.

[1]Hershel B. Sarbin, "The Hottest Issues in Travel—And the Coolest." Talk before the Eastern Council for Travel Research, May 18, 1971.

A $9 million investment—on land worth at least $20 million, has produced Caneel Bay Plantation, St. John, U. S. Virgin Islands, one of the most beautiful resorts in the world. Spread over 200 acres of a former Danish sugar plantation, resort has only 120 guest rooms ($95 to $105 room rate for two, American plan, in season); its occupancy rate is unusually high. It is owned by a foundation devoted to conservation and managed by Rockresorts.

Considered by many to be the "greatest" hotel in the world, the Mauna Kea Beach Hotel was built at Kamuela, Hawaii. As is true with most of the Rockresorts, the hotel was built both as a fine resort and as a means of bringing life to an economically depressed area. The hotel sits on the dry side of the large island of Hawaii. Though the area gets less than 20 in. of rainfall a year, plenty of water is available by pipeline from the nearby mountains. The resort is assured of almost year round sunshine without the usual concomitant water shortage. It is reputed to have cost $100,000 per room. The kitchen alone is said to have cost $1 million. (For pictures of two other Rockresorts, see page 118 and page 100.)

THE TRAVEL AGENT

Travel agents in this country produce an annual sales volume in excess of $4 billion—over $2 billion in domestic air sales, more than $1 billion in international air, and at least another billion in hotels, sightseeing and other ground services.[1] Erwin Robinson, publishing director of the *Travel Weekly,* the source for these figures, further states that this country has some 6000 travel agencies, employing more than 30,000 sales and clerical persons.

The travel agent, according to Robert A. Peattie, Jr., is responsible for booking about two-thirds of all overseas and international airline trips as well as for about 40 percent of domestic airline travel.[2]

The travel agency business represents opportunity for women. Some 80 percent of all the employees are women and about 2000 agencies in the U.S. are owned wholly or in part or are managed by women.

A worldwide study of 224 hotel operations outside the U. S. showed that travel agents and tour operators handled reservations for about 35 percent of these hotels. The range was wide. Less than 10 percent of reservations to Central America were arranged by travel agents and tour operators; more than 50 percent of the reservations were handled for travelers to Africa. Reservations systems accounted for 20 percent of the reservations; about 1/3 of the reservations were made directly by the traveler.[3]

Thos. Cook and Son

Persons with knowledge about travel have been arranging trips for others for centuries but it was Thomas Cook who is credited with being the first bona fide travel agent to work as a full-time professional.

A wood-turner by trade, Cook was deeply religious and a temperance enthusiast. In 1841, he chartered a train to carry 540 people on a round trip to a temperance convention. Cook arranged the trip at a shilling each for the round trip from Leicester to Loughborough, a distance of 22 miles. Cook did the arrangements for the trip with no profit for himself, but soon saw the potential of what could be done in arranging travel for others.

In 1845, Cook became a full-time excursion organizer. The travel business, as he saw it from the outset, was more than a business, it was an opportunity for education and enlightenment. The five percent commission he received from the Midland Counties Railroad was not enough to maintain a solvent business. Besides selling day excursions, he became a tour operator, and later a retailer of tours.

Cook, dedicated to making the tours as convenient and interesting as possible to the "tourist," printed a "handbook of the trip" for an 1845 tour from Leicester to Liverpool. Soon after, he produced coupons which could be used by the traveler to cover his hotel expenses. In 1846, he took 350 people by steamer and train on a tour of Scotland. A specially designed tour-guide, the first of its kind, was made for the trip.

By 1851, no less than 165,000 people were using Mr. Cook's lodging and transportation plans to go to London for the first World's Exposition at the Crystal Palace.

Later, Cook moved his offices to London and began conjuring up all sorts of imaginative trips for people to take hither and yon. Soon he was arranging "grand circular tours of Europe," itineraries involving visits to four different countries.

He helped popularize Switzerland as a

[1]Erwin Robinson, "The Distributive Environment in Travel," *Proceedings First Annual Conference, Travel Research Assn.,* Salt Lake City, 1970, p. 158.
[2]Robert A. Peattie, Jr., "Measuring Travel Trends Through Travel Agents," *Ibid.* p. 95.
[3]*World Wide Operating Statistics of the Hotel Industry, 1972.* (New York: Horwath and Horwath International, 1972).

touring center by taking a group through the country in 1863. Soon after the Civil War, his son, John M. Cook, was in America with a group traveling to New York, Washington, and some of the Civil War battlefields.

In 1872, Cook achieved another first: an around-the-world trip with nine tour members. Thoughtfully, his impressions were recorded in letters to the *Times,* the great English newspaper. As he circled the globe, time elapsed, 222 days (the trip was said to have inspired Jules Verne to write *Around the World in Eighty Days).* Today, the same trip can be taken over a weekend.

A Cook's tour was likely to turn up just about anywhere. Long before Florida became a winter resort, Cook and his clientele escaped English chill by sailing up and down the Nile, viewing the wonders of ancient Egypt.

Centuries before, the Venetians had done well by arranging transport for Crusaders to the Holy Land. In 1884, John Cook arranged for the transportation of the entire expeditionary force of 18,000 men up the Nile for the attempted relief of General Charles George Gordon at Khartoum. Like many tours, the relief "tour" arrived late. General Gordon had already died from a stabbing pain in the chest. Khartoum had fallen.

No Spot Too Remote

The Cook's interest in geography was universal in scope. John arranged trips into Yellowstone Park, soon after the park opened. In 1875, tours were arranged in Norway. In collaboration with the P&O Steamship Line, travel to India was made "posh." The traveler, as soon as he arrived in Bombay, was escorted to spacious compartments on Indian trains and served complete meals while en route to visit the Taj Mahal. The traveler could visit the Himalayas, Mt. Everest or travel to the Vale of Kashmir.

In the 1890's, they ran pioneering trips across Europe to Asia via the Trans-Siberian Railroad. Cook undertook the difficult: a trip to Jerusalem in 1890 needed armed guards, mules, horses, cooks and tents. It also needed a great deal of bargaining with local sheiks and pashas to permit travel through their domains. Cook, or his son,

arranged everything and went along as an escort.

In 1874, Cook provided "circular notes," credentials which would be accepted by banks, hotels, shops and restaurants around the world. Just who gets credit for introducing the traveler's check (British spelling is cheque) is debatable because the American Express Co. introduced money orders in 1882 and the travel check, by that name, was adopted by British banks and the travel agency, replacing their own circular notes.

The important feature of these notes or "traveler-cheques" was that they were insured against loss. In selling a $100 traveler's check, the selling company acquires $100 which it can invest or loan at interest. The American Express Co. has $750 million in its "float," acquired from selling traveler's checks. The American Express Co. states that, while it makes little or nothing on its travel agency business, it makes considerable money with the use of its float. The same is no doubt true of the Thos. Cook Co.

Cook's only son, John Mason Cook, continued the work of his father and, in 1878, became manager of the firm. (Thomas' later years were passed in blindness.)

The Cooks were well aware of the elasticity of demand for travel. If the cost of travel could be reduced, more people would travel. The more people travel by a particular mode of transportation, the more likely that type of transportation can be reduced in cost. By chartering whole trains and steamers and by booking large blocks of rooms, Cook was able to reduce the cost of travel. It costs only a little more to operate a train, a steamship, or an airplane that is 100 percent full than one that is 25 percent full. With crowds, cost per seat can be drastically reduced. Convenience of travel offered by the Cooks was also important.

Another reason for the Cook's success was their enthusiasm for travel as an enlightening venture, one for the masses, not just for the elite. Cook, and later his son, must have been inordinately energetic. John often worked 18 hours a day. The Cook's Tour, throughout the second half of the 19th century, meant an escorted group tour, very often conducted by John or one of his sons.

Tours came in for their snide remarks from the outset. Some people, like Mark Twain, were enthusiastic about the tour group, feeling that the traveler had a ready-made group of friends wherever he went. The first tour groups tended to be solidly middle class, which did not protect them from being caricatured by the travel snob:

"It seems some enterprising and unscrupulous man has devised the project of conducting some 40 or 50 persons from London to Naples and back for a fixed sum (referring to Thomas Cook). He contracts to carry, feed, lodge, and amuse them. They are to be found in diet, theatricals, sculpture, carved wood, frescoes, washing, and roulette. You see them, 40 in number, pouring along the street with a director—now in front, now at the rear—circling them like a sheep dog. Europe, in their eyes, is a great spectacle, like a show-piece at Covent Gardens; and it is theirs to criticize the performance and laugh at the performers at will.

"When foreigners first inquired of me what this strange invasion might mean I bethought myself to take aside the most gossip-loving of my acquaintances and told him that our Australian colonies had made such a rumpus of late about being made convict settlements that we had adopted the cheap expedient of sending our rogues abroad to the Continent, apparently as tourists. The knaves, after a few weeks, take themselves off in various directions as tastes or inclinations suggest. Then that fussy little bald man that took such trouble about them will return to England for more."[1]

It is doubtful Cook, being a serious, self-determined man, took much note of such ridicule. He went about his business, improvising, promoting, being his ingenious self. On an Italian tour featuring Holy Week in Rome, the hotel reneged on reservations for his party of 50. Cook promptly hired a Prince's palace for the period of ten days at $2500 and arranged meals at neighboring restaurants. The trip produced a deficit which led the tour members to volunteer a contribution of $1000, probably the first and last such contribution. Ever the improvisor, when on a trip to New York City, he hired a wagon to haul his and his friends' luggage to the hotel at a fraction of the cost

This picture of Thomas Cook (1808-1893), pioneer in developing the business of pleasure travel, is seen on all of Cook's Traveler's Cheques.

charged by the horse cabbies.

The Cooks pioneered the "travel conglomerate" (one company engaging in a number of the aspects of the travel business) long before the term was used. Before 1875, the firm had acquired and operated the railway up Mount Vesuvius in southern Italy. Later, the company acquired the exclusive right to carry the mails, as well as special travelers and government officials, between Assiont and Assonan on the Nile. The company also operated ships and a ship repair service in Egypt.

On John Cook's death at 83, in 1898, management of the firm passed to his three sons. The business by that time had grown to include three divisions: tourist, banking and shipping.

The around-the-world-tour was introduced by a Cook-chartered Cunard liner in 1923. In 1927, the company arranged for a special plane flight from New York to Chicago for fans attending the Dempsey-Tunney world championship prize fight. Box lunches were supplied by Louis Sherry, the fashionable New York caterer. In 1931, Thos. Cook merged with the Wagon-Lits Com-

[1] K. C. Tessendorf, "Prophet of Mass Marketing," *The Travel Agent*, Oct. 16, 1972.

pany, operators of the sleeping car and express trains in Europe and also a large travel agency company.

The Cooks continued to do everything possible to make the trip easy for the traveler. Cook's agents often met planes with a car. They waited at the custom's entrance to whisk the traveler directly to a reception or anywhere else he wanted to go. The all-inclusive price for a tour made it much easier for people to plan vacations and to budget their time and money.

Following World War II, the British government acquired the principal interest in Thos. Cook and Son, and policy was determined by the British Government through the Transport Holding Company. Wagon-Lits is an affiliate. The Company today has over 625 offices and 10,000 employees around the world. The Company operates as five more or less independent divisions. Sales in 1969 were $360 million.

The Company, considered to be the largest of its kind, today has manifold interests other than in the sale of travel as such. It owns Prestatyn Holiday Camp in North Wales which caters to 30,000 holidaymakers each year.[1] In the period 1970-1972 Cook sustained losses on his travel arrangements, but made substantial profits on traveler's checks and the foreign currency business. In 1972, the British government sold Thos. Cook and Son to a Midland bank consortium for $858.5 million. Trust Houses Forte and the Automobile Association (of Britain) were part of the consortium.[2]

The American Express Company

The American Express Company (Amexco) is another well-known worldwide travel agency. It grew out of the old Wells-Fargo Company of Pony Express and Wild West fame. By 1945, the Company had revenue of $75 million annually, primarily from arranging tours and selling traveler's checks.[3] By 1968, Amexco had diversified to become a travel and financial conglomerate. Almost half of its earnings came from casualty, life and property insurance. The Company is a major factor in international currency transactions, buying and selling on each working day $100 million in foreign currency, for corporations and individual customers. A-

merican Express may best be described as a travel-oriented bank.

The sale of traveler's checks in itself is not very profitable. What is profitable is the use of the $750 million which travelers, in effect, loan to Amexco until the checks they buy are cashed.

The company is integrating travel services in that it not only arranges tours but also sells traveler's checks; publishes Travel & Camera Magazine; sells the American Express credit card; teaches foreign languages; has bought an interest in the Club Mediterranee, a chain of sea and ski resorts for the budget-minded.

American Express credit card holders charged $1.7 billion for purchases in 1969, enough to warrant employment of a 300-man international security staff to fight theft of cards and checks.[4]

Computerized Reservations

The Company is also in the business of selling mutual funds outside of the U. S. and, in 1969, started a computerized reservation service. The service may be one of the Amexco's most important ventures. The service, called Express Reservations, comprises a computer network that can be used by any traveler to secure hotel reservations in major cities throughout the world. The computer subsidiary is headed by the same person who put together the vast computer system for Holiday Inns. Not coincidentally, the computer itself and its "spacebank" of over a quarter of a million rooms is housed in Memphis, the headquarters city of Holiday Inns. Computer terminals are located in Express Reservations sales centers throughout the world. Confirmations of reservations can be secured in only 15 seconds.

The traveler wishing a reservation calls the Express Reservations Office in his area at no charge. Managers of hotels who wish to be part of the system pay 5 percent of

[1]"The Story of Travel, 1841-1966." *The New York Times,* Feb. 6, 1966; *Dictionary of National Biography,* Vol. XXII, Supp. Oxford University, 1921-22; "Cook's—Still Evolving After a Hundred Years in Travel," *World,* Dec., 1969, pp. 18-19.
[2]*The Travel Agent,* June 4, 1972.
[3]"A License to Print Money," *Time,* 1969, p. 94.
[4]"Tourists Gone Giddy, Lose Senses, Dollars," *Springfield Union,* July 4, 1970.

the total reserved unit cost of a minimum of $1, plus a minimal monthly listing fee.

Promotion of the system should be relatively easy. There are three million American Express Credit Card holders who are a likely market for the system; any charge made can be placed on their Express card account. National advertising is also carried in such magazines as *Time, Life* and *Newsweek*. Full-page ads are carried in the major airline magazines.

Apparently the reservations business is not profitable for in 1974 American Express announced that the 5 percent commission being charged lodging firms using the Space Bank was not enough to keep the operation in the black.

Amexco spokesmen said that in the future they would book reservations through airline reservations systems.

As mentioned, American Express owns an interest in Club Mediterranee. Other Mediterranee stockholders include its managers and Edmond de Rothschild of France. In 1970, the Club Mediterranee merged with the Club European to form an organization which owns 58 resorts with more than 40,000 beds. Membership in the two clubs is estimated at nearly one million and, in 1969, more than 250,000 persons vacationed at the villages which are sponsored by the two clubs.[1] (Club Mediterranee was described in greater detail on p. 43.)

Surge in Travel and Growth of Travel Agencies

Other travel organizations appeared in Britain and the United States before 1900. Brownell's, operating out of Birmingham, Ala., became a tour operator, selling tours to other agents, in the 1890's. (Today, it is a retail travel agency only.)

In the 1920's, the American Express Co. along with Thos. Cook and Wagon-Lits, the Belgian-based company, were the big names in the travel sales business. In 1928, Exprinter Travel Service, now in Los Angeles and New York City, became the first non-competitive travel wholesaler, selling tours only to travel agents.

With the arrival of scheduled airlines, the travel agency business began to change. In the 1930's, the Pan American World Air-

ways, so small that they could not afford a ticket office, ended up by borrowing three feet of counter space from Thos. Cook and Son in New York City. Commissions of ten percent on all ticket sales were paid by Pan Am to American Express and Cook; other travel agents received five percent.

Following World War II, the travel urge broke loose and numbers of people set themselves up in business as travel agents. The idea of opening a travel agency has natural appeal to many people. They are likely to think (wrongly) that the business requires only limited capital, a minimum of travel information, and will satisfy their desire to "meet people" and see the world themselves. A number of agents set themselves up as part-time business people, operating out of their homes or working as teachers, clerks or what have you. (A home is, strictly speaking, not a sufficient office for appointment as an airline agent.)

Today, there is a vast network of 17,000 travel agencies around the world which are approved by the International Air Transport Association. About 100,000 people work in these agencies. Within the United States and Canada, some 7500 retailers of travel are in operation, including clubs, banks, department stores, airlines and hotels. Over 800 travel agencies and tour wholesalers in the U. S. and Canada grossed sales of $1 million or more in 1971. American Express, the American Automobile Association and Ask Mr. Foster ranked as the largest of the travel agencies in the U. S.

The Agent as a Professional

The travel agent is a businessman selling travel services. He is an agent in that he acts for carriers, hotels and other people selling travel services, but he is much more than that. A more descriptive term would be travel advisor or consultant. Perhaps "broker" is a more apt term. He is an entrepreneur in that he usually is in business for himself; he is a professional in that he draws upon a body of knowledge and skills to help the traveler get the pleasures, the conveniences and experiences that he wants, or thinks he wants.

---

[1]*Travel Weekly,* March 27, 1970.

A good agent is something of a personal counselor, a psychologist and an expert in the art and science of travel. He not only knows the advantages and disadvantages of the various modes of travel, their costs as well as travel schedules; he is, in many cases, the counselor to adjust travel services to fit the client.

The travel agent must base his recommendations on the answers to such questions as: How old and energetic is the client? Should the client travel by tour group or independently? Shouldn't the travel schedule be arranged so that the client arrives at a destination in the early evening, rather than at night? What about the effect of crossing time zones, effects of altitude in South American cities, the dangers of food poisoning in the tropics—the list of considerations stretches on and on.

The major part of the business for most travel agents in this country is arranging air travel both for the business man and the vacationer, although this is not all the travel agent does. The business traveler turns to the travel agent to handle the details of making reservations and writing up tickets. And why not? Such arrangements are time-consuming and may involve long distance calls. The travel agent usually makes such arrangements at no charge to the traveler but receives a 7 percent commission from the airline.

Trip Arrangements Vary

How trips are arranged to particular vacation destinations varies widely. For isolated resort hotels, sometimes 90 percent or more of the business booked is through a travel agent; for resorts that can be reached by auto and are close to metropolitan centers, as much as 90 percent of the business is booked directly between guest and hotel. Arrangements for Hawaii, in 1968, were made largely by wholesale travel agents and retail travel agents, with each segment doing about half of the total business. About 35,000 people arranged their own accommodations directly, and 5000 had their arrangements made through an airline.

Tour business is growing rapidly and constitutes a major portion of many travel agents' time and income. People who travel on tours are likely to be less sophisticated, less aggressive, and less secure than the independent traveler. Oftentimes, the traveler to a completely strange part of the world will elect a tour to familiarize himself with the area, afterwards going there on his own.

According to the director of a large market research company, travelers can be classified as "cosmopolitans" versus "locals." The cosmopolites are more widely traveled, better educated, and enjoy testing themselves in strange environments. Even their feelings about guilt are different. They have a greater capacity to let themselves go without feeling guilty. They work hard and play hard. "Since they are more sure of themselves they have less anxiety about being away from home. Let Aunt Susie take care of the kids."[1] They use travel agents but are not dependent upon them.

The "locals" have less confidence in themselves, particularly in unfamiliar situations. The tour is a readymade mobile environment, predictable and safe. According to this authority, there are many more "locals" in America than "cosmopolitans," which means a growing market for travel agents and, in particular, for tour groups.

Like any professional, the agent follows a code of ethics which at times may not favor him economically. Usually he belongs to one or more trade associations and carries bonds to protect the traveler and the carriers he acts for.

The travel agent must be able to react easily and quickly to people who are searching for answers and who many times are under a great deal of stress. Bad weather cancels hundreds of flights causing a log jam of travelers waiting at home for a flight to clear. The agents' office phone never stops ringing, hour after hour. It is only human nature to somehow shift some of the blame for the delays on to the innocent agent. Would it be a bad pun to say that the travel counselor becomes a "cooling agent"?

The range and diversity of fares seem to increase each year. In 1970, United States travelers were offered a choice of almost 50 different Atlantic fares, more than

[1] Russ Johnston, "Motivation in a Changing Environment," *Operations Bulletin,* American Hotel and Motel Assn., Sept., 1970.

enough to confuse them, and possibly the agent as well. One Los Angeles to Europe round trip fare, for affinity groups of 80 or more traveling together, was $300. But independents who joined a group of 40 could have a flight for $305, provided they paid $100 or more for two weeks of sight-seeing and London hotel rooms. Available tours are almost endless, including a "singles tour for 40 on a sail," one to Austria for concert enthusiasts, another to go fishing in Alaska.

A two-year study of travel agent operation throughout this country, done by Touche, Ross, Bailey and Smart, accountants, showed that point-to-point air tickets accounted for 63 percent of the travel agent's transactions. According to the study, the agent lost $2.64 on each transaction because of the cost of processing the ticket and doing business in general. The agent made less than half of one percent on the 30-day Discover America excursion tickets, about 1.3 percent on family-plan coupons, and about 1.25 percent on tours. Of course, the cost of doing business varies considerably from the small town agent doing business in his own home to the luxury office within a city. The big profit for travel agents came from the sale of international transportation, the sale of FIT's (foreign independent tours) and group tours.

Figuring Air Fares Takes Expertise

The computation of airline fares is no job for amateurs. Some of the joint fares, the variations between 21-day excursions and other types of group fares, are so complicated that even veteran travel agents often refer particular fare computations to an airline. Many an irate traveler has found that his friendly travel agent, or even the airline clerk, has figured his fare so that it cost him more than necessary. Unless the agent is really on top of the fare changes, which occur frequently, the best fare may not be the one which is produced.

A sample audit by the Civil Aeronautics Board in 1973 of airline tickets sold by travel agents for multi-carrier trips showed that only 69 percent were correct. Those issued by air carriers showed only slightly fewer errors: 75 percent were correctly priced.[1]

Changes in airline schedules and the addition of new flights make the agent's job one of constant challenge; he must be alert to keep abreast of every new change, even though he has the schedule published by the airlines to follow.

Quite naturally many—perhaps most—travel agents are themselves wide travelers, taking every opportunity to visit new and different places. If he is careful in his selection of a travel plan, the agent travels at a reduced rate and is often given complimentary rooms by hotels.

Special "familiarization tours" are often arranged for agents at little or no cost to the agent. Some 500 travel agents were guests of the Bahamian Tourist Board in 1969. Some 2000 agents were brought by United Airlines to Hawaii in 1969; another 800 in 1970. Various other tourist agencies are pleased to arrange trips to the areas they represent, most of the trips at reduced or minimal cost to the travel agent. The airlines are pleased to cooperate on reduced fares when there is government approval. The more he travels, the better informed he is and, presumably, the better travel agent he becomes.

A sense of geography is part of his equipment. Every year, names which were unknown to the general public suddenly become the places to go. The Seychelles (islands in the Indian Ocean), the Algarve (Southern Portugal), Costa del Sol (Spain), St. Martin (Caribbean) are names to conjure with, and part of the agent's bag of knowledge.

The travel agent's range of expertise is large and is constantly growing. A job description would include the following tasks:[2]

Prepares individual pre-planned itineraries, personally-escorted tours and group tours and sells prepared package tours.

Arranges for hotels, motels, resort accommodations, meals, car rentals, sight-seeing, transfers of passengers and luggage between terminals and hotels, and special features such as music festivals and theatre tickets.

Handles and advises on the many details involved in modern day travel, e. g.—travel and baggage in-

[1]*Travel Trade,* March 5, 1973.
[2]*Honolulu Magazine,* Feb., 1967.

surance, language study material, traveler's checks, auto garaging, foreign currency exchange, documentary requirements (visas and passports), and health requirements (immunization and other inoculations).

Uses professional know-how and experience, e. g.— usually has schedules of train connections, rates of hotels, their quality, whether rooms have baths, whether their rates include local taxes and gratuities. All of this is information which the traveler can spend days or weeks of endless phone calls, letters and visits to secure, and still may not get it right.

Arranges reservations for special-interest activities such as religious pilgrimages, conventions and business travel, gourmet tours and sporting trips.

The lexicon of the travel agent is especially concerned with tours:

PACKAGE TOURS. A package tour is designed to fit the requirements of a particular group of travelers. Some tours cater to special interest groups such as gourmets, accountants, students or art lovers.

Package tours may be either escorted or unescorted. They are advertised in brochures, which contain the cost, terms and conditions of the offered package.

ESCORTED TOURS. An experienced tour director travels with the group. He handles all basic details—hotel reservations, transportation, sight-seeing, baggage, customs, language interpretation when necessary, etc. He is responsible for maintaining the overall schedule of the tour. By and large, escorted tours are "all inclusive."

UNESCORTED PACKAGE TOURS (FIT or DIT) are more flexible. They enable the traveler to purchase an arranged package with transportation, transfers, sight-seeing, hotel accommodations, and usually some meals, according to the custom of the country, but he does not travel with a group led by a tour director. Sight-seeing excursions may or may not be arranged. The predetermined cost allows the traveler to budget most of his expenses in advance.

The basic advantage of a package tour is convenience. Also, since the package is arranged by a specialist who buys in large volume, his suppliers—the hotels, sight-seeing companies and others—are anxious to please him by providing high-quality service for those who have bought the package.

GROUP TOURS (GIT). A group tour is 15 or more people traveling together who are members of a club, business organization, or other affiliated group who have pooled their purchasing power to realize savings, particularly on transportation.

Group tours are offered to almost any destination—a month's trip to the Antarctic, a Land Rover run across the Sahara, a tour of public gardens in Europe, a group of gourmets eating their way through the world's fine restaurants.

Inclusive Tour Charter Operations

The Inclusive Tour Charter, ITC, is a large part of some agents' business. By chartering an entire aircraft from one of the supplemental carriers, the cost per traveler is drastically reduced for the longer trip. (It represents little savings for shorter trips, in many cases.) ITC began their existence in the United States in late 1966. Requirements for such a trip, as of 1970, included the following:

Tour must last longer than seven days.

Tour operator must post a $10,000 bond for tour.

The tour must provide overnight accommodations at a minimum of three places, each at least 50 miles from the others.

Tour price must include, as a minimum, all hotel accommodations and necessary air and surface transportation between all places on the itinerary.

Total tour charge must be at least 110 percent of the lowest scheduled air fare for the same trip.

Cost for chartering a large plane seems surprisingly high to the uninitiated: cost may range as high as $49,000 for a plane seating 195 passengers for a round trip between New York and Hawaii, over $100,000 New York City to Australia and back.

The big advantage for the traveler is that the air fare costs may be up to 50 percent less than the equivalent scheduled fare. ITC success is attested to by the fact that load factors for the supplemental airlines have averaged more than 80 percent, as compared with 50 to 60 percent for scheduled air carriers. (Supplemental air carriers get more use of their planes averaging 14 hours per day in-flight aircraft utilization, as compared with 10 hours for the scheduled airlines.)

Charter Flights

The charter flight, flight by so-called affinity groups, has shaken up the overseas travel picture considerably. In 1969, about 100,000 United States tourists traveled to all parts of the globe by charter flight.[1] By signing up for the special charter flights, savings from 30 to 45 percent on transportation costs were achieved.

A typical round-trip charter fare between Los Angeles and Frankfurt, Germany, 1970, cost between $270 and $280. The comparable individual, economy class, excursion rate ticket on a Pan American plane cost $467 to $512, depending upon the season.

In 1969, about 70 percent of all transatlantic passengers who flew from the West Coast used chartered flights.

In the early 1960's, the Civil Aeronautics Board authorized approximately a dozen then small airlines to offer their planes for commercial charter, classified as "supplemental," meaning that they did not fly regular schedules. The Civil Aeronautics Board permitted these airlines to lease whole planes for trips by established social, fraternal or charitable organizations.

Charters Fastest-Growing Segment

Because of the possibility of sizable reductions in fares, charter flights became the fastest growing segment of the travel business. Scheduled carriers cried foul; the supplemental airlines were delighted; so too were the passengers, if everything worked out for them on the flight.

Everything does not always work out for the passenger, especially if he is not, in the eyes of the Civil Aeronautics Board, a bona fide member of the organization which has chartered the flight. In 1969, about 100 charter flights were cancelled by the Civil Aeronautics Board and on many flights a number of passengers were scratched from the passenger lists as having no connection with the sponsoring organization.

The rules covering charter flights, in effect, include these points:

1. The passenger must be a registered member of his sponsoring group for at least six months before the flight departs.

2. The sponsoring group may not solicit outsiders to join simply to take part in the charter flights.

3. The group or club must exist for some other purpose than for travel alone.

4. Only the member of the group who ordered it may use the ticket which has been purchased. Exceptions are sometimes made for resale to another member of the group.

5. The purpose of the flight cannot be for profit; total costs are divided among the travelers. A small administrative fee is allowable.

Why then are travel agents interested in charter flights? (1) A five percent commission to the travel agent who arranges the flight with an airline is permissible; and (2) huge profits have been made by persons operating outside of the rules.

Travel clubs have been put together and members charged a fee of some $14 to $20 to join the club. The applications have been back-dated to take care of the Civil Aeronautics Board rule that members must have belonged for at least six months before taking the trip. According to *U. S. News and World Report,* some entrepreneurs have divided the cost of leasing a plane among the passengers, then added on an extra $20 per ticket for themselves.[2] With the 5 percent commission and the extra charge, plus the membership fee, the arranger can gross at least $6000 and as much as $15,000 on a 250-passenger DC-8 jetliner flight.

Not all charter flights are profitable and many do not materialize. In 1969, 47 percent of the ITC (Inclusive Tour Charters) did not materialize. Eighteen operators, who filed for 413 tours, cancelled every one of them.[3]

Travel Agency Commissions

The amount of money paid to the travel agent by the transportation company, and sometimes by the traveler himself, has

[1]"If You Are Planning a Charter Flight," *U. S. News and World Report,* Mar. 9, 1970.
[2]*Ibid.*
[3]Erwin Robinson, "The Distributive Environment in Travel," *Proceedings First Annual Conference,* Travel Research Assn., Salt Lake City, 1970, p. 159.

varied through time, and will probably continue to do so.

Commissions paid to travel agents of 20 percent and higher are sometimes paid by Caribbean hotel operators. Some hotels pay commission on the total rate, whether it be European plan, modified American plan, or American plan. Others do not.

For point to point travel within the United States, the travel agent receives a commission of 7 percent. The schedule reproduced on page 92 was current as of 1970 and gives an idea as to the range of commissions received by the agent who is recognized by the hotel or the transportation company.

Travel agents may also sell money orders, which are commissionable by the firms offering them, American Express, Thos. Cook, First National City Bank and Bank of America. The commission averages about $.50 for each $100 sold. Travel insurance may also be sold. Commission rates are 25 to 40 percent.

Setting Up an Agency

Like any other business, the travel agency business has a body of information and a number of skills connected with it that should be learned by the agency operator. Most of the training is done on the job, during time spent in an established agency, for a year or as long as it takes to master the requisite information and skills. As is true of the restaurant business, many people feel that they can enter the travel agency business without prior experience. It is easy to imagine the chaos that could result if the public carriers recognized anyone who applied as an agent.

Appointment to the various transportation conferences is necessary, if the travel agent is to be recognized and successful. Each conference (association of carriers) establishes its own requirements for appointment. The agent must make application to each conference separately. The principal U. S. conferences are listed at right above.

To insure continuity and competency, the carriers have established well defined rules and standards for the agents who have been accepted and publicly represent them. One such set of rules are those laid down by

PASSENGER CONFERENCES

Air Traffic Conferences

International Air Transport Association (IATA)
Traffic Service Office
Montreal 113, Canada
(514) 866-1011

500 Fifth Avenue
New York, New York 10036
(212) OXford 5-0862
John H. Krasman, Mgr.

Air Traffic Conference (ATC)
(Domestic USA)
1000 Connecticut Avenue, N. W.
Washington, D. C. 20036
(212) 296-5800
George A. Buchanan, Executive Secretary
Richard R. Saunders, Director, Agencies
Nestor N. Pylypec, Asst. Dir., Agencies

Rail Conferences

Rail Travel Promotion Agency (RTPA)
436 Union Station, Chicago, Ill. 60606
(312) 726-6900
H. B. Siddall, Chairman
N. S. Landgraff, Vice Chairman
Lawrence Rubin, Manager

Ship Conferences

Transatlantic Passenger Steamship Conferences
17 Battery Place
New York, New York 10004
(212) 425-7400
Wm. J. Armstrong, Secretary
R. J. Wortnik, Asst. Sec.

Trans-Pacific Passenger Conference
2 Pine Street
San Francisco, California 94111
(415) 981-5370
Ronald C. Lord, Gen. Mgr.

the Trans-Pacific Passenger Conference, an organization representing the passenger ships serving the Pacific area.[1] Among the standards that must be met by the applicant wishing to be recognized by the Conference are those listed on the facing page.

[1] "Rules of the Trans-Pacific Conference Affecting Travel Agencies," Trans-Pacific Conference, San Francisco, 1969.

The applicant's place of business must be at an address in an area capable of producing steamship travel business.

The activities of the staff of the applicant's agency must be confined primarily to the sale of travel. At least one member of the staff must have had at least one year of experience in the sale of travel, including steamship travel.

Each location maintained by the travel agent must be bonded. A fee of $25 is paid to the conference each year for each location.

The agency must maintain ethical standards of business in the conduct of the agency in all promotional and advertising activities, and all dealings with passengers or purchases of passage and with the Conference and its lines.

Carriers Require Bonding

It is readily apparent why a travel agent must be thoroughly scrutinized and bonded before being accepted by the carrier. As an agent, he is a holder of thousands of dollars worth of tickets and monies which are the property of the carrier.

The carriers insist that agents representing them keep up-to-date accounts and records of all transactions. In the case of the Trans-Pacific Passenger Conference, the agent must permit an inspection of his accounts and records at any time by the Conference Secretary or his representative, or by a representative of any of the lines represented by the Conference.

A major area of controversy between agent and carrier is the amount of commission due the agent for his services. The Trans-Pacific Passenger Conference specified that the commission be 7½ percent between all ports within the jurisdiction of the Conference and allows 10 percent on all round trips, circle tours, special cruises and inclusive tours initiated by the member lines. An additional override incentive commission of 2½ percent is given agents who sell inclusive tours which are published under a special folder.

The rules specifically prohibit the agent from dividing part of his commission with the purchaser of the ticket or with anyone else. No commission is allowed on reduced rate passages, or on bookings made by a line on the strength of leads, letters or cards of introduction furnished by the agent. In other words, the agent must actually make the sale of the service or passage. The Conference also specifies a number of reasons for which the agreement with the agency may be cancelled.

The American Society of Travel Agents

The largest association of travel agents is the American Society of Travel Agents (ASTA), headquartered in New York City. ASTA has 24 chapters, each with its own elected officers and appointed committees. Membership totals more than 12,000 of which some 3600 are travel agents. Allied members include airline and steamship companies, railroads, buslines, car rental firms, hotels, and government tourist offices.

Founded in 1936 as the American Steamship Travel Association, it has sponsored such activities as conferences on various travel matters, conducts research into travel preferences and works with various governmental agencies concerned with travel. Persons wishing full membership in the society must have completed three years of experience in the travel field. The Society also conducts a number of training courses and seminars.

An organization which has splintered off of ASTA is the Association of Retail Travel Agents (ARTA). A number of agents, feeling that ASTA and other associations representing the retail travel agent are not aggressive enough in behalf of the agent, formed ARTA. In 1970, ARTA had about 500 members.

The ARTA group questions the legality of the immunity of the International Air Transport Association from the United States anti-trust laws, feeling that the IATA is in the nature of a monopoly in its control of overseas flight fares. It also feels that a common automated reservation system is in the nature of a monopoly. ARTA is against banks acting as travel agents. The organization conducts "town meetings" and periodic "sales seminars."[1]

[1]The Association of Retail Travel Agents, Croton-on-Hudson, New York, New York.

TABLE VII—TRANSPORTATION COMMISSION SCHEDULE FOR TRAVEL AGENTS

Domestic air	Family plan and 30-day Discover America excursion	8%
Domestic air	Advertised, independent tour	11%
International air	Point to point and excursion	7%
International air	Groups (depending on type and whether tour is sold in conjunction with plane ticket)	7 to 10%
International air	Inclusive tour package for individual traveler	10%
Air charter		5%
In-plant		3%
Hotels and Resorts		5 to 15% (few pay no commissions)
Tours (ground arrangements for independent itineraries)	Agent adds mark-up to cover cost of preparing itinerary and to give a profit. Amount is usually not disclosed.	Recent, varies up to 30%
Tours (ground arrangements for published trips)	Commission depends on the destination and the wholesaler's policy	10 to 18%
Cruises	Higher rates are customary for special sailings	10%
Atlantic scheduled voyages	Point to point	7 to 7½%
Atlantic scheduled voyages	When approved tour is involved	10%
Car rental	Varies with operator and whether client is a business or pleasure traveler	10 to 18%
Rail ticket		5% (tours bring more)
Rail tour, including ticket and tour		10%
Bus lines, including ticket and tour		10%
(Foreign)		5 to 10%
Insurance		25 to 40%
Money Orders		varies

Another agency-related organization is the Creative Tour Operators Association (CTOA), an organization of "manufacturers" whose members package and market tours. In 1970, the organization had 23 members.

Travel agents, like many other semi-professional groups, are seeking to upgrade and to professionalize their jobs. A basic course in the mechanics of being a travel agent is available by correspondence from the American Society of Travel Agents. In 1964, an Institute of Certified Travel Agents was established to provide an educational program in the field of tourism. The Institute offers a certification program, leading to a CTC, Certified Traveler Counselor. To receive the designation, the candidate must successfully pass examinations covering travel agency business management, passenger traffic management, marketing and sales management and international travel and tourism. An individual research paper is also required. The candidate must be at least 25 years of age and have had five years of practical experience in a travel agency.[1]

European Travel Agencies

In the United Kingdom, travel agents do most of the airlines sales and inclusive tour sales. They even sell 14 percent of the seats on the British Railroad. (U. S. travel agents sell very little railroad business.) Business there is concentrated in the hands of a few agents; 50 percent of the bookings come from fewer than 100 agents. The Association of British Travel Agents (ABTA) represents 2670 offices. Average sales per employee are about $37,000 a year. In order to be really profitable, according to Michael Peters, agency employees should take in close to $72,000 a year.[2]

In Germany, large numbers of tours are sold by mail order. Quelle and Neckermann, two large mail-order concerns, went into the travel business in the 1960's. These companies also operate department stores. Catalogues are sent out to mail-order customers who can ask for advice and make their bookings at any of the company department stores. Most important towns in Germany have one of the stores.

These firms concentrate on a relatively limited number of well-tried holiday resorts, and by so doing have cut prices by nearly a quarter. Some of the tours are sold as "loss leaders," with compensatory profits being made on the sales of other goods to tourist clients. A large number of Neckermann tours go to Roumania; Quelle send many of theirs to Portugal. The government of the Cameroons, and other governments, have cooperated with the firms by reducing air travel and destination-facility prices.

Germany has about 1200 professional travel agencies. A number of European countries require travel agencies to be licensed; among these countries are Austria, Belgium, Bulgaria, France and Italy.

Around 80 percent of all overseas tour expenditures are in connection with tours that have been put together by fewer than 100 companies in North America. These tour "manufacturers" are tour wholesalers. Package tours of various prices, lengths and purposes are assembled by direct negotiation with airlines, shipping lines, hotels, restaurants and other travel-affiliated services. (Most tour wholesalers also operate tours themselves.)

These tours are then sold to the travel agents who, in turn, sell them to the traveler. In recent years, some of the tour wholesalers have also purchased ownership or interest in resort hotels. Similarly, some of the hotel chains have purchased tour wholesalers or set up their own tour sales companies. The advantages to the hotel owners are plain: all the tour groups can be routed through the owner's hotels.

Tour Operators

Services offered by a tour operator vary widely and are limited only by the imagination. Services may include meeting the client with fanfare and ceremony upon his arrival at a destination. In Hawaii, the tour operator is on hand to place the traditional lei around the neck of the visitor as he arrives in the airport building. The lei with the traditional kiss serves to unnerve some

---

[1] American Society of Travel Agents, 360 Lexington Avenue, New York, 10017.
[2] Michael Peters, *International Tourism*. (London: Hutchinson, 1969), p. 229.

visitors but the custom is pleasantly startling to most. Travelers who may have been on the plane many hours need the reassurance, and sometimes the physical support, of the escort to the waiting tour vehicle. Older clients are glad the operator makes all the arrangements for transporting the luggage from the airport to the hotel.

The tour operator may accept the complete responsibility for the tour, from beginning to end. The tour cost may cover everything which the traveler would ordinarily have to pay: porterage, baggage gratuities, accommodations, air fares, meals, sight-seeing and entertainment. Prices for a tour package range from $100 to $10,000, and tours may last from a few days to a three-month cruise. A package tour can be put together for almost any trip imaginable.

Tour operation involves a multitude of details and demands a variety of skills, including sales ability. The tour operator must be administratively capable, able to speak and write well. He must have the talent for visualizing the step-by-step details of a complicated tour arrangement. He is constantly planning for the future and anticipating changes in markets and tour details. At times he works under tremendous pressure. Some tour operators own their own transport; others lease or contract for transport services.

Some tour operators concentrate largely or completely on certain travel destinations. MacKenzie, All Travel, Robinson's, Hawaiian Holidays, Island Holidays and Tradewind offer tours only to Hawaii. Two wholesalers, AITS and Berry, are each responsible for bringing about 50,000 people annually to Hawaii. Three of the major wholesalers own hotels in Hawaii. Some 376,000 people buy all or a portion of their trip to Hawaii as a wholesale tour. About 30 of the largest wholesalers account for most of the sales.

FITS—Foreign Independent Travelers

Travelers who "buy a tour" do not necessarily travel in a particular tour group. Large numbers of tour purchasers are classified as foreign independent travelers (FIT). They purchase a completely planned itinerary and may have a string of coupons which serve to buy all of the services needed on the trip—but they are not part of a scheduled tour group. Parts of the tour will be taken with other tour groups; they may move from one group to another for portions of the trip. The FIT's benefit by being able to purchase a completely planned trip and, in many instances, get the package of travel accommodations, services, ground transportation and entertainment at a total price which is less than if they had assembled the package for themselves.

There are also DITs, domestic inclusive tours.

Tour Wholesalers

Tour wholesalers sometimes have segments of their business which include retail travel agencies. This practice is not welcomed by the retail travel agent since he rightly feels that the wholesaler is competing with him.

Tour wholesalers can be local, national or international. The local wholesaler packages tours for his area, then sells them to retail travel agents wherever possible. He may have regional offices in other countries. In the United States, a regional office costs about $45,000 a year minimum to operate. If a market area does not justify a complete office, the wholesaler may arrange to be represented in an area.

The best known of the tour wholesalers are Thos. Cook Co. and American Express Co. The airlines also package tours and sell them to the retail travel agent who, in turn, sells them to the travelers as individuals or for group travel.

The hotel chains are likely to spell out what is commissionable and what is not.

Commissions are usually paid on extended stay accommodations, that is, when clients, pre-booked by a travel agency, extend their stay at a hotel. The commission of 10 percent on meals is applicable only if clients are pre-booked on a full or modified American plan basis; that is, for two or more meals. No commissions are applicable on drop-in meals if clients are pre-booked on a European Plan basis.

The major airlines in the United States are owners of hotels and quite naturally are interested in selling hotel space as well as airplane seats. The major airlines also are large bookers of space at the better known hotels even though a particular airline may have no financial interest in the hotel. Pan American Airways, for example, reserves blocks of rooms in major hotels. Travelers can be sold an air ticket and a reservation to a particular hotel at the same time, an advantage to the traveler and a service by the airlines. Only after the block of rooms have been sold out do the airlines need to make individual requests for additional rooms. The traveler, in effect, bypasses the travel agent and purchases both ticket and room at the same time through the airlines.

As indicated elsewhere, the airlines are moving into the hotel business and many provide rooms as well as plane seats. The airline can profit two ways. The airlines have a huge stake in the tourist business at certain destinations. For example, in 1967, airline revenues from Hawaiian tourism reached $380 million. Tourists spent another $400 million after arrival on the islands.

The Small Agency Gives Way to the Large

The travel agency business, looked at as a whole, is still a business of many small operators. A 1970 survey by The Travel Agent Magazine counted 739 retailers and wholesalers among the travel firms that had sales in excess of $1 million. According to the survey, there are about 7500 American and Canadian agencies holding appointment in the principal transportation conferences. American Express is the largest, with sales of over $200 million. The American Automobile Club is second in sales volume. New York, California and Florida lead in the number of travel firms with over $1 million in sales.[1]

It can be expected that a number of agencies will grow and establish branches. This has already been done and as outside investors, such as conglomerates, buy up agencies, multi-officed agencies can be expected to grow in number. Several attempts to franchise agencies have been made; some have failed. Vertical integration with a parent company owning agencies, airplanes, resorts, and other destination facilities can be expected. The Aga Khan on the Island of Sardinia is an example. The corporation of which he is a part owns a series of resorts on the island as well as an airline which transports guests to the resorts from Italy and elsewhere. American International Travel Service, Boston-based, is another example of large-scale integration of travel. The company owns agencies which sell its tours to Hawaii, Europe and elsewhere.

Wages for agency staff are comparatively low. the average wage being under $6000 a year, in 1967. Gross sales, by all travel agencies with a payroll, exceeded $7 billion in 1972.[2]

Travel Agency Profit and Loss

A profit and loss statement for the "average" travel agency is not available nor would it be representative of the profitable agency. Dick Cook, travel agency consultant, speaking before the Eastern Council for Travel Research, presented this profit and loss statement for "the average agency selling $1,000,000 worth of travel." According to Cook, the simulated agency would be close to an average for the largest agents, about a third of the total number, in the U. S.[3] Here is his statement:

Total Sales		$1,000,000
Total Commissions (Earnings)		80,000
Expenses:		
Salary—Owner, Manager	$12,000	
Salary—Employees	32,000	
Advertising and Promotion	5,500	
Occupancy	8,000	
Office Supplies/ Equipment	5,000	
Telephone and Telegraph	4,000	
Postage, Freight, Delivery	2,700	
Legal, Acct. Ins. Misc.	4,800	
	$74,000	
Net Profit	$ 6,000	

---

[1] "Million Dollar Agencies: The Annual Survey," *The Travel Agent,* Mar. 29, 1971, p. 32.
[2] Louis Harris Survey, 1973, *Travel Weekly.*
[3] Dick Cook, "Can Research Help the Travel Agent?" Address, Eastern Council for Travel Research, Warwick Hotel, Dec. 8, 1970.

A rule of thumb for computing the gross profit of a travel agency is to multiply gross sales by 8 percent. If an agency grosses $1,000,000 in sales a year, its gross profit for that year would be $80,000. After all expenses the net profit would vary, depending on how much the owner pays himself as a manager. From a tax viewpoint, the owner should take a large salary, leaving no profit to be taxed at corporate rates. If the business is a corporation, the owner is well advised to think of various ways of reducing profit, diverting income into his own pocket. Some of the ways of doing this include:

1. Driving a company-owned car and charging all or most of the expenses to the company.

2. Having the company cover the cost of a paid-up life insurance policy on the manager.

3. Arranging for the company to provide loans at no interest charge to the manager.

4. Arranging a medical insurance plan paid for by the company.

5. Instituting a profit-sharing plan which permits a sizable percentage of profits to be tax-sheltered until the beneficiary retires and is in a lower income tax bracket.

How Much Is a Travel Agency Worth?

The value of a travel agency hinges on its ability to produce profits, now or later. It may also have value as a tax shelter for a person in a high income tax bracket who can use a tax write-off for several years with the expectation that the agency will increase in value and can be sold at a profit. Such profits of course are taxed as capital gains and not as earnings. Usually the buyer is interested in an agency producing a livelihood for him and his family immediately, or within a short time. He will want a record of sales and commissions for at least three years. From such records he can see if his sales and profits are trending up, down or sideways. He will also analyze the sales mix to learn what percentage of sales is of minimal profit (point to point commercial air sales), what percentages produce higher profits such as that from tours, hotels, and reservations, car rentals, and large-ticket vacation sales.

The location is always important. If the agency depends upon volume commercial sales, a street level location is an asset. Is the neighborhood changing for the better or for the worse? Are the agency's clients moving into the neighborhood or out of it? Is the character of the neighborhood changing so that it is attractive, or at least suitable, for the clientele?

A rule of thumb regarding the value of a travel agency as proposed by Laurence Stevens is that a retail travel agency is worth somewhere between 4 and 10 percent of the average annual gross sales.[1] According to this rule an agency grossing $1,000,000 in sales and with a favorable sales mix to produce maximum profit would be worth about $100,000 to the buyer. Some agencies would be liabilities from the date of purchase. Mr. Stevens recommends a provision in the contract to permit the buyer to participate in the business during a transition period. The buyer would naturally be interested in retaining customers and building new business while he becomes familiar with the agency. He suggests that the seller may wish to receive payment over a number of years to avoid falling into an unnecessarily high tax bracket in a given year.

Like any business, travel agency management must perform cost-accounting and cost-analysis. Profitability of a particular travel agency is much related to the type of business it does, the so-called business mix. As seen earlier, commissions vary from 3 percent for services performed for an industrial organization, up to 20 percent, or more when the agency puts together and sells a chartered flight.

The cost of doing business varies widely also. Cost of booking a short domestic air trip, for example, is much higher percentage wise than booking the usual overseas travel. The operation of a travel agency has a problem similar to any other business selling a service; it must determine which items are most profitable, which are less profitable. Some may result in a loss when all costs are considered. Some travel agency managers or owners concentrate on tour

---

[1] Laurence Stevens, "Agency Management," *The Travel Agent,* May 29, 1973.

sales where the percentage of profit is high. Domestic airline sales are considered a break-even service, and for this reason domestic airline sales are played down. Ernst and Ernst, the international accounting firm, has computed the cost of selling domestic airline tickets as seen below. The annual employee cost of $5000 used in the example is, of course, out of date, but the method of analysis is sound.

COST OF SELLING DOMESTIC AIRLINE TICKETS

Average time to process a ticket	5 hours
Effective time utilization	75%
Handling inquiries, changes, cancellations 20% of effective time	
Effective average time to process a ticket	8
Number of tickets that can be processed per day	10
Annual employee cost	$5000.00
Estimated annual employee overhead (50%)	$2500.00
Total annual employee cost	$7500.00
Employee cost per day (based on 230 working days per year)	$ 33.00
Employee cost per ticket	$ 3.30
Minimum break-even ticket price (on the basis of 7% commission)	$ 47.00

ERNST & ERNST

The travel agency manager is urged to break down his income from sales so that he knows what he is selling, what it costs him to sell each item, and the profit from each segment of sales. The break-down as seen on the following page may not be applicable to a particular agency, but it illustrates a method of analysis which will produce useful information on which management can make decisions.

A word of caution; it is often impossible to sell only those parts of travel which are most profitable. The usual travel agency must provide domestic airline sales even though such sales are less profitable percentage wise than tour or charter sales. Domestic air sales will produce revenue which helps the agency meet the fixed costs of rental, some salaries, telephone, and other costs. Such sales might be considered as necessary to help reach the break-even point in the agency operation.

Beginning in the late 1950's, some of the major hotel systems introduced computerized reservation systems which permitted anyone, a travel agent or a traveler, to request a room and receive a confirmation (if a room is available) within a few minutes. The use of the computer speeded up the reservation process considerably over the use of long distance telephone and, of course, is much faster than correspondence. Notable among the systems were those developed by Sheraton Hotels, Holiday Inns and Hilton Hotels.

The computerized reservation system, independent of any particular hotel system, was started in 1966 by Telemax. Later the American Express Bank System was introduced.

Mass Merchandising of Travel

As previously mentioned, travel is being merchandised by mail order and department stores in Germany. An I.U.O.T.O. technical bulletin points out that tourism is being successfully marketed by correspondence, and on a large scale, in nearly every tourist-generating country, but especially in France, the United Kingdom, the Federal Republic of Germany, Canada and the United States. Several years ago, Montgomery Ward in this country tried and failed at selling travel via mail order. The company will try again by sending a 32-page color brochure, listing twelve inclusive tours of 17 days to Spain and Mediterranean areas. The brochures will go to more than 3.5 million of their customers in the Chicago-Albany-Baltimore triangle, our prime travel market.[1]

More recently, some of the large publishers, such as *Holiday Magazine,* have moved into the travel field. *Playboy Magazine,* a company that also operates a club network here and abroad and is in the hotel business, is also promoting tours. Chicago's radio and TV station, WGN, has moved into the retail agency trade. Newspapers from time to time have offered special-interest tours.

---

[1] "European Operators Invade U. S. Market," *The Travel Agent,* Jan. 25, 1971, pp. 38-39.

TABLE VIII—SALES AND COMMISSION INCOME

	Sales $	Commission Income		Time Cost
		% of Sales	Amount $	at $ Per Hour
Transportation (FIT)				
Sea				
Air-domestic				
Air-foreign				
Rail				
Bus				
Hotels/Meals (FIT)				
Sight-seeing and Sidetrips				
Transfers (FIT)				
Cruises				
Conducted Tours				
College Tours				
Reservation Costs/Income				
Other Sales (Travelers Checks, etc.)				
TOTAL				
Destination				
Domestic				
Hawaii				
Canada				
Mexico				
Caribbean				
Europe				
Africa				
Asia				
Australia/New Zealand				
Pacific				
Round the world				
Near East				
Combination trips				
TOTAL				

Large existing media organizations have built-in advantages for merchandising travel. They have management skills and its large, well organized staff of personnel presumably could move into the travel field with comparative ease. A number of banks have added sales of travel to their services. Banks are in a position to loan money for travel and probably profit more from lending the money than from the actual sales of travel. As of 1973, the American Society of Travel Agents was successful in preventing banks that were not already in travel from entering the travel business.

Whether or not to require that travel agencies be bonded is likely to become academic as pressures from government mount to require that every travel agency be bonded so that the traveler is protected in case of financial default on the part of the agency. The Better Business Bureau of Metropolitan New York reported 445 complaints against travel agents in 1969.

In the summer of 1970, some 3000 students were stranded in Europe when an agency failed. Indications were that the students would lose about 75 percent of their advance payments.

Most of the hotels in Barbados are small, many of them guest houses, and some of them old estate houses. This scene from Bathsheba on the Atlantic side of Barbados shows the breakers pouring in from the ocean. On the other side of the island the vegetation is dense and tropical and the water placid.

ROLE OF THE AGENT IN THE TOURIST BUSINESS

More and more, the travel agent is seen as an important nexus in the travel chain, the link in the series of events that stimulates and makes travel convenient and satisfying. Ideally, the agent is a professional, well-traveled and currently informed on schedules, accommodations, entertainment and costs. The trend is to larger agencies, operating multiple offices in a number of cities. The company itself may be owned by a larger company, often as part of a conglomerate. Vertical integration seems inevitable, with hotel companies owning travel agencies that will feed business to hotels within the system. Government permitting, airlines are also likely to buy or create multi-office travel agencies.

The small independent travel agent, like the small restaurant operator, will probably always have a place, especially in the smaller community. As with any business that is easy to operate, the travel agency business is likely to continue to have numerous members who make only a modest and, in many cases, even a sub-standard income. The small independent will be competing against the larger, multi-officed agency that can develop its own tours and has the capital to invest in the best accounting and other office equipment. Other competitors on the horizon include insurance companies and mail order houses.

The rewards of being a travel agent are several, including inexpensive travel for the agent, contact with interesting people and the constant challenge of keeping up with changes in schedules and fares. The whole world is his field of study—its geography, peoples, political conditions, foods and history.

The Dorado Beach Hotel, a Rockresort in Puerto Rico, caters to both the golf lover and the person who appreciates a tropical beach.

Freeport, Grand Bahama Island, where much of the tourist business in the Bahamas is centered. As recently as 1960, Grand Bahama was almost completely undeveloped. Special tax concessions, gambling privileges and the right to import expatriate workers all help to account for the rapid development.

WHY TOURISTS TRAVEL

The emphasis in this chapter is on trying to identify the reasons why people choose to travel when some necessity does not compel them to do so. In the course of history, motivation for most travel has been fairly obvious: religious conviction, economic gain, war, escape, migration. It would seem that what is left—travel for pleasure—is straightforward and plainly understandable. This, however, is not the case.

Research evidence showing the reasons why people travel and vacation would be helpful. Unfortunately, little such research has been reported, and what has been done has not been related to a well established theory of human motivation, primarily because such a theory is not presently in existence.[1] Because research and established theory are lacking, the comments included here are necessarily impressionistic and made principally to stimulate investigation.

The most widely quoted theory of motivation is that presented by H. A. Maslow in his book, *Motivation and Personality*.[2] Maslow posits a hierarchy of needs as being the determinants of behavior. According to Maslow, these needs are universal, found in every human being. At the base of the hierarchy are the physiological needs, such as hunger, thirst and the need for air. They are overriding needs, blocking out all others if not satisfied.

Next in line, but not quite as potent in their effect on human behavior, are the needs for security and safety. These needs may be satisfied by buying insurance, seeking tenure in a position, owning a home or putting money away for a rainy day.

Above the level of the survival needs are the needs to belong, to be loved and accepted by a social group. Closely related to these needs for affection and acceptance are the needs for self esteem, self respect and the esteem of others.

At the very top of the hierarchy are the self-actualization or self-realization needs, the need to develop one's own potential, the need for aesthetic stimulation, the need to create or to build one's own personality and character.

If we hypothesize the need for change, for divertissement, for new scenery, for new experiences, for a certain amount of change —then travel and vacationing take their place somewhere near the top in the hierarchy of universal needs.

Certainly, there are tremendous variations in what is needed by individuals at the self-actualization level. Millions of people prefer not to travel or vacation because they are more comfortable in their present circumstances, or are afraid to leave them, or to take the chance of being injured while traveling or at a strange destination. Other persons seem to thrive on travel and change. Some need the letdown brought on by a quiet vacation; others seek the same pitch of excitement as exists in their work-a-day world.

The observations that follow make no claim to validity other than a validity based on observation and reflection.

John A. Thomas, writing in *ASTA Travel News*,[3] lists 18 motivations he believes to be most important in causing people to travel:

Education and Cultural Motives

(1) To see how people in other countries live, work and play.

(2) To see particular sights.

(3) To gain a better understanding of

[1]For a comprehensive review and analysis of motivation theory, see N. C. Cofer and M. H. Appley, *Motivation: Theory and Research* (New York: John Wiley & Son, 1964).
[2]A. H. Maslow, *Motivation and Personality* (New York: Harper, 1954).
(The author wishes to express special appreciation to Dr. Charles Metelka, Assistant Professor, School of Travel Industry Management, University of Hawaii, for several suggestions and the use of several of his ideas in this chapter.)
[3]"What Makes People Travel," *ASTA Travel News*, Aug. 1964, pp. 64-65.

what goes on in the news.

(4) To attend special events.

Relaxation and Pleasure

(5) To get away from everyday routine.

(6) To have a good time.

(7) To achieve some sort of sexual or romantic experience.

Ethnic

(8) To visit places your family came from.

(9) To visit places your family, or friends, have gone to.

Other

(10) Weather (for instance to avoid winter).

(11) Health (sun, dry climate, and so on).

(12) Sports (to swim, ski, fish or sail).

(13) Economy (inexpensive living).

(14) Adventure (new areas, people, experiences).

(15) One-upsmanship.

(16) Conformity (keeping up with the Joneses).

(17) To participate in history (ancient temples and ruins, current history).

(18) Sociological motives (get to know the world).

Surveys conducted among tourists have tended to classify reasons for travel in terms of experiences enjoyed or disliked. A consumer marketing study of tourists to the Pacific, *Pacific Visitors Survey*,[1] classified tourist experiences according to various experiences that were satisfying. See table, facing page.

In the same survey, it was reported that the factors which motivate Pacific tourists in the selection of a place to visit are essentially the same as those that motivate visitors to go to Europe. Tourists seek a variety of satisfactions, each in its own way contributing to the richness of the travel experience. The "vacationers" are more concerned with creature comforts such as accommodations and climate, but do show at least some interest in recreational facilities; "vacationers" have less interest in cultural items, such as buildings, temples and churches.

The twelve most important reasons for choosing a place to visit fell into three groupings, the most important group including these factors:

"warm, friendly people"

"comfortable accommodations"

"beautiful, natural scenery"

"reasonable prices"

Next in importance were:

"attractive customs and way of life"

"good climate"

"beautiful creations of man"

"outstanding food"

Least important, although still important enough to be included in the top twelve, were these factors:

"good shopping"

"exotic environment"

"historical or family ties"

"exceptional recreational facilities"

Travel survey results, of course, are partly determined by the manner in which the survey is conducted, the wording of the survey and the population sample used.

Vacation Attitude Survey

A vacation travel attitude survey, based on 1005 structured personal interviews of a nation-wide sample of heads of households, showed that the most important factor in determining where Americans go on their vacation trip is the desire—or obligation—to visit friends and relatives.[2] The most important reason for choosing a vacation destination, as revealed in this study, was what the report labeled "the nostalgia/habit factor." In other words, a vacationer was likely to go where he had been before. When the nostalgia/habit factor was removed from consideration, the leading motives for choosing a vacation destination turned out to be:

Beautiful scenery

A chance to get a good rest

Good sports or recreational facilities

A chance to meet congenial people

Outstanding food.

Some marketing studies attempt to discover the reasons why travelers, and especially vacationers, select a particular destination area. One such study, done for a large land-holding company in Hawaii, conducted extensive research into the ques-

---

[1] Pacific Area Travel Association, *Pacific Visitors Survey*, San Francisco, 1967.

[2] Travel Research International, *Vacation Travel Attitude Survey*, New York City, 1967.

TABLE IX—KINDS OF EXPERIENCES CONSIDERED SATISFYING
BY TOURISTS TRAVELING IN THE PACIFIC AREA

DESTINATION

	Pacific (1084)	Hawaii and Return (384)	Europe (255)
Educational, Interesting New Experience			
New experience, saw new places, new things	15%	9%	18%
Educational, broadening, interesting	13	4	11
Different cultures, way of life	11	2	11
Interesting sights, buildings	5	3	4
Satisfactory Personal Contacts			
Met, made contact with interesting people	22	23	15
Traveled with congenial, friendly people	8	5	4
Visited home, family, friends	7	4	12
Good Tour Management			
Well planned, well organized tour	19	14	16
Excellent tour leader, guide	4	1	
Physical Comfort and Satisfaction			
Good hotels and accommodations	7	8	4
Beautiful scenery, beaches	8	17	7
Good weather	4	25	7
Relaxed atmosphere, casual living	3	16	1
Good food	3	4	5
Miscellaneous Satisfaction			
Enjoyable (no further explanation)	13	24	20
Like to travel	14	7	13

tion. The study was based on depth interviews and a questionnaire answered by consumers and members of the travel industry.[1] The researchers soon found that most people viewed a vacation as a real extension of their personality. Because this was so, they were reluctant, or unable, to verbalize directly their attitudes about vacations. The depth interview approach circumvented this barrier to learning what travelers really feel.

According to the study, there seemed to be four principal determinants of vacation plans:

(1) Financial. Vacation trips are shaped, or curbed, by the amount of money the person has, or wants to spend on a vacation.

(2) Obligation to visit. Selection of a large number of vacation destinations was determined by the fact that the person felt it necessary to visit relatives residing in the area chosen for vacation or during a stopover on the vacation trip.

(3) Advertising. Travel advertising affected the choice of a vacation spot when the cost was not such as to exclude it from consideration.

(4) Family status. The more people in the family, the more it was necessary to consider the cost of travel and the opinions of the children. In many cases, it appeared that, within financial limits, the children chose the trip.

The Kay Study supported the view that vacationers tend to idealize the vacation area. If the area lives up to the expectations of the traveler, he is well satisfied; if not, he is dissatisfied. Should this theory be true, then much travel is motivated by the creation of an image or an ideal in the traveler's mind. The image may take form over a short period of time or over a number of years.

The story is told of a stewardess who remarks to a passenger flying from New York to Miami, "We have just crossed the Georgia line." The passenger peers out the window and enthuses, "Yes, I can recognize the Florida moon."

Even though a destination area may not remotely resemble the expectations of the traveler, the expectations provide the basic stimulus for the trip. The promise of balmy breezes, friendly people, gorgeous scenery is what counts, at least, for the first trip.

Business Versus Pleasure Travel

Tourists, as defined, travel mainly for reasons of business and pleasure. Travel for business reasons implies motivation for economic gain. Something like 16 percent of all the travel done by U. S. citizens is for the purpose of doing business and attending conventions.

Another 39.6 percent is done for pleasure.[2]

Of airline travel, about half or more is done by business travelers. A Pan American study shows the business-pleasure mix to vary widely, according to destination area. Over 90 percent of the travel between the U. S. and the Caribbean is for pleasure.

The figure for Mainland-Hawaii pleasure travel is over 80 percent. For the U. S.-transatlantic flights, it is a little less than 80 percent; about 70 percent for the U. S.-Latin American flights. Pleasure is the dominant reason for slightly over 60 percent of the passengers flying between the U. S. and the trans-pacific area.[3]

About 60 to 70 percent of the guests who check into Sheraton hotels around the world are traveling for business reasons. Much business travel is plain hard work, whether it is travel in one's own automobile, by bus or rail, or in the luxury of a first-class seat aboard an airline. On the other hand, much business travel is mixed with pleasure.

It is difficult to say where business begins or pleasure ends when the business traveler is attending a convention in Las Vegas or Florida where as much as half of his time will be spent gambling or gamboling. The trip to Europe may involve contacting potential customers but it also may involve sight-seeing or an evening at the Folies Bergere. To further confuse the distinction, his wife may be along on the "business trip."

Differentiating business from pleasure travel has presented difficulties for some time. During the 30's, many hotels permit-

[1]John S. Kay, *Land Development Plan and Program for C. Brewer and Co., Ltd., 1969-1982* (Honolulu, 1968).
[2]U. S. Dept. of Commerce, *1967 Census of Transportation.*
[3]John R. Summerfield, Address, Urban Land Institute, Honolulu, April, 1970.

ted the business traveler to share his room with his wife at no additional charge. Family fares on the airlines also allowed the wife and other family members to travel at reduced rates with the head of the family.

The convention business, a business unto itself, is growing in size and importance each year. Is a conventioner traveling on business or pleasure? Probably both. Shouldn't business be pleasurable? According to a 1967 study, "From a psychological standpoint, we can expect a leveling out of business travel and a huge increase in pleasure travel."[1]

Travel for Pleasure

Pleasure is a state of mind. One man's meat is another man's poison. Pleasure depends partly upon existing prior conditions or the anticipation of good things to come. Pleasure is indeed relative. It may come from the relief of pain, respite from boredom, escape from the routine of life. It may be the feelings that come with sensual gratification—a warm bath, basking in the sun, eating, drinking, sex play or the thought of it. Play is generally thought to be exciting and associated with pleasure.

What is pleasurable changes with time and the culture. Most of the present older generation have been programmed into believing that work in itself is one of the highest goods; sensual gratification has not been of over-riding importance. The Puritan Ethic, however, is fading; sensual gratification is back in favor. Life can be fun. Work becomes fused or interwoven with pleasure.

Vacationing for pleasure has changed and will continue to do so. In the 1890's, travel in the summer to a mountain resort was highly pleasurable. The table and the rocking chair on the resort porch constituted an escape from the hot city, offered gratification for the stomach, rest and rustication, and a chance to be with one's peers, or hopefully one's betters. The railroad took you there in some style.

Until the 1940's, travel abroad was necessarily by ship.* Shipboard activities proved exciting enough for some, relentlessly banal to others. During the five- or six-day trip from New York City to England or France, there was a plethora of food and a

round of activities planned by the cruise director. The trans-atlantic traveler could sit in a deck chair, wrapped in a blanket, shivering against the cold Atlantic winds. If he found no pleasure in this, at least he could think about how much better off he was than his friends and neighbors back home. Seasickness is best forgotten.

Today, it may be a jet flight to Las Vegas for gambling, Hawaii for surfing, Florida for the dog track, Greece for the Parthenon, or London for the theatre. There may be movies at 40,000 feet to distract passenger attention from the small seats in the plane.

What is pleasurable in travel and vacation varies within a family and also changes for an individual as time passes. Surf-riding is one of the most exciting sports imaginable, but only for the conditioned athlete and the young. A trip to Paris may mean the Lido and bare-breasted damsels for the husband; for the wife, the highlight may be a tour of Notre Dame Cathedral or dinner at the Tour D'Argent restaurant. For the college student in Bermuda, it is the mating game and the motorbike. Later in life, Bermuda can be a place of relaxation and an opportunity to view nature.

Oh, the Pain of It All

Observers of the human condition are wont to deplore the convenience of modern travel. Ruskin resented being shipped around "like a parcel." The word "travel" is from the same root as travail; some people apparently need more travail than others. Some moderns regret that travel is packaged and safe, leaving little room for challenge in getting around. The challenge of travel is still there, especially for those who need it. Try the food in Mexico or Tahiti for a soul-searching experience with intestinal illness.

A certain amount of discomfort may be enjoyable, if mixed properly with new and interesting experiences. As one elderly tour traveler put it, "I have never been so

---

[1]"The Exploding Travel Market in Affluent America," *Newsweek,* Apr., 1967, p. 32.
*The first transatlantic flight to be regularly scheduled was in 1939; nonstop flights began in 1953.

uncomfortable in my life. It's either too hot, too cold, it rains or it's dusty or muddy or the planes and things we have to see are dirty, miserable and I wonder why we ever take these trips.

"But don't misunderstand me. I wouldn't think of going home."[1]

The proponents of challenge and inconvenience in travel get short shrift from the bulk of travelers. A Harris survey of 1972 of American international travelers showed that the traveler ranked safety, personal security, and convenience at the top of the list of attributes most desired in travel. For ground travel abroad, safe drinking water, clean sanitary facilities and safety from personal harm were prime considerations. Regarding plane travel itself, the traveler wanted ease in making reservations, fast ground service (check-in and baggage collection). As regards the plane itself, they demanded a good maintenance and safety record, able pilots. Adventure be damned if it concerned health, threat to the person, or inconvenience.[2]

Travel for Health

Travel and vacationing appeal to primitive instincts. The search for health and longevity has fostered the spa, bathing in the sea, and more recently, the flight to the sun. Sun worship comes easily to those who live in the temperate zone. The tropic dweller may welcome the cool and changing climate of the temperate zone.

The compulsion to acquire and display a vacation tan may be seated in snobbery but basking in the sun is pleasant to many an animal, including man. If not overdone, the resulting vitamin D and relaxation of muscles is beneficial for most, legal and non-fattening. To the newly-arrived tourist at a sun resort, the sun and sand connote purity. The beach or the pool is almost a place of worship and healing.

Vacationing for many people, and from the viewpoint of industry, can be thought of as an investment in health, a matter that lends itself to cost-benefit analysis. The individual's physician urges not one all-out vacation per year but a series of vacations as a means of recouping one's energies, interest and enthusiasm for the job. Schedule your health, say the health counselors, just as you schedule work activities.

Three one-week vacations are likely to be more healthful than one three-week vacation. Persons highly tuned to an achievement drive often become bored with a vacation after a few days. Spacing vacations, summer, fall and winter, can be more satisfying to the vacationer, and to the tourist operator as well. The peaks and valleys of the business are leveled out.

The Need for Change

The primitive motives that drive the world—fear, greed, lust and love—are basic, but these are overlaid with a need for stimulation which can be brought on by change, novelty, excitement, doing or seeing something different.[3] Travel and vacationing can provide diversity, getting away from present, familiar surroundings to something that is new and, because it is new, pleasantly exciting.

Humans apparently need stimulation and travel can stimulate. Sensory deprivation studies show what happens to the mind when deprived of adequate stimulation. The brain ceases to function in a normal way. Hallucinations and other aberrations become normal. Once the creature comforts have been met, the mind seeks stimulation and titillation.

Aldous Huxley and others have noted an over-riding boredom that overtakes mankind, a sense of universal futility that arouses a complementary desire to get away from where one is at the moment.

Perhaps the bulk of mankind is too busy scratching out a living to develop the kind of ennui Huxley ascribes to mankind, but certainly the feeling that "I must have a change," comes to many who can afford it. Variety may be more than the spice of life; it may be a necessity.

A marketing research director puts it more simply, "The greatest reason for travel can be summed up in one word, 'Escape.'

---

[1]*ASTA Travel News,* June, 1964.
[2]*The Travel Agent,* Sept. 2, 1971.
[3]N. C. Cofer and M. H. Appley, *Motivation: Theory and Research,*" "Hedonic and Activation Theories of Emotion," (New York: John Wiley & Sons, 1967), ch. 8.

Escape from the dull, daily routine. Escape from the familiar, the commonplace, the ordinary. Escape from the job, the boss, the customers, the commuting, the house, the lawn, the leaky faucets."[1]

Everyone, according to him, is searching for change even though some do it actively, others passively. The "actives" are people who like to go, explore and to experience new things. The "passives" are those who like to hide and lie on the beach. Both want change.

Leisure, great massive chunks of leisure, is scheduled to become available for millions in the affluent nations in the upcoming years. The workweek is scheduled to decline and the number of days of vacation is forecasted to rise.

Disposable income, money left after paying taxes, is predicted to rise to $673 billion in the United States in 1970. The term, millionaire, was first used not so long ago, 1843, describing Pierre Lorillard, prince of snuff and tobacco. In 1970, one out of every 2000 persons in the United States is now such a "rara avis."

Leisure time can be used for good or ill. At least people will have more opportunity for the happy life and less necessity to compete for their daily bread. Philosophers, like Bertrand Russell, hold that, given the opportunity of a happy life, people will become more kindly and less suspicious of each other.[2] The taste for war will die out, partly for this reason, partly because war involves unending and hard work for all who engage in it.

Other commentators foresee a vast restiveness resulting from leisure which bodes ill for all. No matter what the viewpoint, it seems clear that there will be more money, more time, and a greater inclination for travel and vacationing.

As Mark Twain pointed out long ago, even heaven is boring after a time. When the anxiety that comes from trying to build security against middle age is overcome, the color TV, the swimming pool and the perfectly controlled temperature of a suburban home get monotonous. The normally gratifying rewards lose much of their potency.

Travel can be a socially acceptable, almost limitless source of reward for those with the time, the money and the energy to undertake it. Travel is innocuous and for many people a relatively inexpensive way to experience both challenge and change. Among large groups, it is almost a necessity if one is to keep up with his neighbors.

The human organism needs change to operate optimally. The level of change that is desirable depends upon a number of things: age, conditioning, energy-level and the expectations of one's associates. It is well established that younger, better-educated, more energetic persons travel more than the elderly and the less educated. What is challenging to one is frustration to another. What was fun at twenty is overpowering at sixty.

Expectations spin the world, especially the travel world. Much of travel advertising is designed to tap the mood for escape and the need for change. One is invited to leave the strictures of suburbia, and "for once in a lifetime, get into this world."

Today's Search for the Exotic

What formerly was a trip to a hot spring or to the mountains has lost its luster for something more exotic. The person is urged to take off for Mexico, Spain, Hawaii or Hong Kong. A foreign country, a new culture, a new cuisine is exciting for those who want safe adventure. Television reaches millions and calls forth a desire to travel.

Any change for many people is a welcome change. The physician who, with his wife, travels 20 miles from his home to stay overnight on the weekend is traveling to get away from the routines and demands of a family and of his profession. The retired carpenter who regularly travels to Reno to gamble is seeking a change from dull routine. The secretary in Chicago who goes to San Juan or Miami Beach for a week in the summer is experiencing a whole new world.

Man is so plastic, so adaptable, so able to be conditioned to his surroundings that it is difficult to say what evokes pleasure in

---

[1] Russ Johnston, "Motivation in a Changing Environment," *Operations Bulletin,* American Hotel and Motel Assn., Sept. 1970.
[2] Bertrand Russell, *In Praise of Idleness and Other Essays,* (London: George Allen and Unurin, 1935).

any particular person. There must be wide individual differences in the amount of change which is experienced as pleasurable. Some people learn to be comfortable only in the office, the coal mine, the classroom, or in the hurly-burly of a downtown section. Even prisoners become conditioned to their cells, or at least some do.

Frequent exposure to any stimuli tends to become pleasurable, or at least comfortable to a person. We like the foods eaten at home while growing up. We like the music of our own particular culture, the architectural style of our own society and time. Even so, most of us wlecome change if not too drastic or demanding, and provided all of the creature comforts are supplied. Travel and vacationing can provide such a change.

Evidence that the North American traveler wants change, but not too much change, is seen in the hotel he selects when abroad. Does he stay at an old established hotel in Madrid, Istanbul or Rome? No, he is likely to have reserved a room at the new Hilton. The rooms at any Hilton are pretty much alike, the food is expected to be safe and they serve hamburgers.

Returning to his room at the end of a day of sight-seeing, the tourist welcomes the Hilton rooms which to him represent safety and the familiar. He will sally forth each morning to see strange people, smell new smells and hear exotic sounds; at night he wants security.

Let the room have a few lamps and pictures reflecting the local color. Okay. But the bed, the bed must be large and American. The lobby decor can contain whatever symbolizes the locale; the dining room, too. But make the menu American. We don't play around with our stomachs.

It has been pointed out that balconies on hotels are popular because the insecure traveler can sit on them, safe and secure, while participating vicariously in a strange environment. Not too unlike the British duke who enjoyed sitting in his club, looking out the window, "to see the damned people getting caught in the rain." A Kenyan hotel carries the balcony idea a step further: the guest rooms are built on tree tops looking over an area where wild animals congregate.

Travel for Learning

The urge to learn is probably innate and can blossom into a persistent search for knowledge, truth and understanding. Travel and vacationing offer an opportunity to satisfy the urge to learn. Twelve million persons visit the Smithsonian Institution in Washington, D. C. each year. Why? To learn. Thousands of people tour the stately homes of England at Chatsworth, Blenheim, Beaulieu, Woburn Abbey, Longleat and dozens of other palaces. Long lines of tourists filing through room after room, viewing furnishings of another epoch and innumerable portraits of aristocratic former owners.

The sense of history is quickened by a tour of Westminster Abbey or the ancient village church. Historic buildings, battlefields and shrines are a means of communicating with the past, of feeling at one with those who came before.

Europe has a particular appeal to the North American; his ancestors probably came from there; his history classes were full of it. In Europe, he can participate in a culture by viewing its cities, visiting its cathredals and castles. More than that, he may have the feeling of becoming part of the culture by attending a London theater or drinking at the local pub. In Spain, he can merge with the bullfight crowd; in France, he can bet on the races; in Munich, join the beer drinkers at Fasching time.

The urge to learn, to explore and to delve into things accounts for much of the tourist's curiosity. Once an interest has rooted itself in a person, he is likely to enjoy pursuing it. Interest reinforces interest. The interest can be almost anything, a people, a language, history, geography, old churches, Roman ruins, travel itself. The urge to meld oneself with the past, to understand it, to re-live it must run strong in millions of people.

North Americans traveling to Britain are likely to be attracted to the Islands for their culture, history and scenery. A British Tourist Authority study of Canadians and U. S. citizens in Great Britain found that the aspects most enjoyed about the islands were the friendly and hospitable people and the historical aspects, with old places and buildings ranking at the same level of interest. Some 400 stately homes are open to the public in Britain. More than 500,000 visitors a year go to some of them. The Tower of London heads the list. Longleat, Tudor mansion of the Marquis of Bath, has been visited by hundreds of thousands of tourists. Woburn Abbey, home of the Duke and Duchess of Bedford, Blenheim Palace, the Marlborough mansion, Chatsworth, the ducal residence of Devonshire, are educational experiences as well as being architecturally interesting.

In contrast, the big appeal for Spain is the sun, sea and sand, similar to the Caribbean.

Once an interest has been developed in a destination area, the urge to see that area or country emerges; the interest grows as knowledge increases. Advertising, of course, sparks interest in a destination—but how much more persuasive and compelling is the interest created by a good book, movie or TV program. James Michener's *Hawaii* undoubtedly caused thousands of readers to want to visit the islands. His *Iberia* is worth tens of thousands of dollars to Spain in tourist receipts.

Some books obviously create interest in an area; others are thought to dampen any such interest. The Sherlock Holmes books created interest in London but whether or not it is the kind of interest which stimulates a desire to visit the city is not known. The London of Sherlock Holmes seems a rather grim place. The book and the movie, *How Green Was My Valley*, was thought by some to discourage interest in Wales as being a sad, depressing place whereas, in reality, the natural beauty is inspiring.

Such inputs are difficult to calculate; they may work on a subliminal level of awareness for the reader or viewer. Over the years, a person reads a book about a place, sees a TV program with the place as backdrop, hears a radio program from the place, and suddenly finds he desperately wants to go there.

This is not to say that every traveler learns. He may be a mere spectator on his journeys. Humans learn from an environment only to the extent they respond to it. The trip to Rome may bring forth only

the response that "Italians are notorious cheats." The traveler can be overwhelmed by the squalor of a destination or by the frustrations he suffered while he was getting there.

The propensity to travel abroad increases with education. In America, 25 percent of the adults who have a college education account for 50 percent of the total flying to Europe each year—even though only 3 percent of them actually do so.[1] Education presumably broadens one's perspective, stimulates curiosity and, quite naturally, arouses an interest in travel, especially travel abroad.

School teachers have long constituted a sizable part of the camera-carrying crowd of Americans in Europe each summer. The college student is also seen in sizable numbers, both on his own, and as part of study groups sponsored by universities. Many universities have arrangements with European universities through which summer session courses are offered for American students. The student combines travel with systematic learning, and receives academic credit for doing so.

Travel Offers Power, Beauty

Travel can give the traveler a sense of power and freedom that is lacking in work-a-day life. Merely sitting behind the wheel of a limousine, driving across a state, presents not only a series of visual impressions, but a sense of mastery, of control. Soaring through the sky may not represent a "conquest of space" but it can provide a sense of awe, a time for philosophizing on man's insignificance in relation to nature. Ocean travel, particularly during a storm, is both fearful and thrilling.

Natural beauty—a sunset, the mountains, fall foliage, a deep valley, trees—is usually pleasurable to the viewer. Ralph Waldo Emerson and others, before and after him, see a mutuality or commonality between man and nature, nature being the whole of the universe including nature's handicraft of Planet Earth. Most people are inspired, or at least awed, by the grand sweeps of nature, otherwise how can we account for the

---

[1]Brian MacCabe, "A Place for Retailers Is Assured in Travel's Future," *Travel World Management,* Feb., 1970.

75 million visitors to our national parks each year. The mass exodus on weekends from the city and suburbs to the country is another evidence of man's need to be with trees and grass, streams and the open sky.

Maslow, the motivation theorist referred to earlier, calls attention to a "mystic experience or the oceanic feeling" which is universal in man. According to him, these are the experiences which may arise in a variety of settings; they are "the feelings of limitless horizons opening up to the vision, the feeling of being simultaneously more powerful and also more helpless than one ever was before, the feeling of great ecstasy and wonder and awe, the loss of placing in time and space, with, finally, the conviction that something extremely important and valuable has happened . . ."[1]

Ego Enhancement, Sensual Indulgence

Travel presents the opportunity for many to indulge themselves in the sensual with the possibility of ego enhancement. Travel to a poor country provides the traveler with a feeling of superiority, if that is what he needs. To be escorted personally by an assistant manager to one's room in a hotel where there are three employees for each guest, to merely clap one's hands to receive instant service, is ego enhancing, to say the least.

Much of the pleasure of the old-fashioned resort centered around the table. For many people food still plays an important part in vacationing. A principal reason for visiting France is to experience its culinary tradition. In a marketing study of tourists to the Pacific,[2] "outstanding food" was "very important" to 28 percent of Pacific tourists; "fairly important" to 52 percent. Forty percent of the visitors to Hong Kong listed "outstanding food" as important to them. For travelers to Japan, the figure was 39 percent and to Hawaii, 37 percent.

The principal motivation for large numbers of vacationers is rest and relaxation, as expressed in the answer to the question, "What do you count on doing during your vacation?"

Take it easy.
Breathe fresh air.
Take naps.
Eat and sleep well.
Enjoy the view.

Some 55 percent of the respondents in a study, conducted in 1947 by the French Institute of Public Opinion, answered in this manner.[3]

The New England mountain resort was primarily a place of respite and good food. The routine, bed to rocking chair to table, varied little from day to day. Guests came for several weeks, or the season. The fishing lodge, the beach cottage, the camping trip are rugged in some details, but are probably thought of as a chance to take it easy and relax.

While many seek rest, others search for excitement. They want anything but repose. They are only happy if the vacation environment is similar to the environment they have left behind. Otherwise, how can we explain such places as Las Vegas and Miami Beach which are crowded and hyperactive. The crowded resort, beach or campsite is substituted for the crowded city.

Many people are disappointed if the vacation destination does not have the same sorts of excitement and even the same people as back home. They want to get away from it all as long as everything is practically the same at the vacation spot as it was at home, and their friends can witness that they have "gotten away."

The Sporting Life

Much travel has a sporting event as its raison d'etre. Millions attend a variety of games—basketball, football, baseball in the U.S., soccer and other games in Europe and Latin America. The Olympic games occasion the movement of millions.

Interest in sports, either as a participant or spectator, is absorbing for large segments of the population. Dumazedier, a French social scientist, interprets much of this interest in "play life" as having a "secondary reality," one which is recognized as such, with a kind of unreality in relation to

[1]A. H. Maslow, *Motivation and Personality* (New York: Harper, 1954), p. 216.
[2]Pacific Area Travel Assn., *Pacific Visitors Survey*, San Francisco, 1967.
[3]Joffre Dumazedier, *Toward a Society of Leisure* (New York: The Free Press, 1967), p. 135.

ordinary life.[1]   Vacationing, he suggests, has something of this same lack of reality, an occasion where for a relatively brief period of time, we play at being rich or primitive or some other role completely different from ours in everyday life.

The Urge to Shop

Could the urge to shop, to gather and collect, be instinctual, relating to the nesting behavior seen in many animals and, perhaps, man? To be able to peruse, to examine, to feel, and think of the joys derived from purchasing certain merchandise is indeed pleasurable to millions of people, and may for them be a minor, if not a major, reason for travel. Hordes of cruise passengers descend upon Kingston, Jamaica, St. Thomas, Curacao, Hong Kong, Freeport, the Bahamas, Singapore and other tax-free emporiums to give witness to the strength of the shopping drive. Nearly everyone likes a bargain; nearly everyone likes to buy; nearly everyone likes to have a reason for going some place different to do so.

The tourist who has just spent $500 vacationing in St. Thomas gleefully totes his five fifths of rum at considerable effort to the plane, through customs, and finally home. You "save" $20-30 in the process. The suit purchased in Hong Kong, says Charles Metalka of the University of Hawaii, is some kind of prize to be exhibited for years to come. The bizarre straw hat acquired in Jamaica labels the owner as a true traveler. What better evidence of a trip to Hawaii than an aloha shirt? A sombrero and serape have got to mean that the owner has been to Mexico. The gift of Chanel No. 5 to a female friend takes on added glamour when the perfume is purchased in an exotic port (besides it doesn't cost as much).

Bargain hunting can be an end in itself. Go to Portugal for a fisherman's sweater; Chile has bargains in copper; blankets are cheap in Ireland, and everybody knows about those hand-tailored suits from Hong Kong for $50. Buy your reading glasses in Germany, your tweeds in Scotland, and your leather goods in Mexico. Being able to get special merchandise at low cost adds purpose to the trip.

For persons living in high cost areas, travel and vacationing in low cost countries can indeed save money. It is possible for an Englishman to rent his home in London for say $200 a month and live in Spain or Portugal for little more than his rental income. Tourists are forever seeking out those places that are inexpensive.

Following the war, Austria was a low cost vacation spot. Supply and demand raised the prices somewhat and the budget-conscious switched to Spain and Portugal. Within the same country, costs may vary widely and the true bargain hunter is soon informed about the differences. Dublin hotels are about as expensive as hotels in New York City but a room in the Irish farmhouse costs only three dollars with breakfast.

Within an area, rates may vary tremendously. Hotel tariffs in Puerto Rico and the Bahamas are high while relatively inexpensive on some of the other islands and in Costa Rica. Acquiring such knowledge is part of the travel game and is fun in itself.

Shopping in a native bazaar has its own allure; the sounds, sights and smells are different. Somehow, the fruit purchased from the floating market in Bangkok or Singapore is more romantic than that bought at the local supermarket back home.

Travel for Travel's Sake

Travel for travel's sake is a self-perpetuating phenomenon: "We just got into our car and drove." The idea of movement, of making good time, of being on the highway or in a plane, in itself can be pleasurable and is to millions of people. The highways of Britain are dotted with weekend picnickers, sitting beside their cars alongside a road as other picnickers whiz by. Much of travel has no real excuse other than the pleasure of travel itself.

"Let's take a trip to Plymouth Rock."

"We threw our camping gear into the car and took off for Yosemite."

"We bought a new car and took off for the West Coast."

Travel en route to a destination can be fun, or a great bore. Shipboard travel is supposed to be one long gala, with champagne, bon voyage parties, Captain's parties, games

---

[1]*Ibid*, p. 21.

galore. In between resting or drinking, there is the ever-groaning table to be attacked. Formerly, there was likely to be differentiation by social class aboard ship. The traveler could feel comfortable by being with his own class. A certain glamour was added to new friendships made aboard ship. Friendships could be made which might last over several years, at least by correspondence.

Travel by plane in the 50's and earlier partook of some of the same glamour, especially when en route to romantic, far-off places for vacations. Conversations between socially acceptable seat-mates and the strangeness of the air travel added luster to acquaintances made in flight. That luster has been tarnished by the nature of air travel nowadays. All social classes travel and seat-mates in the same row may include a company president, a service man and a young wife with a small baby. The commonality of interest is limited, so too is the conversation.

The shuttle planes between Boston, New York and Washington on the East Coast, and between San Francisco and Los Angeles on the West Coast are likely to be filled with businessmen or sales personnel who have ridden planes so much that the trip is little different than riding a subway.

As pointed out by sociologists, there is little conversation between passengers.[1] When the plane lands, the movement of the passengers is galvanized in one direction, getting off the plane as fast as possible. This exit-orientation appears almost to be an escape. The flight is over, "Let's get out of here as quickly as possible." In spite of admonitions from the stewardesses to remain in one's seat "until the plane has reached the terminal and the engines have been stopped," many passengers scramble out of their seats, frantically reaching for coats and hats, poised ready for the dash to the exit door.

When Getting There Is Fun

On flights to obvious vacation destinations, such as the Virgin Islands, and where the dress and behavior of the passenger identifies him clearly, there is a certain camaraderie reminiscent of shipboard travel. Where there are extended meals served in flight,

along with "complimentary champagne," the atmosphere becomes noticeably more relaxed as the flight progresses. In such cases, getting there may be half the fun.

The tourist traveling first class often begins the experience of the destination as soon as he steps aboard the transporting vehicle. A flight to Japan via Japan Airlines is promoted as a Japanese experience. The trip is an extension of Japan with kimonoed stewardesses, Japanese food and drink, decor and music.

The Chinese Airlines present themselves as "the world's first flying Chinese restaurant." The Aloha flights to Hawaii are of the same nature, the first-class passenger being plied with goodies representative of the Islands. The idea is not new. Some of the super trains between New York City and Florida were giving the "Florida experience" to their first-class passengers in the 30's.

The experience en route may be more exciting to the passenger than the destination area. Many shipboard passengers remember the fun and games and the good life aboard ship as much or more than they do the ports of call, or the arrival in Europe or someplace else. People who wish to be immersed in the British Isles are likely to take a British ship; going to Germany means making reservations aboard a German ship.

Several shipping lines have presented their accommodations not as transport but as "floating hotels" or as resort hotels, which in effect they are, especially if they are cruising Mediterranean or Caribbean waters. The ship experience can be as exciting, as novel and as pleasurable as time spent at a vacation destination.

For many people, the vacation begins at the airport, continues with the flight to the destination and only ends when the person steps off the plane upon arrival back at the starting point. The same can be true of other modes of transportation, especially the ship. The chartered bus, full of sports enthusiasts going to a game, may be as much a part of the total experience as the game itself. Travel can indeed be something more

[1]For further discussion of this concept see Morris Davis and Sol Levine, "Toward a Sociology of Public Transit," *Social Problems*, Vol. 15, No. 1, Summer 1967, pp. 84-91.

than an empty experience or one of waiting to get someplace. It need not be a void, a hiatus between home and destination.

According to Charles Metalka, the pleasures of travel can be divided into three phases: ante-trip, the trip and post trip. Each can bring its own distinctive pleasures. Thought and preparation for travel can be as pleasurable as the trip itself. Planning a trip is half the fun. Studies have shown that for extended trips, people often plan and arrange for a trip six months or even a year in advance.

Pleasures of Pre and Post Travel

Talking about the trip, learning about the destination can be an extensive and elaborate procedure, partaking of the nature of a ritual, involving the reading of books, going to dinner parties with people who have already been to the destination—even leading to an attempt to learn the language of the destination's people. (One is tempted to ask if planning the trip is half the fun, what is left upon arrival at the destination?)

Many people, it turns out, plan for a trip, take the trip and even before the current trip is completed, are planning the next one. Travel becomes a way of life. Indeed, for many people of the middle class who are over 45, travel and the thought of travel becomes a major interest. Children are grown up and away from home; financial security is assured; career goals have lost their potency. Travel can be the major interest.

Sales managers are well aware of the magic appeal of travel. The prizes awarded for winning sales contests are often in the form of a trip to the Bahamas, Puerto Rico, Greece, or some other romantic spot. Such iridescent prizes radiate an allure not possible when the reward is an automobile, a color TV set, or a swimming pool The contestants already have them.

Travel can feed on itself. Persons who have learned to travel may develop an accentuated appetite for the stuff. Californians are notably more mobile people in and around the state; they also travel abroad much more than the average U. S. citizen.

The more a person travels, the more he may want to travel. The more knowledge he acquires about travel and geography and peoples, the more fascinated he may become about little-known cultures and faraway places.

The wealthy widow may start her travel out of loneliness or a secret yearning to rekindle youth. The talks given to local women's clubs following the trip brings recognition and some attention. One trip opens the way for others and there is the opportunity to become known as an expert on that little island, or the tiny village in Spain.

While not a primary urge to travel, ownership of a vacation cottage, or second home, reinforces the need to travel and vacation. The fishing lodge, the hunting camp, the place at the beach have long played a part in the vacationing behavior of thousands of North Americans.

Vacation Homes Spur Travel

Part of being very rich is to have more than one domicile, an apartment in Manhattan, a winter home in Palm Beach, a place in Cannes. At the turn of the century, it was a "cottage" (mansion) at Newport, Rhode Island. With the upper middle class, it might be a home on Lake Kezar in Maine or a small frame cottage on Lake George in New York. The fishing camp in Minnesota or in Canada appeals to the Midwesterner and involves only an automobile trip.

The middle class American can now own a home or a condominium in the Caribbean. The Connecticut restaurant operator has a summer home in Barbados; the professor buys a condominium in St. Croix. While not using the house or apartment himself, he can have it rented by an agent. Hopefully, the rental payments cover the cost of the mortgage payment and maintenance fee. The fact that a physician owns a condominium in Honolulu gives him a very good reason for spending his vacation there. It may also be an excellent investment because of inflation and the growth of tourism on the islands.

Thousands of apartments in Florida are owned by New Yorkers and Midwesterners who spend winters there and rent the apartments for the rest of the year. The cost of the trip to Florida is taken as a business trip for income tax purposes. As affluence continues and grows, hundreds of thousands of vacation homes or apartments can be expected in the Caribbean, Central America, the Mediterranean, other subtropical and tropical areas around the world, all of them inducing travel that combines business and pleasure.

Travel to Gamble

Travel for the purpose of gambling is growing in importance. Some 15 million people go to the remote, desert town of Las Vegas each year for the opportunity of losing their money in nice, clean surroundings. Other millions go to the race tracks, to Puerto Rico, London, Reno, Monaco, the Bahamas and other destinations where various games of chance are legal. Gambling on the horses was a major appeal of Saratoga Springs in its hey-day. Hot Springs, Ark. was also known for its gambling (although not strictly legal). The dog track at Hialeah and fronton courts are a major appeal of South Florida.

The urge to gamble, to take a risk, is found in nearly every culture, from the most primitive to the most advanced. Gambling can provide an excitement not found in the safe and sanitary confines of suburbia. For the poor, it offers a chance to get a lot for a little. For some, it develops into a sickness, an addiction as strong as that for drugs.

The customer of the casino in Reno or Las Vegas does not qualify as chic, one of the elite. The gambler pulling the lever of the slot machine is likely to be a little old lady. The man playing black jack could well be a retired plumber who plans a monthly trip to Vegas as a fillip in an otherwise prosy life.

Travel as a Challenge

Travel appeals to the competitive instinct in man, especially travel to remote places or travel involving ingenuity or hardship on the part of the traveler. To travel the length of the Pan American Highway is no easy task. Several thousand Americans visit Katmandu, capitol of Nepal, each year. They may not be particularly happy with what they find (especially the food) but the trip represents a challenge to be overcome.

Travel still can involve a number of risks, tropical diseases, food poisoning, immense frustrations over delays and inconveniences. Anyone who has "stacked up" in a plane over Kennedy, O'Hare or other airports for hours wonders why he did not stay home. Nearly everyone who goes to Acapulco reports experiencing the "Mexican two-step," resulting from food poisoning. Not that the traveler enjoyed the diarrhea and the vomiting; perhaps it was a sign of courage, a merit badge for doing something relatively dangerous. Fear of air travel, of experiencing sickness while traveling, of being alone in a strange hotel or other dangers associated with being away from home are still major deterrents to travel.

Some commentators deplore the conveniences and lack of problems presented by modern day travel. Apparently, they would like us all to undertake travel only for the work and hardship that it can offer. Such inducements to travel are not widely welcomed.

To some people, however, travel is a test of endurance. Whole families pack themselves into a Volkswagon bus and take off cross-country. "We made 700 miles today driving" is meant to be partly a commentary on one's stamina. To climb the Matterhorn is remembered as a thrilling accomplishment. Skiing is a constant challenge to life and limb, especially as most enthusiasts attempt the more difficult.

Who would travel for the purpose of jumping out of a plane at 10,000 feet? Skydiving addicts, that's who. Forget the fact that the chute may not open. Think of the impact of landing and the possibility of broken legs or ankles.

Perhaps every man has a touch of the "Ulysses factor," a label for the exploring instinct said, by writer J. R. L. Anderson, to be genetically rooted in some supermen.[1] According to Anderson, the great explorers run to a type patterned after the Homeric hero, Ulysses. Such heroes pit themselves against the unknown, to glory in their own endurance and self-sufficiency. Driven by curiosity and imagination, they dare to seek

---

[1] J. R. L. Anderson, *The Ulysses Factor* (New York: Harcourt Brace, Jovanovich, 1970).

out adventure and challenge. (Hopefully, not everyone has the anti-social elements ascribed to Anderson's hero figure, those traits of cunning, unscrupulousness and selfishness.)

According to Walter Matthews, a travel consultant, the urge and confidence to travel grows with experience. Few North Americans travel to the Orient as a first trip. Rather they first try out Britain or Europe. As they gain confidence they seek out more distance and more exotic spots—Russia, Africa, Japan, Hong Kong. The travel market can thus be segmented into levels of traveler sophistication. One destination will appeal to the novice traveler; the more exotic destination to the sophisticated traveler. Airline marketers would probably do well to classify their prospective clients according to the number of trips they have already taken and where they have previously gone. Advertising for a destination such as New Zealand or Australia then would be directed to the veteran traveler rather than to the person just coming into the travel stream. The person living on the Eastern Seaboard might first be urged to go to the Caribbean, then to Europe, then to the Orient, and, finally, to Nepal or Nairobi.

The Social Nature of Travel

Much of travel grows out of man's social nature. Man, the social animal, feels comfortable in a tour group. He is with others of his kind who are predictable, a camaraderie develops; he is "safe and secure from all alarm," as the hymn goes.

If a tour is of a special nature, the traveler may develop friendships which last for years. Some tour groups have reunions years after the tour took place. The Christmas greeting contains a reference to "the time Nellie Smith fell in the pool with her clothes on," or "I'll never forget Jack in that hula skirt."

The affluent of yesteryear were just as herd-bound as the tour group of today. The enclaves of the wealthy on the Riviera, Newport, Bar Harbor and Palm Beach were evidence, if any is needed, that most people want to be with others of their own kind. The "tour group" of the jet set or of the "400" is the gathering at the destination.

In a highly competitive society, man abhors loneliness. He usually needs the support of a group. Then there is always the possibility of meeting compatible persons, or even the dream person. The package tour makes it possible for the timid, or those not-up-to-coping with the rigors of independent travel, to travel in the comfort and safety of a group, with all arrangements being made by the tour host.

In some subcultures, such as found in a university faculty, travel is the accepted way of spending one's vacation. Just about every university faculty member has visited a foreign country and has a set of color slides ready to prove it. Sabbatical leaves, and the foreign assignments possible for university teachers, encourage travel and the development of a passion for it.

According to Charles Metelka, travel increases the "sociability resources" of the individual. It builds his fund of impressions, refreshes his reservoir of anecdotes, and widens his range of knowledge, thus making him a more interesting person, to himself and to his social group. Instead of name dropping, the traveler "trip drops." He has a ready supply of stories of what happened at Miami Beach, or Tijuana or on Cape Cod.

Undoubtedly much travel is done merely for the sake of keeping up with the Joneses, and being able to appear knowledgeable about foreign places. Indeed, travel one-upsmanship can be an exciting game, the most widely traveled person receiving some sort of accolade from those who value travel as a way of life. Travel snobbery can be just as gratifying as money snobbery, educational snobbery or family snobbery. It takes a certain amount of wealth, ingenuity and energy to travel widely.

The Travel Snob

The travel snob would like to be able to tell about places he has seen, the hotels where he stopped, the restaurants he patronized, places that he hopes his listener has not encountered.

"Of course, you have been to see the bulls run at Pamplona."

The perfect put-down: "Of course. I run with the bulls at Pamplona every year."

Travel snobbery has its own rewards.

Among large groups of people, the main reason for taking a trip is to be able to tell the folks back home about it.

Being "well-traveled" has similar status to being well-educated. The recent "trip to Yucatan" enriches the traveler, adds the glow of glamour to him as a personality. Travel talk is in, especially if it is travel to an out-of-the-ordinary destination.

The wise traveler exploits his trip while traveling, when newly returned home, and for years thereafter. On the trip, there are the "postcards from Paris," the souvenir from Hong Kong, sent to the right people. As Metalka points out, post-trip, the traveler has the opportunity of making points with the right stories. Nor need the story concern only that magnificent Chinese food, it can be a horror tale of being stacked up over London, lost baggage, the $300 lost camera, or any other experience of the journey. The "recount value" of travel and vacationing is part of the appeal, a part of the total travel package. Post-travel benefits extend over a lifetime.

Travel for "Acceptance"

Another reason for travel comes in the desire to be where one is accepted and comfortable socially. Until recently, Negroes in the U. S. did not travel much because they lacked the money to do so and because within the country it was embarrassing and difficult to get first-class accommodations. The Negro, until recently, was not seen at any of the well-known resort areas, except as an employee.

In the South, there were a few resorts and motels catering to Negroes. More recently, large numbers of Negroes can and do travel and a number of travel agencies have opened in black neighborhoods. New York City has at least 12 such agencies.

The U. S. Negro traveler naturally favors the destinations that receive him well—Jamaica, the Bahamas, Puerto Rico, the Virgin Islands and the other Caribbean Islands. Haiti, as an example of Black governing Black, is favored. He is also traveling to Europe, going to the major cities, especially the historic ones. Negroes are somewhat of a curiosity in Scandinavia and are well received. They are also welcomed in Mexico and Canada. Travel is one of the newest status symbols for the Black just as it has been for the White in the past.

Vacation Travel and Urbanization

Vacation travel is linked with the degree of urbanization. A French study showed that Paris, with 18 percent of the population of France, accounted for 51 percent of expenditures on vacation. Seventy-two percent of the inhabitants of Paris or the Paris area took vacations. Figures collected by the National Institute of Statistics and Economic Studies indicate that only 19 percent of people living in the country went on vacation in France in 1957.[1] Perhaps the need for the outdoors, the sun and for vigorous exercise is already met in rural life.

Vacationing as a Cultural Norm

Travel and vacationing as a cultural norm cannot be overlooked. France, in 1936, decreed that 12 days of paid vacation were mandatory. A Holiday With Pay Act was passed in Britain in 1938. Such statutes tend to establish vacationing as a norm.

Seventy-five percent of the Swedish people take at least one annual trip away from home which lasts three to four days. The reasons seem plain enough. The Swedes have one of the highest per capita incomes; their long winters induce sun worship and send them flying off to Spain, Portugal, Greece and St. Barts in search of beaches and warmth.

In England, the figure is 55 percent. The "holiday" in England is a must, superseding all else, the subject of conversation year around. Plans for the holiday are made months or even years in advance and when the time comes, nothing is allowed to get in its way.

In France, the figure is 45 percent.[2] In the month of August, business in Paris almost comes to a standstill. A large percentage of the residents have gone on a holiday.

With their new affluence, West Germans have also become big vacationers.

[1] Joffre Dumazedier, *Toward a Society of Leisure* (New York: The Free Press, 1967), p. 125.

[2] "The Big Picture," *ASTA Travel News*, June, 1969, p. 80.

Forty percent take at least one annual trip away from home which lasts three to four days. Where vacationing is a cultural norm, not to vacation is an aberration.

Sociological influences condition some groups to travel more than others. Blue-collar workers do not associate, to the same extent, with people who talk about travel as do white-collar workers or students. The two million Jews of New York City are a highly traveled subculture and account for much of the house count of the resort hotels in Atlantic City, Sullivan County, Miami Beach, Puerto Rico and the Bahamas.

Travel Can Sharpen Perspective

Travel can awaken the senses and heighten awareness of one's own milieu. A trip to a foreign country is likely to provide new perspective and often more appreciation in viewing one's own community.

"One thing that the trip made me realize is how lucky we are in our own country."

"I was glad to make the trip but even gladder to get back home."

"I never realized how small Marshalltown was until I visited Tokyo."

Travel exposures and experiences can provide new standards, art forms, and even new systems of belief. By viewing a range and diversity of societies, the person is likely to develop a wider tolerance for cultures other than his own. Removed from his own culture, perceptions are often sharpened and the personal "data bank" enlarged.

Spiritual Value of Travel

The Catholic Church sums up many of the benefits and dangers of tourism to the individual in a "General Directory of the Pastoral Tourism."[1] "If a man," says the Pastoral, "lacks a healthy moral formation, by using tourism he may become a careless and dissipated human being, a hasty traveler, who is a slave of the powerful means by which he may enjoy the benefits owing to the growing technical progress, a superficial creature incapable of dialogue, heedless of the beauties of nature and of the riches that spring forth out of man's labour, a meddling seeker of pleasures and degrading experiences, until he gets to the point of abusing

the hospitality that is offered to him."

On the other hand, according to the same source, tourism can, if properly used:

". . . . Contribute to the mutual knowledge of man and to the development of the sense of hospitality,

". . . . Reduce distances between the social classes and the human races,

". . . . Overcome the isolation of peoples by encouraging them to banish inauspicious prejudices through the encounter of civilization and culture,

". . . . Constitute one of the principal economic resources for many nations and promote new sources of labour. . . . ."

Tourism, the Pastoral explains, can stimulate man's touch with nature and improve natural resources. It presents the manifold beauty of creation as a common heritage to all mankind. It can be an instrument of peace and brotherhood, a means of unifying the human family, a means of increasing the solidarity of man with the universe and of restoring the person as an individual.

After cataloging the varied and numerous reasons for travel and the expected joys to be derived from it, it must be pointed out that even with the best travel agent, the most convenient and fastest form of transportation and the most glorious of destinations, the returning tourist does not always measure up to the picture of the ecstatic satisfied vacationer. A distressingly large number of returning travelers look harassed and over-extended. Travel and vacationing can still be an exhausting and demanding experience.

Although the pleasures are there, or can be; so, too, are the frustrations. While some national leaders inveigh against tourism as an affliction to be endured, bringing thousands of unwanted visitors who pollute the environment, ruin the ecology and cause pain for the residents, other national leaders sing its praises. Prime Minister Pierre Trudeau of Canada believes that travel stirs national unity and pride and he encouraged the nation in 1971 to establish 96 hostels for some 120,000 young people to use in

---

[1]Abbr. from *Technical Bulletin,* International Union of Official Travel Organizations, Sept. 1969.

traveling throughout Canada. In 1972, $1.2 million was spent in opening 120 hostels. Travel, as well as tourism generally, is very much a matter of "the eye of the beholder."

Pitirim Sorokin, the well known sociologist, examined the effects of travel on the personality and found pluses and minuses. Spatial mobility, he believed, encouraged more plastic and versatile behavior, decreased narrow-mindedness, facilitated innovation. On the negative side, travel encouraged superficiality and decreased sensitivity, made for impatience and touch-and-go habits. It generated skepticism and aversion to theory. Travel, according to Sorokin, drove the uneducated to sudden dogmas, diminished intimacy with others, increased loneliness, restlessness, sensual pleasures—and suicide.[1]

Undoubtedly the urge to travel and vacation is touched off by instinctual needs, present in all mankind. Overlaid upon these basic needs are those learned or culturally determined activators, varying from culture to culture and within a society, which give rise to the movement of millions of people within and around the world each year.

Why do people travel? There are a number of answers, depending upon the individual and his cultural conditioning. The answers are psychological and sociological. What the traveler says are his motivations for traveling may be only reflections of deeper needs, needs which he himself does not understand, nor wish to articulate.

[1]George W. Pierson, *The Moving Americans* (New York: Alfred A. Knopf, 1973), p. 249.

Another Rockresort, Little Dix Bay in Virgin Gordo, British Virgin Islands, spacious and remote, the resort permits complete relaxation on a beautiful white sand beach in tropical waters.

THE ECONOMIC AND SOCIAL IMPACTS OF TOURISM

That tourism affects the economy of a destination area cannot be questioned; however, the extent of its effect, its implications and repercussions are debatable. Much of the research in tourism is concerned with the economic impact made by tourism on a state, nation, island or community. Since there are countervailing forces at play within an economy, the costs and benefits accruing from tourism are not immediately quantifiable. Cost-benefits study involves the collection of masses of data and the use of highly sophisticated analytical techniques. The statistical analyses are sometimes complicated and results are often disputed among the experts.

Costs and benefits are not evenly distributed. What may be a benefit to one group may be a cost to another group within the same community. Hotel and restaurant operators may benefit from tourism but the permanent residents may suffer a cost in terms of crowding, pollution, noise and, in some cases, a changed way of life. In some areas, immigrants must be invited in to serve the tourists and these constitute a cost to the community since they increase the use of schools, hospitals, roads, water systems, sewage systems and, in some cases, welfare funds.

Two Sides to Tourism

In well developed areas, tourism may enrich the community by providing additional shops, theaters and restaurants. The permanent resident is offered entertainment and social options previously unavailable. In less developed areas, enclaves of tourism may be the source of frustration and resentment. Small areas are given good roads, adequate water supply and other utilities; the rest of the community remains as it was.

The jet airport on a Caribbean island is fine but the native cannot afford to fly. He cannot afford to eat in the new restaurant or buy at the boutique. The native who receives a marginal income can only observe; he cannot participate. His position vis-a-vis the tourist accentuates his poverty and may lead to violence.

Does tourism bring into the economy more than it takes out? Are the benefits evenly distributed or do they go to a relatively small minority? Do the increases in government revenue generated by tourism pay for the added cost of government services?

As dollars brought in to an economy by tourism stimulate that economy, costs of goods and services increase; the price of land may skyrocket. In some areas the economy is overheated. Landowners and developers may become rich but the cost to the average citizen usually multiplies because of the increased cost of housing.

Should tourism be encouraged and expanded? How much public funds should be used to market and advertise tourism? What is the power per dollar of advertising? How many tourist dollars will be returned for each dollar invested in tourist promotion?

In many communities and areas, whether tourism is beneficial to the area is academic. The area may have almost no other options. Most communities would probably like to have a "smokeless," clean economic base such as provided by tourism, research or service industries. For areas that have natural beauty, pleasant climate and yet are remote from the skilled labor markets and raw materials needed for manufacturing, tourism development may be a necessary choice. Bermuda, situated hundreds of miles from a land mass, was once a small agricultural producer. With the growth of population, tourism was an obvious choice to improve the island's economy and is now the major and almost only industry. In 1972, the island attracted 339,782 visitors.

Annual occupancy in hotels was 66.6 percent, average length of stay, 5.4 nights. Another 81,168 persons visited from cruise ships. The principal market is the U. S.; some 85 percent of the regular visitors coming from the U. S.; 8.8 percent from Canada and 3.2 percent from the U. K.[1]

The Bahamas and most of the smaller Caribbean Islands can barely subsist as agricultural economies. Per capita income on some of the islands is less than $400 a year. They are too remote to be competitive as small manufacturers. They have little choice but to consider tourism for future development. Yet some of the leaders and many of the natives resent tourism, feeling that it degrades the worker. It has been said that the worker is exchanging one kind of servitude for another. The white man continues to give the orders, the blacks to take them.

Tourism Major Force in Mixed Economy

Puerto Rico is an example of a mixed economy in which tourism is a major force. The economic mix of a country shifts with time. Barbados, a few years ago, was dependent upon sugar; tourism now shares the economic limelight. Tourism in Jamaica is growing rapidly, and necessarily so, to replace the declining importance of agriculture.

Cape Cod is an instance of an area forced to rely to a large extent on tourism. Although it was originally an agricultural and fishing community, by the 1930's these industries were no longer competitive. Nantucket Island and Martha's Vineyard were once whaling centers, now tourism is the principal industry.

Tourism is not necessarily an "either-or" proposition. It often blends well with a mixed economy. The largest concentration of hotel rooms in the world is in New York City; tourism is a sizable part of the City's economy. London is more likely to be thought of as a huge financial and industrial center; it is also a major tourist center. Nearly 95 percent of all American visitors to England spend some time in London. Chicago, San Francisco, Los Angeles, Houston and Boston are also tourist centers. Florida is a mixed economy, resting upon three legs: agriculture, tourism, industry.

Some nations are self-sufficient to a large degree but need the foreign exchange developed by tourism. Mexico, Ireland, Greece, Austria, England, France, Italy and many other small agricultural countries are examples. Spain and Portugal are two prominent instances of countries that need tourism income for the foreign exchange necessary to balance their economies.

Nations and communities in today's world must import. Tourism can be a major export, used to offset the cost of imports.

Who Benefits from Tourism and by How Much?

The first beneficiaries of tourism are likely to be the land developers, the land owners and the entrepreneurs (who are successful) that provide transport, accommodations, food and beverage service, sight-seeing and other entertainment for the traveler.

Land owners and speculators are likely to benefit the most immediately and, in many cases, the most impressively. When a tourist industry is being developed, the price of land skyrockets in and around the tourist facility and sometimes for miles around it.

Land cost along the Gold Coast of San Juan is fantastically high as compared with its cost following World War II. Land cost in Honolulu may run as high as $5 million an acre. Tourism-fueled land prices rise even in the remote Caribbean Islands such as Grenada, Barbados and Saint Lucia. Beach property and areas close by are priced around $40,000 an acre and up. In some islands, such as the Grand Caymans, there are no available large blocks of land left for home or tourist development. This drives up the value of the land that is available.

Contractors who build tourist facilities are likely to be big beneficiaries of tourist booms. Another highly visible group of beneficiaries from tourism are those engaged in transporting tourists to and around the destination—airlines, tour bus companies, taxi and rent-a-car agencies.

What benefits accrue to the rest of the population of the tourist destination area? Do the 20 million plus travelers to Florida

---

[1]*The Travel Agent,* Mar. 15, 1973.

each year bring benefits other than to South Florida and especially to the Miami Beach area? Does the citizen living in Jacksonville benefit from the tourist industry which is centered 300 or 400 miles south of it? What good is the tourist industry to the retired person living in Florida? In what way does tourism affect the school teacher in Honolulu? In some communities, such as Las Vegas, most of the population is dependent upon tourism in one way or another.

Tourism in a Mixed Economy

In a mixed economy, does tourism pay its own way for government services? Of a dollar spent by a tourist at a destination area, how much will remain in the area after a few weeks? On an island location, where nearly everything, including food, beverage, furniture and building supplies, has to be imported, perhaps less than 25 percent of the tourist dollar remains in the local economy. The rest is "leaked" out of the economy. In other economies, the dollar is spent and re-spent within the economy, creating a "multiplier effect," increasing the ultimate impact of the tourist expenditure.

Within the United States, income from tourism varies from state to state. States such as Florida, California, New York and Massachusetts are destination areas; others such as Iowa and Nebraska are "pass through" states. Eleven states have reported receiving more than $1 billion in income from tourist expenditures.[1] The table, page 122, shows the estimated expenditures, in millions of dollars, made by visitors within several of the states for the year 1969.[2] The statistics are not necessarily comparable since the assumptions and methods on which the research is based vary widely.

Persons concerned with developing a visitor industry—whether government or privately sponsored—want to know the extent of benefits likely to occur, and their costs. For every tourist dollar, how many dollars can be expected to be returned to the private sector, the residents, and to the public sector, the government? Benefits divided by costs equals the benefit-cost ratio. Benefit-cost ratios for both private and public sectors are desirable.

To arrive at these ratios, the following

steps are required:

1. The determination of where the tourist dollar is spent, its allocation by expenditure.

2. The determination of what percentage of each expenditure goes out of the local economy, "the import propensity."

3. The derivation of a "multiplier effect," a ratio applied to income which reflects multiple spending within an economy (explained later).

4. Application of the multiplier effect to the tourist expenditures to arrive at the total benefits in dollars of tourist expenditures.

5. The derivation of a benefit-cost ratio, expressed as dollars received/dollars spent.

6. Application of the benefit-cost ratios to tourist expenditures to provide estimates of income and costs of the tourist business to a community, for both the private and public sectors.

The "Multiplier Effect" of Tourist Spending

When a "fresh" dollar enters an economy, it affects that economy in various ways. Some of the dollar immediately leaves the economy as profit, savings, in various purchases of imports. Technically these are lumped together as "leakages."

The part of the dollar that remains in the economy may be saved, invested, or used for purchases. Technically, these are referred to as "a first round of spending." Part of what is spent is re-spent for a "second round of spending." Other rounds of spending take place.

As the money which stays within the economy is re-spent it stimulates the economy, causing other spending.

The tourist dollar is a fresh dollar to the economy: in economic terms an export, bringing in new money. The part that remains in the economy is spent and re-spent, setting up a Tourist Income Multiplier. The more of the tourist dollar that remains in the economy and the faster it is re-spent,

---

[1]*Travel Trends in the United States and Canada,* University of Colorado, Business Research Division, in cooperation with The Travel Research Assn., Boulder, 1971, p. 36.
[2]*Ibid.*

TABLE X.–ESTIMATED VISITOR OR TOURIST EXPENDITURES, 1971
(In Millions of Dollars)

State	1970	1971
Alabama	$ 512.0	$ 545.0
Alaska[a]	42.0	45.0
Arizona	565.0	610.0
Arkansas	623.8	806.0
Colorado	570.0	600.0
Connecticut	N.A.	385.0[a]
Delaware	142.0	151.0
District of Columbia	642.0	645.0
Florida	3600.0 [a, g]	N.A.
Georgia	763.0	839.4
Hawaii[a]	570.0	645.0
Illinois	N.A.	2820.0
Iowa	577.0	610.0
Kentucky	N.A.	585.0
Louisiana	614.0	650.0
Maine[a]	540.0	594.0
Minnesota	810.0	860.0
Mississippi	402.9	N.A.
Missouri	N.A.	955.6
Montana	198.0	210.5
New Hampshire	338.0	N.A.
New York	3500.0	3600.0
North Carolina	802.0	850.0
North Dakota[d]	106.0	125.0
Oklahoma	430.0	455.0
Oregon[a]	339.5	438.3
Pennsylvania	4100.0	4200.0
South Carolina	382.0	405.0
Tennessee	N.A.	730.0
Texas	1469.1[c]	1305.4[h]
Utah[a]	135.0	153.0
Vermont[a]	200.0	220.0
Washington[a]	394.0	450.0

[a] Out-of-state visitors only. [b] Summer season only. [c] Includes commercial carriers. [d] Estimates. [e] New series beginning 1966. [f] New series beginning 1968. [g] New series beginning 1970. [h] Auto visitors only.

Source: *Travel Trends in the United States and Canada* (University of Colorado, Business Research Division, 1973).

the greater its effect in "heating" the economy.

When a visitor arrives at a destination area, he may have already spent a sizable amount of money for transportation. Suppose he came by plane. The airlines will spend a certain amount of the traveler's money in the destination area. Some of the pilots and stewardesses may live there. Airplane mechanics are needed there. The gasoline for the planes may have been purchased through a local supplier who makes a profit on the gasoline and also employs local people. The multiplier effect has already started. The airline employees and the suppliers spend a certain amount of the money they receive within the local economy; they may deposit some of it in the bank to be loaned out at interest. The bank profits and, at the same time, the money may be used to build a home or start a business in the destination area.

If the visitor stays at a hotel, between 20 and 40 percent of the hotel bill will go to local employees of the htoel. They are likely to spend a large proportion of what they earn within the destination area. Again the multiplier effect: each time the money is spent, it stimulates the economy.

The tourist pays $10 to take a tour of the destination area. The tour operator buys gasoline. Most of the purchase price goes out of the economy. But he also pays local drivers, makes a profit for himself and will spend some or most of it within the economy.

The tourist rents a boat to go sailing on. If the boat was built within the destination area, much of the cost would have remained in the economy. Profit to the

The Holiday Inn, Freeport, Grand Bahama Island; 800-room resort is largest in the Caribbean.

MODEL OF ESTIMATED TOURIST EXPENDITURES FOR FOOD AND BEVERAGE

(Note: Arrows Point To Dollars Changing Hands.)

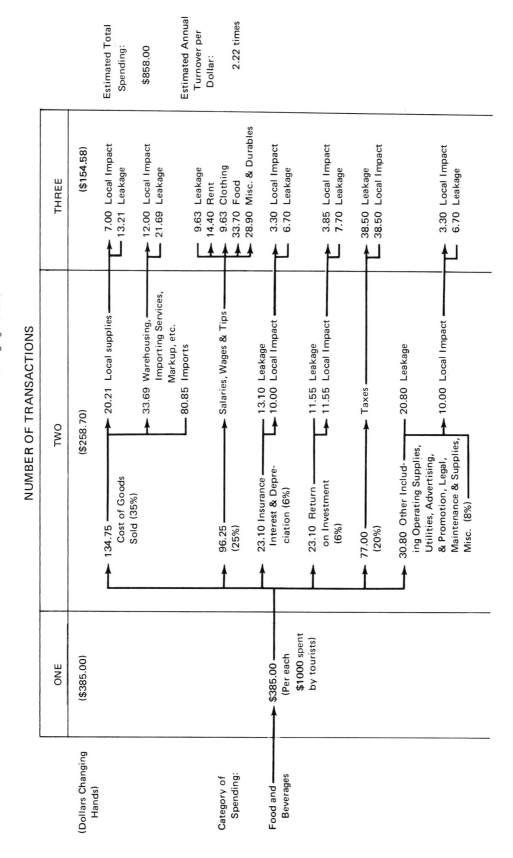

NUMBER OF TRANSACTIONS

(Dollars Changing Hands)	ONE	TWO	THREE
	($385.00)	($258.70)	($154.58)

Category of Spending:

Food and Beverages

$385.00 (Per each $1000 spent by tourists)

134.75 Cost of Goods Sold (35%)
→ 20.21 Local supplies → 7.00 Local Impact
   13.21 Leakage
→ 33.69 Warehousing, Importing Services, Markup, etc. → 12.00 Local Impact
   21.69 Leakage
→ 80.85 Imports
   9.63 Leakage
   14.40 Rent
   9.63 Clothing
   33.70 Food
   28.90 Misc. & Durables

96.25 Salaries, Wages & Tips (25%)

23.10 Insurance Interest & Depreciation (6%)
   13.10 Leakage
→ 10.00 Local Impact → 3.30 Local Impact
   6.70 Leakage

23.10 Return on Investment (6%)
   11.55 Leakage
→ 11.55 Local Impact → 3.85 Local Impact
   7.70 Leakage

77.00 Taxes (20%)
   38.50 Leakage
→ 38.50 Local Impact

30.80 Other Including Operating Supplies, Utilities, Advertising, & Promotion, Legal, Maintenance & Supplies, Misc. (8%)
   20.80 Leakage
→ 10.00 Local Impact → 3.30 Local Impact
   6.70 Leakage

Estimated Total Spending:

$858.00

Estimated Annual Turnover per Dollar:

2.22 times

MODEL OF ESTIMATED TOURIST EXPENDITURES FOR ACCOMMODATIONS

(Note: Arrows Point To Dollars Changing Hands.)

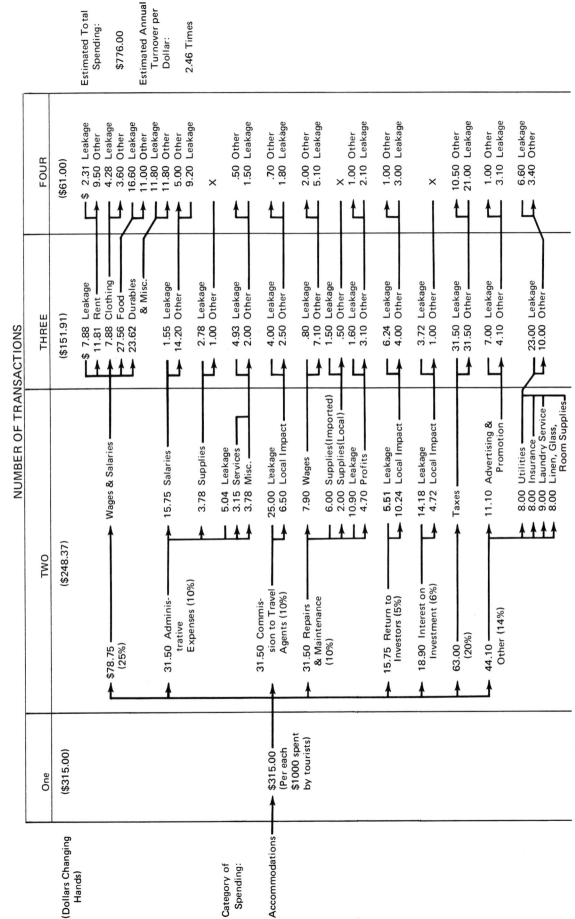

owner would remain in the economy. He, in turn, would spend most of his profit.

A large part of the rent paid by a tourist to an apartment owner is likely to remain in the community. The illustrations can continue but it is plain to see that there are "rounds" of spending kicked off by the "injection" of the tourist dollar into a destination economy. There are also "leakages," dollars which leave the economy for purchases of goods and services outside of the community. Other leakages occur when profits go out of an area.

The charts on pages 124 and 125 are models which graphically illustrate what happens to the tourist dollar spent for accommodations and what happens to a tourist dollar spent for food and beverages. At each round of spending, "leakages" occur, money leaves the economy of the area. The charts were drawn up by H. Zinder and Associates, Washington, D. C. and form part of a study done for the Agency for International Development, Washington, D. C.[1]

Import Propensities

To establish what part of the tourist dollar remains at the destination, it is necessary to find out where it is spent and how much of it is sent out of the destination area.

The "import propensity" of the tourist dollar is the percent that is sent to another area for purchases or other reasons. The import propensity represents a leakage from an area.

The table on page 126 shows import propensities of tourist dollars spent on various things in Hawaii. The table is presented only as an example. Tourist spending is broken down as to where it was spent—hotel, restaurant, food store, etc. Then the percent of that expenditure that goes out of Hawaii is figured as its import propensity.

Import propensities are necessarily estimates but are needed to arrive at a multiplier effect for either the private or public sectors. The estimates would not hold true for a different destination area. The effect of the dollars spent in travel to Hawaii that end up in Hawaii was not considered.

From an economic viewpoint, services performed in tourism are "exports." This concept is somewhat difficult to grasp, since services are not tangible like a shipment of machinery or wheat. Nevertheless, the result of offering services to tourists serves to produce income for the tourist destination area the same as a tangible good shipped from the area.

Items which must be imported to support tourism are, indeed, imports and are charged against the benefits of tourism to the economy. If a tourist spends $100 in an American hotel, about $40 of that money goes to the employees. That $40 would be considered economically as an export. If food were brought into the hotel from outside the community, its cost is an import. Ireland and Spain, for example, are pleased with tourism insofar as it produces exportable services, and brings in foreign exchange. The more of the tourism dollar that qualifies as an export, the better it is for the economy.

Expressed in arithmetical terms, the tourism multiplier is:

$$TIM = \frac{1-TPI}{MPS + MPI}$$

Where: TIM = Tourism Income Multiplier, or factor by which tourist expenditures should be multiplied to determine the tourist income generated by these expenditures.

TPI = Tourists' Propensity to Import or buy imported goods and services which do not create income for the Bahamas.

MPS = The Marginal Propensity to save or the individual's decision not to spend an extra dollar of income.

MPI = The Marginal Propensity to Import or the individual's decision to buy imported goods or spend his money abroad.

A large scale study of the effect of tourist spending on the economy of the Bahamas was completed in 1969 by the Checchi Company of Washington, D. C.[1] In this study the multiplier effect derived was .894. It was estimated that of the dollar spent by the tourist, about 34¢ went to import or

[1]*A Plan for Managing the Growth of Tourism in the Commonwealth of the Bahama Islands* (Washington, D. C.: Checchi and Company, 1969).

TABLE XI—THE APPORTIONMENTS OF VISITOR EXPENDITURES BY TYPES OF BUSINESS ESTABLISHMENT AND THE IMPACT PROPENSITIES ASSOCIATED WITH EACH TYPE OF ESTABLISHMENT[1]

Type of Business Establishment	Apportionment of Visitor Expenditures 1965-66 Survey	Import Propensity
Hotels	24.6%	38%
Hotel Apartments and Apartments	4.1	39
Restaurants	31.4	41
Food Stores	0.6	49
Liquor Stores	6.0	66
Clothing and Accessory Stores	9.3	44
Jewelry, Gift, and Souvenir Stores	5.2	60
Department and Variety Stores	1.7	54
Drug Stores	0.3	65
Photography Stores	1.1	57
Inter-Island Transportation	4.5	39
Ground Transportation	4.9	37
Tour Agents	1.8	29
Miscellaneous	4.8	45
TOTALS	100.0	—

Note: Figures do not necessarily add to totals because of rounding.

Source: First National Bank of Hawaii, *The Impact of Exports on Income in Hawaii* (1964), p. 38

buy imported goods and services which created no income for the Bahamas. It was also estimated that 46¢ of every dollar spent by Bahamian-based companies and individuals was spent on imported goods and services. Another 28¢ went for savings and investment. Stated in economic terms, the economy's marginal propensity to import was .456; its marginal propensity to save was .281 and the tourist propensity to import was .341. Using the Tourist Income Multiplier formula, the arithmetic is:[2]

$$TIM = \frac{1 - .341}{.281 + .456} = \frac{.659}{.737} = .8942$$

In other words, in the Bahamas study, it was estimated that each tourist dollar spent in the Bahamas generated the effect of spending 89¢ within the Bahamas economy. (Again, it should be pointed out that arriving at the "propensity to import" and the "propensity to save" may be extremely difficult. Two researchers may well come out with two different estimates.)

The multiplier effect found as regards tourist spending varies widely:[3]

---

[1] Charts (pp. 124-25) are presented only as illustrations of how rounds of spending take place in a destination area. The "multiplier effect" as developed in the Zinder Report has been sharply criticized in the article "Income Effect of Tourist Spending: Mystification Multiplied," a critical comment on the Zinder Report, Kari Kivett and Iqbal Gulati, *Social and Economic Studies,* Institute of Social and Economic Research, University of the West Indies, Jamaica, Vol. 19, No. 3, Sept. 1970, pp. 326-343.
[2] *Ibid.,* appendix B-3.
[3] Michael Peters, *International Tourism* (London: Hutchinson, 1969), p. 240.

DISTRIBUTION OF THE TOURIST DOLLAR IN FLORIDA

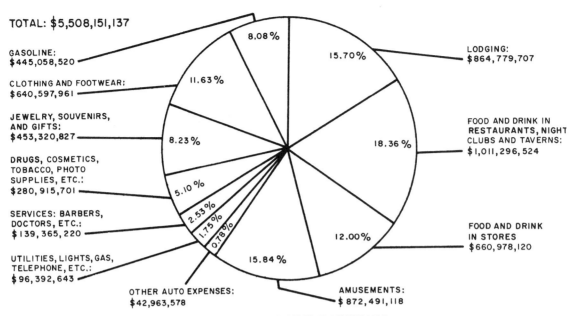

TOTAL: $5,508,151,137

GASOLINE: $445,058,520

CLOTHING AND FOOTWEAR: $640,597,961

JEWELRY, SOUVENIRS, AND GIFTS: $453,320,827

DRUGS, COSMETICS, TOBACCO, PHOTO SUPPLIES, ETC.: $280,915,701

SERVICES: BARBERS, DOCTORS, ETC.: $139,365,220

UTILITIES, LIGHTS, GAS, TELEPHONE, ETC.: $96,392,643

OTHER AUTO EXPENSES: $42,963,578

8.08%

11.63%

15.70%

8.23%

5.10%

2.53%

1.75%

0.78%

15.84%

18.36%

12.00%

LODGING: $864,779,707

FOOD AND DRINK IN RESTAURANTS, NIGHT CLUBS AND TAVERNS: $1,011,296,524

FOOD AND DRINK IN STORES $660,978,120

AMUSEMENTS: $872,491,118

SOURCE: FLORIDA TOURIST STUDY — 1968, FLORIDA DEVELOPMENT COMMISSION

New Hampshire	1.6 to 1.7
Hawaii	.9 to 1.3
Greece	1.2 to 1.4
Ireland	2.7
Canada[1]	2.43

The estimate of the economic impact of tourist spending on the destination area, of course, is greatly influenced by the multiplier effect which applies. The larger the multiplier, the greater the economic impact of a tourist dollar on an area.

The key to understanding the size of the multiplier effect is the amount of the tourist dollar that goes out of the economy as compared with the percentage that remains in the economy to be spent over and over again. The more that goes out, the lower the multiplier effect; the higher the amount that remains in the economy, the larger the multiplier effect. Another factor is how many times the tourist dollar is respent within the economy. Studies vary in assuming turnover of the tourist dollar from once or twice to as high as twelve times.

In highly developed destination areas, such as New York and Hawaii, many of the purchases needed to support tourism are made within the area. The tourist dollar is spread throughout the economy. A siz-

able part of the tourist dollar remains for use by the government to build roads, schools, hospitals and to supply the other necessary social services.

Distribution of Spending by Tourists

The American Hotel and Motel Association, quoting U. S. Dept. of Commerce Studies, says that a 300-room hotel will generate $10.5 million worth of business for the community. The hotel, operating at a 60 percent occupancy, with a $12 average room rate, generates $788,400 in annual room sales. These, in turn, generate $2.2 million in other sales, enabling the hotel to have an economic impact on the community comparable to that of an industrial plant with a $3 million payroll. The studies assume that there is a 3.6 multiplier effect in a U. S. community. The new wave of purchasing power created by the multiplier effect has the effect of generating $10.5 million worth of new business for the community.

Expenditures per visitor in the desti-

[1]Lawrence G. Ecroyd, "What's New in Canadian Travel Research," *Proceedings First Annual Conference* (Salt Lake City: Travel Research Assn., 1970), p. 39.

nation area vary greatly; they are determined by the number of days spent on the visit, the cost of accommodations and meals and the general level of cost in the area. Some destination areas have many attractions, each with a cost; other areas are relatively devoid of places of entertainment and places in which to spend money. For example, as compared with Florida or Hawaii, there are few man-made tourist attractions in Maine.

A 1968 study by the Florida Development Commission showed the daily average expenditure of visitors to Florida to be $17.59 per day. During the summer, the average length of the stay is about 12 days; 19 days in the winter. Average expenditure per stay was $275. Food and lodging accounted for the majority of expenses, although spending for amusements, souvenirs and gifts represented 24 percent of the traveler's budget.

The pie chart shows how a tourist dollar is distributed in Florida. According to the estimate, visitors spend more than $445 million on gasoline, over $640 million on clothing and footwear. An amazing $453 million was spent on jewelry, souvenirs and gifts, and about $281 million on drugs, cosmetics, tobacco, photo supplies and similar purchases. Various service personnel, in locations other than hotels and restaurants, received over $139 million. (See chart, facing page)

If the benefits from tourism can be personalized, expressed in simple terms, residents of the area are more likely to favor the development of tourism. In the previously mentioned study for the Bahama Islands, the consultant explained how tourist income could be translated into tangible benefits for the residents. According to the Checchi Company,[1] the construction of two condominiums in the islands would generate enough government income to pay for one schoolroom. Customs duties on materials and furnishings, and income from spending by tourists who would stay in the condominiums would generate $11,200 in government revenues, enough to pay for one new schoolroom.

It was pointed out that each two hotel rooms that were built would mean 200 tourists coming to the islands each year who would leave $8200 in government taxes, enough to pay one teacher's salary.

To overcome resentment against expatriate hotel workers needed to man the new hotels, it was explained that each expatriate hotel employee generated more than $16,400 in taxes each year, enough to pay for a new hospital room.

Import duties may be more acceptable since less visible, than direct taxes on income. Import duties bring revenue to the government regardless of other benefits from tourism. Campers, for example, may generate little employment but would contribute to the public sector if import duties are exacted on purchases made by the campers for food, beverage, gasoline and the like.

Costs of Tourism to the Public Sector

The economic impact of the tourist dollar has two broad effects: the impact on the private economy of the destination area and the impact on the government sector. Impacts can be widely different. Tourist dollars spent in a developing country may be sent out of the country almost immediately as profit to absentee owners and for imported goods and services. The labor force may contain large numbers of imported laborers who send much or most of their money home to their families. An example is the U.S. Virgin Islands where about 16,000 workers, mostly from British islands, are employed. In some areas, most of the food and beverages sold to tourists have to be imported, as is the case in many island economies and in countries with undiversified economies. The multiplier effect for the private sector is low.

It can also be low for the government sector, depending on its tax policies. In most developed countries, central government revenues vary between 30 percent and 50 percent of national income depending on the social policies of the country.[2] If the government has granted import tax holidays on construction materials, furnishings, and food and beverage imports, tax income

---

[1]*A Plan for Managing the Growth of Tourism in the Commonwealth of the Bahama Islands* (Washington, D. C.: Checchi and Company, 1969), p. 153.
[2]Michael Peters, *International Tourism* (London: Hutchinson, 1969), p. 243.

to the government is small. Many developing countries rely most heavily on import duties for their revenues. The individual income tax is little used or difficult to enforce. Tourism in such an economy brings fewer dollars which remain in the economy, either in the public or private sectors. Heavy import duties on goods used by tourists, directly or indirectly, is one way of increasing the public sector benefit from tourism.

Import duties may be more acceptable since less visible than direct taxes on income. Import duties bring revenue to the government regardless of other benefits from tourism. Campers, for example, may generate little employment but would contribute to the public sector if import duties are exacted on purchases made by the campers for food, beverages, gasoline and the like.

Costs of Public Services

Tourists increase the costs of various public services. These vary widely from an under-developed area, such as the island of Grenada, to a highly sophisticated city like Honolulu. The table, below, is an attempt to allocate various public service costs to a visitor day in Hawaii. The chart is presented only as an example of the kinds of public costs engendered by tourism.

TABLE XII—COST PER VISITOR DAY OF PUBLIC SERVICES RENDERED DIRECTLY TO VISITORS TO HAWAII IN 1968

	Function	State-Local Own General Expenditure (millions of $)	Per Capita Annual Cost	Cost per Visitor Day
(1)	Highways	$38.8	$68.88	$0.189
(2)	Airports	7.4	c	.249
(3)	Police Protection	15.7	21.24	.058
(4)	Fire Protection	8.7	11.77	.032
(5)	Sewerage	13.2	17.86	.049
(6)	Natural Resources	13.1	17.72	.049
(7)	Local Parks and Recreation	16.6	22.45	.062
	Total Variable Cost per Visitor Day			.688

Sources: Table V-3: "Bank of Hawaii," *Hawaii '69* (Aug. 1969), p. 37; Dept. of Planning and Economic Development, *Hawaii Tourism Data Book: 1969* (1969), pp. 13, 14 and 16.
"The Visitor Industry and Hawaii's Economy: A Cost-Benefit Analysis," Mathematica, Princeton, 1970, p. 162.

Public Costs of Immigrant Workers

Some tourist areas already have full employment, or the residents do not choose to work in hotels, restaurants and other tourist-related businesses, as is the case in the Bahamas and the U. S. Virgin Islands. If workers must be brought in to man the tourist facilities, the initial cost to the community is high. Additional public services of all kinds are needed. Such social costs as education are rising much more sharply than general costs. The cost of public education for students over the post war period up to 1968 rose at nearly 7 percent per year, as compared with the wholesale price level which rose at a rate of 1.5 percent a year.[1]

---

[1] "The Visitor Industry and Hawaii's Economy: A Cost-Benefit Analysis," Mathematica, 1970, p. 3.

As the proportion of immigrants in a labor force rises, the benefit-cost ratio for visitors falls sharply. The public service cost of an immigrant family of four was estimated in the Hawaiian study to range from $1557 (no public school children) to $3041 (one child in public school and one going half-time to the University of Hawaii).[1]

Much hotel employment is of a semi-skilled nature, work that requires a minimum of education. In eating and drinking places, about 30 percent of the employees are waiters and waitresses. General help constitutes another 14 percent of the jobs. More highly skilled workers, primarily cooks, make up 15 percent of eating and drinking establishment employment. Bartenders represent another 7 percent. In laundries and gasoline stations, over half the employees are unskilled.[2] Such unskilled and semi-skilled employees are usually paid at the bottom of the wage scale and make the smallest tax contributions.

The costs indicated above are relatively observable; other social costs are not. At what point does crowding of an area become so pronounced as to make the area intolerable for the permanent residents? What is the social cost of attracting an element of people such as the hippies to an area? What about the "cost" of inflation to permanent residents whose incomes are insufficient to maintain a high standard of living? Social costs in terms of psychological tensions produced by tourism were mentioned earlier in the chapter.

Benefit-Cost Ratios Vary According to the Type of Visitor

Numbers of visitors are one thing; "quality," according to particular standards, is something else. An area conceivably could attract large numbers of low-spenders or it may attract only the wealthy few. Other areas attract mixed groups.

Which groups are best from a benefit-cost viewpoint? Will the "bad drive out the good?" Are campers a desirable market? Or is the area of such a nature that all groups can enjoy themselves amicably at certain spots and separate by class in others? In Bermuda, the spring months are given over to thousands of college students; at other times of the year, older and more affluent groups predominate. Formerly, distance from population centers tended to make the more remote tourist areas exclusive. Not many student groups or non-affluent can afford to go to Tahiti, but the non-affluent appear in numbers at many spots formerly considered exclusive. Mass follows class.

Find Best Markets

The tourist planner is interested in identifying the markets which are most beneficial to the tourist area. Social costs and benefits were figured for Hawaii for different groups, breaking them down by region, age and income. Income for the State produced by each group was compared with the social cost for each group. Benefit-cost ratios were figured for various levels of immigrant workers. The higher the percentage of immigrant workers, the higher the social cost. The range in benefit-cost ratios was extreme, varying from 1.39 to 12.02. The table, page 133, shows some of the benefit-cost ratios for various visitor categories to Hawaii.[3] Benefit-cost ratios were computed assuming three levels of immigrant workers (last three columns).

It can be seen from the table that the "big spenders" are from the Northeast, in the age group 31 to 49, with incomes of $15,000 and over. They stayed an average of 10.2 days and spent $81.99 a day. The group benefiting the state the least, in terms of dollars spent, were those from the North Central area, a group who were over 50 years old with incomes of less than $7500 a year.

The authors of the Hawaiian study state, however, that big-spending visitors may not benefit Hawaii the most. High income visitors characteristically stay in luxury hotels which are relatively labor intensive. If more immigrants are needed to man these hotels, the social costs of servicing the immigrants would increase to partially offset the benefits resulting from the high rate of visitor spending.

[1] *Ibid*, p. 170.
[2] *Estimates of Private Employment in Mass. Directly Generated by Tourist Vacation Travel.* Supp. for 1968 and 1969, U. S. Dept. of Labor, April 16, 1969, p. 4.
[3] "The Visitor Industry and Hawaii's Economy: A Cost-Benefit Analysis," Mathematica, 1970, p. 181.

As a general statement, the Hawaiian study found that, for every dollar spent by a tourist, the state and county governments received between 19 and 23 cents and the private sector received nearly a dollar additionally. Almost another dollar was generated for the private sector for each tourist dollar spent. Similar studies of other destination areas have found higher ratios.

The costs and benefits of tourism should be considered for everyone concerned, including the residents of the tourist area. Spain's 85 paradors and other government inns enrich the lives of the middle class Spaniards who vacation in them, as well as bringing cash to the country via the foreign visitor. Social tourism, which makes provision for low cost tourist facilities to be subsidized by a government, is intended largely for the well being of the working class of the nation. Social tourism is a cost to the government but a benefit to its lower income citizens.

Governments Make Choices

Some governments avowedly want nothing but the so-called "quality" market, the affluent usually in the 50-plus age brackets. Other governments prefer a mix of tourists ranging from the low-spending student to the rich. Puerto Rico, for example, has encouraged the development of hotels to appeal to the quality market. Campers are not allowed on any of the island's beaches. As of 1971, the government of the Bahamas had not allowed camping but was considering the possibility of doing so on some of the more sparsely populated islands of the Bahamas. Some governments are not interested in attracting travel clubs like the Club Mediterranee because they believe that such clubs do little to improve the economy of an area. Other governments welcome them.

It is seen in some areas that catering only to the quality market leaves something to be desired. And several governments are now pursuing a policy of developing second line hotels, one step below the deluxe or luxury standard. By doing so, they tap vast new tourist markets.

Some tourist development projects must be viewed as demonstration models that will encourage others to build and develop. Club Mediterranee villages might be considered as pump primers for tourism. The villages are enclaves which leave little income for the local economy. Much of the food used in the clubs is imported and most of the work done by "working members." Even so, the clubs stimulate tourist interest in an area and encourage other tourist development. (As of 1970, Club Mediterranee had 48 resort villages and some 200,000 members).

Residents Have Second Thoughts

While tourism admittedly brings money and stimulates an economy, uncontrolled or too-rapid growth of tourism often results in second thoughts by residents of the area. The Cape Cod Planning and Economic Development Commission recommends a limit on the number of hotels and restaurants on Cape Cod. Route 28 and other parts of the Cape are disastrously clogged during the height of the summer season. Oregon's Department of Economic Development and its governor, Tom McCall, want to keep Oregon for Oregonians. The governor invites people to "come and visit us again and again. But, for heaven's sake, don't come here to live."

The government of Puerto Rico is attempting to disperse tourism from around the downtown San Juan area to other parts of the island. In Hawaii, one faction feels that tourism has already been overdone and has changed the "quality" of life unfavorably for the permanent residents. One wag puts it "There's so much concrete on Waikiki that the island of Oahu is likely to tip over into the ocean."

Economic impact studies, of course, cannot quantify such variables as lifestyle, the effect of tourism on the psychology of the serving personnel, the cost of air pollution and noise. What is exciting and wonderful to one person may be gross and vulgar to another. While one person seeks peace and quiet and a low cost of living, another wants crowds, entertainment and does not mind high costs. The quantifiable benefits of tourism usually (although not always) favor its development, especially for underdeveloped areas. Most tourist experts favor controlled development and, for

TABLE XIII—BENEFIT-COST RATIOS AND BACKGROUND INFORMATION FOR THE 5 "BEST" AND THE 5 "WORST" CATEGORIES OF VISITORS WITH THE AVERAGE BENEFIT-COST RATIOS FOR ALL VISITOR CATEGORIES

Cell No.	Region	Age	Income	Average Length of stay	Number in Party	Total Expenditure per day of stay	Benefit-Cost Ratios Benefits for 20% Costs for =		
							0.2	0.4	0.6
(1) 29	South	under 30	7,501-14,999	8.9	1.1	$51.76	6.98	5.18	4.12
(2) 24	North East	31-49	over 15,000	10.2	1.8	81.99	6.51	4.73	3.72
(3) 33	South	31-49	over 15,000	10.8	1.6	73.55	6.51	4.67	3.65
(4) 31	South	31-49	under 7,500	9.1	1.2	55.16	6.13	4.38	3.39
(5) 15	North Central	31-49	over 15,000	12.5	1.9	78.55	6.09	4.41	3.47
(6) Weighted Averages for All Categories of Visitors									
(7) 13	North Central	31-49	under 7,500	11.1	1.4	35.14	4.21	3.27	2.68
(8) 25	North East	over 50	under 7,500	12.2	1.5	34.31	3.88	3.02	2.47
(9) 7	West	over 50	under 7,500	13.2	1.4	31.42	3.86	2.99	2.44
(10) 1	West	under 30	under 7,500	10.4	1.2	28.19	3.81	2.94	2.38
(11) 16	North Central	over 50	under 7,500	18.8	1.6	27.80	3.14	2.45	2.00

Source: "The Visitor Industry and Hawaii's Economy: A Cost-Benefit Analysis," Mathematica, Princeton, 1970, p. 3.

some destinations, even a leveling off of expansion.

Sociological Implications of Tourism

This chapter has been concerned primarily with the economic implications of tourism. Perhaps of even greater significance to the lifestyle of the people in the tourist area are the sociological implications of having thousands and even millions of travelers visiting an area. The sociological impact has not been well documented, however, and a discussion will not be attempted here.

It is obvious to most visitors to the Bahamas, Jamaica, Puerto Rico and several other Caribbean islands that all is not right between visitor and resident, especially the poor black resident. Travelers complain about indifference or even outright insolence on the part of waiters, taxicab drivers and others.

An incident reported in the *New York Times* illustrates the kind of resentment that tourism has brought in some places.[1] An order for "Our Chef's Specialty, Steaming Hot French Soup, with a crusty crouton" brought cold, canned soup, no crouton. When it was sent back, its replacement—steaming hot—landed on the gentleman's suit. No apologies.   •

Similar stories are common concerning tourist experiences in other parts of the Caribbean. What infuriates the tourist is that he may be spending $50 to $100 a day and expects better treatment.

The Bahamian government, well aware of the hostility and also of the vital importance of tourism to the economy, is trying to overcome these feelings by a "Friendliness Through Understanding" courtesy program. Sidney Poitier, who went to school in the Bahamas and is a friend of Premier Pindling, regularly reads letters from U. S. travelers on the radio, letters which describe instances of rudeness and usually statements that they will not return to the Bahamas. Courtesy contests and bonuses for politeness are being tried.

A somewhat different impact is reported by Dr. Frances Cottington, a psychiatrist who points to evidence that, on the island of Hawaii, tourism has brought ulcers and divorce.[2] The island, formerly almost com-

pletely agricultural, has seen a large growth in luxury hotels and the number of farm wives hiring out as waitresses and maids.

According to the psychiatrist, the farm wives can make up to $1000 a month in salary and tips while their husbands "back on the farm" make only half that. The husbands frequently become suspicious of their wives' improved grooming and dress and accuse them of interest in other men. Presumably such accusations and the stresses in the new way of life cause ulcers in the women. The divorce rate on the island of Hawaii also increased 180 percent between 1963 and 1970, compared with a 52 percent increase for the entire state of Hawaii. Leaving the little grass shack, apparently, introduces problems as well as benefits.

While it is common to castigate tourism as a diluter of culture and a source of tension among the residents of a destination area, such a view must be carefully qualified. Cosmopolitan centers like New York City, London, and countries like Switzerland, Denmark, and France have cultures which seem to suffer little as a consequence of a large influx of tourists. Communities like Monaco, Las Vegas and Miami Beach have tourism as their reason for being. The residents, far from resenting visitors, are most unhappy when they stay away.

It is a truism to say that travel and tourism induce change. The real question becomes one of its acceptance or rejection and by whom. Social change influences different groups at a destination area differently. Certainly where the travel intensity index is high, economic, social and psychological changes take place. Where the visitor and the resident are of a similar economic, educational and cultural level, social change is less. Where there are sharp differences in culture and economics between visitor and resident, more social change can be expected. The assumption is often made that such changes are always unfavorable. The "natives" resent the display of wealth by the tourist, the tourist is rude and unsympathetic to the native, the native becomes highly dissatisfied with his economic status,

[1]*The New York Times,* Travel and Resorts Sec., Aug. 23, 1970, p. 1.
[2]*The New York Times,* Aug. 9, 1970.

and so on. Such is not always the case.

Dr. Philip McKean, an anthropologist who studied the impact of tourism on cultural patterns in Bali, concluded that the culture change brought about by tourism actually strengthened several of the folk traditions.[1] Beginning in 1969, when a jet port was opened in Bali, tens of thousands of tourists arrived to enjoy the island and to be entertained by Balinese temple performances of dancing and religious rites. In 1971, some 65,000 tourists were offered programs of dance music and drama. They purchased handicrafts, paintings, and carvings. They enjoyed the scenery and the accommodations and the people of the island. Interactions between tourists and the Balinese were, for the most part, formalized and well-structured via the staffs of hotels and tour agencies, who essentially served as "culture brokers."

Making Tourists Welcome

In exchange for his money, the tourist was allowed to enter the mythic realm of the Balinese cosmos. He was welcomed as a spectator at well staged aesthetic events. Rather than diluting the island's culture and fostering the development of "psuedo cultural events" which would have destroyed the indigenous tradition or "homogenized" the cultures, the Balinese culture suffered not at all. The people welcomed outside participants in their ritual performances which in the Balinese tradition enhanced their ceremonial value. The income from tourist tickets to such temple performances was welcomed and used to improve both performances and equipment needed for them.

Another anthropologist, James Bodine, studied the changes made as a result of tourism at Taos where the Taos Pueblo Indians and the Angelos, the Whites, have mutually benefited from tourism. A "cultural symbiosis" developed between the White motel and shop operators and the Indians, because of their mutual dependence on the visitor. Both groups understood that if the ethnic distinctiveness of the Indian culture disappeared, so too would the tourist.[2]

Further comments on cultural change appear in a following chapter on Caribbean Tourism. On several of the islands—Jamaica, the Bahamas, Puerto Rico, the U. S. Virgin Islands, Trinidad-Tobago and Curacao—tourism tends to be seen by some leaders as disruptive, intrusive, and generally unfavorable. Much of the discontent hinges on racism and nationalism. Surprisingly little scientific study of the impact of tourism on social change has been done.

The effect of rising nationalism, pride in self and country, has not been studied in any depth. It has been pointed out that nationalism can be favorable or unfavorable to tourism development. New nations often complicate and extend customs clearance rituals. It can be viewed as a ritual, which in effect announces to the visitor, "Look how important we are. Look at how difficult it is for you to get into our country." The "busy" customs inspector takes on greater importance if the visitor is made to queue up, is asked a series of questions (usually of little importance). The official stamping of the passport adds to the ritualistic value.

The effect of political leadership on tourism is always important. In developing nations it may be overriding. The leader can trigger feelings of hostility—or welcome. He can encourage pride in work in a hotel, or resentment. He can exacerbate feelings of inferiority or inspire confidence. He can encourage law and order or permissiveness and hooliganism. He can urge planned growth or himself participate in quick profits from tourism. Political climate of a destination can do much for or against tourism.

In weighing benefits and costs of tourism, the obvious benefits to measure are economic. Perhaps what is more important are the sociological and psychological changes that result from increasing tourism in an area. Ideally, tourism can benefit all concerned—the traveler, the entrepreneur, the worker and the area resident. We shall see that in some places tourism has brought as many problems as benefits.

---

[1]*Tourism, Culture Change, and Culture Conservation in Bali,* paper delivered at the 71st Annual Meeting of the American Anthropological Assn., Toronto, 1972.

[2]James Bodine, "Symbiosis at Taos and the Impact of Tourism on the Pueblo: A Case of Unplanned Economic Development," manuscript read at Symposium of the Central States Anthropological Society, 1964. Quoted by Philip McKean.

Paradise Island, Nassau, Bahamas, a resort complex (largely owned by what was formerly the Mary Carter Paint Co.) is linked to Nassau by a toll bridge. The tourist must pay $2 for the privilege of crossing the bridge and gambling in the Casino.

SOCIAL TOURISM

Social tourism, though not well defined, implies at least a partial subsidy of travel itself or of the destination experience. The most obvious examples of social tourism are the government owned and operated tourist businesses in the communist countries. Tourism is a government monopoly; trains, airlines, destination facilities, are all owned and operated by the state or by agencies of the state including unions. The entire apparatus of tourism may be heavily subsidized for the resident of the country and in many cases for those from abroad.

The government of Yugoslavia, for example, can decree the construction of a number of resort hotels and operate them at a loss with the justification that foreign exchange is needed. A Soviet citizen may be assigned "a vacation" in a Black Sea resort for his health or as a reward. The real cost of the vacation is borne by the state.

In Europe subsidized vacations take a number of forms. Employees may draw upon "holiday" funds set up jointly by a trade union and the employer. In the Netherlands and the United Kingdom, holiday bonuses may be provided by an employer. In Belgium employers sometimes grant cash benefits for travel. In New Zealand state employees receive price reductions in hotels.

Tax benefits are granted some nonprofit associations for tourism ventures, and the state gives assistance in the form of equipment for camps and for youth organizations. A special fund has been established by the Danish government to subsidize the development of holiday centers. The Norwegian government makes interest free loans at a reduced rate for the same purpose.[1]

In the U. S., social tourism has existed in fact, if not in name, for some time. Church camps, Y.M.C.A. and Y.W.C.A. camps, Boy Scout camps, and various fresh-air camps would have to be included under the label of social tourism if defined as subsidized vacationing. Far more important, however, is the social tourism engaged in by Federal and state governments.

Social tourism, as usually defined, implies that a government or other organization in some way subsidizes a vacation or a vacation facility for someone, usually the working class. In the U. S., many of the lodging facilities built in state parks since 1965 have been first class and the rates charged are such that they are not apt to be used by a low income family or individual—social tourism with a twist. With room rates at $20 or higher and with first-class hotel facilities, the new tourism might be called social tourism for the middle class. Nevertheless it is subsidized tourism. Since 1965 this type of tourism has flourished remarkably. It is the purpose here to discuss its growth and some of the implications.

Tourism as seen in the National Parks and U. S. Forests is probably the most obvious example of subsidized tourism in the U. S. The National Park Service has contracted with more than 250 concessionaires to operate facilities within the parks. About 175 of the concessionaires have invested something like $104 million in facilities which they operate. The U. S. Dept. of the Interior has invested about $10 million in facilities and supports the concession operations with utilities, roads, and trails.[2] The U. S. Forest Service has 369 lodges under permit which are owned privately plus 16 owned by the Forest Service.[3]

The Kentucky State Park Resorts

Large as the tourist facilities are in Federal parks and forests, the spectacular growth of subsidized tourism has taken place within the states and within a brief span of time. Funded either by bond issue or massive support by the Federal government, several states have moved into the resort business in a big way. Some of the resort facilities recently built are spectacularly beautiful and highly successful economically.

The State of Kentucky has led the way in constructing lodge and restaurant facilities which compete with the best of private enterprise. According to C. F. Smith, Jr.

[1]Robert W. McIntosh, *Tourism: Principles, Practices, Philosophies* (Columbus: Grid, Inc., 1972), p. 49.
[2]Telephone conversation with Andrew Wolfe, Chief, Concessions Management, National Park Service, Washington, D. C.
[3]Telephone conversation with Mel Loveridge, U. S. Forest Service, Washington, D. C.

TABLE XIV—KENTUCKY STATE PARKS

FACILITIES GUIDE—KENTUCKY STATE PARKS AND SHRINES
DEPARTMENT OF PARKS, COMMONWEALTH OF KENTUCKY

FULL OFFICIAL NAME / MAJOR RESORT PARKS	LOCATION	YEAR OPENED	PARK ACREAGE	LAKE ACREAGE	VISITORS 1970 (THOUSANDS)	LODGE ROOMS	TWO BEDROOM SUITES	OPEN YEAR AROUND	OPENING DATES—LODGE	CLOSING DATES—LODGE	DINING ROOM SEATING CAPACITY	COFFEE SHOP	GIFT SHOP	HANDCRAFT SHOPS	EFFICIENCY COTTAGES	1 BEDROOM AND LIVING ROOM COTTAGES	2 BEDROOM AND LIVING ROOM COTTAGES
BARREN RIVER LAKE STATE RESORT PARK	BARREN	1967	1,500	10,000 CE	533	51	X				250	X	X				
BUCKHORN LAKE STATE RESORT PARK	PERRY	1962	750	1,200 CE	351	24			5/1	10/31	200		X				
CARTER CAVE STATE RESORT PARK	CARTER	1952	1,000	36 S	823	28	X				200		X			8	2
CUMBERLAND FALLS STATE RESORT PARK	WHITLEY	1931	1,720		2,263	60	X				212	X	X		11	6	10
GENERAL BUTLER STATE RESORT PARK	CARROLL	1931	809	30 S	1,042	33	X				170		X		12	3	
GREENBO LAKE STATE RESORT PARK	GREENUP	1960	3,330	225 S	244	36	X				150		X				
JENNY WILEY STATE RESORT PARK	FLOYD	1962	1,700	1,150 CE	1,486	48	X				225		X			8	10
KENLAKE STATE RESORT PARK	MARSHALL	1948	1,800	128,807 TVA	1,084	56			4/1	10/31	156		X		9	10	8
KENTUCKY DAM VILLAGE STATE RESORT PARK	MARSHALL	1948	1,200	128,807 TVA	6,138	95	X				250	X	X	X	10		27
LAKE BARKLEY STATE RESORT PARK	TRIGG	1967	3,600	57,920 CE	854	120	4	X			350	X	X				
LAKE CUMBERLAND STATE RESORT PARK	RUSSELL	1954	3,000	50,250 CE	470	60	X				160		X			6	14
NATURAL BRIDGE STATE RESORT PARK	POWELL	1933	1,500	50 S	885	35	X				150		X	X	6	4	
PENNYRILE FOREST STATE RESORT PARK	CHRISTIAN	1937	435	55 S	497	24			5/1	9/30	180				3	3	9
PINE MOUNTAIN STATE RESORT PARK	BELL	1926	2,500	35 S	392	30			5/1	10/31	134		X	X	7	3	10
ROUGH RIVER DAM STATE RESORT PARK	GRAYSON	1962	377	4,860 CE	1,185	40			4/1	10/31	200						15

(until recently executive assistant for the Department of Parks of the Commonwealth of Kentucky), the total investment by the state in 15 lodge structures is on the order of $20 million. This amount does not include the cost of support facilities or the value of the land. It is interesting to note that about two-thirds of the funding for these resorts has been received from the Bureau of Outdoor Recreation of the U. S. Dept. of the Interior and from the Economic Development Administration of the U. S. Dept. of Commerce.[1]

The lodge structures are indeed first class. The newest, Lake Barkley Lodge, designed by Edward Durell Stone, was built at a cost of approximately $50,000 per room (total cost of building divided by number of rooms). Most of the lodges were built at a cost of $12,000 to $15,000 per unit. (Pictures of facilities on pp. 146-49.)

It must be emphasized that the Kentucky Resort Parks represent a new concept for state parks; they are total resorts which include a range of facilities: first-class lodges (hotels), beaches, pools and tennis courts. Two of the resorts have 18-hole golf courses, six include 9-hole courses, others 3-hole and miniature courses. Most have convention rooms. All but two have boat docks. Two have chair lifts. Besides the lodges, all but one has camping spaces, one for 200 tents. One has a landing strip for small planes. Others have riding stables.

Some of the lakes in the parks are enormous. Two parks are located at Marshall, a lake of 128,807 acres. Two others have park areas of 3600 acres. (See a list of major resort parks and their facilities above.)

Apparently the resort park concept has been a tremendous success from the viewpoint of stimulating statewide tourism and travel. Occupancy rates range from close

[1]Telephone conversation with C. F. Smith, Director of Publicity and Public Relations, Dept. of Parks, Frankfort, Ky., Dec. 23, 1971.

3 BEDROOM AND LIVING ROOM COTTAGES	LODGE COTTAGES	EXECUTIVE COTTAGE 2 BEDROOM	EXECUTIVE COTTAGE 3 BEDROOM	BATHHOUSE	BEACH	COMMUNITY POOL	LODGE POOL	PAR 3 GOLF COURSE	9 HOLE REGULATION GOLF COURSE	18 HOLE REGULATION GOLF COURSE	MINIATURE GOLF	HORSEBACK RIDING	SUPERVISED RECREATION*	PLAYGROUND	HIKING TRAILS	TENNIS	SHUFFLEBOARD	AIRSTRIP	SHRINE OR MUSEUM	AMPHITHEATER SEATING CAPACITY	FISHING	CAMPING SPACES	CENTRAL SERVICE BUILDING IN CAMP AREAS	GROUP CAMPING	PICNIC SHELTER WITH RESTROOM	PICNIC SHELTER WITHOUT RESTROOM	GROCERY	BOAT DOCK	OPEN SLIPS	COVERED SLIPS	PADDLE BOATS	BOAT LAUNCHES	CHAIR LIFT	MEETING ROOMS SEATING CAPACITY	RECREATION ROOMS SEATING CAPACITY	CONCESSION STANDS
		12		X	X			X	X				X	XX	X				X		X	111	2		1			X	50	40			X	350	125	
				X	X								X	X	X						X	26				1		X	30				X			
				X	X				X				X	XX	X	X			X		X	82	1		1	1		X			X			260		X
	20			X			X	X					X	XX	X	X			X		X	73	2		1		X							100	40	
3				X	X		X		X			X	X	XX	X	X	X		X		X	154	3	X	1		X	X			X			100	150	X
				X	X		X						X	XX	X	X			X		X	74	1		1		X	X	65				X	150	150	
				X			X	X	X				X	XX	X	X			X	900	X				1	2		X2	199	40		X	X	100	250	X
1				X	X		X		X				X	X	X	X	X	X		2000	X	120	1		1			X	70	140			X	200	190	X
13		20		X	X		X			X	X2		X	XX	X	X	X	X	X		X	200	4		4		X	X2	93	138			X	175	400	X
		9		X	2		X				X		X	XX	X	X	X	X			X	80			1			X	46	80			X	400		
				X			X	X	X				X	XX	X	X	X				X	145	2				X	X	50	40			X	80	100	X
				X	X		X		X				X	XX	X	X	X				X	77	2		1	1	X	X				X	X	100		X
				X	X		X		X			X	X	X	X	X			X		X	65	1			2	X	X			X	X				X
				X			X				X	X	X	XX	X		X			4000	X	32			1	1									250	
				X	X		X				X	X	X	X	X	X	X	X	X		X	50	1			1		X	38	18			X	225		X

to 100 percent in the summer to 45 percent in the winter in the 10 resort parks that are open year around. Rates range from $14 single to $35 double.

Another interesting aspect of the development of the Kentucky resort parks is that a number of them have been built on land leased for 99 years at no rental cost to the state by the U. S. Army Corps of Engineers. The Engineers have built a number of reservoirs and, as a part of the reservoir development, acquired additional land for recreation purposes (land for some of the parks has been donated by individuals). Water-oriented sports are the biggest tourist attraction throughout the Kentucky parks system. Because of the many man-made lakes, Kentucky has more navigable and fishable water than any other state in the Union, except Alaska.

The larger resort parks pay their way, according to Mr. Smith. The smaller state parks were developed to seed tourism in a particular area, a function which has demonstrated its efficacy in the fact that numerous other tourist facilities have been built soon after the seeding operation opened. The Kentucky Parks have generated an impressive amount of taxes for the state.

A 1970 survey of travel in Kentucky reported that some $43 million was received by the Commonwealth of Kentucky in state taxes from tourist expenditures. Travel and tourism ranks number two as an income producer for the state. Table XVI, page 140, shows the spectacular growth of tourism and the tax return to the government.

A breakdown of the taxes received from the resort parks has not been made but "a good part of the $43 million collected in sales tax from out of state visitors to Kentucky comes from tourists using the resort parks."[1]

[1] Dr. Lewis C. Copeland, *1970 Survey of Travel in Kentucky,* Dept. of Statistics, College of Business, University of Tennessee.

TABLE XV–KENTUCKY: GROWTH IN TOURISM AND TAX BENEFITS FROM TOURISM, 1960-1970[1]

(Amounts in Millions)

	1960	1965	1966	1967	1968	1969	1970
Contribution of Out-of-State Tourists to: Kentucky State Government Revenue	$ 12	$ 22	$ 24	$ 26	$ 33	$ 38	$ 43
Expenditures by Out-of-State Travelers: Total Expenditures	187	260	295	316	345	370	394
Expenditures for Vacation and Recreational Travel	132	182	205	220	240	260	278
Total Expenditures for All In-State Travel by both Kentuckians and Out-of-State Visitors	280	378	425	440	483	510	542

TABLE XVI– TOTAL KENTUCKY STATE PARK[1] VISITATION

(No. of Visitor Days)

1962	8,532,075
1963	11,083,087
1964	14,243,691
1965	15,449,993
1966	16,189,321
1967	18,750,969
1968	19,404,082
1969	20,225,843
1970	23,746,795
1971 (est.)	25,000,000

In Kentucky the resort parks are operated by the state. The resort parks are promoted and advertised by a state agency, The Public Information Agency. Reservations are made in the state capitol for accommodations in the state parks. Free use of a WATS line to the reservation center in Frankfort is made available to residents of adjoining states. Promotion of the parks is done through publicity releases, folders distributed through travel agents, and highway information booths. Package plans—lodging, entertainment and all meals—have been promoted. (Table III above notes impressive growth in visitor days spent in Kentucky's state parks.)

The Kentucky State Park system represents a cooperative effort among several state agencies, among them being the Department of Highways, Public Information, Natural Resources, Health, Public Safety, Commerce, Aeronautics, Finance and Fish and Wildlife.

None of the lodges in Kentucky's parks is concessioned. Salaries for managers are surprisingly low, about $9000 a year. The larger resort parks employ full-time recreation directors.

The Ohio State Park Experience

Ohio, perhaps observing the success of the Kentucky Resort Park operation, has forged ahead building several large resorts with lodges. The Army Corps of Engineers has helped Ohio practically double its park system during the past five years. The Engineers have purchased land, dammed rivers, and turned the land over to the state.

Salt Fork State Park will have a lodge with 148 guest rooms, a dining room with a capacity of 300, indoor and outdoor pools, two sauna baths, meeting rooms, barber and beauty shops, and a coffee shop. There will also be 54 cabins with parking space for 150 cars and 212 camp sites. Another large lodging complex at Portsmouth State Park will include a $2 million lodge and motel and a $500,000 complex with 25 cabins.

All of the major lodges are open year around; occupancy runs 90 to 95 percent in the summer, about 40 percent during the four to five winter months.

Four of the lodges in Ohio state parks are operated by Ohio Inns, a concessionaire. The new political administration in office would like to operate them with state employees so as to better control prices, especially food and beverage prices about which there have been many complaints. The lodges in several of the park facilities have been made possible by issuing revenue bonds. Curiously, the state has not taken advantage of funds available from the Federal sources.

Facilities in the state parks, however, are more likely to be used by Ohioans rather than by visitors to the state.[2]

[1]Dr. Lewis C. Copeland, "Travel Survey in Kentucky," Dept. of Public Information, Commonwealth of Kentucky, 1971.
[2]Conversation with a spokesman for the Ohio Department of Natural Resources, Division of Parks and Recreation, Columbus.

The West Virginia Park Experience

West Virginia is another eastern state well known for its park facilities. The Sports Foundation of America, in February 1971, presented the State Parks Division with an award for being the second best park system in the U. S. The state now has nine lodges, and all but one have 55 rooms or less. The Pipestem Resort State Park features two lodges with a total of 140 rooms. It also has an aerial tramway, an 18-hole golf course and a nine-hole par-3 course. In addition, there is an Olympic size swimming pool and tennis courts. Convention and meeting facilities accommodate up to 500 people.

The lodge sits in a 4000 acre park. Its total cost was $13 million.

The Department of Natural Resources in West Virginia began planning for the park development in 1963. It was aided in its feasibility studies by grants from the Economic Development Administration's predecessor, the Area Redevelopment Administration. That agency made a $7 million grant and $16 million was made available in loans. Two other parks were funded later by the same agency. Since that time the EDA has provided further grants of about $4 million to finish Pipestem and other facilities.

The Oklahoma Experience

Oklahoma has one of the most successful state-operated lodge systems, dating back to the early 1930s. With a total of 995 rental units (625 lodges, 368 cottages), the state has invested approximately $12 million in accommodation facilities. The lodge properties are operated strictly on income. Original funding came from a bond issue of $7 million which was paid off out of income 18 months ahead of schedule.[1] The largest property has 200 lodge units with 22 cottage units; the smallest has a lodge with 20 units and 14 cottage units.

Arrowhead Lodge is one of the more spectacular properties in this country, complete with soaring lobby, "tree house," cabins raised from the ground on stilts, and a lounge which has an underwater view of the swimming pool. The resort has a 9-hole golf course and can accommodate groups as large as 400.

Fountainhead Lodge with 180 rooms (plus 22 cottages) is located in a 3400 acre park, adjacent to Lake Eufaula which covers over 100,000 acres. The seven Oklahoma State Lodges are listed below:

1. Quartz Mountain Lodge: 40 rooms, 2 youth camps
2. Roman Nose Lodge: 20 rooms, kitchen equipped cottages, 2 youth camps
3. Lake Murray Lodge: 54 rooms, 86 cottages, 4 youth camps
4. Texoma Lodge: 103 rooms, 68 cottages
5. Arrowhead Lodge: 104 rooms, 100 cottages
6. Fountainhead Lodge: 180 rooms, 22 cottages
7. Western Hills Lodge: 102 rooms, 62 cottages and a youth camp.

A unique feature of the Oklahoma State Lodge system is that four of the units provide lighted air strips for private planes.

California Experience

In California, the state has taken a different tack in the development of lodge and other tourist facilities within the state parks. The private sector has been encouraged to build and operate facilities within the parks. Encouragement is given by the granting of long term leases and an abatement of rent in lieu of real property improvements. Lodges presently exist at Asilomar Conference Grounds in Pacific Grove; Pfeiffer Big Sur State Park, Big Sur, and Olympic Village in Olympic Valley. Cash rentals paid to the state in the fiscal year 1969/1970 came to more than $700,000.

Concessionaire investments in real property improvements which become State Property reached $6,293,000.[2] At Point Mugu, concessionaire investment in facilities is expected to exceed $9 million and Lake Perris will probably involve even larger concessionaire investments.[3] Total investment in facilities by concessionaires, says a state

[1]Letter from John C. Reeves, Assistant Director of Oklahoma Lodges, Oklahoma Industrial Development and Park Department, Oklahoma City, Apr. 7, 1972.
[2]*Concessions in the California State Park System, 1969-70, fiscal year,* Dept. of Parks and Recreation, Sacramento, Ca., 1971, p. 3.
[3]*Ibid*, p. V.

publication, may approach $40 million during the next 10 years.

Role of the U. S. Army Corps of Engineers

As previously mentioned, the U. S. Army Corps of Engineers has played a prominent part in the expansion of state parks throughout the U. S., especially during the last few years.   Funds for these developments are available under the Federal Water Project Recreation Act of 1965 (PL-89-72). Under the terms of this Act, a non-Federal agency must agree to assume one-half of the separable costs of recreation development and all costs of operating, maintenance and replacement, and administer the project lands and waters for recreation and fish and wildlife purposes.[1]

The Secretary of the Army is authorized to grant leases of project lands, including structures or facilities thereon, to non-Federal governmental bodies without charge. Leases to non-profit organizations for park or recreational purposes may be granted at reduced or nominal consideration.[2]

Many of the Engineer projects were developed primarily for the purpose of flood control. Some have also been developed for low-flow augmentation, recreation and local protection (flood control for a particular community).

Role of the Economic Development Administration

Another important government agency involved in funding the state resort parks has been the Economic Development Administration.   Under the Public Works and Economic Development Act of 1965, EDA is authorized to provide financial assistance to areas of high unemployment (interpreted to be those with an unemployment rate of 6 percent or greater):

Public Works Grant & Loan Assistance may be extended to Tourism or Recreational Projects if it is shown that such a project directly contributes to the fundamental growth of tourism in an area where tourism was previously unimportant or that there is a lack of sufficient private capital to overcome a shortage of accommodations in an area already dependent on tourism.

According to the Annual Report, Fiscal 1971, of the Economic Development Administration, "Jobs for America," $10.320 million was made available in loans for hotels and motels in the period 1966-71. These covered nine projects.   Under the terms of the "obligated business loan projects," the local investor must put up 35 percent of the money. EDA will advance 50 percent of the money. A local development non-profit organization puts up 5 percent, and the applicant, 10 percent. As of February 1972, these loans were being made at a 5¾ percent interest rate.   Public works projects for tourism, says the same publication, involve $69.707 million in Federal government money, covering 117 projects. These public works grants and loans were made to states and municipalities for such items as convention centers and marinas during the period 1966-71.

The same Public Works Development Act authorizes the establishment of economic development commissions with members from a common region.   The New England Regional Commission, as an example, has members from each New England state. The commissions are co-chaired, one chairman from the Federal government, the other elected by the state members.

Regional commissioners map and carry out long-range economic development plans. They can assist outdoor recreation projects with supplemental grants up to 80 percent of the total project cost.

Indian Reservations

Tourism-Recreation projects on Indian reservations have been funded by EDA in excess of $35 million.   Expenditures have been made for marinas, docks, trailer parks, parks, lakes, gas stations, campgrounds and arts and crafts centers.   Fifteen motels or lodges have been built on Indian land, ranging in size from 20 units to 120 units, as shown in Table XVII on facing page.

Another Federal agency which has been much involved in the development of state resort parks is the Bureau of Outdoor Rec-

---

[1]Federal Assistance in Outdoor Recreation, Publication No. 1, rev. 1970 (Washington, D. C.: Supt. of Documents).
[2]Ibid, p. 44.

TABLE XVII—TOURISM AND RECREATION PROJECTS ON INDIAN RESERVATIONS FUNDED BY THE ECONOMIC DEVELOPMENT ADMINISTRATION

State	Reservation	Project Description	Total Project Cost	Completion Date	EDA Input
Arizona	Fort Apache	106-unit motel, ski lodge and facilities and trailer park	$3,221,000	7-1-72	$1,588,000 96,000 1,116,000
Arizona	Hopi	20-unit motel, restaurant, arts and crafts	977,000	3-1-71	582,000 59,000 129,600
Colorado	Southern Ute	40-unit motel, restaurant, arts and crafts	695,000	2-1-72	556,000
Idaho	Nez Perce	50-unit motel, museum, restaurant, trading post	1,532,000 838,000	2-1-73 2-1-73	1,154,000 378,000
Montana	Blackfeet	55-unit lodge, 40-unit tepee village, 100-unit campground, 180-seat restaurant, marina and swimming pool	1,794,000	5-1-73 5-1-73	488,000 1,306,000
Montana	Crow	60-unit lodge, restaurant, grandstand	887,500	5-15-71 11-1-71	770,000 32,750 682,400
Montana	Fort Peck	50-unit motel, craft center, museum	1,054,000	12-1-72 12-1-72	862,000 192,000
New Mexico	Jicarilla	20-room lodge, trailer park, game park (Stone Lake)	1,568,700	8-15-72	968,000 358,960
New Mexico	Mescalero	Dam and lake—Phase I; 140-room hotel, 18-hole golf course, marina, swimming pool—Phase II	4,282,000 3,073,000	6-73 6-73 *	2,297,600 1,088,000 897,000
N. Dakota	Ft. Berthold	40-unit motel, restaurant, marina, trailer park	1,607,100	3-72 3-72 3-72 3-72	21,000 214,000 887,420 409,000 46,550
N. Dakota	Standing Rock	46-unit lodge, marina, restaurant	1,509,400	3-1-73 3-1-73 3-1-73	1,219,000 50,000 300,000
Oregon	Warm Springs	110-unit motel, restaurant, golf course	5,159,500	3-1-72 3-1-72 3-1-72	3,080,000 1,220,000 568,000
S. Dakota	Crow Creek	Motel, restaurant, marina	1,109,500	3-4-72	164,000 723,600
Utah	Uintah Ouray	Motel, restaurant, arts and crafts, marina, cultural center	1,490,000	7-5-71 7-5-71	18,780 16,294

*Completion date not determined—Project not put out to bid.

reation, U. S. Dept. of the Interior. The Bureau was established in 1962: "The Bureau maintains liaison with state and local governments, Federal agencies, and a private sector to promote maximum coordinated effort in accessing needs and providing increased outdoor recreation opportunities."[1]

Role of the Bureau of Outdoor Recreation, U. S. Dept. of Interior

Under the terms of the Land and Water Conservation Fund Act of 1965, grants have been made to states and, through states, to their political subdivisions, for planning, acquisition, and the development of outdoor recreation areas and facilities. Planning grants and technical assistance are also available.

Present policy of the Bureau is not to fund lodges since they are classified as "elaborate facilities." Facilities supporting a lodge, however, can be funded, usually on a 50-50 basis with state support. Grants are available for campgrounds, picnic grounds, swimming pools and the like. Some 8000 projects have been approved involving $400 million of Federal money.

The construction of resort parks by states represents an aspect of social tourism which has become a significant part of tourism in the U. S. It indicates that government priorities are shifting to include greater concern for and the encouragement of favorable vacationing experiences for the American people.

To say "government concern" may be misleading in that, theoretically at least, the voters influence government priorities. To be more precise, Congress and several of the state legislatures have enacted legislation which either provides money for state parks through government agencies or permits the state to raise money by means of bond issues. In the last analysis, these acts have the effect of permitting large segments of the U. S. population to enjoy first-class accommodations and other facilities at resort parks operated by the states or, by concessionaires in state parks.

Several factors permit rates which are less than would be charged by private entrepreneurs. Aside from the outright grants made by the Federal government and the development of lakes and roads by the U. S. Army Corps of Engineers, the cost of land is zero. The cost of money raised by state bond issues is less than the cost of money to a private enterprise. This constitutes social tourism or subsidized tourism.

Is social tourism desirable? The answer, of course, depends upon one's political philosophy. Can we not say, however, that swimming in a beautiful lake, tramping through a well-kept forest, staying at an attractive lodge or eating in a fine restaurant overlooking natural beauty is desirable and should be encouraged by the government? Are not such experiences helpful and "recreational?"

Wilderness advocates might object to the building of resort parks believing that any intrusion on nature is desecration. Some "forever wilders" would not even allow access to wilderness areas by hikers or for the removal of fallen timber. Such an argument is hard to swallow when such areas can be used by thousands of people enjoyably and healthfully. The alternative is to crowd people into urban areas, saving the wilderness areas for a few back-packers or for "the future." Wilderness advocates can be seen as an elitist group determined to retain for themselves an environment which they alone prize and use to the exclusion of many times their numbers who may enjoy a different environment.

Certainly, with increased population, the day may come when the state parks are as crowded as some of the Federal parks and steps will have to be taken to ration their use and to control the environment to avoid several kinds of pollution. It may be necessary to exclude automobiles from sections of such parks as is being done in some of the Federal parks. It may be necessary to spread parks throughout a state to avoid over-aggregating people. Such comments would suggest the need for planning and building of a number of such parks spread throughout the U. S. but particularly near population centers.

Most of the Federal parks are located in the western states, removed from the great population centers of the east. They represent social tourism but social tourism for those who can afford to travel considerable distances. State resort parks can make recreational experiences available to vast new numbers of people, hopefully at prices which they can afford. For the really poor, the facilities and accommodations in such state parks could be made available at reduced rates or at no charge at all.

Philosophically speaking, individuals constantly strive for preferment no matter what level of society they are in. Because of differences in native capacity and circumstances, some individuals and their families achieve more benefits from society than others. Among those preferred benefits have been the wherewithal to travel, the ownership of sites of natural beauty and the time to enjoy nature. Some get, others don't. Some get a great deal. Social tourism is an attempt to redress the disparities in distribution of goods, making it possible for large segments of the society to enjoy many of the pleasures hitherto had by a few. State forests presumably are owned by the people as a whole. Why should they not be "facilitated" to be enjoyed by all or most of the people?

Conference facilities of the Illinois Beach State Park.
Several states have entered the tourist business directly by constructing lodges, dining rooms and other tourist facilities which are maintained and operated by the state.

The Giant City Lodge, Restaurant and Cabins. Like the facilities at Illinois Beach State Park this facility is operated by the Department of Conservation of the State of Illinois.

Yosemite Lodge, at the foot of Yosemite Falls, is operated by The Yosemite Park and Curry Co. The company also operates hotels, cottages and cabins within the park. Other services offered in this popular national park are food service, transportation, souvenirs, American Indian arts and crafts, general supplies, groceries, horse rentals, garages and health services.

Aerial view of Lake Barkley Lodge in Kentucky, built at a cost of $5.6 million in 1967. The Lodge has 124 guest rooms in the main structure, dining room seating 550, a meeting room for 400, and nine two-bedroom "executive" cottages. The State of Kentucky operates the "resort parks" as if they were private resorts, offering first class accommodations, restaurants, gift shops and a variety of recreational facilities. This is "social tourism" on a high level.

Vaulted end of Barkley Lodge, called the largest wooden structure built since 1917. The steps lead to the swimming pool piazza and the boat dock beyond.

The lofty, beamed ceiling dining room at Barkley Lodge, Ky. has a magnificent view of the 57,920-acre Lake Barkley.

Fountainhead Lodge in Oklahoma is located on the 100,000-acre Lake Eufaula. The resort has 180 rooms in the main lodge and 22 cottages. As the climate is suitable to year around recreation, visitors are attracted from neighboring states and from all over the North Central region for water sports, fishing, hunting and golf. The park has its own landing strip for private planes.

Ohio's new Salt Fork State Lodge will have 142 guest rooms, a dining room seating 300, a coffee shop, a meeting room, and 54 deluxe cabins.

Hueston Woods Lodge is another facility in the Ohio state park system. Revenue bonds have been used to finance several of the lodges in the system. No federal funds have been used.

INDIAN RESERVATIONS PROMOTE TOURISM

Indian tribes have turned to tourism as an avenue to provide income and employment for their members. Those living on reservations find that rugged areas with natural scenic beauty are a magnet for tourists, especially when overnight accommodations and sports facilities can be added. Moreover, tourists are fascinated with Indian lore and rituals, a boost to maintaining Indian culture, and they buy the craft work made by older members of the tribes.

The Mescaleros' Tourism Triad

By turning their New Mexico hunting ground into a 100,000-acre recreation area for the white man, the Mescalero Apaches are making tourism a major industry that will bring economic growth and year around job stability to their tribe. This is the lead of an article published in the September 4 issue of *Commerce Today*, a biweekly magazine of the U. S. Dept. of Commerce.

The article, prepared by the Economic Development Administration, goes on to say that the "proud descendants of Geronimo and Cochise have turned their sacred mountain into a ski resort. The Sierra Blanca Ski Area in northwestern New Mexico was started six years ago through tribal planning and investment. Each year for the past five years, the ski facility's revenue has increased by about 30 percent, a record not shared by other Rocky Mountain ski operations."

The success of the Mescaleros in developing their own tourism resources has encouraged the Economic Development Administration to designate them as one of the first tribes to be given assistance under the Selected Reservations Program.

At the Sierra Blanca Ski Area, the Mescaleros will build their first resort complex, the first of three to be developed. If Ciengita, the new resort's name, is as successful as hoped, the next projects will include the Rinconada Dude Ranch and a hunting lodge. The EDA has financed $4,282,600 of the cost for the $6 million Ciengita complex, which is scheduled to be completed in June, 1973. The Ciengita will include a 100-acre lake, a 140-room resort hotel with meeting facilities which will cost $4 million, and an 18-hole golf course. The project also involves such public works as access roads, water and sewage systems, and recreation areas around the lake and hotel.

From this first resort complex, the Mescaleros hope to expand tourism to their other two projects in the planning stage. The concept is that visitors attracted to Ciengita will go from there to visit the dude ranch and hunting lodge. The case for tourism development is attested by the rise in median family incomes at Sierra Blanca Ski Area, which doubled between 1967 and 1970 and almost wiped out unemployment in the area. For the Mescaleros, however, the average family income is only $1000 per family annually, a figure which the tribe hopes to upgrade substantially through its own members' efforts.

The EDA investment was made primarily to create year around jobs and economic stability for the Indians. Tourism as a means of earning a livelihood was first considered by the Mescaleros nearly ten years ago. As there is a population of about 9 million within traveling distance of their reservation, tourism may well become one of the solutions for the tribe. The idea is for the Indians to encourage non-Indians to come and enjoy their reservation on their (the Indians') terms. In addition to skiing, the attractions include hunting, fishing and other outdoor sports along with the area's scenic beauty and the tribal culture and festivities of the Mescaleros.

Tourism on Other Indian Reservations

Among the other EDA investments in Indian tourism are those which are described in the following paragraphs:

ALABAMA-COUSHATTA. In the Big Thicket of Southeast Texas, the Indians of the Alabama-Coushatta Reservation have re-created examples of their ancient culture in the development of a tourism complex. A museum reflecting the culture and heritage of the two related tribes and the natural beauty of the area has been constructed.

The Na-Ski-La Dancers give daily performances in the summer on the authentic dance square. A restaurant offers authentic Indian food and the nearby trading post sells locally made arts and crafts. Major attractions are the Big Thicket Tour in four-wheel drive vehicles and rides on the "Indian Chief" Railroad. Construction of a dam resulted in a 30-acre lake. Camping, trailer and picnic sites have been developed. Future plans include an amphitheatre and a museum.

An estimated 125,000 tourists visit the reservation annually. The existing program provides nearly 150 part-time and seasonal jobs to tribal members. Planned new construction will enable the tribe to operate year around, developing full-time job opportunities. EDA has assisted in development of this complex by providing $495,000 in public works funds.

SOUTHERN UTE. In Scenic Southwestern Colorado, the Southern Ute Indian Reservation contains some of the finest hunting and fishing in the state. To attract tourists to their reservation, tribal leaders decided to construct a complex outside the town of Ignacio. It includes a motel, restaurant, convention center, arts and crafts center with gift shop and museum.

Local Indian craftsmen work in the center and their products are sold in the gift shop. Ute history can be traced in the museum and authentic Indian dances are performed throughout the summer. The tribe has hired a manager with experience in this field and 38 tribal members are employed in the complex. EDA provided $550,000 toward the cost of this project.

CROW. With an economic base largely founded on agriculture, the Crow Tribe is seeking to diversify its economy by entering into the tourism field. The Custer Battlefield National Monument, site of Custer's famous "Last Stand," is on the Crow Reservation and draws over 300,000 tourists annually.

Each July, the Crow Tribe re-enacts the battle as a tourist attraction. In anticipation of developing a major tourism complex, the tribe's plans include construction of a lodge, restaurant, teepee village, Heritage Village, concessions, grandstand and parking areas. EDA provided $1.450 million toward this project. Although some of the construction is not completed, the tribe operates the motel and restaurant under temporary management. An estimated 50 to 70 tribal members will be employed at the complex.

ISLETA. Location of the Isleta Pueblo Reservation in New Mexico on Interstate 25—just south of Albuquerque and adjacent to the Rio Grande—led tribal leaders to begin developing major tourism facilities on their reservation. Plans call for a motel, restaurant, golf course, and trailer camping and picnic facility. The first phase involved construction of fish ponds with adjoining picnic and camping facilities, and a concession building.

EDA put $350,000 into this project which has proved so successful that the Tribe is planning major expansion. The project manager and seven employees are all tribal members.

HOPI. Around 1275 A. D., various clans of Indians began an exodus to the spiritual center of the Hopi ancestral homeland. Old Oraibi, already established and today believed to be the oldest continuously inhabited community in the United States, became the busy scene of the "Gathering of the Clans," according to Oraibi tradition. Today, there are 12 villages in unique geographic settings, each displaying the Hopi culture and friendliness.

To accommodate the thousands of visitors to the Hopi Reservation, the tribal leaders built a "Cultural Center" with the assistance of EDA which provided $770,000 toward the total cost. Facilities included a motel, restaurant, craft shops and museum. The motel and restaurant have been leased by a family experienced in this field, using all-Indian employees. Meanwhile, the craft shops are operated by individual tribal members while the tribe manages the museum.

An example of the way Portugal encourages tourism is the interior court of the Pousada de Obidos. The government-owned inn is a restored convent. Room and meal rates are low.

The Pousada da Ria, near Aveiro, Portugal was built by the national government and leased to a private operator. Rates and services are government controlled.

TOURIST DESTINATION DEVELOPMENT

Large scale land developments require comprehensive planning by a number of experts; it is not unusual for 50 to 100 people to be involved in the master plan. The costs may range from $100,000 to $300,000, for such a plan and the graphic presentation prepared for the project. The master plan usually includes something of the history of the land holdings involved and a description of the ownership and of the zoning regulations which apply.

A statement is also included which covers the original cost of the land, the development cost, cash flow which is expected year by year and the final capital gains expected from the entire project. A market and feasibility study is done separately but parts of the study are abstracted to the master plan. Drawings, usually in color, include the entire area in perspective; drawings of each of the amenities, such as the hotel, golf course and beach club, are also included. Most projects call for multiple use of the land—resorts, apartments, condominiums, vacation estates (free standing residences) and worker housing.

Construction costs per square foot, per hotel room, and so forth, are included. The management organization which will operate the project, as it is being built and when finished, is also outlined, including organization charts and details of financial controls, compensation methods, performance incentives and budgets.

For those who are interested in the details of a master plan for a destination area, or other large land development project, the appendix on pages 285 to 287 includes an information Check List for Large-Scale Land Development Projects.

Balancing Hotel Rooms with Guests

One of the problems of a government planner or a resort developer is to have enough hotel rooms available to accommodate the numbers of tourists arriving. It would be easy to say that the capitalistic system is such that entrepreneurs seeing the need for more rooms will build them. Such is not always the case. One reason is that authentic current occupancy figures are sometimes hard to come by. Present owners are not eager for more hotel construction because of the increased competition it will offer. Also, private capital is reluctant to pioneer development in an area, preferring to let the government or someone else test the water first. On the other hand, once an area shows high occupancy, more rooms than can be filled are likely to be built. In some cases, Singapore is an instance, entrepreneurs have overbuilt and private capital needs to be cautioned about building more hotel rooms.

Government agencies and consultants are often called upon to produce a projection of rooms needed next year and for other intervals in the future. These projections are extremely difficult to make because of factors which cannot be controlled. Just because a destination has been growing at a 20 percent rate in the past does not mean that it will continue to do so. Each year the base becomes larger and the 20 percent projected increase can soon assume great magnitude.

It makes no sense to say that any destination area will indefinitely increase at a fixed rate of growth. The business recession in 1969-70 played havoc with forecasts of tourist growth in several destination areas. Instead of increases of 10 to 20 percent as predicted, many areas experienced declines.

Forecasts of growth are much easier in some destination areas than others. For example, Bermuda is a fairly well saturated island as regards tourist accommodations. The government has decided to limit growth to about 12 percent a year. Other destination areas are highly dependent upon inexpensive air fares for continued growth. Still others cater only to a luxury market.

According to an Eastern Airlines forecast, the number of rooms available per visitor in the Bahamas, Bermuda, Jamaica and Puerto Rico will change markedly with time.[1] The number of rooms is not projected to increase at the same rate as the number of visitors. In 1969, the Bahamas had 10,000 rooms and 1.717 million visitors, or one room for about every 112 visitors. By 1980, according to the forecast, there will be about one room for every 145 visitors. Jamaica, in 1970, had one room for every 100 visitors and will have one for every 73 visitors by 1980. Bermuda apparently can be expected to decrease the number of rooms from one for every 80 visitors to one for every 95 by 1980. Puerto Rico is the only island projected to continue at about the same rooms-to-visitors ratio, 160. A factor in determining the number of guest rooms needed for a particular area is the average number of days the guest stays at an area. This varies tremendously from one or two days up to 13 days, and more. Other factors are occupancy rate and the pattern of occupancy.

At an island destination, many of the visitors may be from cruise ships, shoppers who spend a few hours ashore but who require no hotel rooms. Destination areas that show wide variations in occupancy rates must plan for the high occupancy season. Places like Austria or Scandinavia need a large inventory of rooms for summer visitors; the same rooms are unoccupied during the rest of the year.

Forecasting manpower requirements as the destination area grows is also a government function, or is done by a consulting firm. Direct hotel employment depends partly upon the degree of luxury and the occupancy rate offered by the hotel. In some areas, as many as three employees are on the payroll for each guest room. The Savoy of London is an example of such a high employee/guest ratio. Luxury resorts, as represented by Rockresorts, have an employee/guest ratio of about two to one.

In commercial hotels the ratio is likely to be less than one. Where minimum service is offered, the ratio may be as low as one-quarter employee per guest room. For large commercial hotels, the ratio is likely to be about eight employees per ten guest rooms.

In Hawaii, guest rooms in 1970 totaled about 28,000 while direct hotel employment was about 16,000, a low ratio but understandable, partly because about 3000 apartment hotel rooms are included in the inventory of rooms. Another 15,000 persons were employed in visitor-related enterprises. The chart on the facing page shows the actual and projected growth pattern of hotel rooms, direct hotel employment and its relation to total employment in the State of Hawaii from 1960 to 1980. Related employment was projected to increase to about 27,000.

Hotel-related employment includes persons employed in non-hotel restaurants, bars and entertainment, retail stores, beauty shops, barbers, sight-seeing, visitor attractions, taxi, auto rental, tour bus, etc.

Professors Jonish and Peterson of the University of Hawaii have correlated future growth in hotel rooms in Hawaii with occupancy rates and come up with a rather alarming conclusion.[2] They assume that even though more visitors will come to Hawaii, the length of stay will continue to decline. In the period 1952-72, the average duration of stay fell from 25 days to 9 days, an average of 11 hours a year. The two professors predict that if there is a zero hotel room growth, occupancy rates will not fall below 70 percent until 1982. If, however, 1000 new hotel rooms are built each year, as has been true, occupancy will fall below 70 percent in 1976. Such occupancy, say the authors, can be interpreted as meaning failure for a number of hotels since there is likely to be rate cutting and costs will exceed income. That rate cutting is likely to occur was borne out in the experience of 1970 in Hawaii when the minimum average price of a room in almost any Waikiki hotel dropped from $20 to $15 and in 1971 airline-affiliated hotels were selling rooms for $8, $10 and $12.

[1]*Land: Recreation and Leisure* (Washington, D. C.: Urban Land Inst., 1970), p. 43.
[2]James E. Jonish and Richard E. Peterson, *The Impact of Tourism in Hawaii* (University of Hawaii, College of Business Administration, 1972).

The cost of zero tourism growth in Hawaii, according to the authors, would be high: hotel employment could drop by over 6000 persons. The wage income of the private sector would fall by $404 million and unemployment would rise by 48 percent. Since about 20 percent of visitor expenditures go into tax revenue collections, the average revenue loss if there is zero tourism growth in Hawaii would be $81 million. The authors found that, during the period 1954-71, an increase of 1000 hotel rooms in Hawaii lowered the occupancy rate by 3 percentage points. When visitor days were increased by 1 million during the same period, occupancy rates jumped 5 percentage points.

In 25 years, tourism has changed the face of Honolulu, especially in the Waikiki area. Not so long ago Waikiki had a few cottages, a few people and one or two hotels. It was quiet and serene. What visitors came were usually the old and the well to do, traveling by Matson steamship from Los Angeles or San Francisco. The remarkable change in scene is evident in the pictures of Waikiki Beach—before and after—one taken in 1952, the other, twenty years later. (See pages 258 and 259.) The contrast is spectacular, thrilling, or appalling, depending upon one's viewpoint.

Before 1930, it required 165 hours or more to travel from New York to Honolulu. In 1973, the same trip takes 10 hours. The visitor has changed. He is a shorter-stay, less affluent type. Many are Japanese traveling in a group. By 1975, it is expected 500,000 Japanese will be coming to Hawaii.

Investment Models

The sophisticated investor is well aware of the two key advantages of real estate investments that are not available for most other investments. The principal advantage is leverage: the investor can borrow a large amount, up to 90 percent in some cases in the past, of the equity money needed for the investment in a hotel or land development.

The lender has good collateral in the land and in the real estate improvements and so is willing to loan a much higher percentage of the value than he would on other types of investment. The other advantage is the tax shelter offered by anything which is depreciable, such as the building, furnishings and equipment of a resort hotel.

The analysis of a particular resort development is especially detailed and usually turned over to a consulting firm. Or the consulting firm's analysis is used as a comparison against one's own analysis. Even though a company has complete confidence in its own analysis, it will usually buy an

TABLE XVIII—DIRECT HOTEL EMPLOYMENT GROWTH IN HAWAII*

YEAR	Total Hotel Units	Direct Hotel Employment	Total State Labor Force	% Direct Hotel to Total State
1960	9,522u	7,618	235,140	3.2%
1970	28,116u	15,666	333,600	4.7%
1972	37,500u	20,530	350,600	5.8%
1974	43,000u	23,255	369,000	6.3%
1976	47,500u	25,245	390,500	6.5%
1978	52,500u	27,135	415,500	6.5%
1980	61,000u	29,739	445,500	6.7%

*Source: *Hotel Manpower Requirements Study,* The Hawaii State Dept. of Labor and Industrial Relations, Honolulu, 1970.

analysis from a consulting firm. The analysis is then used as a supporting document in making a request for a loan from a lending institution. The lending institution almost invariably insists upon an independent market and feasibility study.

The paper and pencil work involved in arriving at a rate of return on investment for a resort project is tremendous. Computer programs have been developed by some of the consulting firms which take only a fraction of the time formerly required. Built into the computer programs are provisions for discounting the investment money over a period of years, reflecting various rates of depreciation for building, furnishings and equipment and arriving at an estimated sale price after a specified period of time.

The models reflect all taxes that will be paid year after year, Federal income tax, excise tax and other types of taxes which may apply. An allowance is made for time elapsing before an income stream begins, usually at least two years in the case of a major project. Maximum depreciation is taken according to the depreciation regulations in effect. As of 1970, the double declining balance method of computing depreciation was no longer allowed for commercial type buildings, such as hotels, but continues to be permissible for apartment buildings and private residences.

In the late 60's, the cost of money had increased to a historical high in the United States. In addition to charging high interest rates, lenders were also demanding and getting "points," premium interest or a percentage of gross revenue. These "extras" can be amortized and also reflected in the program for the model. By projecting all income, cost, depreciation and taxes over a definite period of time, such as ten years, the entrepreneur is able to arrive at a more accurate guess as to his return on investment.

As in the case with all models, the resort model is built using assumptions which may or may not approximate reality. No one can predict the future in the business world with a high degree of certainty. By using the model, the potential investor takes into account factors which may be overlooked.

The use of the computer permits computation in a matter of seconds whereas, without the computer, days of paper-and-pencil work would be necessary. The model can be used for investment projections for hotels, golf courses, marinas, condominiums, restaurants or any tourist attraction. The model reflects a long-term income stream which varies from year to year depending upon depreciation policy, the effect of various taxes and the cost of capital at the moment.

Usually such financial analysis is done by a consulting firm, among the better known ones being Laventhol, Krekstein, Horwath and Horwath; Peat, Marwick, Mitchell and Co.; and Harris, Kerr, Forster Co. Each firm has its own techniques of analysis developed over a number of years of conducting market and feasibility studies.

Thomas L. Sander, of Peat, Marwick, Mitchell and Co., has given special permission to include the detailed explanation of how his firm performs an economic analysis of a proposed resort development. His approach and a description of the system used by Peat, Marwick, Mitchell and Co. follows:

ECONOMIC ANALYSIS OF RESORT DEVELOPMENTS
An Interdisciplinary Approach

In recent years, development of resorts and recreation-oriented real estate has received much attention from corporate, institutional and private investors. It is clear that "leisure time" industries today represent attractive opportunities for developers. It is equally clear that better integrated, well-planned resorts will be necessary to satisfy the sophisticated traveler of the 70's. In order to retain a theme or flavor for their particular resort, corporate developers have moved increasingly to the acquisition of larger areas of land which they can control and develop according to a carefully created master plan which allows them to protect and enhance the environment. This type of approach to resort development requires major investments of cash and, therefore, the project investment evaluation process has become increasingly rigorous and a more sophisticated planning process has been imposed.

Whereas, formerly, decisions to pursue a modest real estate investment were made by "back of napkin" calculations, today's destination resort developments, involving $200 to $300 million gross investment, require careful and systematic planning.

Within the area of real estate development, destination resorts, hotels and recreational resorts are big business in Hawaii and the Pacific. In Hawaii, where I am based, our main real estate-oriented work is concerned with resort development. Some of the major resort developers in Hawaii are such firms as Dillingham Corporation, Continental Airlines, Inter-Island Resorts, C. Brewer & Co., Boise Cascade and Del E. Webb Corporation.

The Interdisciplinary Approach

What is the scope of an interdisciplinary approach when applied to resort development planning? Exhibit 1 (page 158) describes one approach which encompasses the role of different functional or technical specialists during the resort development cycle. Typical participants in the planning phase of a resort are:

Market and financial analysis
Architects
Engineers and/or potential contractors
Urban planners

These groups normally work closely together and interact with each other during the planning cycle. Emphasis during particular phases may be on one or another of the participants, but all become involved at some stage.

One newcomer to the interdisciplinary approach is the sociologist/psychologist team. It is only very recently that developers rather than academicians have undertaken the responsibility for analyses of such subjects as the impact of resort developments on social patterns. Even today only the most enlightened developer has engaged sociologists/psychologists to study such issues as environment and social patterns. In many cases the economic benefit of such action is not clear to a developer, although in many cases such explicit concern can aid a controversial zoning application.

Typical of the interdisciplinary approach would be the heavy inputs from urban planners and architects at the early stages of the analysis. They set the tone for the resort development by a conceptual master plan (for example, see Exhibit 2, page 159) and set the stage for the type of inputs which market analysts can provide. They define the physical development potential of the resort in planning terms. It is now the responsibility of market and economic analysts to determine if the development plan in terms of size and timing can be justified in economic terms. Exhibit 3 (page 160) indicates a preliminary resort master plan which might have been prepared by urban planners. It indicates two resort hotels, a golf course, a racquet club and some resort condominiums. The market analysts must respond to the nature, sizing and timing of this scheme in terms of market support. The preliminary plan may be modified to account for this input.

Role of the Market Analyst

The market analyst must examine those factors which will give him an indication of the probable success of the resort development.

What is the total visitor market to this region?

Which resorts compete for this market?

What drawing cards does this resort have by comparison with competitors?

How successful are comparable resorts in terms of hotel occupancy, golf course and racquet club utilization and other revenue-producing areas?

Has the sales velocity of resort condominiums been good?

In what quality and price range?

In the final analysis, the market specialist will address such issues as:

Which year should the hotel come on-stream?

How many rooms should it have?

What is the appropriate room rate?

What occupancy level can the hotel achieve?

How fast can resort condominiums be absorbed?

What type of condominiums can readily be absorbed?

What should be the price range of the condominiums?

EXHIBIT I

THE RESORT DEVELOPMENT CYCLE
AN INTERDISCIPLINARY APPROACH

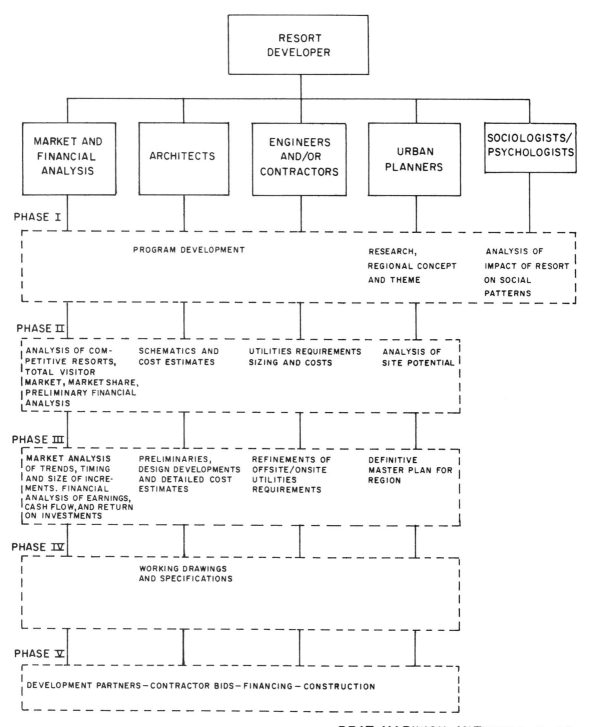

PEAT, MARWICK, MITCHELL & CO.

EXHIBIT 2

CONCEPTUAL MASTER PLAN FOR
HYPOTHETICAL RESORT REGION

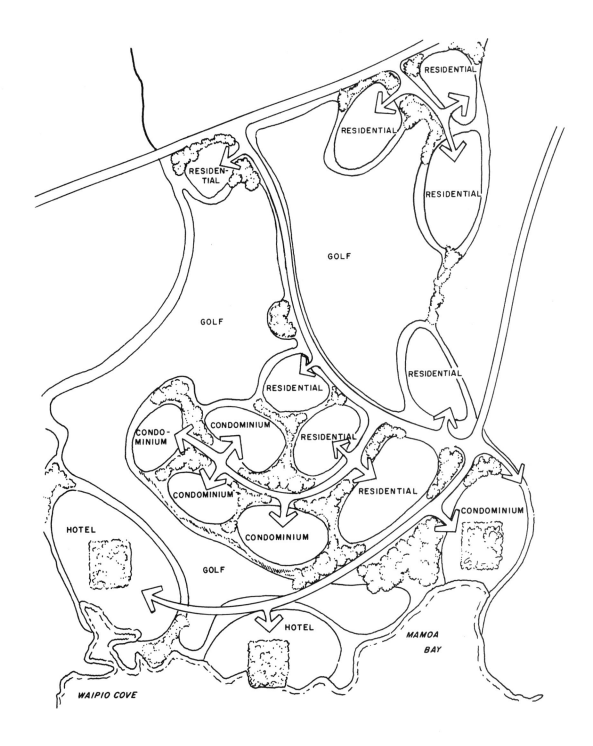

PEAT, MARWICK, MITCHELL & CO.

EXHIBIT 3

HYPOTHETICAL RESORT DEVELOPMENT SCHEDULE

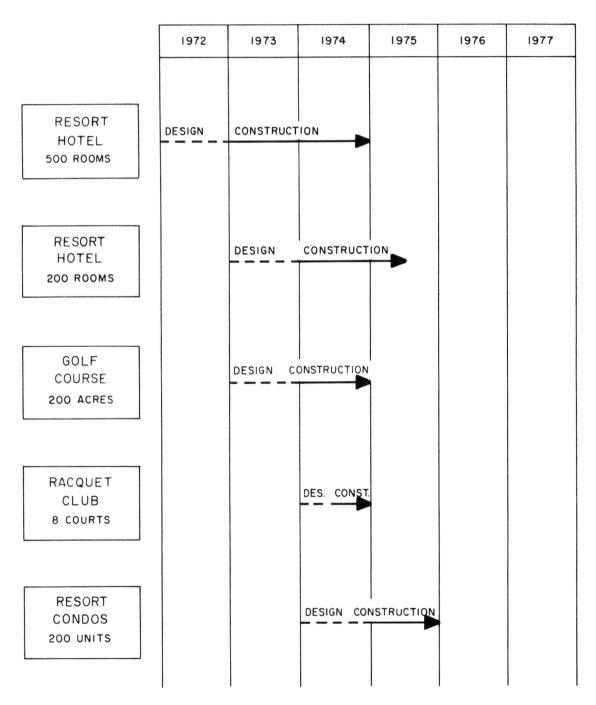

PEAT, MARWICK, MITCHELL & CO.

Role of the Economic Analyst

A thorough analyst will now check back with engineers and architects to determine the expected land improvement and construction costs to examine how these fit with the pricing structure indicated by the market.

As one example, how does the indicated room rate or condominium selling price fit with estimated construction costs? It is at this point that some preliminary economic analysis is brought into play.

If there is not a good fit between construction costs and market pricing trends, then the market analyst, architect, engineer will meet with the developer to pursue alternative strategies such as:

How much quality has to be sacrificed in order to lower the construction costs?

Can we create a unique resort to justify the higher pricing?

How will either of these alternatives affect the marketability of our product?

Should we reduce the recreation facilities to minimize cost?

Can the golf course, a $2 million investment, which is often a "loss leader" in the resort, be justified in economic terms by its enhancement of the resort environment?

After these discussions, the basic development plan may be modified to meet the requirements of a highly competitive market or it may be decided that the uniqueness of this new development will make the higher pricing acceptable to the consumer.

If there is a good fit between cost and market pricing trends, the economic analyst will work with architects and engineers to develop detailed cost data for the project. This data will be broken down in several ways:

Gross project investment

Construction cost by depreciation basis

Quarterly capital requirement schedule

Quarterly cash equity requirements and maximum cash exposure for the project.

These schedules will allow the developer to estimate total investment expected for the project, how much of that amount will be covered by interim financing and how much of the cost and expenses will have to be provided in cash equity during the construction phase of the project.

When the market parameters of the resort are defined and the cost factors involved are detailed, it remains only to identify other financial inputs before moving to the computerized projection of project profitability.

Resort Development Computer Model

The following inputs must be defined in preparing the computer model:

Relationship and amounts of hotel departments and other revenues and expenses.

Debt structure (interest rate, loan to value ratio, amortization period)

Tax rate of investor

Depreciation method

Other operating expenses.

Having detailed these inputs, we can undertake the first computer run. The computer run shown in Exhibit 5 (pp. 164-69) is provided by an investment model developed some years ago by PMM & Co. in response to the needs of the real estate industry.

It provides the developer with the key indicators of real estate development profitability, namely:

After-tax cash flow

Return on equity investment

In the case of a corporation whose stock is publicly traded, potential earnings will also be a key criterion; however, cash flow still remains the major indicator by which real estate investments are evaluated. Cash flow takes into account two of the major advantages of real estate over other investment opportunities:

The opportunity to leverage an investment so as to minimize the actual equity investment. Even in today's high interest market, 80 percent loan to value ratio with 30-year amortization can be obtained.

The opportunity to use accelerated depreciation methods and capital-gain tax rates to minimize the after-tax cash yield from the project.

Data from Computer Run

The computer run of Exhibit 5 for the Honokaa Beach Hotel shows a ten-year pro-forma profit and loss statement on the first page, after-tax cash flow and other outputs

A closeup view of the center of the La Grande Motte resort on the French Mediterranean. The pyramidal design adds interest and gives each room a balcony-terrace.

on the second page, the calculation of discounted cash flow and return on investment on the third page, and diagnostic data with regard to depreciation and principal and interest retirement on the fourth page. The computer run shown is for a 500-room resort hotel operating at 70 percent occupancy. It indicates a very satisfactory 18 percent return on equity investment. (Exhibit 5, pages 164 to 167.)

After separate analysis for the resort hotel, other computer runs may be made for the other income-producing recreation attractions such as the golf course, racquet club and for the condominiums for sale. These total cash flows are then shown in graph form. (Exhibit 6, page 169.)

This exhibit details an optimistic and

A general view of La Grande Motte in the Herault area of the French Mediterranean. The French Government has actively encouraged tourism in the area. The architecture, which might be described as "beehive modern," is unique in tourist hotel construction.

conservative range of results for cash flow and return on investment, which might reflect a range of occupancy, utilization and condominium absorption rate assumptions.

Destination development usually involves sizable investment, often running into millions of dollars. In large part, they are real estate investments where traditional measures of profit and loss are obscured by the depreciation and tax shelter factors. They represent heavy debt, high capital investment, and low "book profit" in the early years. Provided that the land on which a project will stand is subordinated to the loan, as much as 100 percent of the development cost is often available. Generally a project is financed by a combination of debt and equity. The developer often "leverages" his investment by borrowing as much as possible. The relationship of debt to equity is described as the leverage of that project. For example, a $20 million project with $16 million debt and $4 million of equity financing is referred to as being 80 percent leveraged.[1]

Most of the debt financing from major destination developments comes from insurance companies, real estate investment trusts, and pensioned funds. According to Mr. Lee, there is plenty of money around for quality projects. "Unfortunately," he says, "there is also plenty of money around, albeit at a higher rate, for poorly designed, cookie cutter projects." Mr. Lee feels that it has been almost too easy to fund a project which turns out to be basically unsound.

[1] Lecture by Robert Lee, *Statler Lecture Series,* 1973.

EXHIBIT 5

HONOKAA BEACH HOTEL

NUMBER OF YEARS= 10   INCOME TAX RATE=0.5400
INITIAL EQUITY INVESTMENT= $2587800.

YR	TOTAL REVENUE	OPERATING EXP. EXCL. DEPREC. AND INT.	DEPRECIATION EXPENSE	INTEREST EXPENSE	AMORT. EXPENSE	BEFORE TAX NET INCOME
1	3957188.	3012276.	659714.	983459.	0.	-698262.
2	5033700.	3809972.	601400.	976889.	0.	-354560.
3.	5335470.	4033583.	550309.	969695.	0.	-218117.
4	5655825.	4270966.	505414.	961817.	0.	-82373.
5	5995080.	4522354.	483152.	953191.	0.	36383.
6	6354810.	4788914	471525.	943745.	0.	150625.
7	6735960.	5071346.	460334.	933402.	0.	270877.
8	7140105.	5370818.	449563.	922077.	0.	397647.
9	7568505.	5688262.	439195.	909676.	0.	531372.
10	8022735.	6024847.	429217.	896096.	0.	672575.

ACCUMULATED VALUES AT END OF YEAR 10

| 10 | 61799378. | 46593339. | 5049823. | 9450047. | 0. | 11318991. |

INVESTMENT TAX CREDIT IN FIRST YEAR = 0.00

PEAT, MARWICK, MITCHELL & CO.

EXHIBIT 5 (Cont.)

HONOKAA BEACH HOTEL

PROFIT (LOSS) AFTER TAXES (BEFORE AVAIL. TAX LOSSES)	TAX SHELTER AVAILABLE	PRINCIPAL AMORT.	BEFORE TAX CASH FLOW	AFTER TAX CASH FLOW	CUMULATIVE AFTER TAX CASH FLOW	AFTER TAX DEBT SERVICE COVERAGE RATIO
-698261.	698262.	69159.	-107706.	-107706.	-107706.	0.8977
-354559.	1052822.	75729.	171111.	171111.	63404.	1.1626
-218116.	1270939.	82923.	249269	249269.	312673.	1.2368
-82372.	1353311.	90801.	332241.	332241.	644914.	1.3158
16736.	1316928.	99427.	420108.	420108.	1065022.	1.3991
69288.	1166303.	108872.	513278.	420108.	1578300.	1.4876
124603.	384173.	119215.	611996.	513278.	2190296.	1.5814
182918.	0.	130541.	716669.	611996.	2854500.	1.6310
2443				664204.	3395184.	1.5137
244431.	0.	142942.	827625.	540684.	2977264.	1.5530
309385	0.	156522.	945271.	582080.		

CUMULATED VALUES AT END OF YEAR 10

-405950   1076130.   4679861.

PEAT, MARWICK, MITCHELL & CO.

HONOKAA BEACH HOTEL

EXHIBIT 5 (Cont.)

	ANNUAL DISCOUNTED AFTER TAX CASH FLOWS	ACCUMULATED ANNUAL DISCOUNTED AFTER TAX CASH FLOWS	AFTER TAX EARNINGS PER SHARE
1	-2687065.	-2687065.	-
2	133844.	-2553421	-
3	164990,	-2388430.	-
4	186364.	-2202066.	-
5	199704.	-2002362.	-
6	206775.	-1795588.	-
7	208935.	-1586653.	-
8	192168.	-1394484.	-
9	132569.	-1261915.	-
10	120948.	-1140967.	-

	DISCOUNTED VALUE OF AFTER TAX CASH FROM SALE	FINAL PRESENT VALUE OF ALL AFTER TAX CASH FLOWS, DISCOUNTED AT 18.0%
10	1181483.	40516.

ANNUAL DEBT SERVICE FOR--

FIRST MORTGAGE	1052618.
SECOND MORTGAGE	0.
THIRD MORTGAGE	0.
FOURTH MORTGAGE	0.
SALE PRICE OF INVESTMENT	19978884.
SALE PRICE LESS DEBT OUT-STANDING LESS CLOSING EXP.	9878659.
CAPITAL GAIN	11264551.
RECAPTURE AMOUNT	651729.
ACTUAL CAPITAL GAIN	10612822.
FED. AND STATE CAPITAL GAIN TAX	3343039.
RECAPTURE TAX	351934.
AFTER TAX CASH FROM SALE IN YEAR 10	6183685.

PEAT, MARWICK, MITCHELL & CO.

EXHIBIT 5 (Cont.)

HONOKAA BEACH HOTEL

YR	DEPNI	DEPN2	DEPN3	FPRINS	FINIRS	SPRINS	SINIRS
1	361270.	0.	298444.	69159.	983459.	0.	0.
2	347723.	0.	253677.	75729.	976889.	0.	0.
3	334683.	0.	215626.	82923.	969695.	0.	0.
4	322132.	0.	183282.	90801.	961817.	0.	0.
5	310052.	0.	173099.	99427.	953191.	0.	0.
6	298426.	0.	173099.	108872.	943745.	0.	0.
7	287235.	0.	173099.	119215.	933402.	0.	0.
8	276463.	0.	173099.	130541.	922077.	0.	0.
9	266096.	0.	173099.	142942.	909676.	0.	0.
10	256117.	0.	173099.	156522.	896096.	0.	0.

PEAT, MARWICK, MITCHELL & CO.

EXHIBIT 6

CONSOLIDATED + RESORT DEVELOPMENT AFTER-TAX CASH FLOWS AND RETURNS ON INVESTMENT

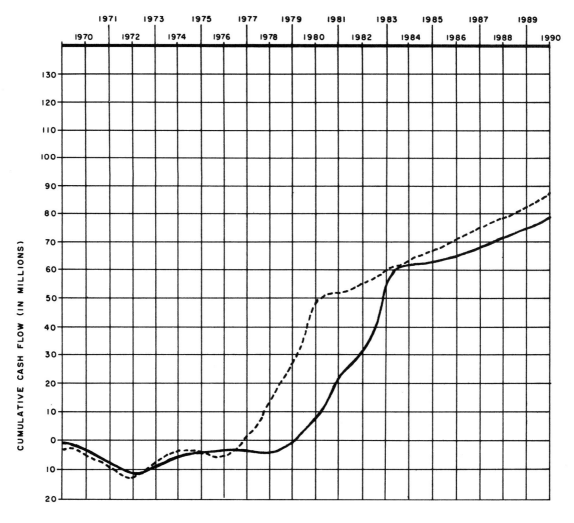

OPTIMISTIC ----------   RETURN ON EQUITY INVESTMENT OF 29.5%
CONSERVATIVE ————   RETURN ON EQUITY INVESTMENT OF 23.5%

PEAT, MARWICK, MITCHELL & CO.

EXAMPLES OF DEVELOPMENT PLANNING

Walt Disney World

The development of Walt Disney World represents one of the most complicated, comprehensive and costly land developments undertaken in the U. S. In scope and imagination, it deserves to be called fabulous. Announced in 1965, part of phase 1 of the project opened in 1971.

Planning and development of the first phase has involved dozens of consultants and the expenditure of about $300 million. Although Walt Disney World is said to be a never-ending project, present plans call for an expenditure of about a billion dollars when the pleasure-living complex will include, in addition to the present entertainment complex, an experimental community with 20,000 people and an industrial park, all located near Orlando, Florida.

The land development for this tremendous project has fascinating financial aspects. Bought originally for about $200 an acre, much of the land was in swamp and covered with snake-infested palmetto. The swamps fitted in with the Disney plan of building their "Magic Kingdom" around water. About $12 million had to be spent for flood and water control which included some 40 miles of winding canals and 15 miles of levees. Land in and around the project quite naturally skyrocketed so that, by 1970, surrounding land was already selling for $10,000 an acre. The company does not conceal plans to sell some of its holdings later and reap a financial harvest on land appreciation.

First Phase of Plan

The first phase, the construction of the "Magic Kingdom" of entertainment, is patterned after Disneyland in Anaheim, California. Disneyland, a 30-acre amusement park which represents an investment of $125 million and offers 53 major attractions, is the most successful tourist attraction in the world. The initial investment was $17 million. Its annual attendance is close to 9.5 million people with a ratio of 4 adults to 1 child.

It has provided impetus for the construction of a convention center, an American League baseball park and close to 7000 hotel/motel rooms. About 40 percent of all people who visit California visit Disneyland. It employs 3000 permanent employees, 3000 more during peak seasons. When completed, the Florida project will dwarf Disneyland in size and scope. Eight million visitors are expected the first year of operation. The market is the family. Walt Disney believed that the strength of America is the family.

Located 15 miles southwest of Orlando, in about the middle of the state of Florida, it will cover 43 square miles, an area twice the size of Manhattan Island, and about the same size as San Francisco. Where Walt Disney World, in its first phase, differs from Disneyland is that in addition to the "Magic Kingdom," in adjoining Theme Park five Theme Resorts have been planned, to be linked with the entertainment complex by monorail, water craft and land vehicles.

There will be 4½ miles of beaches with more than 150 water craft ranging from submarines to paddle wheel steamers. Plans are also being developed for golf courses, stables and bridle trails, nature tours and recreational activities including swimming, tennis, archery, bicycling and camping.

The five Theme Resorts are large hotels, each offering a different style of living and architecture. The Contemporary Resort will feature an open-mall lobby longer than a football field, with an 80-foot ceiling. A monorail train connecting all parts of the park will travel directly through the lobby to the station located inside. An Asian hotel will feature a Thai motif; a Polynesian style hotel will carry out the Islander theme with all rooms facing the water. A Venetian hotel will be reminiscent of St. Mark's Square in Venice with an 120-foot campanile. A Persian style hotel will complete the theme resorts. The Contemporary and Polynesian resorts, the first to be built, were constructed and are owned by U. S. Steel.

The 1565 rooms in these resorts will be of unitized or modular construction, each hotel room completely assembled at ground level and hoisted into place. The modules—

30 by 15 feet—include a bathroom and air climate control fixtures. The rooms will be secured to the structural frame of the hotel by an interlock system, and the plumbing and utility lines simply plugged in. Total weight for each module is about 8 tons.

The Florida State Road Dept. has constructed highway interchanges off major highways and has widened local public roads to afford easy access to the project. A 200-acre, 14 foot lagoon was built. There is a STOL port (short take-off and landing) which is operating on a regular basis.

A central energy plant supplies power, air conditioning, hot water and compressed air. The system will be driven by two 6000-kilowatt, gas turbine generators. Waste heat from these generators passes to large boilers which produce high temperature hot water; the water energizes 4 1500-ton absorption chillers at 40°F. used to air condition the Park and 2 hotels. Most of the working parts of the project are underground, including utility conduits, warehousing, refrigeration, employee wardrobe and lounge areas and space for the delivery of food, merchandise and supplies. There is an 8-acre basement which is above water level and a 3½ mile monorail—a very costly installation.

Waste Collection and Removal

The collection and removal of trash has been automated and uses underground pneumatic tubes to transfer trash quickly, economically and hygienically, from collection stations to a central disposal site   A 20-in. pipe carries the receptacles which transport waste at 60 m.p.h.   System is based on AVAC system of vacuum collection of solid waste that has been used in Sweden for several years.

Linking and controlling the entire project is a comprehensive information-communication system encompassing computer systems, telephone systems, automatic monitoring and control systems, mobile communications, television and wideband systems. Guests can make reservations for hotel rooms, entertainment and recreation before and during their stay. A special Walt Disney World credit card may be provided to hotel guests for use throughout their stay.

The hotels are all designed to handle convention business and will be connected by a closed-circuit television system, making it possible for conventions to be held simultaneously in two or more locations. Conventions will be courted during the off season, expected to be about six months of the year.

Beyond Phase One is Epcot—experimental prototype community—an ultramodern city for 20,000 persons.

Evidence of the thought and planning which have gone into Walt Disney World was the establishment of a 40-acre flora research center, near the Walt Disney World site. Because Florida's flora has a "sameness" about it, the center was established to try out scores of new plants and trees to see if they would adapt to the ecology of Central Florida. Thousands of bushes and trees not indigenous to the area were planted and many of them then used in the Walt Disney World project.

Development for Walt Disney World is phased over a 20-year period. Phase one is scheduled for completion in 1971; Phase two, in 1975; Phase three, in 1980. The last stage is planned for the 20th year, or 1990. Because the development is so unique, the plan for each phase is shown on pages 171 to 174.*

---

*All of the drawings are copyrighted by Walt Disney Productions and used by special permission.

THE MASTER PLAN, WALT DISNEY WORLD

The total development of Walt Disney World will be phased over a 20-year period. The schedules for the various stages of development are graphically presented on the following pages.

The initial phase, comprising the resort complex and the associated recreation area, will serve as the economic base from which the other elements of Walt Disney World will grow.

Pertinent statistics for the four stages of development are shown to indicate their proposed growth over the 20-year period.

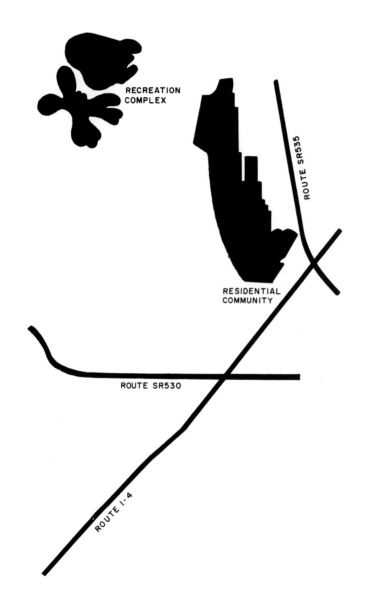

RECREATION COMPLEX

RESIDENTIAL COMMUNITY

ROUTE SR535

ROUTE SR530

ROUTE I-4

RECREATION COMPLEX

6500 Employees
1500 Hotel/Motel Units

RESIDENTIAL COMMUNITY

625 Residents
1000 Employees
1000 Motel Units
250 Residential Units

25,000 Visitors—Annual Daily Average

Development Plan—Year 1 (1971)

Source: Walt Disney Productions, Anaheim, Calif.

YEAR 5, WALT DISNEY WORLD

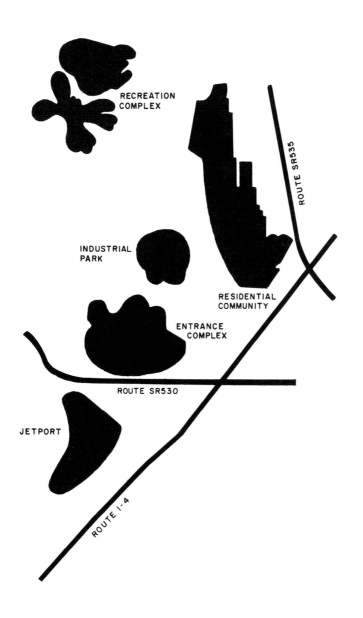

RECREATION
COMPLEX

ROUTE SR535

INDUSTRIAL
PARK

RESIDENTIAL
COMMUNITY

ENTRANCE
COMPLEX

ROUTE SR530

JETPORT

ROUTE I-4

RECREATION COMPLEX

8000 Employees
3000 Hotel/Motel Units

RESIDENTIAL COMMUNITY

4000 Residents
2000 Employees
2000 Motel Units
1500 Residential Units

INDUSTRIAL PARK

2000 Employees

ENTRANCE COMPLEX

500 Employees
500 Motel Units

JETPORT

400 Employees

45,000 Visitors—Annual Daily Average
Development Plan —Year 5

Source: Walt Disney Productions, Anaheim, Calif.

YEAR 10, WALT DISNEY WORLD

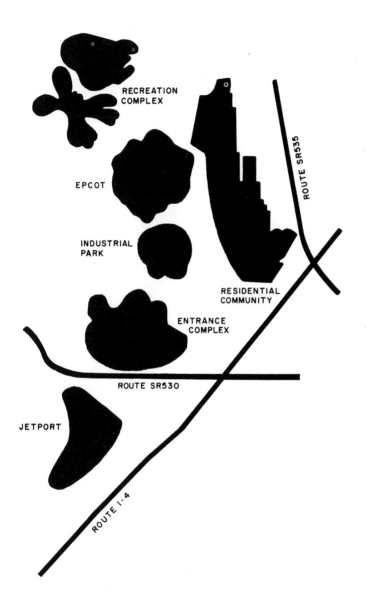

RECREATION
COMPLEX

EPCOT

INDUSTRIAL
PARK

RESIDENTIAL
COMMUNITY

ENTRANCE
COMPLEX

JETPORT

ROUTE SR535

ROUTE SR530

ROUTE I-4

RECREATION COMPLEX

10,000 Employees
4,000 Hotel/Motel Units

EPCOT

3,000 Residents
1,250 Employees
1,000 Residential Units

RESIDENTIAL COMMUNITY

15,000 Residents
3,500 Employees
2,500 Motel Units
4,000 Residential Units

INDUSTRIAL PARK

10,000 Employees

ENTRANCE COMPLEX

2,000 Employees
2,500 Motel Units

JETPORT

800 Employees
200 Motel Units

65,000 Visitors—Annual Daily Average

Development Plan—Year 10

YEAR 20, WALT DISNEY WORLD

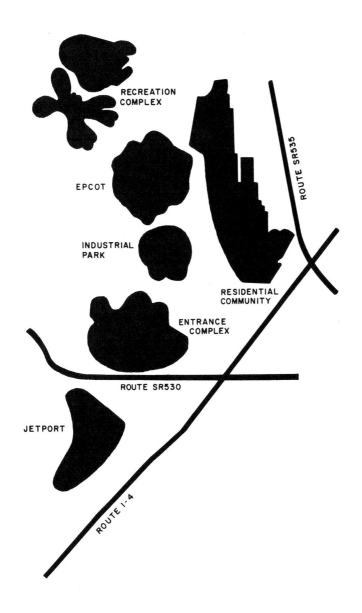

RECREATION
COMPLEX

EPCOT

INDUSTRIAL
PARK

RESIDENTIAL
COMMUNITY

ENTRANCE
COMPLEX

ROUTE SR535

ROUTE SR530

JETPORT

ROUTE I-4

RECREATION COMPLEX

12,500 Employees
 6,000 Hotel/Motel Units

EPCOT

25,000 Residents
10,000 Employees
 4,000 Hotel Units
 7,500 Residential Units

RESIDENTIAL COMMUNITY

16,500 Residents
 4,000 Employees
 3,000 Motel Units
 4,500 Residential Units

INDUSTRIAL PARK

20,000 Employees

ENTRANCE COMPLEX

4,000 Employees
5,000 Motel Units

JETPORT

2,000 Employees
 500 Motel Units

100,000 Visitors—Annual Daily Average
Development Plan—Year 20

Source: Walt Disney Productions, Anaheim, Calif.

Rockresorts

Imagine yourself a very rich man with a fine sensibility for natural beauty and an urge to preserve and cultivate that beauty and to share it with others. Your name might be Laurance Rockefeller, with access to one of the great fortunes of the world and a sense of stewardship inherited from the family.

What better way to share and conserve natural beauty than to create a resort in the midst of that beauty? This is what Laurance Rockefeller has done on the island of Hawaii, in the Virgin Islands, Puerto Rico and Vermont. The resorts created are among the most beautiful in the world; many people believe they are the ultimate in blending resort facilities into a natural environment in such a way as to enhance the quality of the environment.

Rockresorts have been described as a view with a room, a haven for the governmental, monied and intellectual elite, a vehicle for developing depressed economies. Rockresorts partake of all of these descriptions. They are of such a scale, quality and remoteness from the usual markets that only a Rockefeller would undertake them. The Aga Khan, with his resort complex on the island of Sardinia, is the only resort operator who can claim membership in the same league.

The hotels were gestating in Rockefeller's mind in the late 1940's when he explored the Caribbean, island by island. In 1952, Caneel Bay Plantation on the island of St. John, in the U. S. Virgin Islands, was purchased. St. John, nine miles long and no more than five miles wide, had almost no industry, almost no agriculture. Long before, it had been a productive sugar plantation but, because of the unevenness of the land, sugar was no longer profitable.

A World Away

The island had no electricity, no water system and a small, unskilled population. Everything for the resort had to be brought in or developed from scratch. Submarine power cables were laid, tanks and the water to fill them were barged in. Vocational education programs for future employees were put into effect.

Rockefeller bought a good part of the island and donated it to the U. S. Government; this area has become the Virgin Islands National Park. The Plantation itself comprises some 400 acres, seven beaches, and a number of cottages hidden behind sea grape hedges. It is not for the swinger or the tourist who wants a little bit of Manhattan in a tropical setting.

Rather, in season, the guest pays from $90 to $105 a day American-plan for two. He eats at one of two al fresco dining rooms. Beautiful tennis courts, snorkeling and lying on the beach constitute the day's effort. Talks by National Park rangers edify him in the evening or he may rent a jeep for $15 a day and explore the island. A dozen or so Sunfish are used, mainly by the employees; there are 300 employees, an unusually large number for the 130 guest rooms, about one employee for each guest.

While only a small percentage of the world's population can afford the rates at the Caneel Bay Plantation, a few miles down the road the same sort of natural beauty can be enjoyed for from $2 to $10 a day. Cinnamon Bay was opened in 1964 by the Park Service; in 1969, it was taken over by Rockresort management and $1 million invested in it by Rockresorts for improving the facilities.

Caneel Bay Plantation, Inc. was given to Jackson Hole Preserve, Inc., a non-profit conservation foundation. Income is devoted to conservation purposes at Jackson Hole Preserve in Wyoming and for other conservation purposes. It is managed by Rockresorts, with headquarters in New York City.

Rockefeller's next venture took him to Puerto Rico where the government felt that tourism should be encouraged in locations other than San Juan. Dorado Beach, built in a swamp and on the grounds of a former grapefruit plantation, was the result. More than a million tons of earth were removed to reclaim much of the area used for the guest units and the 36-hole golf course. The swamps were either drained or turned into lagoons, streams and other water hazards for the golf course. As happened at Caneel Bay, it was necessary to teach waiters, who had never before used silverware, to skillfully serve clientele with gourmet tastes.

Guest rooms in beach houses and cabanas make up the 306 rooms spread on either side of a central building. Twenty miles west of San Juan, the 1500-acre estate includes two miles of the Atlantic coast and two Robert Trent Jones golf courses.

Financially, Dorado Beach, with an occupancy rate of 92 percent over a 4-year period, has been the most successful of the two 18-hole golf courses together with a casino. Cerromar Beach, completed in 1971, has become a sister resort. It has another two 18-hole golf courses together with a casino, supper club, shopping arcade, sauna and 508 guest rooms and suites. Condominiums will be a part of Dorado Beach and Cerromar. The two resorts have a total of 800 rooms, enough to cater to large conventions.

A resort hideaway, Little Dix Bay, resembling St. John in its relative inaccessibility, was built on British Virgin Gordo, only eight square miles in size, with work starting in 1958. The kind of problems encountered at Little Dix Bay help to explain why only a person of perseverance and great wealth can succeed with a resort in such a location. A dirt airstrip had to be built. An experimental solar plant to distill sea water failed, an electric desalting plant proved inadequate, and now water is barged from Puerto Rico, 60 miles to the west. All food must be imported, as well as most of the employees.

Little Dix Bay has no telephones, no air-conditioning. It is thought by many to be the perfect resort for getting away from it all. At the thatched huts on the beach are little flags. The guest hoists the flag any time he wants food or drink. The dining room is an open air pavilion under vaulted roofs that angle down close to the floor. The table cloths are clamped to the tables to keep the breezes from blowing them away.

Mauna Kea, on just about everybody's list of great hotels, was built following a request from the governor of Hawaii to develop the island of Hawaii as a tourist area. Mauna Kea is the only highrise among Rockresorts. Like all of them, it is esthetically integrated with the land and water. Built at a reputed cost of $100,000 a room, the kitchen alone is said to have cost $1 million. Even with room rates of $85 a day, the hotel could not be profitable if judged in the usual financial terms.

But Rockresorts cannot be judged in the usual financial frame of reference. The payoff period is not two or three years or even five years, as is often planned for a resort. Rather there is a seven year payoff period, during which the operation is not expected to make a profit. More importantly, each Rockresort is backed up by thousands of acres of land, purchased with a view to keeping the setting pristine. Also, it is well known that a successful resort multiplies the value of the land around it.

Condominiums built on adjacent property can be highly profitable and can also provide customers for the food and beverage operations of the hotels. Rockresorts represent, as one writer put it, "noblesse oblige." They also represent one man's vision of beauty and a desire to share that vision.

Rockresort management has a style, a polish and a grace found in few places. It is not precision service, as stressed by the luxury resorts of Europe. It is even better in that it is somewhat informal and open, the kind of service that is not necessarily appreciated by hereditary aristocracy but is appreciated by an aristocracy based on merit.

Rockresorts, Stimulus to Community Development

The Rockresorts reflect the Rockefeller philosophy that the resort can preserve natural beauty and, at the same time, act to stimulate an under-developed area. Rockresorts have been placed in gorgeous natural settings and the resort structure subordinated to the landscape. Each site has been placed in an under-privileged area and the project is a combination of conservation, economic development and profit venture. Land is comparatively cheap; other costs are high. (See pictures, pp. 80, 110, 118.)

Construction costs in most of the Caribbean Islands are high since almost everything—for construction and daily operations—is imported from the mainland. Construction costs in the U. S. Virgin Islands are a minimum of $22 per square foot. The operational costs are approximately one-third above stateside prices. Land costs too are moving up and have been at a rate of about 10 percent per year during the decade of the 60's.

Like the operations at Dorado and Caneel Bay, Mauna Kea was placed in an economically depressed area and a principal purpose in building was to stimulate tourist development on the Island of Hawaii. With a $68 average rate for a double room, it has maintained a 90 percent and above average occupancy year round. The area around the hotel has prospered; the sleepy little town of Waimea was slowly dying. Now it is a thriving community.

A 500-room facility, costing about $35 million, is planned for a site near the Mauna Kea. It will be part of a much larger plan which will involve the eventual development of a resort community of 50,000 people along the 20 square mile area of the Kawaihae Coast of Hawaii. The complete development will include condominiums, luxury retirement and vacation housing, fairway home sites, a cultural center, marinas, additional golf courses and more hotels.

The total concept envisages developing a planned environment during the next 35 to 50 years, with accommodations running from low-rate camping and inexpensive cabanas to luxury style hotels.

Another feature of the Rockresorts, which is unusual in destination area planning, is the long-range character of the financial planning. Because of the logistics and problems involved in the development of such remote properties, profit projections are usually based on the third year of operation, rather than 18 months as would be the case on the continental United States. Dorado Beach took nearly seven years to make a profit and the Mauna Kea five. Both are now very profitable.[1] In 1969, 40 percent ownership of Rockresorts was acquired by Eastern Airlines.

The Four-Season Resort in the Temperate Zone

Originally northern resorts were designed only for the summer trade. With the mass interest in skiing developing in the 30's, some of the summer resorts attempted to become two-seasonal, introducing small

rope tows and catering to beginning skiers. Some resorts were close enough to major ski areas to be able to operate at least on weekends during the skiing season. Some of the established resort areas, such as Yellowstone National Park, Banff National Park, Jasper Lodge, are now open in the winter. With interest being shown by major corporations, capital has become available to create four-season resorts which may include skiing in the winter; boating, swimming, golf, tennis, hiking and riding during the other seasons.

The new extensive resorts usually include land development as a major or even principal aspect. They may be built around a village core with individual homes, condominiums and commercial lodges. Vail and Snowmass in Colorado have condominiums and lodges with underground garages. It is expected that, in the future, because of the high cost of land, parking, auto and service access and egress and all utilities will be housed two or three levels below the resort village core.[2]

The prime problem facing every developer is how much to build and when. The large developments are almost invariably built in stages with cash flow brought in by sale of land and condominiums financing or helping to finance the next stage of development.

Ski Area Requirements

Selection of a site for a ski area is critical, since weather and availability of snow cover during the ski season are overriding considerations. According to Ted A. Farwell,[3] there are seven factors which a vacation-oriented ski resort must possess:

1. A vertical drop of 1500 feet in the northeastern United States and a 3000 to 4000 vertical foot drop in the West. Base areas must be large enough to accommodate 3000 to 5000 skiers.

2. A location where prevailing winds

[1]Richard E. Holtzman, "Resort Hotels—Their Impact on Underdeveloped Areas," *Land: Recreation and Leisure,* (Washington, D. C.: The Urban Land Inst., 1970)
[2]Ted A. Farwell, "Resort Planning and Development," *The Cornell Hotel and Restaurant Administration Quarterly,* Feb., 1970, p. 36.
[3]*Ibid.*

will not whip away snow, usually a north or northeast exposure.

3. An annual snow fall of 200 inches, coming at frequent intervals. Less snow calls for snowmaking equipment which is expensive.

4. Slopes for both beginners and for experts, ranging from grades of 25 to 75 percent.

5. A climate which is cold enough to maintain the snow, preferably with lots of sunshine.

6. An adequate source of water, if snowmaking equipment is to be used.

7. A base area large enough to accommodate lift terminals, base buildings, parking, lodges and other amenities.

If there is to be a golf course, rolling countryside, water and trees are called for. Water sports require a lake in the vicinity.

Ideally, says Farwell, the four-season resort should focus on a village core with a northeast-facing mountain to the south, a major lake to the north, and rolling, lightly wooded terrain for golf to the southeast.

Vail Village—Prestige Mountain Resort

Vail Village in Colorado has been particularly successful. At an altitude of 8200 to 11,200 feet above sea level, it is 110 miles west of Denver, about a 2½ hour drive. Only a relatively remote sheep pasture in the heart of the Rockies in 1957, it attracted 360,000 skiers during the 1968-69 season. Commercial property values in Vail Village increased from the original value of about $150 an acre to about $6 per square foot. Over 5000 guestrooms have been built in the area and the place attracts over 60,000 convention guests each year.

Because the Village core area totals only about 140 acres, it has been kept primarily for pedestrians by placing parking lots underground. The initial cost of underground parking has been offset, to some extent by the savings resulting from elimination of snow removal. The side effects, not originally planned, have been that the one-day skier is being replaced with the person who stays for a longer period of time. The day-skier has no place to park.

It took four years for the company to turn the corner into the black. Once that

happened, commercial land was leased rather than sold. Leases run for a period of 49 years, with options to extend an additional 49 years. An unusual feature of the lease arrangement is that the lessee pays eight percent of the value of the property, with the property being revalued at the end of the 5th and 10th year. Thereafter, it is revalued every 10 years for the life of the lease.

Combining Snow with Sun

The Carolina-Caribbean Corporation has pioneered in offering club membership to property owners at a ski resort: Beach Mountain in the Blue Ridge Range of western North Carolina, and at St. Croix in the Virgin Islands. A membership club, the Carolina-Caribbean Club is housed in a hotel, the Beach Mountain Inn, at Beach Mountain. Only property owners on either Beach Mountain or St. Croix are permitted to use the facility.

The Beach Mountain development has been particularly successful. Between 1967 and 1969, over $9 million worth of lots were sold. The original $5 stock returned $3.03 in the first year in earnings after taxes. Cash flow was such that the need for borrowing money for future development was minimal.

The Beach Mountain development is unusual in that condominiums were built and used solely for rental. Privately owned chalets are also rented by the owners and the Beach Mountain Lodge provides rental units.

Even though the resort is located on the slopes of Beach Mountain, at a maximum elevation of 5600 feet, snow making equipment was necessary. Over 40,000 feet of waterlines, 62 snow guns, a snow cannon and a 1500-horse power air compressor for making snow were installed. Snow can be manufactured whenever temperatures fall below 28°F. During the 1968-69 season, over 50,000 skiers used the slopes. In the initial year of operation, the demand for rental skis far exceeded the 1400-set inventory on seven occasions.

The property, some 9000 acres, will include four golf courses. Two thousand acres will be set aside as a wilderness area. A summer day camp includes facilities for boating, swimming, sailing and camping. A "Land of Oz" is being contemplated which will include boulders, grotesque trees and life-like moving figures.

A Central American Vacation-Home Development

An example of a land development project involving tourism is the Beaches of Nosara on the Pacific Coast of the little Central American country of Costa Rica. A young lawyer, Alan D. Hutchison, of Washington, D. C. had organized and developed two land companies on the Cayman Islands in 1966. In 1969, Hutchison and others organized a tax-exempt company operating out of the Cayman Islands and, soon after, organized a wholly owned subsidiary, Inversiones Nicoya, S. A. under the laws of Costa Rica. Some 3300 acres of land were purchased or optioned on the remote peninsula of Nicoya, 100 miles northwest of San Jose.

To familiarize himself with local building contractors, surveyors, lawyers and the problems that might arise in Costa Rica, Mr. Hutchison first developed a small acreage near the city of San Jose. The property was subdivided and sold to North Americans who wished to retire in the country. From this experience, he was able to determine which firms to deal with for the larger Nosara Ranch project.

About 1200 half-acre homesites were plotted and a 30-unit hotel planned, also a golf course and marina. Since the area was remote from any population center, arrangements were made with a private plane company in San Jose to transport Nosara passengers on a priority basis. Electricity was brought into the property by the national electric power company, Costa Rican Power and Light Company. The undertaking required construction of 35 kilometers of all-weather roads and the installation of a water system.

The marketing of such a development requires specialized skills and the company turned to Hank C. Schlosberg, a marketing specialist who had successfully marketed 2500 homesites on the Island of Montserrat. The marketing fee was 7½ percent of gross sales. Forty half-acre and larger lots were initially marketed for $5590, payable in terms of $100 down and $100 a month with no interest charges.

An advertisement detailing some of the merits of the development was test run in two newspapers, the *Newark (N. J.) News* and the *New Haven (Conn.) Register*, in February, 1970. Prospective buyers were told about the low cost of living in Costa Rica where T-bone steak costs 60 cents a pound and a substantial 3-bedroom house can be built for $10,000. Later, ads were taken in the *New York Times* and other publications.

Other benefits include a virtually tax-free status for American couples who can prove a minimum income of $300 a month. The development has over two miles of sandy beach on the Pacific Ocean and another two mile frontage on a fresh water river, the Rio Nosara. The company wisely plans to leave much of the area in its natural state, providing horseback riding trails and an environment for birds and wildlife.

Cost per inquiry was less than $4, which is considered low, according to Hutchison, the developer. The usual cost per inquiry says Hutchison, is somewhere between $5 and $10. A letter briefly explains the project. If further interest is shown by the prospect, an additional post card must be mailed in and the inquirer receives a copy of a condensed version of the book, *Costa Rica.* Total marketing cost is budgeted at $1 million, one-ninth of the $9 million which is expected from the project.

The Waimea Village Inn

Many developers are careful to reflect the character of an area. If well done, a development can enhance the natural character of an area rather than destroy it bit by bit. The Waimea Village Inn is a case in point. Waimea is a village completely surrounded by the Parker Ranch on the Island of Hawaii. Completed in 1969, the Inn is a cluster of buildings around two landscaped open spaces. One of the spaces is a courtyard, a focal point for the commercial and social life of the center. Around it are grouped an ice cream parlor, a rustic steak house and bar, a sporting goods store, a craft shop and a gourmet food and liquor store. It includes a 40-room hotel unit and

The Waimea Village complex, comprising a 40 unit inn, office space and restaurant, is an example of unit planning, designed to reflect the environment. Waimea Village is completely surrounded by the Parker Ranch on the big island of Hawaii. Formerly, the village was a tiny cow town and is now used as a base camp for hunting, fishing and tour groups.

Even the Bell Tower design is in keeping with the spirit of the Village

The Waimea Village Gift Shop is evidence that a gift shop can be esthetically attractive and, to a certain extent, reflect the area where it is located.

Astroworld, near Houston, Texas, a sports and entertainment complex covering 350 acres.

several office spaces. Ten of the hotel suites include kitchens. In effect, the Inn comprises a core of a village.

Evidence of the careful planning to maintain a consistent character are the clock tower and other buildings in the photographs on the preceding pages. Evidence that good taste is commercially saleable is the fact that, during its first year, the Inn, which is in an isolated part of Hawaii, ran a 67 percent occupancy.

The Astrodomain of Houston, Texas

The Astrodomain, a 350-acre family entertainment and convention center near Houston, combines elements of a Disneyland and a convention center with the world's largest air-conditioned and completely enclosed sports building, the Astrodome.

According to its developer, Judge Roy Hofheinz, the complex involves an expenditure of $100 million and will never be completed. Presently, the Astrohall convention center is serviced by a Sheraton Inn, a Holiday Inn, and a Howard Johnson Motor Lodge and the Astroworld Hotel. The judge has spared no expense and has introduced air-conditioning viaducts under the seats for outdoor dining in the hot Texas sun.

Total cost of the stadium, which seats 44,000 for football games, and includes 53 private rooms and five restaurants, was over $45 million. The stadium took 6600 tons of air conditioning. In true Texas style, the scoreboard alone cost $2 million. The stadium structure itself cost $20 million but the overall cost of the entire project came to $35 million, of which $31 million came from two county bond issues. The State's highway department and the City of Houston contributed another $3.75 million for offsite improvements, including paved streets, bridges and storm sewers. Over 4 million persons visit the Astrodome annually.

The Costa Smeralda

The Costa Smeralda, the Emerald Coast, is one of the truly large scale resort developments of the world. Located on the Italian island of Sardinia, total cost for the entire development is projected at $300 million. Some 35 hotels are projected and, eventu-

ally, 9000 villas and apartments, 2 golf courses, a polo field and 80 beaches. According to the Aga Khan, hotels are not profitable but land sales are.

After Sicily, Sardinia is the largest island in the Mediterranean, an island that had almost no economic importance or productive capacity until tourism was introduced. In 1961, Prince Karim, later Aga Khan the Fourth, and his friends, began buying land for vacation homes of their own. A consortium of land holders was formed for the purpose of preserving the natural beauty of the island. This syndicate, which was joined by other business acquaintances of the original members, eventually purchased 38 miles of coastline and some 32,000 acres of land. The consortium began building highways and whole villages, clearing out harbors and bringing water from ten miles away.

The whole area will be developed in parts, each part as a cohesive unit, each with its infrastructure of roads and other services. The land has been plotted to contain residential areas of varying population intensity. Some areas will include apartment blocks and villas with little or no space around them; other blocks will have landed villas with one or several acres of land. Large expanses of countryside have been set aside as open space. Some industrial development is being encouraged. An unusual feature of the consortium is the fact that it owns its own airline which transports tourists to and from Sardinia to airports in Nice, Milan, Genoa, Bologna and Rome. Charter flights also fly in from Northern Europe. It is possibly the largest full development ever contemplated.

The Italian government is encouraging the project by exempting some taxes and reducing others. Loans are made by the government for up to 70 percent of a hotel's cost and capital grants for another 15 percent. The interest rate totals only 3 percent.

Controlled Architecture

All of the architecture is controlled by the consortium and is supposed to reflect peasant simplicity, without peasant inconveniences. Five architects, three Italian and

Arcades below the Piazza at Porto Cervo, one of the several developments at Costa Smeralda on the Italian island of Sardinia. Considerable attention has been given to making the architecture reflect what is Sardinian: white plaster walls, lattices and beams of juniper wood, green plants and terraces. The architectural style is described as a "modern interpretation of traditional peasant Sardinian architecture." One commentator has called it "instant ancient."

Hopetown, Abaco, is one of the 700 islands of the Bahamas. Abaco is an "out-island" so Hopetown offers beautiful scenery, sparkling water and not much of anything else. Yachting, among the various islands of the Bahamas, within the Virgin Islands and among the Grenadines is rapidly growing in popularity.

two French, are responsible for the overall design of the development. Some of their buildings are a little startling at first glance. One of the luxury hotels, the Cala di Volpe, is designed as a castle, with a complex of turrets, pillars and cloisters. A series of Moorish arches, and roofs at various levels. add to the complexity of the building which from an operational viewpoint can hardly be considered efficient. The architectural committee exercises close watch on exterior colors, the layouts of the gardens and even the construction of fences.

Costa Smeralda represents, on a grand scale, an attempt to mix the tourist markets, to offer something for everybody. A range of accommodations, from modest to luxury, are part of the planning. The project includes five luxury style hotels and a number of less expensive ones. Costs of apartments and villas also range in price from modest to luxury.

Quechee Lakes, Vermont

Several "vacation villages" are being developed around the country. CNA Financial Corporation, headquartered in Chicago, is developing what was once a Vermont woolen mill town into a 6000-acre vacation home village. Old homes and farmsteads in the area are being restored to retain the New England flavor. Stone fences are being rebuilt and the town mill is being made into a restaurant. The river which passes the mill will be dammed to form a lake.

Large acreage "farmsteads" as well as smaller sites will be available. Farmsteads, or small farms of 4 to 11 acres, are designed for the family that wants a small stable or barn, in addition to a vacation home. Some homes will be clustered to preserve the open land. Architecture within the town itself will be controlled to conform to the New England spirit; houses hidden away in the woods can be of contemporary design. Two-thirds of the area will be left as common land for hiking trails, riding and snowmobiling.

The central recreational facility will include a clubhouse and an 18-hole golf course. In addition, there will be a health club, indoor and outdoor swimming pools, tennis courts, and other amenities. The two

lakes in the area will have beaches and marinas and a family ski area is being developed. Eventually, some 2000 vacation homesites will be available from the Chicago holding company. Quechee is between Woodstock, Vt. and Hanover, N. H.

Second-Home Communities

The U. S. Census of 1967 found that in 1967 about 1.7 million of the 58.8 million households in this country had second homes which were reserved year-around for their use.[1] While not a part of tourism in the generally accepted sense of the word, they do foster travel, and affect the economies where they are located, in a manner similar to tourism. Some of the better known of these communities are Sea Pines Plantation, Hilton Head Island, S. C.; New Seabury, Cape Cod, Mass.; The Sea Ranch, Sonoma County, Calif.; Bryan Beach, Freeport, Texas.[2]

Sea Pines Plantation, Hilton Head Island, South Carolina

It is appropriate to conclude this chapter with a reference to Sea Pines Plantation on Hilton Head Island just off the coast of South Carolina. A resort catering to tennis, golf and ocean lovers, Sea Pines Plantation is one of the tightest, most completely controlled resort developments anywhere, and one of the loveliest. Charles Fraser, its developer, believes strongly that the only way to have aesthetic control is through the power of ownership. Some 40 pages of restrictions are attached to every deed issued to purchasers of some 550 individually owned properties in the Plantation. Mr. Fraser has the legal power to negate any building or landscaping plan proposed by one of the owners.

Most of the houses have cedar-shake roofs and bleached-cypress siding. Most of the houses are in the $40,000 to $50,000 range but some owners have invested up to $300,000 in their houses. Condominium villas, a small town and a series of apart-

[1]*Land: Recreation and Leisure.* (Washington, D. C.: The Urban Land Inst., 1970), p. 12.
[2]"Second-Home Communities," *Architectural Record,* Nov., 1965, pp. 143-160.

ments are included in the Plantation.

Fraser has definite ideas about the seashore and where houses should be located in relationship to the shore. No homes line the beach, for Fraser feels that a road would then go back of the houses and the beach would be limited to those houses which front the ocean. Instead, at the Plantation, dozens of public swaths are interspersed between arterial roads. Walkways are built through the swaths to the ocean so that everyone has easy access to the ocean. Neither the beach nor the line of primary dunes behind it has been built upon. Although there is unusual density of homes, the landscaping is such that each appears well separated and individual. Some houses are set back in the woods along the numerous fairways; others are on narrow drives that lead toward the beach from the principal roads.

Considerable effort has been made to save the trees, roads having been built around them to avoid cutting them down. Fraser, it is said, will not remove a tree until at least two automobiles have crashed into it. Twenty-five percent of the Plantation is left in its natural state, even to the point that alligators are not removed from the ponds and streams until they reach 6 ft. long.[1] Fraser also saved 75 percent of the marsh land. His next venture, on Cumberland Island off Georgia, will be on an even grander scale.

Nantucket: Master Planning by One Individual

The visitor to Nantucket may feel he is stepping into a mid-19th century whaling town. Indeed he is, or at least the town looks like one man's view of what Nantucket was like in 1850. The island, 30 miles off Cape Cod, has been largely redesigned by one man, Walter Beinecke, who has spent millions in buying property on the island, razing run-down buildings, an old ice factory, gas stations, a lumber yard, and rusting fuel tanks. By buying up large parcels of the downtown area and virtually all of the wharf, Beinecke has been able to raise rents, prescribe design and operation of businesses. His holdings include 155 buildings. Beinecke states that he is determined to protect the island from the developers who have taken over much of Cape Cod and

turned it into honky tonk strips of motels, gas stations and fast food stands. He has become the single largest commercial land holder. In place of the buildings which he has torn down he has put in a boat marina, a string of narrow one- and two-story grey shingle shops and a bandstand. To most visitors the island is authentic; others say it is not. One of his companies, the Nantucket Historical Trust, is owner of the Jared Coffin House, a fine restaurant and inn which must, according to its lease, remain open the year around even though it loses money during the winter.

Master Planning a Prerequisite to Success

We have seen in this chapter that by casting the most critical eye possible upon a proposed land or resort development, the planner can better anticipate what will happen to sales and profits. If he is a government planner, he can better forecast cost and benefits to the area. The developer can call for inputs to his plan from a variety of experts. Based upon certain assumptions, he can project cost and return on the investment well into the future.

A master plan allows the planner to stage his investment by increment. Foreseeing the future is not possible and by staging an investment, he can modify it according to what happens in the real world. If projections of visitors or buyers exceed his forecast, he can bring in the second-stage more quickly. If the forecasts prove to be optimistic, the development can be slowed or halted. In this sense, a master plan is a hedge against the future.

With a master plan, the developer is more likely to be able to borrow money from institutional lenders. If the project is sizable, a master plan is mandatory in order to interest the decision makers in the lending institutions. The master plan does not provide prescience but it does force the planner to examine contingencies that otherwise might be overlooked.

Even with the most extensive planning the "best laid plans of mice and men" go awry. Who would have forecast the kinds

---

[1] "Profiles, Encounters with the Archdruid," *New Yorker,* Mar. 27, 1971.

of social problems encountered in Puerto Rico, St. Croix, and Curacao in 1970? The trends all pointed up; economics looked good; everything looked favorable—except that a large percentage of the population was discontented.   One such factor can throw a bombshell into economic forecasts no matter how carefully made.

Le Chateau Champlain, a $25 million luxury hotel that opened in 1967 in Montreal, represents the modern city hotel. Built at a cost of about $40,000 per room, (all costs divided by number of rooms), the hotel is one of the most colorful and luxurious in the world. Note the semi-circular windows.   The Chateau has five specialty restaurants, each with a different decor and cuisine.   Average rate in 1970 was $27.00. Employees number 700.

The modern hotel usually has a number of specialty restaurants and at least one coffee shop style of restaurant.   L'Escapade, the rooftop restaurant of Le Chateau Champlain in Montreal, Canada is one of five specialty restaurants in the hotel.

EXAMPLES OF DESTINATION DEVELOPMENT

In recent years, vast stretches of land have been studied and improved to create new tourist destinations. Most of these developments have taken place in areas where there is mild or subtropical weather prevailing—the Mediterranean, Caribbean, Hawaii, Arizona, California. Some of the developments have taken place in ski country—Vermont, New Hampshire, Maine, Colorado.

By scrutinizing an entire area and the interrelationships taking place within the environment, planners have been able to recommend total community development with all elements in harmony. At the same time, the communities are planned to be economically viable and attractive as tourist destinations. They are more than just real estate developments which are usually done for the profit of a few individuals or a corporation and often prove to be less than satisfactory for the good of the larger community.

Land development is one term being used for this broader type of planning. Often land, raw or in agricultural use, is studied intensively and proposals made for its use. The proposal may include a resort as part of the total plan, or the resort may be the central feature. The plan is likely to include a proposal for a permanent town or village, made up of permanent residents and employees of the resort. Villages for retirees may be included. Land development, unlike real estate development, is likely to deal with unused or agricultural land, rather than already existing residential, business or industrial sections.

The real estate development phrase, "the highest and best possible use" of the property or land, has usually meant the best profit for the developer. Land development planning in its best sense is intended to be best not only for the developer but also the user and the community at large. It takes into consideration the welfare of the people who will be employed in the new facilities—their life style and economic welfare—as well as the visitor and the owner.

Motivation for the development of new tourist destinations has sometimes come from philanthropic-minded individuals or from state or national governments interested in improving the economy and way of life of a large group of people. Ideally, the results are beneficial to everyone concerned.

As the term is beginning to be used, land development may include long range plans for total facilities needed for a tourist destination: water supply, roads, police protection, health protection, tourist reception and accommodations, tourist attractions and other entertainment. It also includes financial planning—short term and long term—shopping facilities, recreational facilities, provisions for schools, churches, sewers, sewerage treatment and flood control. Some of the plans include community clubs and green belts. Recommendations may be made concerning the management of golf courses, hotels, gift shops and tourist attractions. Some plans include marinas, aerial tramways and other facilities of touristic value.

Tourist areas are developed for a number of reasons, among them being:

1. For immediate gain to the developer. The developer assembles a package and sells pieces of it to other entrepreneurs, acquiring a profit in the process.

2. For purposes of long term appreciation of the land. Over a period of time, land almost always appreciates. Profits from the sale of land are taxed as a capital gain at about half the rate charged for ordinary income.

3. A hotel in a land development may be built principally as a means of increasing the value of surrounding property. It is the "frosting on the cake," the lever for appreci-

ating surrounding land. Its value as an operating hotel may be small.

4. An area may be developed by a government principally as a means of increasing employment in an economically stunted section.

5. An area may be built up for political reasons, as a means of granting aid to a region, paying political debts, redistributing income within a nation.

6. A resort may be viewed as a monument to someone's ability or pride, an opportunity to build something beautiful and lasting.

7. Particular hotels have been built in developing nations as a means of expressing national pride. In some of the smaller countries, the new hotel is a showplace, perhaps the most imposing building in the country, a place for government entertainment and an official government facility to house distinguished visitors.

8. Some areas have been developed, at least partially, because an individual or group thinks of a resort as a challenge or a fun business. Several resorts in the Caribbean were built by persons or families for the joy of doing it.

9. The most obvious reason for creating a resort is to operate it at a profit.

Tourist areas fail, aesthetically and financially, for two principal reasons: a lack of market research and a lack of area planning. A hotel or other tourist facility without a market cannot survive. Many facilities have been built with little or no thought given to market feasibility.

Tourist facilities that have not been controlled or master planned become part of a jungle, usually with little beauty, often garish. The "motel rows" found on the outskirts of many U. S. cities are examples of what happens without a master plan. Each motel owner is forced to erect a larger sign and to forego landscaping or other amenities in order to compete. Nobody profits, least of all the traveler. When an area grows without controls or planning, each entrepreneur shifts for himself, with little regard for the area as a whole. The area suffers and, in the long pull, the entrepreneur does not do well, or does less well than if planning and controls had been instituted.

The recreation-land business grew to tremendous proportions in the late 1960's.[1] In California alone, between 50,000 and 100,000 acres of rural lands were subdivided each year into "recreational communities." The stakes are high for the developer, although development cost in the late 60's climbed to more than 50 percent of the market value of the project.

A "full amenity" project, as built by Boise-Cascade, one of the largest of the developers, has become a stereotype for the standard recreation community; a country club with one or two golf courses, a lake and between 2000 and 4000 second-home plots. The average lot price which was $6500 in 1964 climbed to $9000 in 1970. Lot sizes in the usual project range from one-third of an acre to two acres.

Most of the people buying the recreational land do not build immediately. Houses have been built on only 3 percent of all California recreational lots sold in recent years.

By the 1970's, the fervor of land development had cooled considerably. Development costs had climbed steeply and the 1969 recession had cooled the buying ardor. Some land development projects were abandoned completely by developers because of the outcry raised against environmental degradation anticipated for some developments. A development at Lake Edson, 100 miles northeast of San Francisco, was dropped at a loss of $500,000 because of a public campaign which insisted on a comprehensive sewage system as part of the development.

In a Connecticut project, Boise-Cascade was forced to spend over $3 million to convert from septic tank disposal to the more expensive tertiary system, a chemical and filtration means of treating sewage. At its huge project in Hawaii, the Boise-Cascade Company has agreed with an archeological museum to preserve certain ancient Hawaiian artifacts on company property. The planning studies alone connected with the arrangement will cost $80,000.

Usually the developer is required to present detailed plans of the numbers of accommodations to be put up, stage by

[1] *The Wall Street Journal*, New York, Dec. 24, 1970.

stage. Many of the plans include the development of subdivisions of homes with detailed proposals of home design for various types and sizes of dwelling units per acre. Building design must reflect prevailing hazards such as the possibility of hurricanes or tidal waves, floods or other natural catastrophes.

Some of the larger land developments are on such a scale and are so complex that an interdisciplinary approach is necessary. One of the largest and most complex is the C. Brewer development in Hawaii which eventually calls for some $500 million in capital investment. The land under consideration is on several of the Hawaiian islands and taken altogether is larger than the total area of the island of Oahu, location of Honolulu.

Robert Lee, of Peat, Marwick, Mitchell and Co., one of the planning consultants, has explained that experts in sociology, marketing, finance, architecture and in planning were employed to develop a master plan. Representatives of each discipline worked somewhat independently, each bringing his special viewpoint to bear on the problem. Inputs from all of the experts were then brought together to form the master plan. Total cost of the plan itself will eventually reach $2 million.

Ecology and Destination Planning

The ecological view in regional and destination planning is being felt. For the biologist, ecology is a study of organisms in reciprocal relations to their environment within a region. The organisms, including man and lesser species, share a common and finite environment not unlike the crew of a spaceship.

The ecological viewpoint stresses the interdependence of all organisms or systems within an environment. It points out the inevitability that regional planning will be confronted with questions of value, and, ultimately, of ethics. Who is to profit from what, and how much? Will a tourist facility detract or destroy other values held dear by the resident population? Which is to be preferred, a high rise resort or a low rise? Does the tourist want rest and rustication or does he want a wide choice of entertainment and

activity in a relatively small amount of space? What is the good life for one group of tourists may be anathema to another group, or to permanent residents.

Residents may abhor the noise, congestion and pollution generated by tourism. They may resent "their" natural beauty spots being violated by outsiders, even though tourism revives the economy. A flourishing tourist business may remove domestic servants from the labor market and increase the cost of living for permanent residents considerably. In some cases, the growth of tourism destroys many of the values held dear.

Luxury or Low Cost Tourism?

One of the major government decisions concerning tourist development relates to the kind of tourism to be sponsored. Should it be of the luxury type, which brings in people of affluence and high sophistication, or should it be the kind of accommodations appealing to middle and working class markets, low-cost tour groups and students. A luxury hotel, in an area where income is very low, accentuates the vast gulf between the haves and have-nots, often between the tourist and the national. The nationals may resent the rich traveler who may spend more in a week than the national makes in a year. Instances of such resentment are seen in the Bahamas, Puerto Rico, Jamaica and other Caribbean islands.[1]

The establishment of tourist facilities by a government unit to be used at moderate cost by the public is often referred to as social tourism. Examples are the numerous campsites in Europe and large numbers of cabins and campsites in State and Federal parks in this country. Often these facilities are rented at a minimal charge and, in some cases, do not return the cost of construction and maintenance. Such facilities can be justified in terms of offering a public service.

Some communities oppose such facilities on the grounds that they attract only minimum spending visitors or other persons undesirable to the community and to the

[1] "The Uneasy Islands," *The Wall Street Journal,* Dec. 22, 1970.

"quality" tourist. Puerto Rico, for example, allows no camping on its numerous beaches. Cape Cod, as a community, does not favor campsites. It can be argued that campsites attract the hippie type, repugnant to the usual tourist. On the other hand, the usual camper is not necessarily impecunious or a non-conformist. Although he pays little for his tent or trailer parking site and probably eats few meals in local restaurants, he may be a big purchaser of a number of items including food, gasoline, sporting goods and tickets to tourist attractions.

The luxury hotel, on the other hand, becomes a kind of national symbol, headquarters for principal government functions, in effect, an extension of the government and its national pride.

Some areas, such as Tunisia and Guadaloupe, which were relatively untouched by traditional tourism, welcomed the kind of tourism associated with the Club Mediterranee. The Club constructs inexpensive holiday "villages," the investor usually insists that the equipment and services be to the taste and specification of the club member. Corfu and Martinique are other islands that have found social tourism compatible with their touristic goals. In Corfu, for example, the Government ceded the land and, in addition, agreed not to install a similar operation within a certain distance.[1]

Some tourist planners assert that low-cost tourism does very little for the tourist area and that it is very difficult to shift from a low-spending market to a luxury market.

Regional Planning

Tourist destinations may be thought of as specific small areas (Nantucket for example), as towns or cities such as Miami Beach, as states, regions, or nations. Los Angeles is a tourist destination which is also part of Southern California, California, and the Far West. Cape Cod is a destination, also part of Massachusetts and New England. Disneyworld is a destination, a part of Central Florida and of Florida and the Southeast. Planning, promotion and development may be done at the local area level or at some larger regional level.

It is logical to expect that there would be benefits from taking the regional approach although relatively little of this has been done except on a state level. New England—comprised of Maine, Massachusetts, Vermont, New Hampshire, Rhode Island and Connecticut—is a regional destination area based on history and image. It can be planned, packaged, and sold as a region, just as any of its parts, such as the White Mountains, Boston or Mystic River, can be planned and sold as entities. Myrtle Beach can be planned and sold as a destination. There may be several advantages in also planning and selling it as a part of the Golden Strand and as part of South Carolina. California is sold by region and as a state.

States that are primarily "pass-through" or "bridge states" usually have at least a few destinations which can be packaged into a state image. Creating an overall image for a region redounds to the appeal of its parts. Advertising New England helps Boston as well as the little town in Maine. Perhaps more importantly, thinking regionally leads to regional research, regional planning, regional control. While areas within a region may be saturated with tourists, regional planning may divert tourists to those areas that need and welcome them. Regional promotion can be directed to build off-season and shoulder business, the relatively low volume seasons on either side of the high seasons. Analysis of a region will suggest that parts of it may be seeded with a tourist attraction to prime the tourism pump. Other parts may wish to discourage more visitors. Route 28 on Cape Cod is an example of excessive tourism during the summer months, while western Massachusetts offers a vast undeveloped area for tourism. A region may have the finances to develop new markets whereas a smaller area may not. For example, it may be wise to promote New England in Japan, a program which would probably be excessively expensive for single destinations within New England.

By the 1960's, local, state and national governments were beginning to be concerned about the erosion of destination

---

[1]*Tourism Development and Economic Growth,* Organization for Economic Cooperation and Development, Paris, 1967, p. 40.

areas, erosion caused by poor planning, overuse and pollution of various kinds. It was seen that broad scale or macroplanning, for entire islands or even regions, would be necessary to maintain the character and romance of an area, or to change the character of an area in a desirable way.

It was also clear that in many resort areas high-rise structures would be necessary while other areas could be restricted to low-rise buildings. Waikiki, Las Vegas, Miami Beach, San Juan, and other resort areas were already high-rise in character. The solution lay not in eliminating the high-rise but in providing open space and corridors to the sea. In Waikiki, only one low-rise building was left, the Halekulani Hotel and another such property would probably never be economically feasible in that area. Even the rabid urbanist would welcome open-space corridors to the sea and expanses of land surrounding the high-rises. This could only be accomplished by government action.

Around the world, access to the sea has been unplanned. The result is that, by accident or wealth, relatively few people live or can afford to rent accommodations fronting on many of the beauty spots of the world. Long stretches of the coast from Miami, north, are completely blocked from view by contiguous residences and motels. On the Island of Maui, one motel after another, each accommodating only a limited number of people, effectively blocks from view some of the loveliest beaches in the world. The Costa del Sol of Spain is another example of lack of planning. Parts of Cape Cod have developed into what might be called "resort slums."

Access to the Sea for All

Regional planners suggest that open spaces be provided in such areas. They also require that all beach front be public property, and accessible to the public. As one planner put it, to do otherwise is like inviting 100,000 people to a football game but allowing only the tallest and the strongest to force their way to the front row, where only they can see the game.

The elite and the rich have usually acquired the choice land sites of an area, living in enclaves of affluence. The new planning considers all of the people, or at least the middle classes, as well. In some of the less developed countries, there is the danger that the choice views will be acquired by foreigners, to the exclusion of the nationals. To forestall this, Mexico has banned non-Mexicans from buying land within 31 miles of an ocean. Of course, this may only insure that wealthy Mexicans control valuable beach frontages and that beach resort hotels have at least part-Mexican ownership.

It has been found that overuse of an area affects not only the people involved but the microclimate (climate for a limited area) itself. Parts of Greece illustrate the climate effect. During World War II, it was necessary for the Greeks to cut down huge tracts of forests to keep from freezing. With the forests gone, the water fall ran off quickly from the land, eroding it. The lack of trees, which breathe water into the atmosphere, actually reduced the amount of rainfall in certain areas.

Plainly, it is necessary to consider regional planning as part of tourist planning. From a business viewpoint, planning is necessary to prevent the entire environment from eroding, thereby reducing the attractiveness of an area and the larger region.

Touristic planning for islands presents the special problems of climate and space limitations. Because of prevailing winds, most islands have a windward and leeward side. The windward side is usually wet and comparatively cool; the other side is comparatively dry and sunny.

Some planners suggest that dramatic resort accommodations, service and entertainment facilities be built on the favored side, holding the windward side development to low rise buildings and expanses of agricultural and forest lands. Valleys can be used for green space, recreational sites, camping and for wildlife refuges. If necessary, because of the press of tourism, the planners would permit the dry and sunny side to have high-rise hotels, but only if interspersed with open-spaces, gardens, parks and corridors to the sea.

One way to ensure open spaces and

HYPOTHETICAL TRANSECT OF A GEORGIA COASTAL ISLAND

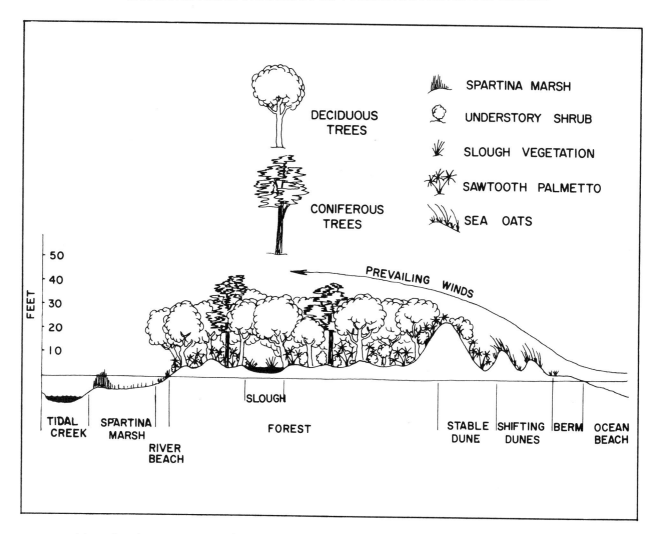

corridors in the concentrated tourist centers when they are part of the area would be to zone for parks and historic preservation sites.

Each area should have an upper limit placed on the number of rooms which can be built, a set number that will not permit overcrowding and erosion of the environment, to the detriment of all. Planners of the Aspen, Colorado ski area have done this. They estimate that between 28,000 and 30,000 skiers can be accommodated on the slopes without undue stress. Working back, they suggest that the number of hotel rooms be limited to the maximum number of skiers that can enjoy the area.

The necessity for government planning is seen clearly along ocean fronts and offshore islands. Sand dunes are necessary to maintain the ecology of coastal islands; the dunes are "the islands' frontal defense against the forces of wind and waves."[1] The prevailing winds which come from the sea tend to move sand dunes inland. To prevent such movement some plant growth, such as that of sea oats, is necessary to disrupt the flow of air and allow the sand to settle out on the top of front of the dunes rather than behind it. The dune grows taller until a critical point is reached where the energy of the wind is no longer sufficient to move the sand to the top. When this happens, a new dune is formed to the windward side of the existing dune and the is-

[1]Clement and Richardson, "Recreation on the Georgia Coast—An Ecological Approach," *Georgia Business*, University of Georgia, May, 1971.

land begins to build seaward rather than inland. The drawing on facing page illustrates how the prevailing winds are raised skyward by the dunes and how trees lift the winds even higher preventing them from moving sand inland.

It is seen that if dune buggies and animal grazing disturb the growth of plant life, the dunes will be swept inland and the beach destroyed. Construction of beachfront cottages, motels, and parking lots occasion the same result. A study by the University of Georgia recommends that any island that is to be used for recreation and residence should have at least one-third of the island kept in its natural state with no more than access trails in the reserve area. Beachfront property extending at least 100 yards back from high water lines should be government controlled and bull dozing of sand dunes prohibited.

Islands need a forest canopy to act as an air foil lifting the wind up and over the island. If clearings are made in the forest, the bordering trees are subjected to abnormal wind pressures which may uproot them. Pine trees, because of their great height, are particularly vulnerable to this danger. Offshore islands continue to expand and contract. Mild summer waves generally add sand to the border or berm of the islands while heavy winter waves more frequently remove sand. In the summer, the islands grow as prevailing on-shore winds move dry sand from the berm to the dunes. In winter, the process is reversed. The border or berm helps to moderate such changes by providing a reservoir of sand available to the dunes and the beach. Where the dune movement is not understood and the dunes destroyed by construction or overuse, large parts of the island may be claimed by the sea and become unavailable for anyone.

Degree of Government Participation in Area Development

Local, state and federal governments participate in every tourist development in one way or another. The degree of participation or intervention represents a wide range. The State of Vermont owns no ski developments but will build access roads to new developments. The State of New Hampshire, alongside Vermont, has built, and operates as a state enterprise, several ski developments. The State of Florida has built interchanges from state highways to link up with Disneyland in Central Florida.

The Federal government has made expensive studies and loans for tourist development in the Ozark region. Federal and state parks encourage tourists to come into the state. In 1968, the American states spent more than $8 million in advertising and promotion to attract tourists.

Most tourist developments require that state and local public money be used to extend sewage systems, water lines, roads and other public utilities. The establishment of State and Federal monuments and historic sites is a public cost.

Abroad, participation in tourist development is often almost completely controlled by the government. In Spain and Portugal, for example, where private enterprise was reluctant to invest in tourism, the governments have stepped in to prime the pump in getting tourism started.

In Spain, there are 85 government owned and operated hostelries, beautifully located, maintained and operated. A number of the "paradors," old castles, fortresses or monasteries, are attractions in themselves. Portugal has about twenty government operated "pousadas," many historically interesting, as well as some small hotels. The Greek government has built hotels, which as soon as they are operating well, are transferred to either the private sector or a mixed company.

The Roussillon-Languedoc tourist project on the Mediterranean in France is one of the more interesting government-sponsored tourist plans, the largest in Europe, perhaps anywhere. The area, amounting to one-twentieth of the national territory of France, expects to attract more than a million people each year, once it is operating. The magnitude of the operation was such that it was necessary to reassure private investors by associating public funds with private to minimize the risk.

The French government began by acquiring 3000 hectares of land which was declared an area of public utility. Provision for the development of the infrastructure—

The Parador Virrey Toledo. Rates in the state inns of Spain are probably the biggest bargains in hoteldom. Full American plan is something less than $10 a day for two persons. Service is outstanding. Quite naturally reservations are hard to come by during the summer season.

Lobby of the National Parador of the Castle of Santa Catalina, Jaen, Spain. The Paradors of Spain are perhaps the most picturesque hostelries in the world. Each is different. Many are converted castles, mansions, or religious houses. Furnishings are authentic antiques or especially made. The Paradors are operated by an autonomous state organization, Administracion Turistica Espaniola. The organization operates wayside inns and upland refuges as well, in all a total of about 85 hostelries.

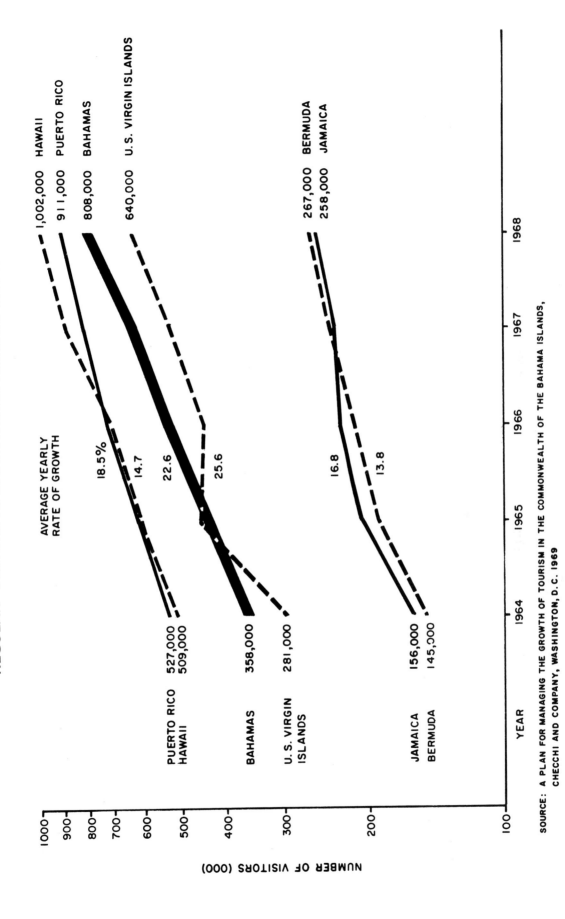

"REGULAR" VISITORS TO MAJOR ISLAND RESORTS 1964-1968

AVERAGE YEARLY
RATE OF GROWTH

HAWAII	1,002,000
PUERTO RICO	911,000
BAHAMAS	808,000
U.S. VIRGIN ISLANDS	640,000
BERMUDA	267,000
JAMAICA	258,000

18.5%
14.7
22.6
25.6
16.8
13.8

PUERTO RICO	527,000
HAWAII	509,000
BAHAMAS	358,000
U. S. VIRGIN ISLANDS	281,000
JAMAICA	156,000
BERMUDA	145,000

NUMBER OF VISITORS (000)

1000
900
800
700
600
500
400
300
200
100

1964   1965   1966   1967   1968

YEAR

SOURCE: A PLAN FOR MANAGING THE GROWTH OF TOURISM IN THE COMMONWEALTH OF THE BAHAMA ISLANDS, CHECCHI AND COMPANY, WASHINGTON, D. C. 1969

four major highways, swamp clearance, port construction, etc.—was contracted to four mixed companies. Government loans were made available to the companies.

Once the infrastructure has been completed, the land will be sold to various users or promoters at a price including the development cost of the infrastructure. Promoters have the obligation to develop the land which they purchase and it is forbidden to resell empty land. Under these arrangements, the government keeps control without exercising a monopoly of execution. The government maintains an overall policy of land acquisition, controls the physical planning and development and maintains financial coordination over the investment in the entire area.[1]

A large number of national governments encourage tourism by providing specific incentives for private investment. In Spain, 25 percent of the total investment in tourism, especially hotels, has been made under special credit arrangements. In Turkey, where tourism investment is only just beginning, the proportion is as high as 80 percent of the total amount of money invested in tourism.

Credit for tourism investment is usually only given to developments approved by the government. Such credits take the form of offering long-term loans at lower than market rates of interest. In most countries, loans for hotel construction are for about 25 years; reconstruction and equipment loans, either 10 or 15 years. Other aids may include reduced custom duties on imported construction materials and equipment needed for tourist services.

Land Speculation

A major problem in nearly every tourist development is that brought about by land speculation. As soon as a hotel goes up on a property, adjoining land jumps in value. One device that can be used by a government is to price the land at its value over a long period previous to the classification of the zone for tourism development. Another is to impose a progressive tax on non-utilization of land in tourism development areas or place a tax on added value. In some cases, the government may buy up the land secretly in advance. The Roussillon-Languedoc project is an example.[2]

Without government aid, tourism in some regions cannot grow substantially. For example, in the Caribbean Islands, a jet airport is an absolute necessity, if large numbers of tourists are to be attracted to the islands. No independent developer is likely to build such an airport.

Inaccessible mountain areas are not likely to be opened for tourist development without access roads being built by the state. Venture capital is notably reluctant to build hotels in developing countries, and for good reasons. Almost invariably, the government finances at least one luxury hotel and hopes that visitors will come as tourists but leave as investors. It also hopes that private capital will build other tourist facilities.

Training for Nationals

Governments have other good reasons for financing at least one or two hotels. Such hotels bring in expert technical advice on construction and operation of the hotel. Outside management is used to train large numbers of nationals, offering training which they would otherwise not have access to. This has happened in widely scattered places including Jamaica, Trinidad, Barbados and the Ivory Coast.

A wide range of government control of development exists. In England and Scotland, government permission is required for almost anything that is built, or any building that is changed. The regulations apply to everyone; Prince Phillip was piqued because he had to get permission to block up a fireplace. Roadsigns are banned completely in Hawaii.

On the Island of St. Croix, the government tells developers what recreational facilities to build, like it or not. Developers of Carolina Reef, a 400-unit luxury condominium, were told to build a 9-hole golf course. The developers were also obliged to supply landscaping, a desalination plant, garbage disposal facilities and a self-contained power generating plant. The reason

[1]Organization for Economic Cooperation and Development, *Tourism Development and Economic Growth* (Paris, 1967), pp. 33-34.
[2]*Ibid.*

for the private utilities is that the capacity of the public utility on the island is already strained; so too are the existing recreation facilities.

Tourist Hotel Economics in a Developing Country*

An economic pattern seems to be developing as the result of experience with new hotels in developing countries, especially some of the island nations in the Caribbean. Typically, the country, eager for tourist dollars, grants extensive tax advantages to hotel entrepreneurs. Import duties are waived and a tax holiday on profits may be given for 10 or more years. Nearly everyone welcomes the new hotel as a boon to the economy. Land owners do not expect huge profits on the sale of their land. Land speculation has not yet set in. Labor is cheap. The nationals who may be unemployed or receiving only a few dollars a day are delighted to work in the hotels at low wages. Tourists are seen as benefactors bringing economic blessings. This is phase I.

Phase II is a halcyon period for all concerned and may last five or ten years. The hotel owner, who has had reasonable land construction and operation costs, does extremely well financially. His labor costs may be only 15 percent or less of his gross sales, as compared with 25 to 40 percent of the sales in the U. S. Local produce and sea food are available at reasonable cost. He pays relatively few taxes and profits can be repatriated without interference from the government. The entrepreneur may have only a small property, 20 to 50 rooms, but, because he can get rates as high as $50 a day, makes a handsome return on his investment and effort.

Storm Clouds Gather

Phase III begins to see storm clouds. The natives begin to resent the tourist who is immeasurably rich by their standards. They also see that relatively few of the locals are benefiting very much from the tourism. Land speculators are getting rich. Perhaps a demagog appears to stir latent feelings of inferiority. The native is told that he is exchanging one role of servitude for another. He has given up the hoe to put on the busboy jacket. He is still servant to the white man. The easy familiarity of many of the tourists makes him wonder if he is not truly as good or better than the tourist.

The government begins to take a hard line on tourism. It seems that perhaps 80 percent of the tourist dollar goes almost immediately out of the country. The economy, which may have been based largely on agriculture, changes character. Tourism may have been pushed at the expense of agriculture, which has been allowed to decline by default. Radical groups may pressure the government and stir completely unrealistic feelings of national pride.

Phase IV also means trouble for the hotel operator, and perhaps the economy generally. The end of the tax holiday period has come. The hotel operator is faced with high or rising fixed costs over which he has no control. The local union may insist upon wages equivalent to those received in a large U. S. city. Labor efficiency, which was never high, drops off even further. The tourist may be insulted or at best treated lackadaisically. Quite naturally, the tourist decides not to return and also to tell his friends of his poor treatment.

The government, seeing that there are few repeat visitors, becomes alarmed and increases its tourist promotion budget. It may use that budget to favor development of certain political constituencies over established areas of tourism. The government, which formerly permitted the entry of skilled personnel, now refuses immigration permits to them. Local produce and seafood prices have been driven up.

The government, being realistic, recognizes that the nationals are not prepared by training or inclination to be effective in resort management. Yet national pride insists that locals hold management positions. The government, reacting to such pressure, opens a hotel school on a vocational level. The nationals resent this and again national pride calls for a hotel school on the management level. The school is opened but few applicants appear. Tourism has reached a plateau and an economic recession in the tourist

---

*The pattern of development was suggested in a lecture by Eric Green at the University of Massachusetts.

market may cause a precipitous drop in tourism to the country.

Phase V means hard times for the resort operator. During the ten-year period when tourism was on the rise, too many hotel rooms were built. Hotels have been built on very expensive land, too highly priced because of land speculation uncontrolled by the government. Little regional planning has been done or the planning has not been implemented. A hodgepodge and clutter of buildings have closed off the beauty spots from the general public and are keeping much natural beauty hidden from the general view. The new hotel operators have had to erect high-rise buildings at high cost often side by side with other high-rises.

The investors in the new hotels see that they themselves cannot operate them and attach their operations to international chains. The international chains, with worldwide marketing facilities, have a tremendous advantage over the independent operator who has relied almost exclusively on word-of-mouth advertising and travel agents for his business. His smaller property may look relatively unattractive when compared to the huge multi-million dollar resort at his side. He must lower his rates to stay in business and is beset by a number of problems which did not exist when he first arrived.

Phase VI completes the developmental pattern of the resort in the newly developed country. At first, it was wonderful—the operator was wanted—he made a fine profit during the first years of operation. Now the area has matured and with maturity have come a number of political and psychological problems that he did not bargain for. There may even be riots as has happened in Bermuda, Curacao and Jamaica. Many of these problems could have been avoided if regional governmental planning had been done initially and enforced as the area developed.

Recreational Towns

The environmental design approach to area planning may include the development of entire towns. Unlike the "new towns" of England, Reston, Va. and Columbia, Md., which are industrially oriented—or bedroom communities—the new communities proposed are recreation rather than work-oriented. They may range in population from a few hundred to a hundred thousand. Havasu City and Sun City, Ariz. are examples.

Most of the residents will be retirees and their families; tourists will add to the numbers. The rest of the people will be those engaged in supplying services to tourists and to the community. Recreational facilities—golf courses, marinas, beaches, riding trails, tennis courts—will serve both resident and tourist. The new community envisages a new lifestyle, blending with nature and outdoor-oriented. Large blocks of land will be left inviolate.

In some cases, for example the Island of Hawaii, the government is working with the private sector in planning the towns. The State, a large landowner in Hawaii, can trade State lands for private lands to make large contiguous acreages available.

The Hawaiian Islands have had a number of large land developments taking place in the late 60's and early 70's. Some are on a grand scale. The South Kohala project, developed by Boise-Cascade, is a 31,000 acre project which will include two Robert Trent Jones golf courses, a recreational village of 5800 house lots and a 10,000-acre recreational open-space area. Some 17 miles of access road had to be improved; several 1200-foot wells drilled; water lines, a recreational center and other facilities built.

As is true of all such developments, the project proceeds in stages. Initially, 4710 acres were left in urban reserve and some 8430 acres left in agricultural and ranching lands. Eventually, the latter will be sold in large parcels. As is also true of most such projects, a resort hotel area is an integral part of the project; an 850-acre section set aside for a resort area surrounding Anaehoomalu Bay is part of the overall plan.

Similarly to most land development, profits are projected to rise sharply as the price of land is raised at each stage of development.

Ski Resort Development

The ski resort has developed from a rope-tow operation to a vast complex of lifts, shops, restaurants and room accommodations. Many ski resorts have become year round operations, having added ancillary facilities such as lakes and golf courses. More importantly for profits, many of the larger new developments include land developments for the sale of lots, second homes or condominiums, often all three.

The market for the modern ski resort has changed from being a relatively small cult of avid sports skiers to include large numbers of affluent young people and entire families. Families now comprise 40 percent of the total market.[1]

Operators of ski resorts have also changed from being individual or small group owners to public corporations. Large sums of money are required for laying out the beautifully sculptured ski runs, the huge lift equipment and the extensive apres ski facilities. Cost is about $500 to $1000 per skier handled on the "design day"—a term referring to the average attendance of the 30 highest days.[2] (If the design day capacity is calculated at 5000 skiers, the ski area will require a capital investment of between $2.5 and $5 million.)

Unfortunately, of the approximately 500 ski areas in the U. S., less than half are consistent profit makers, according to Harrison A. Price, whose company has done extensive planning for ski developments. Price states that three out of four new operators do not generate the kind of profit that would be acceptable to the average investor.

Price divides ski operations into three types: (1) The Day Skier Facility, (2) The Weekend Skier Facility and (3) The Vacation Skier Facility. The travel time necessary to get to the ski area from a precise market determines the class of the area. Generally, the area that depends upon weekend and holiday skiers has the poorest return on investment.

Vacation ski areas, on the other hand, that can maintain a high level of skiing throughout the season are the most profitable. Only the exceptional ski lift operation, says Price, consistently grosses 50 percent or more of the original investment annually. For most operations, the Breakeven point is reached when gross revenue is 28 percent of the original investment.

Real estate sales may be the most profitable part of the vacation ski resort. High land values also attract the non-skiing investor who may desire to speculate on the recreation properties. Such areas also typically have a high rate of summer use. Profitability is coming to depend more and more on dual-season operation.

Sales of lots, vacation homes and condominiums, however, do not help the weekend ski areas because there is little incentive for the day skier to purchase property when he lives so close to the resort.

Government and Consensus in Planning Goals

It is extremely difficult in a capitalistic and relatively free society to legislate into action regional plans, no matter how objective and worthwhile they may be. Vested interests and desire for private gain, if not checked, override public interest. Political action is usually the result of compromise, and often brought on only by crisis.

In the late 60's, the American public became increasingly aware of pollution of the environment and the general deterioration of the "quality" of life in the United States. A natural consequence was to place more value on regional planning. A government must constantly balance the needs of various groups and try to establish consensus, even though it be temporary.

The State of Hawaii offers an example of how priorities concerning tourism changed when scrutinized from a broader viewpoint. Hawaii, with limited land, a rapidly rising resident population, together with a sharp increase in the number of visitors, became alarmed enough to institute group planning for tourism.

In 1970, a Travel Industry Congress was called by Governor John A. Burns to study and make recommendations about tourism and travel. Nearly 400 representative citizens from industry, university and public office, labor and land owners convened at a Travel Industry Congress. Guidelines for development were set forth which could later be enforced by appropriate legislation. Among the recommendations made

[1]Harrison A. Price, "The Ski Resort and Its Feasibility," Address, Economics Research Associates, President, Brown Palace Hotel, Denver, Colo., Oct. 26, 1970.
[2]*Ibid.*

by the Congress were the following:

1. A comprehensive state development plan should be developed.

2. Where a choice must be made between resident goals and visitor goals, the resident must have paramount importance.

3. Substantial areas of land should be donated to the state representing in value an appropriate proportion of the increase in price of land created by rezoning.

4. Free public access to the shorelines must be insured.

5. A major program of public acquisition of shore areas should be undertaken.

6. Beach and improvement programs along Waikiki and Ala Moana Beaches in Honolulu should be such that surfing sites are protected.

7. The development code should encourage resort developers to provide housing and community facilities for their employees.

8. Strict controls should be placed on exhaust pollutants of aircraft.

9. No high-rise construction should be allowed within the sight lines affecting the profile of Diamond Head.

10. The assessment of land should be revised to include non-economic criteria as well as the strictly economic criterion usually used: "the highest and best use" of the land.

11. The number of guest rooms in the Waikiki area should be restricted to 26,000 by the year 1980.[1]

Multiple Use of Land

Planners may often consider "multiple use" of the land. The same area of land may be used for growth of timber, for camping, for fishing and for hunting. Agricultural land may also be used for hunting and fishing.

Reservoirs present many possibilities for recreational development. For example, the reservoirs of the Tennessee Valley Authority have been developed into a national sport fishing area, second only to the Great Lakes among inland waters. The TVA reservoirs have combined shore lines in excess of 10,000 miles and had an annual visitation of over 36 million man-days in the early 1960's.[2]

Utilizing Historical Sites and Treasures

Tourist area developers often find that there are historical and archeological aspects of an area that will enhance the entire project, and especially the tourist development. The Boise-Cascade development, South Kohala, on the Island of Hawaii, has incorporated a number of historical sites into its 31,000 acre development. A Bishop Museum team of archeologists engaged in an eight-month study of the area. A number of important historical finds were reported in the Anaehoomalu Bay area; these the Boise officials plan to restore and preserve.

Travel Relationships to the Proposed Development

Vital to the success of any resort destination area is the available means of transportation. The three critical factors in transportation—cost, convenience and speed—affect the success of every resort, even though it may be intended to be highly exclusive. The closer a development is to population centers containing people of some affluence, the greater the likelihood of success for the development. If several modes of transportation are available for travel to the area, so much the better.

As distance increases between market and destination, the potential number of visitors decreases. Also, as distance increases, the affluence of the potential market must increase for the traveler to be able to afford the cost of the long travel. As previously pointed out, however, absolute distance may not be as important as travel time and convenience.

As advances are made within a mode of transportation and changes in modes come about, the travel flow changes. In the case of Hawaii, the introduction of supersonic planes and the introduction of new routes which bypass the Islands can change the flow map drastically. In 1970, Japan Airlines scheduled direct flights from the West Coast to Japan, bypassing Honolulu. Tourists, who may have considered stopping

[1]Hawaii Visitors Bureau, *Recommended Goals for Hawaii's Visitor Industry* (Honolulu: 1970).
[2]U. S. Dept. of Commerce, The Office of Regional Economic Development, *Tourism and Recreation* (Washington, D. C.: Arthur D. Little, Inc., 1967), p. 101.

over in Hawaii because of the necessity of a stopover there, now have the option of flying direct to Japan and bypassing the Islands.

The Hotel as Part of Area Development

An integral part of any resort development, of course, includes hotels and may include the newer concept of a hotel-condominium. The hotel may be the principal reason that the traveler comes to the area, be it for business, pleasure or convention purposes. If well planned, the hotel adds to the general appearance of the area and can be a major source of employment.

When viewed as part of the total development and as necessary to the development, the investment per room in the hotel is subject to different standards than if the hotel were to stand on its own. Developers are building hotels costing $30,000 to $50,000 per room. The Mauna Kea on the Island of Hawaii is reputed to have cost $100,000 a room. If judged by the rule of thumb that the hotel room rate should be based on $1.00 per $1000 invested, it is seen that such hotels will not be profitable as independent ventures.

Yet the hotel may be highly profitable when viewed as a part of a total complex. The developer recaptures the hotel cost in the sale of land and other facilities. When seen in the perspective of the total development, which may run as high as $500 million to a billion dollars, the cost of the hotel is minimal. Alcoa's Century City in Los Angeles will cost $500 million. Disney World in Central Florida will represent an investment close to $1 billion.[1]

A statement of estimated annual income and expenses is drawn up for the proposed hotel. Such a statement projects costs and profits for varying levels of occupancy. Table XIX on page 206 is for a 200-room destination resort. The example was done for a proposed resort in Australia. The work was done by the international accounting firm of Harris, Kerr, Forster Co. for the Australian Tourist Commission. The statement shows costs and profits for three levels of occupancy—65, 70, 75 percent. The estimates assume a $22 average room rate per day. It can be seen that profits rise more sharply than occupancy once the breakeven point has been reached. In the example, a 65 percent occupancy rate will produce a profit of $602,300 before capital expenses. With an occupancy rate of 75 percent, profit increases to $737,100.

Another projection needed for a feasibility study for a resort hotel is one reflecting the cost of money and depreciation. Such an analysis necessarily assumes a certain average daily rate and annual occupancy of the hotel under consideration. It sets up a schedule based on a particular rate of annual depreciation for the building, another one for the building equipment and a third for furniture and fixtures. It usually assumes that the property is financed by a particular amount of mortgage financing at a certain rate of interest.

A financial analysis of a proposed resort is presented, starting on page 156.

Retail Shopping Plazas as Part of a Resort Destination

Few resort areas can succeed without providing space for resort shops, restaurants, evening entertainment and travel services. Shop facilities should offer a diversity of wearing apparel and items ordinarily not stocked in the usual store. According to Harris, Kerr, Forster, there is a relatively uniform relationship between hotel revenue in a resort area and volume of sales in shops within the resort hotel and near it. In a feasibility study for a resort on the Island of Hawaii, the firm projected sales of $5.1 million per year in the various shops; 20 percent or $1 million sales were forecast for shops within the hotels, while the balance of sales would be developed in separate shopping complexes.[2]

The Condominium as a Means of Financing a Resort

In the 60's, inclusion of the condominium plan in resort hotel financing became fairly common. By selling guest rooms —studios, suites or individual dwelling units

[1]"Hotel as a Catalyst in Development Complexes," *The Cornell Hotel and Restaurant Administration Quarterly* (Nov. 1969), p. 11.
[2]Harris, Kerr, Forster and Company, Land Development Plan, The Kohala Coast Resort Region/Island of Hawaii (Honolulu: 1967), p. 54.

PROJECTED RETURNS FOR CONDOMINIUM OWNER

Year	Rental Income	Operating Expense	Interest	Depreciation	Profit (Loss)	Debt Amortization	Cash Flow	Tax Payment (Shelter)	Net Gain
Super	1500	500	300	500	400	200	500	200	300
Good	1000		300	500	(300)	200	0	(150)	150
Poor	500		300	500	(800)	200	(500)	(400)	(100)

and apartments—as condominiums within a resort, large cash flows were generated for the developer. In some cases, the condominium was sold before the resort was built.

The condominium buyer usually pays 25-35 percent in cash and gets a mortgage on the balance of his debt for the condominium. In other cases, the developer holds the mortgage and receives the prevailing rate of interest for it. In some developments, the condominium owner is required to pool his condominium with the resort complex for rental when he is not occupying the space.

In the case of the Maui Hilton, the developer contracted with the Hilton Corporation to operate the complex, paying Hilton all of the operating expenses, 3 percent of the gross sales and 10 percent of the net profit. Profits are divided among all of the condominium owners. In other condominium hotels, the space owner arranges individually with the management to rent his space when he is not occupying it.

In some cases, the developer leases back the condominium from the buyer for a definite period. At the Ilikai hotel operation in Honolulu, for example, the Ilikai takes a three year lease on the condominium from the new buyer.

The advantage to the developer is that he gets his profit out of the building much sooner than if he attempted to operate it. The space buyer gets a tax advantage; interest which he pays on his mortgage is a tax deductible item on Federal income tax. Although he is charged for the maintenance of his space, he expects to have the charges at least partially off-set by earnings from the rental of his space. In the 60's, nearly all condominium construction appreciated at a 10-15 percent rate a year, another advantage to the space owner.

In the strange way that income taxes are computed in the U. S., the condominium owner, who makes his unit available for rental when he is not occupying it, is allowed the cost of his trip to the condominium in a resort as a business expense. In other words, the condominium owner gets several tax advantages and, in addition, can write off part of his vacation expense for income tax purposes. Little wonder that condominiums have been exceedingly popular in Hawaii, Florida and the Virgin Islands.

Financial Projections

In making financial projections for condominiums, it is often possible to show that few or no further cash expenditures are required after the down payment is made. The buyer, with a minimum amount of current expenditure, can have a second home in a desirable recreational area and, at the same time, build a financial equity by reducing the principal amount of the mortgage. Under favorable circumstances there could even be a cash return.[1]

Robert Lee of Peat, Marwick and Mitchell, the international accounting firm, gives an example of the results a condominium owner (one in a 50 percent tax bracket) can anticipate. This is for a condominium in which the developer maintains and rents the condominium for the owner when the owner is not in residence. (See above.)

Mr. Lee points out that the cash shelter provided by the condominium is most advantageous for persons in high income brackets, especially those whose taxes may constitute as much as 60 or more percent of their income. Such persons are constantly searching for tax shelter investments. Condominium and other real estate ventures have been a popular means of reducing taxes and, at the same time, increasing equity as the property appreciates in value. Thousands of relatively small investors have

---

[1]Ralph Bardoff, "Resort Oriented Hotel Condominiums" (*Transcript*, July, 1970).

bought condominiums and many have experienced appreciation of 100 percent or more over a ten-year period. Experience in South Florida has generally been favorable but the situation could change. In the U. S. Virgin Islands, condominiums during the period 1969-1973 depreciated sharply in value. As Mr. Lee points out: "The tax shelter game really makes sense only for those in the higher tax brackets."[1]

Tax rulings regarding income and losses as a result of condominium ownership are changing and may remove some of the tax shelter advantage. As of 1973 the condominium owner—typically, a prosperous business or professional man—received several advantages from ownership in a well located, well designed and well managed condominium. He could use it as a second home, rent it while not there, offset income with depreciation and deduct any losses from his income tax.

Condominium rentals were usually to people like himself—but about ten years younger, during the popular seasons. For the off-seasons or "shoulder" seasons (between high seasons), the condominium manager can rent his unit to members of a convention or group. The manager can seek assistance in rental from agencies that specialize in condo rentals, among them Venture Inc., Vacation Home Exchange Assn. and Destination Concepts. These latter provide a reservation network assisted by computers similar to hotel reservation networks

Even so, the prospective condo buyer is well advised to read the fine print. Maintenance fees can run as high as $300 a month on two bedroom units. Assessments may be made against owners by the management company. Not all condo units appreciate in value as condo owners in parts of the Caribbean have learned. As in any business venture costly construction delays can occur, markets for renters can be saturated and the character of a destination change for the worse.

Laws covering condominium developments are not clear or, where specific, are difficult to follow. Are condominium developments promoted by promises of rental income subject to the control of the Security and Exchange Commission? The SEC has stated as much since 1963. Because of the cost and time involved and because many properties were originally planned as small developments of seasonal homes, only about 4 percent of the condominium developments by 1973 were registered with the SEC.[2] As long as two years were required for clearance with the SEC in some cases. Prospectuses needed for advertising and clearance by the SEC ran as long as 134 printed pages. In 1973, the SEC agreed to accept 20-page prospectuses.

The Apartotel, an apartment building which is also used as a residential hotel, comes to us from Spain.[3] The Melia Organization in 1970 completed the Melia Castilla in Madrid, a $23 million, 1000-unit, luxury hotel-apartment condominium, the third apartotel owned and operated by the company.

Jose Melia, president of the company, launched his business career in 1947 with two sight-seeing buses converted from ambulances. The apartotel concept started in 1963 with the 171-unit Torremar at Torremolinos on the Costa del Sol in Spain. Under the apartotel concept, a person of moderate means can buy a condominium apartment and have access to full hotel service for $21,230. The down payment is 20 percent—$4246, the balance paid off within four years. He may choose to put his apartment into a rental pool. If so, he receives a dividend from profits on the operation which in the past has amounted to about 9 percent of the investment.

The Apartotel in Spain

In some apartotels, the condominium owner chooses his own furnishings; in the Melia apartotels he does not. The owner of a Melia apartment gains other advantages. He becomes a member of Club Melia which enables him to rent a room in any other Melia hotel, motel, or apartotel at a 20 percent discount and membership also entitles him to a 20 percent discount on Melia rent-

[1]*Statler Lecture Series,* University of Massachusetts, 1973.
[2]"Resort Hotel Condominiums, Guidelines for Resort Development," *Cornell Hotel and Restaurant Administration Quarterly* (May, 1973).
[3]"Spanish Introduce Apartotel Idea," *Lodging and Food Service News* (June 5, 1971).

a-cars and bus tours. The Melia Organization claims to be the fourth largest travel agency in the world with 65 agencies, 125 tour buses, and 500 rental cars. The company operates 17 hotels or motels in Spain and plans to expand into other European countries, Venezuela and Puerto Rico. It also operates in Mexico.

In New York City, Manhattan East has been developed in a manner similar to the apartotel. Twelve buildings in midtown Manhattan were acquired and converted into apartment hotels, with studios and one- and two-bedroom apartments with terraces.

In a very short time, condominiums have exploded all over the United States from Hawaii to Puerto Rico. Spain and Portugal have also seen rapid condominium growth. The buyer can select a second home at a recreational facility which may be much more extensive or attractive than anything he could obtain on a single unit basis. He need have little worry about maintaining the property; in addition, the rental received when he is not in residence may be greater because the condominium as a whole is managed by a professional. He need not worry about vandalism and he may be able to secure better mortgage financing.

Industrial Corporations and Land Development

In the 60's, several factors favored large industrial corporations moving into land development. Profits from industrial operations could be offset by development costs. The developed land continued to rise in value and land itself continued to appreciate year after year, in some places, as much as 10 percent annually. Profit from sale of developed land was taxed at capital gains rate, about half that on the usual corporation profits. A number of U. S. corporations were large owners of agricultural land, and much of it could be converted to resort areas, increasing its value and profitability.

These large corporations had large management staffs and large amounts of money, or access to it. They turned to architects and economic consultants to develop master development plans for land they owned or were interested in.

Following is the list of some major companies in tourist area development.

EXAMPLES OF MAJOR AREA COMPANIES IN TOURIST AREA DEVELOPMENT[1]

Corporation	Development
American Cement Co.	Investor in "Snowmass-at-Aspen," Colorado, developed by the Janss brothers.
AMFAC, Inc.	Owns most of Maui Island, Hawaii and is investor in its hotels. Owns Fred Harvey, Inc., and recently acquired Death Valley, Calif., from Borax.
Atlantic-Richfield	100 acres at Kaanapali and other land in Hawaii
Atlas Chemical Industries	Owns resort community in northeastern Pennsylvania
Boise-Cascade	Former Lake Tarlton Club and other land in New Hampshire for vacation home development.
Cherry-Burrell Corp.	South Caicos, Turk Island, south of the Bahamas.

[1]*The Cornell Hotel and Restaurant Administration Quarterly* (Nov., 1969), pp. 12-13.

Citgo (City Service Oil Co.)	Joint venture with Restaurant Associates to build Citgo Villages along Interstate highways.
Consolidated Oil & Gas, Inc.	Owns land developments in Hawaii, including 11,000 acre ranch on Kauai and on Hawaii island.
W. R. Grace & Co.	Purchased Jacque Borel et Cie Assoc., firm Societe de Promotion Touristique (13 restaurants and 200 motels planned in Europe).
Great Lakes Properties	Investor in resort project in Portugal.
Hamilton Watch Co.	Investor in resort in Lancaster County, Pa., owned by Bush Terminal of New York.
Hamilton Oil Co.	50,000 acres near new Houston airport. 25,000 acres in Clear Lake City.
International Paper Co.	Acquired real estate firm to enter vacation home development.
Kaiser Industries	Investor in Hawaiian resorts.
McCollough Oil. Corp.	Lake Havasu City, Ariz.; Pueblo West, Colo., a 26,000 acre development planned for 60,000 residents.
North American Rockwell	Investor in resorts in Bimini, Bahamas.
Owens-Illinois, Inc.	Owns acreage in Bahamas, an industrial park at Perrysburg, Ohio, and recreational use land in southeastern U. S.
Phelan Sulphur Co.	Bought 24 acres for $240 million development near Montego Bay, Jamaica. Also has New Falmouth resort.
Phillips 66	Expansion of Pier 66 and marina program in several Southeastern states.
Shakespeare Co. (Mfgr. of fishing tackle)	Owns a resort in Michigan.
Shuford Development Co.	Owns Cape Kennedy Hilton.
Signal Oil & Gas	Kona Village Hideaway, Hawaii, 50,000 acres on Hawaii island, 5 to 7 more resort hotels; also Huntington Harbor in Calif.
Disney R.C.A. U. S. Gypsum U. S. Steel	Developers of Disney World, new town, industrial park, suburban housing development on 27,000 acres in central Florida.

TABLE XIX—PROPOSED 200-ROOM DESTINATION RESORT
STATEMENT OF ESTIMATED ANNUAL INCOME AND EXPENSES

73,000 Rooms Available Annually
$22.00 AVERAGE TARIFF PER ROOM PER DAY[1]

	65% Occupancy 47,450 Rooms Occupied			70% Occupancy 51,100 Rooms Occupied			75% Occupancy 54,740 Rooms Occupied		
	Amount	Ratio (1)	Per Available Room	Amount	Ratio (1)	Per Available Room	Amount	Ratio (1)	Per Available Room
Total Sales and Income									
Rooms	$1,043,900	61.7%	$5,220	$1,124,200	61.5%	$5,621	$1,204,500	61.3%	$6,023
Food	410,700	24.3	2,054	447,900	24.5	2,240	485,400	24.7	2,427
Beverages	203,700	12.0	1,018	219,400	12.0	1,097	234,900	12.0	1,175
Other departmental profit and other income	34,200	2.0	171	36,600	2.0	183	39,300	2.0	196
Total Sales and Income	$1,692,500	100.0%	$8,463	$1,828,100	100.0%	$9,141	$1,964,100	100.0%	$9,821
Cost of Goods Sold and Departmental Wages and Expenses									
Rooms	$ 268,300	25.7%	$1,341	$ 284,000	25.2%	$1,420	$ 297,500	24.7%	$1,487
Food and beverages	497,700	81.0%	2,489	537,200	80.5%	2,686	576,200	80.0%	2,881
Telephone	35,600		178	38,300		192	41,100		206
Total Cost of Goods Sold and Departmental Wages and Expenses	$ 801,600	47.4%	$4,008	$ 859,500	47.0%	$4,298	$ 914,800	46.6%	$4,574
Gross Operating Income	$ 890,900	52.6%	$4,455	$ 968,600	53.0%	$4,843	$1,049,300	53.4%	$5,247
Deductions from Gross Operating Income									
Administrative and general expenses	$ 110,000	6.5%	$ 550	$ 115,200	6.3%	$ 576	$ 119,800	6.1%	$ 599
Advertising and business promotion	45,000	2.6	225	45,000	2.5	225	45,000	2.3	225
Heat, light and power	66,000	3.9	330	70,000	3.8	350	72,800	3.7	364
Repairs and maintenance	62,600	3.7	313	65,000	3.6	325	68,700	3.5	344
Total Deductions from Gross Operating Income	$ 283,600	16.7%	$1,418	$ 295,200	16.2%	$1,476	$ 306,300	15.6%	$1,532
House Profit	$ 607,300	35.9%	$3,037	$ 673,400	36.8%	$3,367	$ 743,000	37.8%	$3,715
Store Rentals	33,800	2.0%	269	36,600	2.0	183	39,300	2.0	197
Gross Operating Profit	$ 641,100	37.9%	$3,206	$ 710,000	38.8%	$3,550	$ 782,300	39.8%	$3,912
Land Rental	38,800	2.3	194	41,900	2.3	210	45,200	2.3	226
Profit before Capital Expenses	$ 602,300	35.6%	$3,012	$ 668,100	36.5%	$3,340	$ 737,100	37.5%	$3,686

(1) Rooms and food and beverages cost and expense ratios relate to departmental sales. All other ratios relate to total sales and income.

[1]Harris, Kerr, Forster and Company, *Tourism Plan for Central Australia*, done for Australia Tourist Commission, Melbourne (Honolulu, 1969).

CARIBBEAN TOURISM

Excepting Europe and the Mediterranean, the Caribbean attracts the most U. S. tourists traveling overseas. Some 4.5 million people were counted as tourists to the region during 1971. The Caribbean offers the magic of flip-flopping winter into summer.

It is instant exotica, providing health, change, excitement. For the hotelman, it offers a multitude of problems. For the investor, a number of questions and, more recently, for the tourist, stories of rudeness, resentment and perhaps danger.

For the people of most of the Caribbean Basin, tourism raises a major question, in many places the most important economic question they will face: Should they foster tourism, construct infrastructure, accommodations and attractions and welcome visitors? The natural resources—beaches, climate, natural beauty—are there to be exploited. Can the economic and social problems connected with tourism be solved so that the natural beauty is enhanced; can the benefits of tourism be distributed so as to benefit everyone? A related question: Are there reasonable alternatives to tourism?

Geographically and climatically, the Caribbean ties together; politically, culturally, and economically, the Caribbean is more collage than community. The area is most notably divided between the British Commonwealth states and territories and those which are historically Hispanic, French or Dutch. In much of the area, the Black/ White syndrome, with its roots in slavery, permeates and complicates the differences. Economics, historical and current, serve to further differentiate cultures within the area. Nevertheless, the Caribbean is thought of as a tropical sea with typical tropical flora, mood and sea breezes. The tradewind blows constantly over most of the area; sugar, coconuts, bananas, political instability, languor, passion, and poverty create the image. Psychologically, the Caribbean is often conceived as a unit.

As a tourist attraction, the area is seen as all of a piece, a view which is only partly valid. White sandy beaches, warm ocean water, the opportunity to swim and to sail are major appeals. For North Americans, the Caribbean projects palm trees waving in balmy breezes, the limbo dance, straw markets, new hotels set in scenic beauty. More recently, the Caribbean has become a tropical sea cruised by sleek vessels manned with foreign crews, providing groaning tables and continuous entertainment with a series of one- or two-day stopovers at exotic islands with free port prices.

The Caribbean is a bottle of rum for a dollar, a calypso singer, a steel band and, best of all, an abrupt and exciting change from a humdrum office or plant. The image is of a whole; reality is something else.

For the sophisticate, each island territory or littoral country has a topography, history and culture of its own. Winter temperatures vary. The ocean is sometimes too cool, except for the hardy, for winter swimming north of Puerto Rico. Several of the islands lack attractive beaches; some have only black sand which absorbs the sun and becomes undesirably hot for walking or beach-lazing. Several of the islands offer only the barest of amenities and no entertainment.

The Caribbean as an area provides a fascinating study of tourism: its economics, problems and inter-relationships with politics and social change. Tourism, while holding out the promise of economic salvation to most of the island economies, which otherwise are marginally productive, has also precipitated feelings of inferiority, anxiety and hatred. Reviled and courted, tourism has brought dollars and tensions, spectacular hotels and overcrowding, tax revenues and gambling, employment and exclusion.

For several of the Caribbean islands, tourism could well be the only industry which can be competitive in the world marketplace; yet it is possible, as recent events have shown, that large numbers of people will turn their backs on tourism as degrading to the human condition. More than that, some leaders, and many individuals, have by various means actively discouraged visitors from coming to their islands. Whether leadership in the islands can reconcile feelings with economics remains to be seen. The

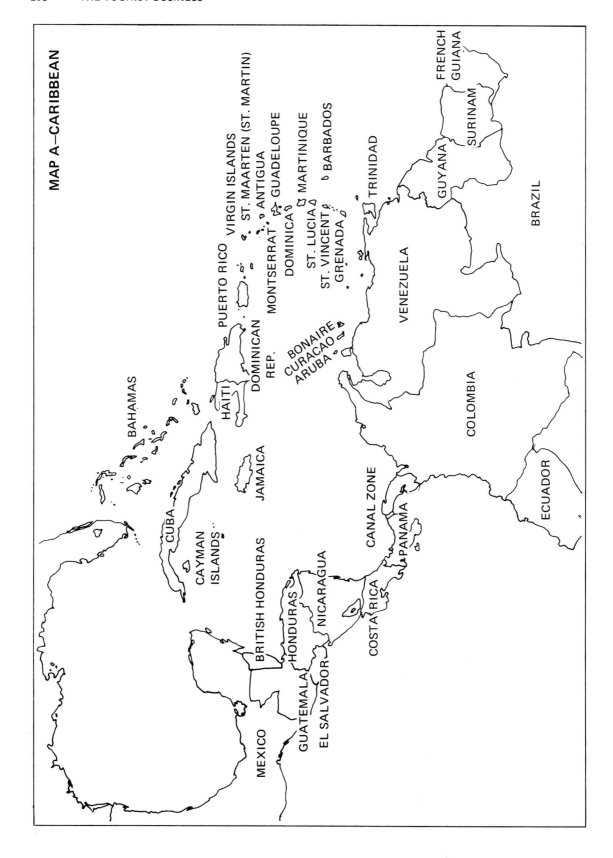

MAP A—CARIBBEAN

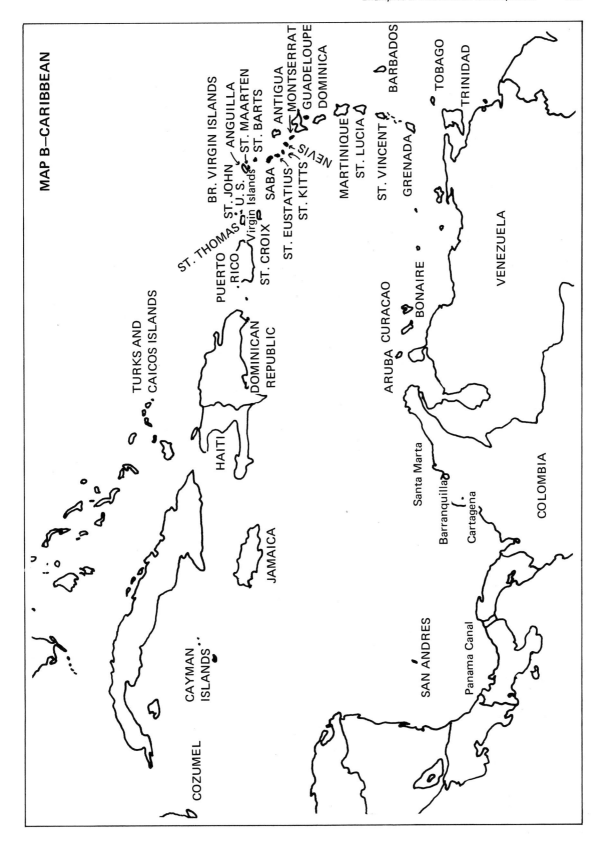

MAP B–CARIBBEAN

story of Caribbean tourism in fascinating because of the conflict and the potential, the clash between cultures, lifestyles and economic reality. It is a story of shifting power, personal values and perspectives.

The Caribbean Sea is an arm of the Atlantic Ocean lying south of the Gulf of Mexico and bounded by the West Indian Islands. By definition, the Bahamas, lying just north, are not a part of the Caribbean but since their economy and history are so similar they are so treated here. The Caribbean Basin, another term used to describe the area, places emphasis on those countries which border the Caribbean as well as on the Islands. The rim nations of Venezuela, Colombia, Panama and Mexico are actively promoting tourism along their Caribbean shores and are a part of the scenario of Caribbean tourism.

The importance of tourism varies from island to island and within the rim countries. Cuba, the largest island, has had almost no tourism since about 1959, and only a single important product, sugar. The Dominican Republic, next largest island in population, has a very small tourist business. It too is dependent largely on sugar for its economic well being. Haiti has not much of anything going for it now, economically or otherwise. Most of its 4 million people are on a subsistence economy. Puerto Rico has a mixed economy: small industry, agriculture and tourism.

Jamaica is the world's largest producer of bauxite. It also has bananas and sugar and tourism. Barbados has sugar and tourism. Trinidad, luckily, has oil and agriculture and is not certain of its feeling regarding tourism. On the little island of Antigua, it is sugar and tourism. St. Kitts has sugar. In the Bahamas, tourism is the big economic product and this is true in the U. S. Virgin Islands, the Cayman Islands, St. Martin and Bonaire. The dry islands of Curacao and Aruba, once good only for salt making, have mixed economies depending largely on oil refining and tourism. Bananas are a mainstay of Costa Rica, Honduras and the Windward Islands. Several of the small British dependencies—Montserrat, St. Vincent, St. Lucia, Dominica, the Caicos—are partly dependent upon grants-in-aid from Britain.

The South American nations of Venezuela and Colombia are only now developing tourism. In Central America, Panama is much interested in increasing tourism. So too is Costa Rica but their Caribbean coast lacks suitable beaches. Mexico is undertaking a large development on their islands off the Yucatan peninsula.

To generalize, some of the larger islands and the large rim countries recognize the importance of tourism. On the smaller islands where there are good beaches, tourism is now the largest industry or may become so. Because of location, distance from markets, small industry so far has not been very successful on the islands without subsidy in one form or another. The kind of social programming which makes the Taiwanese and Hong Kong resident an excellent factory worker seems to be absent in the Caribbean. So too is the business acumen needed to introduce and carry on industry.

The mountainous islands of Montserrat, Dominica, St. Vincent, St. Lucia, Guadeloupe and Martinique are hard put to compete in any economic sphere except tourism. Sugar, once profitable with slave labor cannot be produced to compete with mechanized production on flat lands. The same is true of bananas.

The options are few for several Caribbean communities. The physical assets for successful vacation resorts are excellent on most of the islands, as well as in parts of Caribbean Colombia, Venezuela, Panama and Mexico. Whether the political and managerial assets are available, or can be developed, is less clear.

Effect of Geography and Topography

Climate and topography favor tourism in most of the Caribbean. A general pattern, of sunshine, easterly breezes, puffy cumulus clouds, prevails. Rainy seasons and the hurricane season in the fall mar the otherwise equable climate of most of the Caribbean Basin. December through April brings sunny weather; June, July and August are usually quite pleasant while May, September, October and November more often are wet and humid. Temperature rarely falls below 70° or rises above 90°F.

U. S. CITIZENS DEPARTING OVERSEAS, BY DESTINATION, 1960-1970[1]

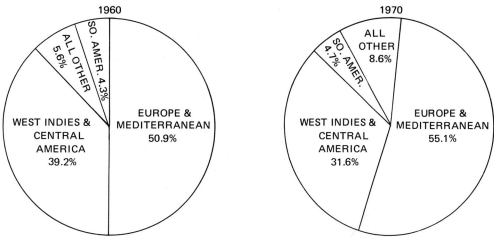

Source: U. S. Dept. of Commerce, Office of Business Economics, based on data of
U. S. Dept. of Justice, Immigration & Naturalization Service.

in most of the sea level areas. Humidity rises during the rainy season, as would be expected. Trade winds blowing from the east vary from about 5 to 20 knots, slowing noticeably during the rainy season.

Because of the constant wind direction, most islands have a windward and a leeward side, the windward side more likely to be lush while the leeward side is drier, especially if mountains are present to force the air up and cool it, precipitating rain. Almost all of the tourist destinations within the Caribbean are associated with beach front; the few "mountain resorts" are small and experience low occupancy. The mountains in the Caribbean mean rain and on a mountainous island like Dominica, where there is a plethora of rain and absence of white sandy beaches, the outlook for tourism on a large scale is bleak.

Flat, small islands in the Caribbean like Curacao, Bonaire and Aruba experience a scarcity of water. Annual average precipitation is only 22 in. or less. One of the problems in establishing Caneel Bay Plantation on the relatively small island of St. John in the U. S. Virgin Islands was the scarcity of water. Water has to be barged in from Puerto Rico, a considerable distance, both to Caneel Bay Plantation on St. John and to the Rockresort, Little Dix Bay on Virgin Gorda in the British Virgin Islands. Solar distillation has as yet not been economically practical.

The availability of relatively large amounts of water for guest use is a major consideration on the smaller islands as the owners of resorts on their own private islands of Petite St. Vincent and Mustique in the Grenadines have found. On the larger islands, or the smaller ones with mountains, rainfall may vary sharply from point to point. Mount Diablotin on Dominica, for example, receives about 300 in. of rain a year, one of the highest rates in the world, while not far away the town of Rosseau receives 70 in.

The origin of an island largely explains its rainfall: those of volcanic origin with high peaks have rainfall. The larger islands also have rainfall, while the small ones, which are exposed reefs formed on the submarine shelf or from reef-capped lateral lava flows, have little rainfall. Where water is at a premium, the roofs of houses are usually used as catch basins, draining into cisterns below the house. In St. Thomas, U. S. Virgin Islands, large expanses of mountainside are surfaced and used for the same purpose. Sea water distillation plants are in use in St. Thomas and Curacao. As technology is improved and the cost reduced, sea water distillation can be a boon to tourism in places with minimal water.

The U. S. and Canada, Source of Tourists

The great source of tourists to the Caribbean, quite naturally, is the Eastern seaboard of the U. S. and Canada. In 1960, about 39 percent of U. S. citizens departing

Source: [1]*Travel Market Yearbook;* carried in *The Cornell Hotel and Restaurant Administration Quarterly,* Nov., 1972.

for overseas destinations went to the West Indies and Central America. While the absolute number of North Americans going to the Caribbean had increased dramatically during the period 1960-1970, the percentage of North Americans traveling overseas to the West Indies and Central America had declined to about 32 percent in 1970. The chart on page 211 shows this relative change.

Europe and the Mediterranean gained from this, as did a number of other spots in the world since North Americans tend to travel almost every place on the globe. In 1960, about 51 percent of the U. S. citizens traveling abroad went to Europe and the Mediterranean; the percentage figure had climbed to 55 percent by 1970.

The Caribbean has been and will continue to be in competition for the North American market. The big competition is Europe and the Mediterranean. Europe offers tough competition—diverse cultures, numerous cities, theaters, history and architecture—which the Caribbean can never match. What Europe and the Mediterranean lack is gorgeous beaches bathed by a warm winter sun.

In absolute number, visitors to the Caribbean increased dramatically as seen on the chart on pp. 216-217. From about 1½ million visitors in 1960, the figure climbed to almost 4½ million in 1970.

The percentage of visitors from the U. S. to the various Caribbean communities, of course, varies. In 1971, 86.5 percent of the almost 1½ million visitors to the Bahamas were from the U. S. A. Another 5 percent came from Canada. Of those from the U. S., more than 60 percent came from the Eastern seaboard, 25.64 percent from Miami alone.[1] Of the more than one million visitors to Puerto Rico in 1971, all but about 22,000 were from the continental United States or the U. S. Virgin Islands. The U. S. was the origin of 292,460 visitors out of a total of 359,323 to Jamaica (not including cruise and shore stay air passengers). About a third of the visitors to Barbados are from the U. S.; Canada is the next biggest market for Barbados tourism.[2]

The 1,736,000 U. S. travelers to the West Indies and Central America in 1971 spent a total of $400 million or about $225 each, exclusive of travel costs. They left $120 million in Barbados, $90 million in Jamaica, $62 million in Bermuda.[3]

The air map on the facing page shows air distances from major cities of the U. S. to San Juan, center of the Caribbean tourist business. Divide by 500 miles per hour to arrive at approximate travel time point to point. Travel time from major Eastern seaboard cities is about 3½ hours by jet, a brief time considering that for a passenger leaving New York City in January, climate changes from mid-winter to pleasant summer.

The air map which shows distances from major cities of the U. S. to San Juan should be read in conjunction with the two maps on page 214 showing air traffic flows as of 1970. These maps developed by McDonnell-Douglas Aircraft Company show both the density of air travel and its extent.

The map showing those routes which carried more than 50,000 revenue passengers highlights the fact that main arteries of travel between the Caribbean and the outside world are between New York and San Juan, Miami and Nassau, and Miami and San Juan. Other routes are also shown illustrating the air links between the various destinations in the Caribbean and a relatively few cities in the U. S. and elsewhere. Outside of the U. S., in 1970, there were direct flights from various Caribbean destinations to Toronto, London, Madrid and Paris.

Most of the Caribbean cruises originate in either New York or Miami. St. Thomas in the U. S. Virgin Islands is the big yachting center of the Caribbean. St. George's on the island of Grenada is an active yachting center for the Grenadines in the Windward Islands to the south.

The three lubricants of travel—economy, speed and convenience, are especially applicable to the Caribbean. Since most of

[1] 1971 *Annual Report of Tourism,* Commonwealth of the Bahama Islands, Nassau, 1972.
[2] *Report of Tourist Travel to the Caribbean for 1972,* Caribbean Travel Association, New York, N. Y., 1972. The report contains comprehensive statistics regarding origin and number of visitors to most of the Caribbean area.
[3] Miller and Smith, "International Travel, Passenger Fares and other Transportation in the U. S. Balance of Payment; 1971," *Journal of Travel Research, Fall, 1972.*

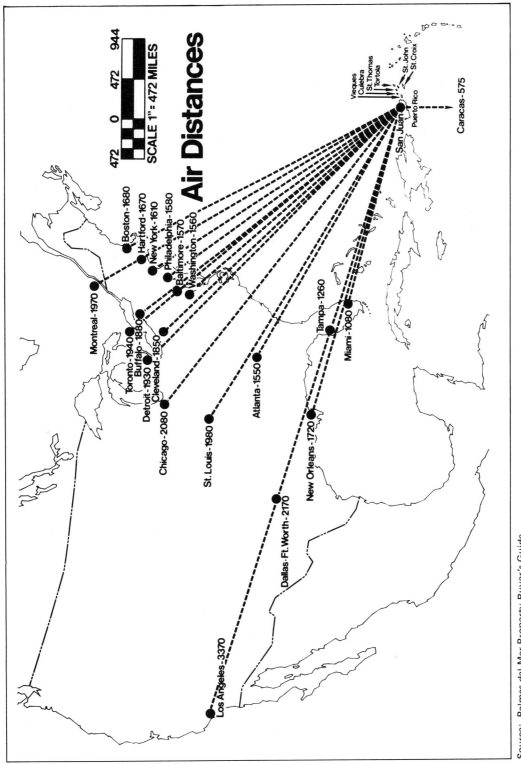

Air Distances

SCALE 1" = 472 MILES

472   0   472   944

Boston - 1680
Hartford - 1670
New York - 1610
Philadelphia - 1580
Baltimore - 1570
Washington - 1560
Montreal - 1970
Toronto - 1940
Buffalo - 1880
Detroit - 1930
Cleveland - 1850
Chicago - 2080
St. Louis - 1980
Atlanta - 1550
Tampa - 1260
Miami - 1080
New Orleans - 1720
Dallas - Ft. Worth - 2170
Los Angeles - 3370

Vieques
Culebra
St. Thomas
Tortola
St. John
St. Croix
San Juan
Puerto Rico
Caracas - 575

Source: Palmas del Mar Property Buyer's Guide

MAIN TRAFFIC FLOWS AND DENSITY

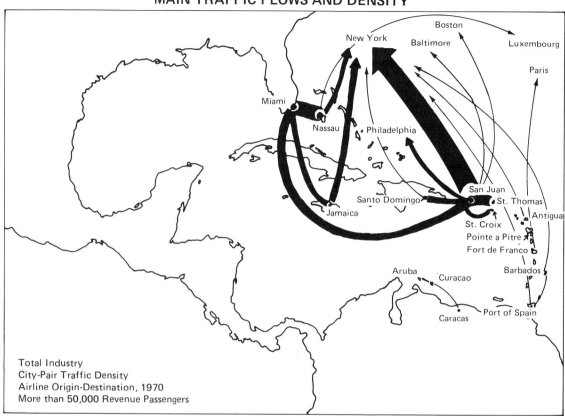

Total Industry
City-Pair Traffic Density
Airline Origin-Destination, 1970
More than 50,000 Revenue Passengers

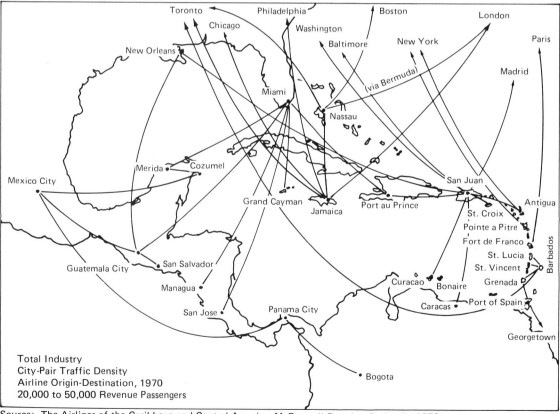

Total Industry
City-Pair Traffic Density
Airline Origin-Destination, 1970
20,000 to 50,000 Revenue Passengers

Source: The Airlines of the Caribbean and Central America, McDonnell-Douglas, St. Louis, 1972

the market is in the northeastern part of the United States, and especially the Northeast, almost any attractive destination in the Caribbean can attract thousands of visitors quickly if an economy package is put together, leaving from one of the major cities on the eastern seaboard, such as Washington, D. C., Philadelphia, Baltimore, New York, Hartford or Boston. The efficacy of such group inclusive tours at reasonable prices has been demonstrated in flights between New York City and Caracas and between New York and Curacao. Other such arrangements which have rapidly accelerated tourism are the Avianca all-inclusive packages between Boston, New York City and Caribbean destinations in Colombia. Assisted by newspaper advertising, such packages have become highly popular.

The Bahamas International Airlines, operated in conjunction with Loftleider airlines of Iceland, has opened up routes between Nassau and Luxembourg. In Barbados, International Caribbean Airways has leased planes for weekly flights to Europe that have been completely sold out.

Change in Visitors to the Caribbean

While the curve representing visitors to the Caribbean increased from a little less than 1½ million to over 4½ million between 1959 and 1971, there has been a marked change in tourist spending habits and in the kinds of visitors to the area. Travel by sea to the Caribbean is declining but cruise ship travel has climbed almost steadily since 1964. Cruise ship passengers live aboard ship and spend much less ashore than tourists living at a destination.

The figures for total visitors to a destination may be misleading. The number of visitors to Puerto Rico, for example, has increased from about 919,000 in 1967 to about 1¼ million in 1971. Visitors from the U. S., however, declined from 928,000 to 861,000 in 1971. The increase was made up mainly of cruise ship visitors and day-trippers from the U. S. Virgin Islands. The same observation can be made about the U. S. Virgin Islands. The number of visitors by air from the U. S. declined sharply from 1969 to 1971 (908,776 to 657,058).

In the same period, cruise ship visitors increased sharply. Interestingly, the typical cruise ship operating in the Caribbean is under a non-U. S. flag. Maritime union wages in the U. S. and building costs have risen so high that a vessel operating under the U. S. flag cannot compete. The usual ship cruising with tourists in the Caribbean flies the Panamanian or Liberian flag, is officered by Italians and manned with natives of several of the Caribbean islands.

As the market for tourism moves from "class" to "mass," the "length of stay" declines. Upper income tourists are likely to be older and to stay at a destination for a longer period. (In Hawaii, for example, average stay declined during the period 1952-1972 from 25 days to 9 days). Average length of stay in the Bahamas in 1971 was 5.9 days.[1]

Competition from Europe

To oversimplify, the commercial jet plane has brought the tourist to the Caribbean. It can also take him away. Instead of a New Yorker taking a direct flight from Kennedy Airport to San Juan, that person can take a similar plane to Europe and spend about the same amount of money for a European vacation as for the Caribbean junket.

The great growth in visitors to the Caribbean in the 1960's was made possible by the commercial jet plane introduced in 1959. The jet doubled air speed, reduced travel time over long distances by half. Travel from major eastern cities to San Juan and elsewhere in the Caribbean was made relatively easy, fast and inexpensive. Travel to the Caribbean soared. As the decade wore on and into the 70's, Caribbean costs rose while European vacations declined. The traveler makes a choice between the culture/scenery/entertainment of Europe and the sun/sand/entertainment of the Caribbean. Or he may decide in favor of Hawaii, glamorous, with equally good or better beaches and, perhaps more important, friendly people.

First-time travelers to an area like the Caribbean are drawn by an image which

---

[1] Janish and Peterson, "The Impact of Tourism in Hawaii," (College of Business Administration: University of Hawaii, 1972). Unpublished.

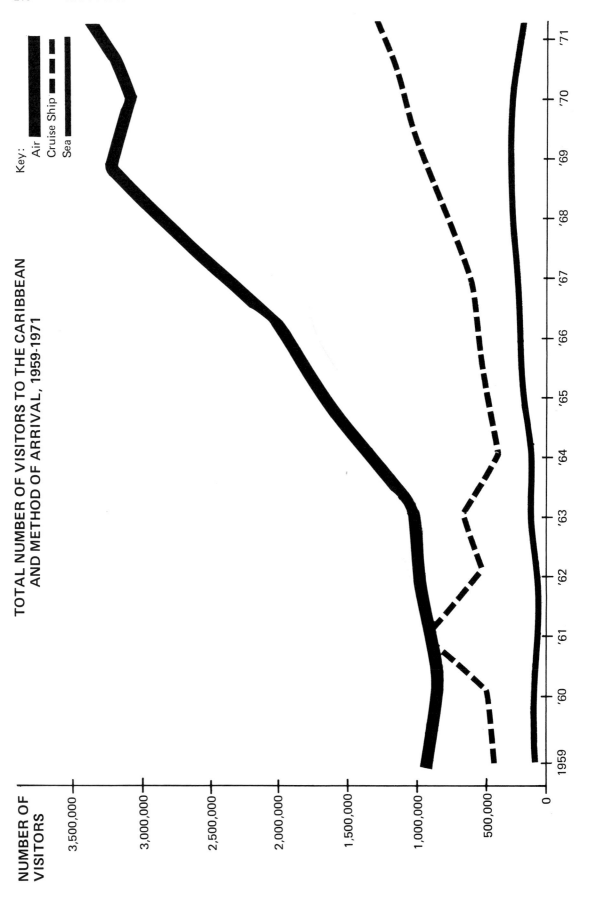

TOTAL NUMBER OF VISITORS TO THE CARIBBEAN
AND METHOD OF ARRIVAL, 1959-1971

Key:
Air
Cruise Ship
Sea

NUMBER OF
VISITORS

3,500,000

3,000,000

2,500,000

2,000,000

1,500,000

1,000,000

500,000

0

1959   '60   '61   '62   '63   '64   '65   '66   '67   '68   '69   '70   '71

FISCAL YEARS

TABLE XX—TOTAL NUMBER OF VISITORS TO THE CARIBBEAN AND METHOD OF ARRIVAL, 1959-1971*

	1959	1960	1961	1962	1963	1964	1965	1966	1967	1968	1969	1970	1971
AIR	932,308	835,468	872,451	999,962	1,076,633	1,257,556	1,506,225	1,743,842	2,226,043	2,798,035	3,131,233	3,038,923	3,279,839
SEA	60,666	54,126	11,861	16,473	124,010	81,701	115,203	118,111	131,038	185,494	238,655	257,861	159,633
CRUISE SHIP	458,669	514,621	896,298	446,191	575,838	423,998	507,486	558,257	673,354	841,897	960,546	1,038,514	1,107,116
TOTAL	1,453,263	1,498,228[1]	1,280,610	1,462,626	1,581,806	1,763,255	2,128,914	2,420,210	3,030,435	3,825,426	4,331,335	4,368,652	4,630,793

*Sources: Official Government Tourist offices as compiled by the Caribbean Travel Association.
Data from these places: Antigua, W. I.; Aruba, N. A.; Barbados, W. I.; Bonaire, N. A.; British V. I.; Cayman Islands, W. I.; Colombia, S. A. (including San Andres); Curacao, N. A.; Dominica, W. I.; Dominican Republic; Grenada, W. I.; Guadeloupe, F. W. I.; Haiti, Jamaica, W. I.; Martinique, F. W. I.; Montserrat, W. I.; Puerto Rico; St. Kitts/Nevis/Anguilla, W. I.; St. Lucia, W. I.; St. Maarten/Saba/St. Eustatius, N. A.; St. Vincent, W. I.; Surinam, S. A.; Trinidad and Tobago, W. I.; U. S. Virgin Islands.

[1] 94,011 not specified included in this figure.

may have been created by advertising, promotion, movies or other means. A particular book or several books may have stirred the imagination and formed a picture of the Caribbean which, in turn, has created expectations about the scenery, people, climate and general ambience. Unfortunately in some respects, the Caribbean tends to be seen as an entity—waving palm trees, friendly natives, golden sandy beaches, quaint houses, straw markets. The traveler may be seeking an exotic experience compounded of TV commercials, promotion brochures and travel guides, all of which carefully avoid mention of the seamy side of life, inconvenience and, in some places hostility.

Enclaves of tourism such as found on St. Thomas, Barbados, St. Lucia and elsewhere can be more pleasurable than the image. Other experiences can be anything but pleasant. The rich have always been attracted to pleasure enclaves such as Baden Baden, the Riviera at one time, Biarritz, Palm Springs, Hilton Head, Lyford Key on Nassau. Several of the Club Mediterranee developments are equally separated from the life of the community—and maybe this is the way tourism should be conducted. Goods and services other than tourism are usually produced in a separate environment from the on-going life of a community.

It may be too idealistic to expect that people from one culture can be intimately mixed with those of another such as is implied by the recommendations of "cottage style" tourism in parts of the Caribbean. The assumption is that residents will operate relatively small hotels or similar establishments and that North Americans will thus be able to mingle and understand the resident population. What is forgotten is that probably only a small percentage of tourists to the Caribbean have a strong desire for such an experience. Intellectuals may yearn for understanding. Social activists may opt for complete integration and a classless society. The average tourist is neither an intellectual nor an activist. He saves his money for a vacation which is directed toward pleasure. To insist that he have other motivations is impractical.

The intellectual decries the phoniness of tourist attractions, the plastic guitar, the ersatz dance performance, the mixing of history and entertainment. The North American traveler to the Caribbean probably is not really concerned as to whether some of the dances, handicraft, costumes and songs are authentic or ersatz. He may enjoy them for what they are. Disney Land and Disney World are phantasies—phony if you like—but the most successful tourist attractions in history. Are Mickey Mouse and Donald Duck phonies? The question is meaningless to most people.

Tourists are invited to visit all parts of the world. In most cases they would not come if they thought they were unwelcome, a "plague," an "affliction," "a pollutant." International travelers represent the more affluent, better educated, probably more socially sensitive segments of a population. If treated well, they respond well. To call them an affliction is a commentary on the commentator.

The North American international traveler is concerned for his safety when abroad. If Caribbean tourism is to attract the North American, the vacation experience must be one where personal security is assured— where there is safety from robbery, abuse, a place where there is safe drinking water, clean sanitary facilities, safety from food poisoning.[1] Such assurance is not always available in several Caribbean locations, including Jamaica, the Bahamas, Puerto Rico, the U. S. Virgin Islands, Barbados, Tobago and Mexico.

Economics and Tourism

A great deal about the Caribbean economics is said in the chart on pp. 220-221.[2] The gross national product of the islands varies tremendously: from an estimated $70 a year in Haiti to in excess of $2500 in the U. S. Virgin Islands. (By comparison, the per capita disposable income,

[1]A Harris survey of 1972 documents this statement. Quoted in the *Cornell Hotel and Restaurant Administration Quarterly*, Nov., 1972, p. 12.
[2]Information for charts from World Bank Atlas, International Bank for Reconstruction and Development, 1971, Washington, D. C. 20433 and the chart of Instant Information, Explore the Caribbean and the Bahamas, ITT Caribbean Directories, P. O. Box 2057, Coral Gables, Fla. 33134, 1970.

income after taxes, in the U. S. was $3954 in 1973).

It is seen that several of the islands have a GNP of less than $500 per year: Cuba, Dominican Republic, St. Lucia, Grenada, St. Vincent, Dominica, Antigua and St. Kitts, Nevis, Anguilla. Of all the islands only Puerto Rico, The Netherlands Antilles and the U. S. Virgins have a GNP which exceeds $1000 a year. In the U. S. in 1969, the year of comparison, the U. S. per capita GNP was $4240.

In other words, most of the Caribbean Islands are poor, most desperately poor; moreover the average annual growth rates in the GNP per capita during the years 1960-1969 show few reasons for optimism. Only the Bahama Islands with a growth rate of 8.2 percent, the U. S. Virgins with a growth rate of 5.7 percent and Puerto Rico with 6.0 percent give much reason for optimism. Four of the islands had negative growth rates: Cuba, Haiti, the Netherland Antilles and Grenada.

Wages on some of the islands are at 19th century levels; on St. Vincent women receive as little as 15 cents an hour; men, $1.50 a day.[1] This dismal economic picture is accented by the fact that in several of the islands there are no natural resources to speak of except for a salubrious climate and beautiful beaches. While most of the islands were once competitive in raising sugar cane, they are no longer. The smaller, flatter islands have the added liability of being short of water.

Income from Tourism

The statistics on expenditures by tourists at the various Caribbean destinations are not precise and are probably computed differently from place to place. The Ministry of Tourism of the Bahamas collected the visitors' expenditures in the Caribbean for 1970 as seen at top of facing column.[2]

The Bahamas lead in visitor expenditures followed closely by Puerto Rico. Both receive more than double the dollars in tourism money than does any other Caribbean or Central American destination. Of the approximately $900 million accruing to Caribbean destinations in tourist expenditures, almost half of it is spent in the Baha-

Countries	1970 Expenditures ($ Millions)*
ANTILLES	
Antigua	23.2
Bahamas	220.8
Barbados	82.6
Dominica	2.8
Grenada	16.0
Jamaica	93.5
Montserrat	30.6
Puerto Rico	217.2
St. Kitts	6.6
St. Lucia	11.8
St. Vincent	6.7
Trinidad and Tobago	23.9
U. S. Virgin Islands	112.3**
CENTRAL AMERICA	
Costa Rica	15.0
El Salvador	3.3
Guatemala	12.4
Honduras	2.1
Nicaragua	11.8
Panama	12.4

*Estimated
**1969 Government of the Virgin Islands report
Sources: Ministry of Tourism, Bahamas, 1970; Zinder and Associates, 1969; SITCA, 1970.

mas and Puerto Rico. It is interesting to note that the highest per capita income in the Caribbean region is found in the Bahamas, Puerto Rico and the U. S. Virgin Islands, areas of highest density tourism.

The economic impact of a tourist dollar varies from place to place within the Caribbean Basin depending upon how much of that dollar must be spent outside of the economy. Almost everything needed to service a visitor to the U. S. Virgins must be imported: food, beverages, building materials, sporting goods and similar items. This is also true for all of the smaller islands. Much of the money spent for labor in the U. S. Virgins goes out of the economy as remittances sent by employees of the hotels to their families on other islands.

The rim countries—such as Venezuela, Colombia and Mexico, have a much higher

[1]*The Wall Street Journal,* Mar. 5, 1973.
[2]*The Airlines of the Caribbean and Central America* (St. Louis: McDonnell-Douglas, 1972).

TABLE XXI—CARIBBEAN AND

	Status	Capital	Language	Population	GNP Percent 1969* (US $)
ANTIGUA	Ind. State associated with U.K.	St. John's	English	65,000	340
ARUBA	N.A.	Oranjestad	Dutch English Papamiento	60,000	(1)
BAHAMAS	Commonwealth with internal self-govt.	Nassau	English	190,000	1880
BARBADOS	Ind. member British Commonwealth	Bridgetown	English	250,000	500
BONAIRE	N.A.	Kraiendijk	Dutch English Papamiento	8,000	(1)
BR. VIRGIN ISLANDS	British Territory	Road Town	English	11,500	N.A.
CAYMAN IS.	British Crown Colony	George Town	English	11,000	N.A.
COLOMBIA	Ind. Republic	Bogota	Spanish	21,100,000	290
CUBA	Ind. Republic	Havana	Spanish	8,000,000	280
CURACAO	N.A.	Willemstad	Dutch English Papamiento	137,000	(1)
DOMINICA	Ind. State associated with U.K.	Roseau	English French patois	70,000	300
DOMINICAN REPUBLIC	Ind. Republic	Santo Domingo	Spanish	3,800,000	280
GRENADA	Ind. State associated with U.K.	St. George's	English	104,000	230
GUADELOUPE	French	Basse-Terre	French	320,000	540

multiplier effect. In Venezuela, as an example, most food and beverage items are produced within the country. The gasoline to fuel the jet plane on its flight out of the country is produced locally. Wheat comes from the country's ranches; fruits and vegetables are grown in the country. In other words, the tourist dollar to Venezuela has a larger impact on the economy than the tourist dollar brought into Puerto Rico and a much larger impact than the same dollar taken in by Jamaica, Bahamas or Barbados.

Moreover, the tourist business in Venezuela, Colombia and Mexico has the effect of balancing the economy as compared with the Bahamas where tourism is the principal and almost only industry.

Observing the development of resort areas around the world, it is seen that often the new destination area develops following a particular pattern. Often the first guest facilities are provided by the government in the form of guest houses or rest houses. The British built such facilities in India and parts of Africa. Governments replacing British control continued the practice. Later the Government often decided to build at least one prestige hotel, usually in its capital city. Some governments have controlled the development of tourism almost completely

BAHAMAS INFORMATION

	Status	Capital	Language	Population	GNP Percent 1969* (US $)
HAITI	Ind. Republic	Port-au-Prince	French	4,000,000	70
JAMAICA	Ind. member British Commonwealth	Kingston	English	2,000,000	550
MARTINIQUE	French	Port de France	French	320,000	690
MEXICO	Ind. Republic	Mexico City	Spanish	51,000,000	640
MONTSERRAT	British Crown Colony	Plymouth	English	14,000	—
PUERTO RICO	Commonwealth associated with U. S.	San Juan	Spanish English	2,700,000	1410
ST. KITTS	Ind. State associated with U.K.	Basseterre	English	40,000	320
ST. LUCIA	Ind. State associated with U.K.	Castiries	English	100,000	240
ST. MAARTEN/ ST. MARTIN	NA/French	Philipsburg and Marigot	Dutch French Papamiento English Spanish	11,000	(1)
ST. VINCENT	Ind. State associated with U.K.	Kingstown	English	90,000	220
SURINAM	Autonomous partner Netherlands	Paramaribo	Dutch English	400,000	560
TRINIDAD & TOBAGO	Ind. member British Commonwealth	Port of Spain	English	1,000,000	890
U.S. VIRGIN ISLANDS	U. S. territory	Charlotte Amalie, St. Thomas	English	65,000	2570
VENEZUELA	Ind. Republic	Caracas	Spanish	10,600,000	1000

Source: *Explore the Caribbean and the Bahamas,* ITT Caribbean Directories, Coral Gables, Florida, 1970.

from its inception to an advanced state, i.e. Spain, Portugal, Greece and Turkey.

After the initial phase of development, usually one of the international hotel companies is called in and invited to participate at favorable terms in the construction of a hotel or given a management contract for operating one or several hotels. Hilton International and InterContinental Hotels Corporation, largely since 1950, have developed to be major components of international travel on this basis.

The next stage of development is seen as large real estate interests and people from outside of the hotel industry move in to develop large destination areas. Examples are: the Rockresorts, the Aga Khan group in Sardinia, Moshe Mayer in East Africa.

Cost of the land is a major factor in every destination development and tends to vary widely, depending upon the stage of development of the area. Professor William

---

*"World Bank Atlas," International Bank for Reconstruction and Development, Washington, D. C., 1971.
(1) GNP for the Netherlands Antilles as a group (Aruba, Bonaire, Curacao and St. Martin) was $1260.

Tabler of the University of Massachusetts whose organization has designed more than 100 hotels around the world has capsulated the increase in land values as a percentage of total construction cost in the table below.

TABLE XXII—COST OF HOTEL[1]

	Under-developed	Developed	Over-developed
Land	1%	10%	20%
Site	5	1½	1
Bldg.	60	50	40
FF&E	15	15	15
Fees	5	5	5
Fin. Tax.	10	10	10
Oper. Eq.	1	1½	2
Pre. Opg.	1	4	4
Invent.	1	1½	1½
Wkg. Cap.	1	1½	1½
	100%	100%	100%

1000 x Room Rate = Room Cost

In the table it is seen that in an underdeveloped destination area land costs may be only one percent of the total cost of development   As the area becomes developed, typically the land costs increase to constitute 10 percent of the total cost of the hotel.   In an overdeveloped area, the land cost will comprise as much as 20 percent of the total cost.

It is fascinating to see how the percentage of capital available for the building itself decreases as a destination area matures.   Initially, 60 percent of the available money can be put into the building construction. As the area attracts more development, land prices increase and only half of the available money may go into the building.   In the overdeveloped destination area, when the land cost is running 20 percent of the total, only 40 percent of the available money can be spent for the building.

Professor Tabler points out that the chart has a sobering effect on would-be investors when they see how little of their money can be spent for the building itself.

Most of the development costs, it is seen, hold fairly constant regardless of the stage of development of the destination area.   Site development itself actually goes down as a percentage of the total.   Furniture, fixtures and equipment remain at 15

percent of the total. Fees take 5 percent of the total and the 10 percent required for financing and taxes remains at about 10 percent. What suffers is the building itself. As land costs shoot up, the entrepreneur has no choice but to build high rise, even though the high rise building may be inimical to the area.[2]

Land Prices in the Caribbean

Land prices in the Caribbean vary tremendously but most beachfront land, almost a necessity for a successful hotel operation, runs $40,000 an acre and higher. It is rather amazing to find these prices in some remote island which is as yet undeveloped. There are exceptions. According to William E. Gilbert, who did a comprehensive study of land suitable for a resort development "prices become almost reasonable on some of the less popular Eastern Caribbean Islands such as Dominica, which appeals to a special sort of person with its wild and rugged beauty and occasional black sand beaches. A hundred acre tract with half a mile of black sand beach and a fresh water river, on the windward side, was recently offered for $500 an acre . . . on Margarita, that lovely island off the coast of Venezuela, the cost of living is still quite low, but the development rush is beginning, and land on the East side, which is the most desirable, is going for $5000 per acre on and near the beach, in large tracts (200 acres) . . . in the Western Caribbean good beachfront land in large tracts can be had at about $1000 per acre on Guanaja, the loveliest of the Bay Islands of Honduras."[3]

Under certain conditions, the Overseas Private Investment Corporation, a U. S. Government entity will issue investment insurance against the possibility that profits cannot be taken out of the country, or against expropriation by a government, war, revolution and insurrection.[4]

Foreign investors in hotels on some of

[1]William Tabler, Statler Lecture Series, University of Massachusetts, 1972.
[2]Statler Lecture Series, 1972.
[3]William E. Gilbert, "Investor's Guide to the Coming Land Boom in the Caribbean-Latin American Waters," (New York: Frederick Fell, 1973).
[4]Overseas Private Investment Corporation, 1129 20th St. N. W., Washington, D. C. 20527.

the islands have had more than their share of problems. At one Tobago hotel two of the locals made a big point of using the hotel's beach, a right which they had since the beach was public property. In reaching the beach, however, instead of walking around the hotel they would march through the lobby. The hotel owner asked the two persons concerned to please go around the hotel instead of using the lobby. There was no question about refusal of access to the beach. The government reacted by interpreting the request to go around the hotel as a refusal of the right to use the beach. As a result the hotel was closed and the owners were given notice to leave within two to three weeks.

At another Tobago hotel there were continuous problems with the water supply and telephone service. At one point, when the hotel was catering to a large group of people, the town's reservoir was emptied for cleaning, which left the hotel without water pressure for four days. On another occasion, after work had been completed on the water line to attempt improvement of the pressure, personal inspection of the line found rocks jammed in it which restricted the water flow.

At the same resort some food which had to be ordered from Trinidad would arrive in Tobago but the resort would not be notified of its arrival. Inquiry brought information that it had not left Trinidad. The food sat on the docks for several days and spoiled. Understandably, on many of the Caribbean islands an attempt is made to fill available positions with natives. The problem arises when there are no local residents qualified to do the work. Government pressure can be brought to bear on a particular operation by revoking work permits of key personnel. Such personnel are often forced to leave on relatively short notice.

Common Elements of Development

Tourist development in the Caribbean has common elements with destination development in other areas:

1. The area must be conveniently accessible to sizable markets. The Caribbean is relatively convenient in terms of flight times and flight schedules to its primary market, the Eastern seaboard of the U. S.

2. The cost of transportation to the destination area must be relatively reasonable. Most of the parts of the Caribbean, including the rim countries, meet this consideration. Convenience and cost of flight to several islands are some of the best travel bargains available. The group inclusive tours packaged by Viasa Airlines of Venezuela, Avianca of Colombia, and others have brought the total cost of the packaged vacation down sharply and have made the trip relatively convenient for those flying from New York City and Miami.

3. Hotel accommodations must be relatively plentiful and preferably available in a range of prices. Some spots in the Caribbean meet this criterion; others do not. Certain islands like Margarita and San Andreas could use many more hotel rooms to meet the demand. Other islands have a surplus of hotel rooms in the luxury category, only a few in the economy group.

4. Promotion and advertising is necessary to keep the destination area in the eye of the potential traveler to the area. Some of the promotion and advertising (examples are included for Jamaica and the Bahamas) for the Caribbean has been outstanding.

5. The destination area must give the traveler the impression that he is welcome and wanted. This has been a great shortcoming in such destinations as the Bahamas, Jamaica, Puerto Rico, the U. S. Virgins, Trinidad and Tobago. Unfortunately, the general public tends to see the Caribbean as an entity; adverse publicity spills over to color the reputation of the Caribbean as a whole.

The destination area must decide whether it really wants tourism; wanting tourism means that at least most of the segments of the population favor tourism, support it and are pleased to have tourists visit their community. Civic groups, taxicab drivers, storekeepers and, particularly, governments must show an active interest. This has not been the case in several parts of the Caribbean. It has been popular among some intellectuals to deride tourism as a demeaning business for those who engage in it and as a pollutant to the environment. Others decry social changes brought on by tourism. The visitor from North America is usually not interested in the social or ecological implications of tourism. If he experiences rudeness, poor service, or becomes concerned about his personal safety, he simply crosses off the Caribbean as a vacation spot.

6. The cost of land, construction and the operation of the hotels must yield a profit to the entrepreneur. When land costs increase to a certain point, only a high rise hotel can be profitable, buildings which may not be in keeping with the environment or the desires of the residents. This has happened on many Caribbean beaches. An alternative is government control or ownership of land. As a result of planning, governments can purchase or set aside lands for tourism development, then restrict their use or lease them under controlled conditions. Another alternative is for governments to build and operate, lease or let on management contracts; this is done in Socialist countries and by several state governments in the U. S. A.

7. The indigenization of tourism away from the high rise hotel, financed with foreign capital and managed by expatriates, is favored by a number of government officials and other leaders in the Caribbean. These leaders favor the small inn that is part of its surroundings, that reflects the local culture, is simply furnished and decorated and serves local dishes. Such a style of tourist facilities can be developed but is probably not attractive for U. S. investors or hotelmen.

It is fairly well accepted that a destination area must offer a variety of experiences for the average visitor, something that an individual inn is ill-equipped to do as compared with a tourist complex offering entertainment, beaches, sports, gambling, night life and shopping. An individual property or a series of small inns would have to be marketed as a group, probably under the sponsorship or coordination of a government, to have an impact on the U.S. market.

It has been suggested that joint ventures be set up with foreign investors. For a U. S. investor this would be hazardous in that he would be 2000 miles away from his investment and unable to exercise direct management control. Some investors will probably want to go ahead anyway. William E. Gilbert, previously mentioned, who has made an intensive study of potential resort locations in the Caribbean, suggests 10 sites for building 25 to 40 room inns.[1] For the larger hotel developments, more self-contained in terms of entertainment, Mr. Gilbert suggests the Northeast shore of Puerto Rico; Cozumel, off Mexico; Puerto Plata, Dominican Republic; Aruba and Bonaire.[2]

Social Tension and Tourism

Some social tension is probably inevitable as tourism moves into a society and changes its structure. Tourism makes for redistribution of income and power. As power shifts from one group to another, resentment is natural on the part of those who lose it. Those who gain it may not know what to do with it. In much of the Caribbean and the Bahamas, political power has shifted from the minority White planter and merchant to the Black politician. Leadership in most Caribbean countries—both those of Spanish and English heritage—is said to be strongly personalized. A politician's charisma is likely to be more important than his ideas. Of course, personalism in politics is universal, but it is a matter of degree. Force of personality of leaders has been particularly important in Puerto Rico, Haiti, Cuba and the Dominican Republic in the past twenty years.

Island governments in transition from dependence to independence can be expected to be less clear about economic goals and how to achieve them. Islands still controlled by Britain, France and the Netherlands can be expected to be burdened with bureaucratic indecision. Leadership may not be able to overcome antipathy to tourism. Certainly leaders who question the value of tourism add to its problems.

As happens, surface calmness may dis-

---

[1]William E. Gilbert, *Investor's Guide to the Coming Land Boom in the Caribbean-Latin American Waters* (New York: Frederick Fell, 1973). San Blas off Panama; Roatan Island off Honduras; Samana Peninsula, Dominican Republic; Aux Cayes Bay, Haiti; Isla Tierra Bomba, Colombia; Margarita, Venezuela; Bourg, St. Anne, Martinique; Hamstead Bay, Dominica; Long Bay, Anguilla; and Mayaguez, Puerto Rico.
[2]*Ibid.*

guise undercurrents of discontent. Curacao, part of the Netherlands Antilles, is an example. Observers felt that of all the islands in the West Indies, the Dutch Islands would have their political problems neatly taken care of. That feeling was abruptly shaken in 1969 when a good share of the downtown tourist shops in Wilhelmstad, Curacao were burned down by rioters.

In the Caribbean, some of the new political leaders have shown little common sense or restraint. Eric Gairy, Prime Minister of Grenada, is an example: "clownish, impudent and often ethically suspect. A personality whose name has more than once been linked to scandal and oppression."[1] His actions toward hotel operators have been capricious. In an episode known to the writer, the owner of a well-run hotel quite reasonably laid off a number of employees because of lack of guests. Mr. Gairy on hearing of the dismissals simply instructed the employees to return to the job. There was no recourse for the owner. Despite the fact that Grenada's Gross National Product is only $230 a year, Mr. Gairy orders "champagne all around" when entertaining and managed to spend several million dollars on an ill-advised trade and cultural fair which was obviously conducted primarily for the aggrandizement of Mr. Gairy.

Several spokesmen for the Black islands say they would rather remain poor than accept tourism.[2] Such an attitude is cavalier since the speaker usually would not suffer economically or socially if tourism is not developed. It is easy for a university lecturer or government bureaucrat to assign people to work in a cane field at a low wage to preserve "their dignity." It might be more just to allow the person the option of cane field versus waiter in an air-conditioned hotel. Unemployment is high on a number of islands (in 1973 it reached 40 percent on Antigua). Would the unemployed man like to work as a bartender rather than have no work at all? And what is so undignified about service employment?

Some Constructive Action

Some leaders in the Caribbean have acted constructively to accommodate tour-

ism. Instead of arousing resentment toward tourists and tourism, they have acted to make tourism work for their people. Michael Manning, Prime Minister of Jamaica, sees no indignity associated with serving tourists: "I've never been able to convince myself that there is a difference in taking an order from a superior in a dull factory or serving somebody a plate of food."[3]

Need for Balanced Economy

It is quite reasonable that a balanced economy is more favorable than one completely dependent upon tourism. At this point in time, however, tourism seems to be the only viable industry possible on many islands. In the U. S. Virgin Islands, Melvin Evans, first popularly-elected Governor, feels that tourism must be balanced with small, non-polluting industry: "We must recognize the fickle nature of tourism and reduce the dependency on this one industry."[4] Evans also feels that tourists may behave in such a way as to violate local customs and habits. This is no doubt true.

Some leaders of developing countries, including some of the Caribbean communities, deplore tourism as an intrusion or displacement of native culture by an outside culture. Instead of an international style of hotel as seen on Miami Beach or Waikiki Beach, they opt for hotels which reflect indigenous ambience. Entertainment, say they, should be drawn from the community's culture and history. Food should be produced locally, as much as possible, and dishes served which are cooked and served in the style of the community.

The traditional marketing approach, to satisfy a consumer in the terms he chooses, apparently is given less value than the need to reflect the authentic character of a community. Prime Minister of St. Vincent, J. F. Mitchell, phrased it this way: "The

[1]Robert D. Crassweller, *The Caribbean Community* (New York: Praeger Publishers, 1972), p. 241. A comprehensive and reasoned statement on Caribbean politics and economics.

[2]*Information Document, Seminar "To Secure a Lasting Tourism,"* Organization of American States, Washington, D. C., 1972.

[3]Horace Sutton, "The Sun Filled Islands: Are They Safe?", *Harper's Bazaar*, Dec., 1972.

[4]"State of the Territory" Message, Jan., 1972.

tourist dollar alone is not worth the devastation of my own people and a country where the people have lost their soul is not worth visiting."[1] The prime minister urged tourists to support the local fishing industry by demanding local fish dishes rather than asking for the usual steaks, roast prime ribs and hamburgers which are often imported. The argument in favor of serving locally produced foods makes good economic sense if the product can be sold; if not, the argument is wasted.

Certain tourist facilities are seen as inimical to the community. The high rise hotel, which operates only six months of the year, leaving severe seasonal unemployment the rest of the year, is an example.

There is support for the small hotel, locally owned and operated. Such hotels are favored in that they reflect the Caribbean lifestyle. While such is likely to be the case, there is no assurance that the small locally owned and operated hotel will satisfy the tourist. Some do; some don't. Those in Jamaica have experienced low occupancy and many complaints of poor service, poor food and poor maintenance. In Barbados, where it is said 60 percent of the island's hotels and transportation services are owned by natives, some of the hotels receive high marks. Many in Bermuda are charming. The small hotel has no apparent occupancy advantage in the off-season. The small hotel in Barbados, Tobago, Jamaica and elsewhere suffers along with the high rise in the off-seasons. Trinidad and Tobago favor cottage style property, owned and operated by nationals and aimed at the Black North American market. Such a development, should it be successful, may have worldwide implications.

Reaction to Rapid Social Change

Rapid social change, no matter what the agent or cause, is almost certain to bring uncertainty and cause resentment from many as adjustments to those changes follow. It has happened in Hawaii, Puerto Rico, the U. S. Virgins, and elsewhere. Tourism skyrocketed land prices in Hawaii. The original owners, the native Hawaiians, however, gained little from the land appreciation. Other groups, among them continen-

tal U. S. residents, Japanese, and especially the Chinese, profited the most. Changes in economic power brought shifts in social status as well.

In Puerto Rico, the old families of landed Dons have given way to the rising middle class, the professional, the entrepreneur and politician. The radical student cries for independence and more power for himself and his friends. In the Bahamas, the political power shift from White oligarchy to Black politician has forced rapid readjustment in social perspective. As power changes from one group to another, the remainder of society often is left wondering just where they fit. New power groups, uncertain of their power, may countenance lawlessness and tolerate a degree of permissiveness unknown previously.

Tourism Causes Dislocation

Tourism can be a basic cause of such dislocation just as industrialization was the cause of upsetting the class structure in Eighteenth Century England as the economy moved from farm to factory. Tourism happens to be the vehicle of change in many of the Caribbean islands, Hawaii, the Bahamas, the Greek Islands and elsewhere.

The scale of dislocation is related to the "travel intensity index": the ratio of visitors to residents. Millions of tourists converge on cities like New York and London where they are absorbed by the huge complex of facilities and merge with the large populations. On an island like New Providence, Barbados, St. Thomas or Oahu, the tourist can overwhelm the facilities and the resident.

It is said there are so many automobiles on the island of Oahu in Hawaii that should all of their owners decide to drive at once they could not physically get on the available roads. Hotels line the beautiful beach at Waikiki so that the beach is not visible from the parallel road. The same is true of Miami Beach. It should be noted that both Waikiki and Miami Beach are considered fairylands by many, deplored by others.

When tourism is introduced into a sizable economy and introduced slowly, the

[1]*Travel Trade,* Nov. 6, 1972.

ripples are small. When, however, tourism replaces another economy within a few years, social, psychological and economic repercussions are inevitable and may be intense.

The expectations of the residents are a key to the degree of dislocation caused by tourism. If a community is created for tourism—as for example Las Vegas, the residents strive to cater to the tourist and are likely to treat them as economic units. Some communities—like Monaco, Bermuda or Nantucket—have over a long period of time come to accommodate to a tourist economy and welcome it as an economic enterprise. Switzerland is a classic case of careful adjustment to tourism over a hundred years. When the adjustments come slowly, they are less likely to be painful.

Even though tourism may bring economic wellbeing to nearly everyone, the relative rewards of tourism are usually experienced unequally. Land speculators, certain politicians, contractors and merchants may acquire considerable wealth. The "man in the street," or more likely, the man and woman in the field, may acquire a relatively cleaner, more desirable job and higher wages but may not be satisfied because of relative income and status. They remain at the bottom of the social ladder. They may feel that the tourist-created job is servile and lacking in human dignity. They will take the job but perform it with less than enthusiasm. Such has been the case in several Caribbean islands.

The long-time resident who has status and income may also resent tourism as prices increase, public utilities are fewer than demand requires, police protection is relaxed, roads become glutted, and hospitals and classrooms overflow. Cape Cod is an example. For such established residents tourism may be a form of affliction.

Regardless of the basic causes, tourism suffered sharply in several Caribbean islands as the result of rudeness (and worse) to tourists. The Jamaican Minister of Industry and Tourism warned that the tourist industry was "in a state of imminent crisis" due to increased crime, "unwarranted racial abuse of visitors" and poor hotel service. Said Minister P. J. Patterson: "One of the

factors in our attitudes toward visitors which has pushed the tourist industry to the point of collapse is the growing tendency in our society—and so within the industry—to view everything exclusively in racial terms . . . . We are no longer a colonial people. We no longer should be subject to the mentality of slaves."[1] Mr. Patterson pointed out that "Many people seem to think there is something funny, or something fashionable, or politically meaningful in shouting abusive racial slogans at people." He called attention to the fact that the number of criminal incidents directed against visitors had been on the increase during the past year and a half, that visitors were badgered by peddlers and that women visitors were being propositioned on the street.

To counteract some of the conditions mentioned, the number of police patrols was increased in resort areas and a hotel inspector concerned with improving service standards was to be appointed. Complaints regarding poor service would result in a warning and possible revocation of the hotel license. (In 1972 the Holiday Inn at Rose Hall was closed down for a period of two weeks by government action.) Appeal could be made to a tribunal comprised of an attorney, a hotelman and a representative of the Jamaica consumer. The Tourist Board also proposed launching a massive internal public education program. Anthony Abrahams, Director of Tourism for Jamaica, warned that if immediate action to save the industry were not taken some 6500 tourism workers would be displaced. He was critical of the shabby appearance of tourist communities and charged government bureaucrats with indifference to the problems.

Hotel Managerial Expertise Lacking

A continuing problem in the entire Caribbean Basin has been the relative absence of managerial know-how and motivation among the residents of the area. Students of the hospitality business generally agree that the management of a hotel, restaurant or resort, especially if it is larger than a family enterprise, requires special-

---

[1] *The Travel Agent,* Aug. 31, 1972.

ized knowledge, of finance, accounting, engineering, maintenance, food and beverage controls and the other subjects taught in a college level course in hotel and restaurant management. Even more important, hotel management requires a particular discipline of the manager and a devotion to the demands of the clock as required by the work ethic.

To be effective, the manager must be achievement motivated, a good organizer of his time and that of others, and use his energies and those of the people who work with him efficiently. He must accept himself as a professional manager, believe in himself and his role as a doer, be profit motivated and ascribe to the belief that management is a profession demanding standards, devotion, skill and creativity. For several reasons few long time residents of the Caribbean are mentally or emotionally equipped for this role.

The fact that few opportunities have existed for residents to become hotel and restaurant managers is only part of the story. The reasons behind this lack of managerial expertise in the Caribbean vary from place to place.

In those islands previously dominated by the British, the individual personality is said to lack identity, to contain more than a little of ambivalence about the self, and overconcern with work in terms of status. The dominance of the mother in the family, the matri-focal family, exists widely in the British Caribbean. For economic and other reasons, the father of the family often is little in evidence and the mother is responsible for holding the family together. Even so, the usual male is said to be ambivalent about women in general: mother and grandmother are accorded high honor; women in general are seen as tempters and given low esteem. In Freudian terms, the boy becomes oedipally attached to the mother and has difficulty in taking on the responsible male role. As compensation for the need to depend on the mother, the male clamors for freedom of all kinds and resents authority.[1] Reinforcing the desire to do as he pleases are the sharp social distinctions carried by various occupations. The doctor or lawyer is independent, free to do as he pleases, accorded high status. The cane worker and small farmer, relatively recently freed from slavery, have the lowest status. The servant, be he in the home or in a hotel, has low status.

In Jamaica, for example, a waiter will often prefer to serve in a hotel located in another past of the island so that his friends and family will not witness his subservience.

Status of Managers

Nowhere in the Commonwealth Caribbean countries has the professional manager been granted the kind of status he holds in the U. S. The governing classes in England avoided anything smacking of the business world, while in the colonies commerce and trade were emphasized rather than industry and manufacturing. Best of all was the absentee owner of the sugar estate who could display his wealth in London, leaving the plantation management to lesser individuals.

It is said that little initiative on the part of those with capital has been seen in the Caribbean. Conservatism and caution are more likely to be the rule. In government as well as business enterprises, it is pointed out that social and communal pressures resist innovation, even at the small farmer level. The innovator is viewed with distrust or resentment. "One man's rise is another man's downfall." There is also the belief in supernatural forces which militates against enterprise. In Jamaica, for example, there is "an almost universal belief that each woman is destined to have a certain number of children and she will not have good health unless she does."[2]

In the British system of things, every occupation is arrayed in a hierarchy, from Duke to dust man. As the Empire spread, the British virus of snobbism was carried with the flag. In Barbados unemployment seems to many preferable to cutting sugar cane. Much of the harvest has been done by workers from even poorer islands like St. Vincent. Education is seen as a leg up in the social structure. The young countryman with an education moves to the town

[1]Robert D. Crassweller, *The Caribbean Community, Changing Societies and U. S. Policy* (New York: Praeger Publishers, 1972).
[2]Commonwealth Caribbean, p. 225.

or city and, though he is desperately poor emulates the dress, manners and speech of those he considers his "betters."

Sharp social distinctions are seen between job classifications within the hotel. The front desk employees, described cuttingly by one commentator as "those little ladies of quality," feel that they are from an upper class and are so accepted by the less educated chambermaid, waiter and cook.

Let no one be bemused into thinking that, because political power has shifted from Whites to Blacks in the Bahamas, Jamaica, Barbados and elsewhere in the Commonwealth Caribbean, there is still not a great deal of class differentiation. As has been pointed out there is ambivalence and tension in the process of upward mobility from peasantry to lower middle or middle class where marriage is the norm. Religion moves from Obeah to conventional Anglican or other religion and there are new attitudes toward the acquisition of wealth.

Expectations rise sharply. Little wonder that the illiterate kitchen worker or bellhop in a hotel is confused in a setting where nearly every one of the hotel guests carry as much money in their pockets as his family has made in the whole year on the small farm. Why, if there is any justice, is he not also affluent? The beach boy with his marvelous physique and aquatic skills may well resent the flaccid vacationer who calls for service. The beach boy has evidence that the lonesome female tourist admires and may welcome his advances. The beach boy may be called on to provide a companion for the lonesome male tourist which does nothing to maintain the social gulf between them.

Generations of denied opportunity develop feelings of fatalism. If one's parents accepted a social station and a way of life as inevitable, which to most it certainly was, that feeling is communicated to the offspring who look upon life as something which is unfair. The postponement of rewards until some future time is not part of the personality, though it is required for capital investment and economic security.

In the Hispanic Caribbean, other factors are at work to militate against managerial development. Individualism is exalted,

limited only by one's obligation to his family and extended clan of intimates who are seen as extensions of the individual. Spanish tradition emphasizes the individual and his extended group, opposing other such groups. Cooperative undertakings are not a part of the Spanish character. The Spanish temperament accepts the dictator, may even feel lost without him. The nobleman, the "caudillo," the patron, the strong man who does as his fancy dictates is part of the Hispanic scene both hated and admired.

Personalism reigns in politics. One is attracted to the daring, the courage, the charisma of an individual leader. Loyalties are more important than logic. Individualism and the attraction to extremes leads to an exalted concept of dignity and honor which leaves little room for the kind of compromise often needed in business.

Positive Factor

A positive factor in the Spanish Caribbean is the relative absence of rigid class and race distinctions. Local managers can be developed, but the fact remains that throughout the Caribbean relatively few hotels are managed by residents. Of those that are, fewer still are well managed.[1] A study of small hotels in Jamaica found that the managers were not profit oriented. Only four of the managers of the 30 hotels reviewed knew how to manage money properly. Most were accused of spending their time on detail instead of planning, organizing and marketing. The vast majority of the kitchens observed would not pass U. S. health inspection. Of all the successful operations not one was managed by a Jamaican. In Puerto Rico only a few Puerto Ricans are in higher management positions in the hotels of the Island. There are a few exceptions, hotels that are excellently managed by native born residents.

The shortage of motivated, trained hotel management personnel may be overcome with the establishment of beyond-high school training programs which have been established in the Bahamas, Jamaica, Puerto Rico, Charlotte Amalie and Barbados. The

[1]The author worked under an AID grant for hotel training in Jamaica in 1962 and was part of a feasibility study team on three other of the Caribbean islands.

new Florida International University at Miami has an active school of Hotel, Restaurant and Travel Services which can serve as a center for the junior and senior university years and welcomes students from abroad.

Puerto Rico Experience

From the American viewpoint, a most interesting government-encouraged tourist destination area is Puerto Rico. Before 1949, Puerto Rico had no luxury hotels, no tourist business worth mentioning. The island economy, largely dependent upon agriculture, was stagnant.

Most observers were highly skeptical that Puerto Rico could be made into a tourist center. When the Caribe Hilton made its debut in 1949, it was dubbed "Moscoso's Folly," a misnomer reminiscent of "Seward's Folly," the sobriquet applied to Seward's purchase of Alaska. Teodoro Moscosov, then director of the Economic Development Administration for Puerto Rico, persuaded the Puerto Rican Government to finance a 335-room luxury hotel. It would be the first luxury hotel on the island and would stimulate the development of tourism in Puerto Rico.

"Ted's Folly" turned to fortune when the Caribe Hilton became what was probably the most profitable hotel of its kind in the world. Several companies were invited to bid for the management of the hotel, but it was Conrad Hilton who took the trouble to negotiate in Spanish and convince the authorities that Hilton International should be given the management contract.

During its first three years, Caribe Hilton occupancy averaged about 58 percent. After that, business skyrocketed. Hilton Hotels International receives 40 percent of the profit; the Government of Puerto Rico, the rest. In 1962, the hotel casino earned $1.6 million while profits from the hotel netted an additional $2 million. The hotel has been expanded to 475 rooms and many times the hotel has operated at 100 percent occupancy.

The Caribe Hilton's success was in large part responsible for further government financing of other hotels. These included an investment of $6.52 million in the La Concha; $1.25 million in the Pierre, $3 million in the Mayaguez Hilton and smaller sums in two other projects. Another factor in the growth of tourism in Puerto Rico was the close-down of Cuba as a tourist area following Castro's take-over of the Cuban government.

As further inducement for investors, the Commonwealth gave generous tax relief. Under the plan, hotels and other business were exempted from taxes during the first 10 years. In the 11th year the exemption dropped to 75 percent; in the 12th year to 50 percent and to 25 percent in the 13th year. The full tax applies in the 14th year.

Hotel Costs

The cost of the newer hotels in Puerto Rico has been $23,000 and up per room. The figure is arrived at by dividing the total cost of the property by the number of rooms. A large part of the cost has been land price. In some cases, cost for land has run as high as $8000 per room. This has forced the construction of high-rise buildings like the Sheraton Hotel and the Ponce de Leon.

Wisely, the Puerto Rico Planning Board has called a halt to all new construction on San Juan's Gold Coast to prevent a "great wall of China" from forming along the beach front. The Planning Board has tried to distribute hotels around the island so that the labor intensive hotels will help the economy of the entire island rather than that of San Juan alone.

Growth of tourism in Puerto Rico following World War II and until 1968 was spectacular. In 1946, only 40,380 visitors came to the Island. That figure rose to 118,401 in 1952. By 1960, the figure was 354,963. The chart on page 231 shows the number of visitors to Puerto Rico in the period 1960-71 rising from 347,000 to a little over a million.

As is true of most visitor statistics, they must be interpreted to be meaningful. In 1972, visitors to Puerto Rico totaled 1,172,885[1] but those staying in hotels and guest houses numbered about half the total, 526,159. The rest stayed with relatives or friends.

[1] *Economy and Finances of Puerto Rico,* Commonwealth of Puerto Rico, San Juan, 1973.

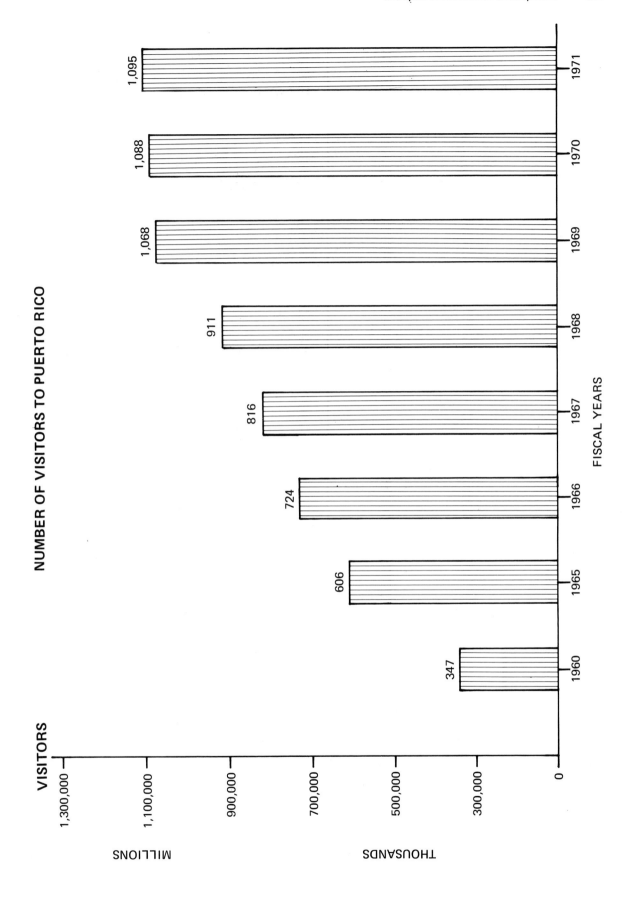

NUMBER OF VISITORS TO PUERTO RICO

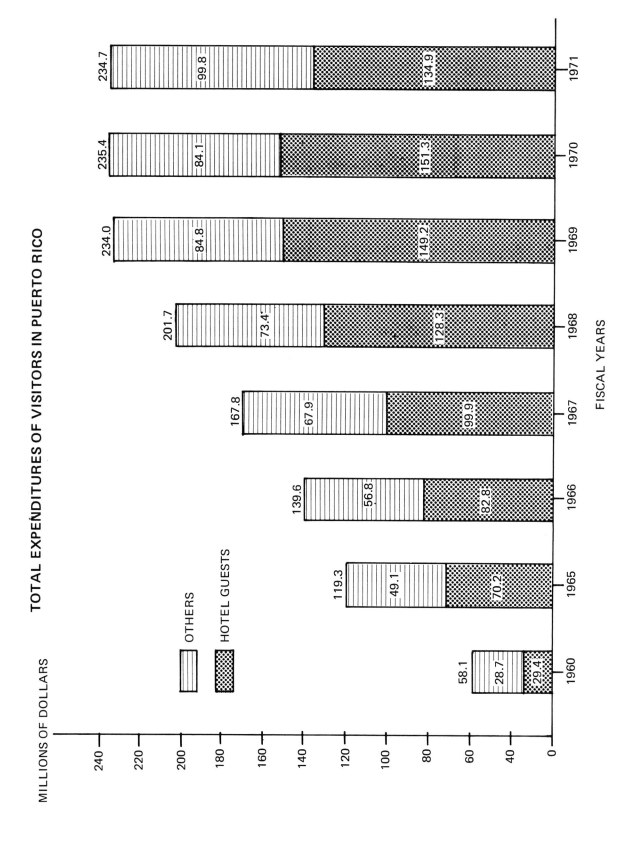

TOTAL EXPENDITURES OF VISITORS IN PUERTO RICO

MILLIONS OF DOLLARS

OTHERS

HOTEL GUESTS

FISCAL YEARS

Expenditures by visitors to Puerto Rico rose in similar dramatic fashion: from 55,681,000 in 1960 to 233,994,000 in 1968.[1] (It is estimated that the average visitor staying in a hotel spent a total of $281 in Puerto Rico during his stay.) Of the non-resident hotel visitors, 82 percent had incomes of over $10,000 a year.

Some of the most spectacular resort hotels in the world have been built in Puerto Rico. The Caribe Hilton, financed by Operation Bootstrap—a government operation, and built in the late forties, set a new pattern for high rise hotels in the tropics. The Dorado Beach built by Laurance Rockefeller in the late 1950's set a tone and standard of design which has influenced tropical hotel keeping around the world.

The importance of convenient location even for a resort was seen in Puerto Rico. The Dorado Beach Hotel, located 22 miles away from San Juan, did not make a profit for several years. The El Conquistador Hotel, another of the most spectacular hotels in the world, waited several years for a profit. Total investment in the hotel exceeded $32 million by 1969. It sits on a gorgeous mountain range overlooking the ocean but is about 40 miles from San Juan. The Barranquitas Hotel was the island government's only attempt at building a mountain resort. It proved a failure. The hotel, financed by the government, was taken back by the government and is now operated as a school for training waiters and cooks.

Gambling Attracts Tourists

As in several of the Caribbean resorts, gambling is a big attraction for the hotel guest. At the Dorado Beach about 95 percent of the guests try their hand at gambling and it takes on a form of guest entertainment. Most of the hotels make from 20 to 25 percent on what the guest spends in buying chips. Odds in favor of the casinos are theoretically only 1¼ percent, but actually work out to about 5 percent, or more. Gambling is carefully supervised and a government inspector must be on hand during the hours of play. TV sets are conspicuously absent in guest rooms. Such entertainment might compete with the casinos for the guest's interest.

A big factor in the sudden spurt in tourism in Puerto Rico in the middle sixties was the extraordinarily low round trip jet fares between major Eastern Seaboard cities and San Juan. The cost of the New York—San Juan round trip jet fare was about $120 which made it one of the least expensive air rides anywhere (less than 4 cents per mile). Paradoxically, at the same time, the round trip fare from New York City to Nassau was $155, and the distance is less. Since then the fares have increased drastically which no doubt constitutes one more reason for the drop-off in number of visitors.

Mid-eastern U. S. constitutes the largest tourist market for Puerto Rico. The state of New York provides more than one-fourth of the total visitors staying in hotels. New Jersey, Pennsylvania and Florida also provide large numbers of visitors. The average guest spends about 66 percent of his budget for food and lodging, 19 percent for amusements and entertainment, 10 percent for shopping and 5 percent for miscellaneous purchases.

A Golden Era for Hotels

In 1969, the resort business in Puerto Rico was booming. Eight Puerto Rican hotels, audited by the firm of Laventhol, Krekstein, Horwath & Horwath, reported an 82.8 percent year-round occupancy, as compared with a 65.4 percent occupancy for 12 southeastern Florida hotels audited by the same firm. U. S. hotels as a whole for that year had a 61 percent occupancy.

What was more interesting for the hotel man was the average room rate achieved in Puerto Rican hotels. The rate was $31.41, compared with $19.62 for southeastern Florida hotels and $17.17 for the larger hotels in the U. S. audited by the LKH&H firm. Tourism was likened to a golden goose and forecasts of growth were highly optimistic.

In 1969, the golden era of Puerto Rican hotel operations seemed to come to an end. Room occupancy for those hotels included in the LKH&H hotel survey for 1970 and 1971 showed fruther declines. Average

[1]These statistics and similar ones come from *Selected Statistics of the Tourism Industry in Puerto Rico*, Tourism Development Company, 1970-71 edition, San Juan, Puerto Rico.

room rate fell as did food and beverage sales. Contributing to the adverse profit picture were rising payroll costs forced in the main by union pressure. Puerto Rico is only part of the larger Caribbean tourist picture which reveals that "the Caribbean hotel industry charges the highest rates per room around the world but makes the lowest profit."[1]

The reasons for the decline in profitability of hotelkeeping in Puerto Rico were several. The employment of hotel non-supervisory workers rose from 3645 in 1961 to 8640 in 1969. Hourly wages ranged far ahead of the consumer price index, increasing from 80¢ in 1959 to $1.94 in 1970.[2] The consumer price index had risen about 35 percent in that period, hotel room rates by about 56.5 percent, hourly wage rates by 142.6 percent. Productivity of employees was low, held down by a number of wage and work stipulations. Annual minimum compensation for 2080 hours was guaranteed to 75 percent of all non-tipped employees, i.e., workers employed more than 20 hours a week but less than 32 hours. If an employee worked less than 20 hours, he was paid for the hours worked on the basis of time and a half the regular rate.

Employees were guaranteed 15 days of vacation with full pay and 15 days of sick leave. Work in excess of 8 hours a day or 48 hours a week was paid at double rate. There were 8 paid holidays plus paid birthday. Employees were given three days' leave with pay in the event of a death of a close member of a family, a 2 percent annual Christmas bonus and other benefits. Fringe benefits in Puerto Rico are about double those found in Miami; effective hourly earnings including fringe benefits range from 14.7 to 47 percent higher than in Miami.[3]

Another factor which makes for low employee productivity is the peculiar expectations of the employee in the Latin-American culture. Under the former plantation system the worker looked at the patron more as a father than employer. The commitment between worker and employer is more than a business relationship. The worker dedicates himself and his family to an employer for life. In return, he expects lifetime security. Once an employee, always an employee. An employee may ad-mit to stealing, drinking on the job or rudeness to guests for which he expects some kind of punishment. But he is never fired.

According to LKH&H, the reasons for the decline in room occupancy in Puerto Rico hotels that began early in 1970 point to four problem areas:

1. Competition for Puerto Rican hotels is severe from other tourist areas and from condominium and apartment developments in Puerto Rico in which the rates are lower than those charged by hotels.

2. Service (or lack of it) appears to be a concern of the tourist; probably the problem is due to the relation between relatively high prices and anticipated services in an industry that grew so fast that training facilities could not keep pace.

3. The market for Puerto Rico should be broader than that represented by the visitor to the luxury resort/gambling-casino.

4. Lack of financing for hotels with fiscal difficulty and for promotion to broaden the market.

It has been pointed out also that the rapid growth of air/sea cruises leaves many unused hotel beds on the islands since the tourist sleeps aboard ship, coming to shore only to shop or to remain for a day. The LKH&H report points out that "The people of Puerto Rico must take a philosophical stand regarding the economic gain from tourism as opposed to the possible loss of some of their cultural values and idiosyncrasies."[4]

Interplay Between Politics and Tourism

Tourism, of course, is always affected by politics, either directly or indirectly. Where there is political pluralism, it can be expected that some groups would express antagonism to tourism, even though the majority favors it. Where there is one party or one man rule, tourism is favored or not fa-

[1]Worldwide Operating Statistics of the Hotel Industry, 1971, LKH&H, 1972. Some hotels in Puerto Rico have done well financially including the Caribe Hilton, The Holiday Inn and The Howard Johnson Motor Lodge. Many have not.
[2]"Cracks in the Golden Egg," Cornell Hotel and Restaurant Administration Quarterly, Nov., 1971, p. 7.
[3]Ibid, p. 11.
[4]Florida, Puerto Rico Lodging Industry, LKH&H, 1972, Philadelphia, 1972, p. 17.

vored; opposition is likely to be muted or suppressed. In Puerto Rico, tourism has been the target of a small but vigorous political group, the "independentistas," those who favor complete separation from the U.S.

True or not, the "independentistas" take credit for several bombings of resort hotels in 1971, acts probably calculated as much to call attention to the independence movement as to destroy tourism or to frighten off tourists. Though a small minority (the parties favoring independence received only 3 percent of the vote in the 1968 elections), the movement is magnified by acts of terror.[1] Though few in number, partisans of the movement include prominent people, four former presidents of the Puerto Rican Bar Association, sophisticated lawyers and wealthy individuals. Members of the movement boast of their connections with Peking and Moscow, claim the authorship of as many as 150 acts of violence in the period 1970-1972.

Technically, Puerto Rico is a self-governing territory established by Act of Congress as a Commonwealth in 1952. Economically at least, independence makes little sense in that the flow of benefits from U. S. federal government would likely be cut off if independence came. The island, 105 miles long and 35 miles wide, has limited natural resources and a high birth rate. Unlike other countries with small resources, such as Switzerland, Puerto Rico has no history of industrial, trade or banking enterprise. Much of the industry in Puerto Rico is there because of tax advantages made possible by the U. S. federal government. While reaping benefits from their limited American citizenship, Puerto Ricans pay no federal taxes and have complete freedom of movement within the U. S. In 1970, in a population of 2,700,000 people, 100,000 chose to leave, most of them for New York City.

Causes of Visitor Dropoff

Much of the dropoff in visitors from the U. S. to Puerto Rico can be attributed to rudeness and worse experienced by visitors to that island. A number of incidents have been reported in the press; no doubt numerous others have occurred. The president of a large hotel firm told the writer that he received each day from Puerto Rico an average of three or four guest complaints about employee behaviour. Incidents of lewd behaviour on public beaches were said to be commonplace.

Strikes Despite High Wages

Although hotel employees in Puerto Rican hotels are among the highest paid employees in the Caribbean region, this has not prevented a number of strikes. The Dorado Beach and the Cerromar hotels were struck just before Christmas, 1972, by 1200 employees to enforce demands for a two-week Christmas bonus which had been given in the past.[2] A few guests who attempted to check out of the hotel said they were threatened with violence by picketing employees. The two-day walkout and picketing was ended, without incident, by court order.

Probably the two most important causes of the decline in tourism have been the threat of danger to visitors and the high rates charged. Several hotels, including the El Conquistador, have been bombed. As pointed out previously, the international traveler places personal safety at the head of his list of desiderata for a destination. The mere threat of danger is more than enough to cause a change in destination choice.

While a small minority rages against things North American, including tourism, the Commonwealth government continues to promote tourism through advertising and other means. Because several hotels have experienced serious financial difficulty the government has taken over some of them.[3] Two of them, the Hotel Barranquitas in the mountains and the Racquet Club, are being used as hotels and, at the same time, as hotel schools. While catering to guests, the Hotel Barranquitas trains cooks and waiters and the Racquet Club is used for supervisory and management level training.

Although the average room rate in the bigger hotels in Puerto Rico declined in 1971 to $32.51, this figure is still the high-

[1]"There are few independentistas in Puerto Rico but . . ." *The New York Times Magazine,* May 21, 1972.
[2]*Lodging and Food Service News,* Dec. 23, 1972.
[3]"Puerto Rico Steps Up Tourism Rescue Effort, Plans Loans to Habits," *The Wall Street Journal,* April 21, 1971.

Master Plan
PALMAS DEL MAR COMPANY
A SEA PINES RESORT IN PUERTO RICO   October 1972

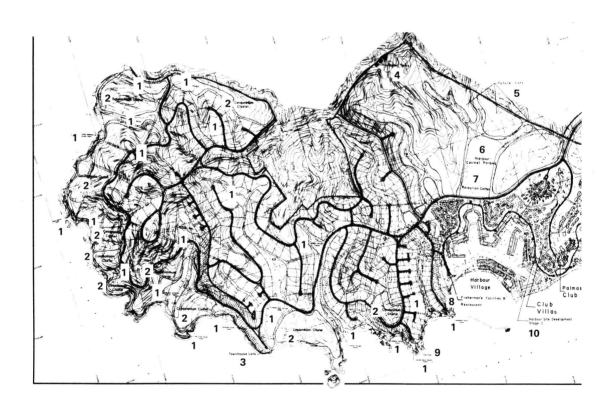

1	Park	**8**	Fisherman's Facilities and Restaurant	**13**	Palmas Botanical Garden
2	Condominium Cluster			**14**	Future Development
3	Townhouse Lots	**9**	Fish Cove	**15**	Environmental Treatment Plant
4	Water Tanks	**10**	Harbour Site Development (Stage 1) also Beach Village		
5	Future Lots			**16**	Lake
6	Harbour Central Parking	**11**	Racquet Club	**17**	Commercial
7	Reception Center	**12**	Driving Range	**18**	Future Housing

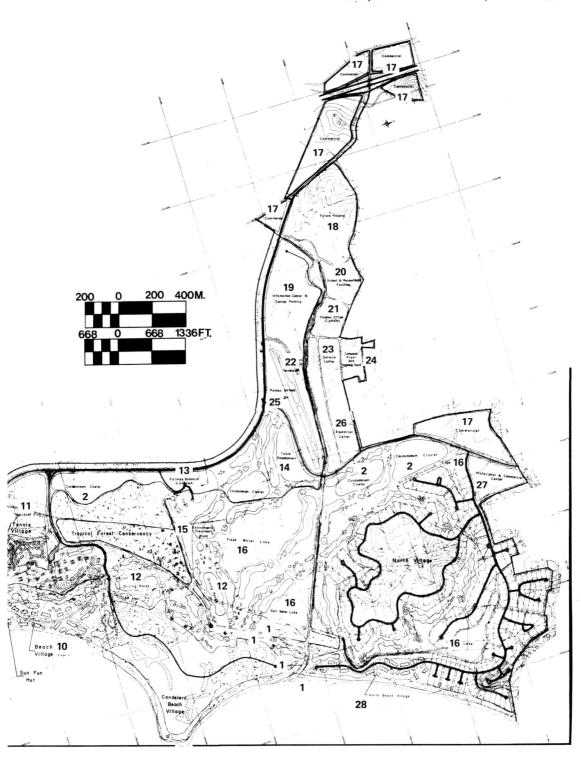

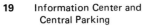

19	Information Center and Central Parking	**24**	Concrete Plant
20	School and Recreational Facilities	**25**	Palmas Airfield
21	Palmas Office Complex	**26**	Equestrian Center
22	Terminal	**27**	Professional and Commercial Center
23	Service Center	**28**	North Beach Village

LEGEND:
EXISTING ROADS
PROPOSED ROADS
MINI-TRANSIT SYSTEM
PEDESTRIAN TRAILS
PROPERTY LINE
ELECTRIC BOAT TRAIL

est in the world.[1]   With Puerto Rico in a competitive position with Europe and the Mediterranean countries, these room rates place Puerto Rico at a distinct disadvantage. As transatlantic fares are reduced, the disadvantage increases.

Leisure Community Under Development

The eastern coast of Puerto Rico is the scene of a new leisure/resort community development which, if successful financially, will no doubt constitute a model for similar developments elsewhere in Puerto Rico and in the Caribbean. Palmas Del Mar, six miles from the town of Humacao, and 45 miles from San Juan, will eventually become a leisure community. It will encompass some 4750 villas and 850 homes, housing tourists, retirees, and permanent residents who are there primarily for sport fishing, ocean swimming, tennis, golf, and vacation living. The project faces some six miles of ocean front and will have as focal points two 18-hole golf courses, a 40-court tennis center, and a harbor area with some 800 boat slips. Movement around Palmas will be primarily by walking, biking, and horseback riding. Electric vehicles are planned for longer distances within Palmas. (See plan, pp. 236-237.)

Like Sea Pines and Hilton Head in South Carolina, developed by the same person, Charles Fraser, about 40 percent of the total land area, 700 acres, will be devoted to green belts, golf, recreation areas, and beach connected by walkways and bike paths. The complex will take on aspects of a Mediterranean village minus industrial activity. A Club will contain a restaurant, pool, and guest suites. A Sun Fun Hut will be the center of beach activities. Some 50 shops will cluster around the harbor.

Palmas will be very much in the hotel business in that condominiums, or villas as they are called, will be rented in the absence of the owners. Every villa owner is also a proportionate owner of communal land such as yards, gardens, parking areas, recreational facilities, and so on. The scale and sweep of the plan is magnificent and pace-setting. The principal architect, Charles Fraser, has developments going at Amelia Island Plantation, Fla.; South Point, S. C.; River Hills, near Charlotte, N. C.; and Big Canoe, Ga.

He has demonstrated what can be done in the way of beautifying an already beautiful area.

A number of condominium developments are operating on the Caribbean islands, including Sun Crest Manor in Barbados and several on St. Thomas and St. Croix. When well constructed and managed, they are adjuncts to the traditional hotel, in fact are more like hotels than apartment houses. Condominiums are a device for raising capital and spreading risks. Under present tax laws in the U. S., they are a tax shelter. They will probably grow to be a sizable part of the tourist plant in the Caribbean.

The Bahamas Experience*

The Commonwealth of the Bahama Islands comprises some 700 islands stretching south and east off the coast of Florida. Only a few are inhabited. Sun-drenched and comprised of limestone and coral, these islands rise barely a few feet out of the ocean and are surrounded by sparkling clear waters that are bathed in sunshine most of the time. For natural beauty and for those who love water sports and fishing, the appeal is tremendous.

Tourism is a natural product which is being developed and sold mostly to North Americans, a large number coming from Florida and New York State. Jet travel has made the islands easily accessible to the U. S. and what was once a playground for the wealthy few is now available for large numbers to enjoy. Large numbers do enjoy the Bahamas, some who come do not. In 1972, 1,391,343 visitors went to the islands, 435,825 of whom were cruise visitors. They spent about $277 million while on the islands, providing about 70 percent of the national income, and more than 50

[1]*Florida, Puerto Rico Lodging Industry,* 1972, LKH&H, 1972.
*Information for this section is largely based on these publications:
A Plan for Managing the Growth of Tourism in the Commonwealth of the Bahama Islands (Washington, D. C: Checchi and Company, 1969).
Annual Reports, Tourism and the Commonwealth of the Bahama Islands, 1967, 1968.
Bahama Islands Visitor Statistics, 1968, 1969, 1971; Ministry of Tourism, Nassau. Some of the statements are based on personal observation.

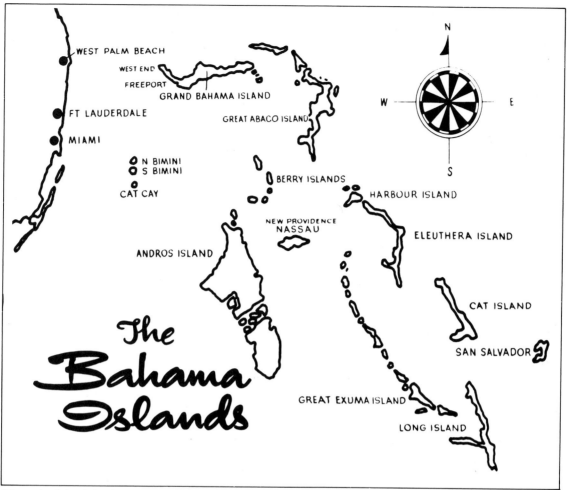

The major islands in the Bahamas chain stretch across 90,000 sq. mi. of the Atlantic Ocean. Nassau, New Providence Is., the Bahamian capital, is a half-hour flight from Miami, 2½ hours from New York.

percent of the government revenue.[1]

The economy of the Bahamas revolves around tourism, necessarily so. Throughout its history, its economy has been feast or famine. Periods of prosperity were built on privateering, ship wrecking, sea island cotton, running the northern blockade of the Confederacy, rum-running and the military activities centered there during World War II. Now it is tourism. Per capita income in 1969 was $1880, second highest, after the U. S. Virgin Islands, in the Caribbean and higher than any Latin American nation.

In 1949, slightly more than 32,000 visitors came to the Bahamas and it was decided by the government that the islands could become a successful year-round resort area. Tourism in neighboring Florida spurred the Development Board to take a firm stand on promotion and branch offices were opened in five North American cities. In two years, the number of visitors to Nassau more than doubled and, by 1954, the 100,000 mark was passed. In 1959, many of the estimated 400,000 visitors who had in previous years visited Cuba began going to other Caribbean islands including the Bahamas. Jet travel was also an important factor in spurring tourism.

Promotion Attracts Visitors

Promotion and public relations have also played a large part in attracting visi-

[1]U. S. Dept. of the Interior, *The 1969 Annual Report, Virgin Islands* (Washington, D. C.: Government Printing Office, 1970), p. 5.

tors. Visitor spending per capita is one of the highest of any tourist area, reaching as much as $6 per visitor. In 1969, the total number of visitors dropped a few points, the drop being attributed to the economic recession in the United States, but also in part due to the high cost of vacationing in the Bahamas and because a reputation for rudeness and inhospitable attitudes had developed. This latter factor is discussed later.

Initially, almost all tourism to the Bahamas was concentrated around and in Nassau on New Providence Island. The first tourist hotel, the Royal Victoria, built there in 1862, catered to blockade runners to the Confederacy. It was not until the 1960's that Grand Bahama Island was developed and the Freeport resort area made into one of the major island resorts.

Today, the Bahamas have about 11,000 hotel rooms. In 1972, roughly 47 percent of all tourist accommodations were on New Providence, about 36 percent on Grand Bahama and the rest on the Out Islands.

Tourism generates some 41,000 jobs. The Out Islands, comprising all those except Grand Bahama and New Providence, are hampered in their tourism development by lack of modern transportation. Few of their airports have lights for night operation and airlines catering to the Out Islands have not been particularly successful.

Much of tourism in the Bahamas piggybacks on Florida tourism—many of the visitors to Florida fly over to spend a few days in the Bahamas. In 1968, the Bahamas received one visitor for every 18.7 visitors received by Florida. Contrary to what might be expected, the Bahamas, except for a low fall season, have a relatively even flow of visitors the year around. The Bahamas draw 87 percent of their business from the United States, 5 percent from Canada, and 7 percent from other countries. About one-fourth of all U. S. tourists to the Bahamas are from Florida; about 18 percent from New York State.

The growth rate of the Bahamas during 1964-68 was one of the highest in the world, an annual compound rate of 22.6 percent. The chart on page 195 compares the growth of visitors to major island resorts during the period.

The Lucaya-Freeport development on Grand Bahama is an example of what political advantage and gambling can do for a resort development. It also shows what can happen when governments change. In 1955, Grand Bahama Island, on which Freeport is located, had little to offer as a tourist attraction. Some 80 miles off the Florida coast, it was flat and barren, except for scattered patches of scrub trees. The island does have some fine beaches and the promoters had the advantage of having virgin land, almost no government restrictions, few people and no roads. The planners could move in any direction.[1]

Planning Island Development

In plotting out the island, the planners placed heavy and light industrial areas on the rocky coastline, downwind of the sandy beach areas. Residential and resort areas were laid out for the beaches. To keep the beaches clear, the town of Freeport was developed inland—Bahamas' only inland town.

In 1955, Wallace Groves, the island's developer, went to the Bahamian Government, then a white oligarchy in a black community, and was able to receive a number of concessions. The entire area would be free from property taxes or levies, personal property taxes, capital gains taxes, taxes on earnings, and taxes on bonuses and salaries until the year 1990. Import duties, export taxes and excise taxes were guaranteed exemption until 2054. In effect, it was "a country within a country," based upon a series of incredibly generous concessions. The phrase "country within a country" was used by Lyden O. Pindling who became prime minister in 1967.

As reported in Business Week[2] "If you came to Freeport to live, you would use Groves' Airport, Groves' Harbor, Groves' roads, Groves' Schools, Groves' land, Groves' Supermarket, Groves' electricity and water. You would operate a business only if Groves gave you a license, and you would pay him a license fee that might run as high as 10 percent of your gross receipts."

[1]"Freeport—a Leisure Community in the Bahamas," *Land: Recreation and Leisure*, (Washington, D. C.: The Urban Land Institute, 1970), pp. 79-84.
[2]*Business Week,* Aug. 1, 1970, p. 55.

The tax advantages offered at Freeport began luring potential investors to the scene. Once arrived, they were disappointed. The place entirely lacked infrastructure: medical facilities, restaurants, theaters, churches, shops and the rest of the amenities. As a result, industry was not attracted.

Groves returned again to the Bahamian Government. Further concessions were made. His Grand Bahama Port Authority Company was granted the exclusive power to license businesses and to import skilled and semi-skilled labor when no skilled Bahamians were available. Even the choice of a name for his company, Grand Bahama Port Authority, had the ring of being a government agency. Things began to change fast.

The Authority and a group of investors together created the Grand Bahama Development Corporation which built the Lucayan Beach Hotel and a top quality golf course. Even more important, legalized gambling was introduced.

Unintentionally, a great deal of free publicity was given Freeport in major American newspapers and magazines because of its gambling activities. The media were critical; nevertheless, Freeport was introduced and kept before the public eye.

The fact that Freeport is only a 26-minute jet flight from Miami, and the other factors mentioned, triggered a massive influx of tourists to the island. The number of visitors jumped from 26,000 in 1963 to over 518,000 in 1969. Some 3400 hotel rooms were built between 1963 and 1969. An International Bazaar was an added tourist attraction. Constructed like a miniature world's fair, it consists of 57 shops where a wide variety of items can be purchased. Because of the overall development, some 20 real estate firms spurred the sale of Freeport real estate. Population jumped from 2000 to over 40,000. U. S. investors by 1970 had poured over $900 million into Freeport.[1]

Condominium development has been rapid and may have set the pattern for condominium development and sales generally. The first condominium in Freeport, a 30-unit project built in 1965, sold out immediately. The second, a 500-unit complex, was also quickly sold out and a third built.

The rooms in some of the condominiums are configured as studio and one-bedroom apartments, but can be combined to form two- and three-bedroom units. Prices, in 1968, ranged from $16,000 to $20,000 for the studio apartments; the one-bedroom units ranged from $25,000 to $30,000.

Unique Condominium Plan

The ownership and rental plan is unusual. Each apartment owner shares in the profit from the rentals and leases of all the apartments, shops, bars, restaurants and concessions, even though he does not choose to rent his own property. Those who rent their apartments receive a share of the net rental income, in addition to the common property income.

The Freeport venture initially was built on the idea of including light and heavy industry as a part of the development plan, but only after the resort complex was built was there any development in the industrial area. Then Syntex, U. S. steel, and an oil refinery were built, among other industrial plants.

The Freeport development may be a lesson in the merits and demerits of depending upon government concessions. A number of questions were raised about the legality and probity of the manner in which the concessions were granted.

Many visitors to the Bahamas have experienced discourtesy and a general attitude of resentment on the part of the natives. Political control, formerly vested in a small white clique known as the Bay Street Boys, is now more widely diffused, but apparently less predictable. As a result, many investors are pulling out of the Bahamas, and from Freeport in particular.

What the government giveth, it can also take away, as has been demonstrated at Grand Bahama. The Pindling government made no bones about its lack of friendliness for the quasi-governmental authority given to the developers of Grand Bahama by the "Bay's" White-dominated government. In March 1969, a freeze on work permits for skilled foreigners was clamped on and, in February 1970, the Black govern-

---

[1]*The Wall Street Journal*, Feb. 2, 1971, p. 1.

**Bahamas Tourism Budgets
and Costs per Visitor (000 omitted)
1961-1971**

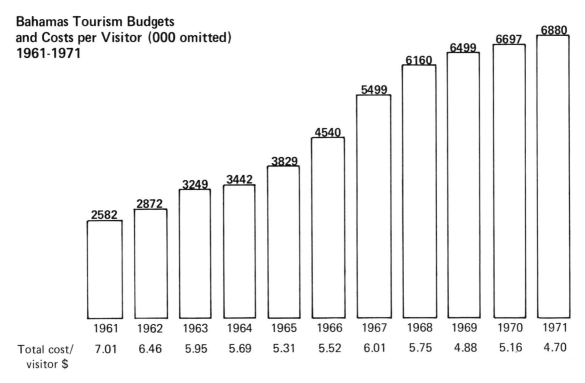

	1961	1962	1963	1964	1965	1966	1967	1968	1969	1970	1971
	2582	2872	3249	3442	3829	4540	5499	6160	6499	6697	6880
Total cost/ visitor $	7.01	6.46	5.95	5.69	5.31	5.52	6.01	5.75	4.88	5.16	4.70

ment of the Bahamas took back its control over immigration at Freeport, in effect a nullification of a key portion of the agreement made with the developers under the previous government.

Although there is almost no unemployment among the 190,000 Bahamians in all of the 700 Bahama Islands, few Black Bahamians, who constitute 85 percent of the population, hold responsible positions in the tourist business. According to some hotel operators in the islands, few are trained or motivated for such positions. The new government could seriously hamper hotel and restaurant operations on the islands by refusing, or delaying for long periods, immigration permits for the skilled employees needed to operate the hotels and restaurants.

By 1970, the Bahamian government was taking action to counteract lack of courtesy to tourists on the part of natives and was publicizing the benefits of tourism to the local resident. Tourism in the Bahamas, in 1970, declined about 2.6 percent, to 1.3 million visitors. Prior to that time there was almost no unemployment but, in 1970, the jobless rate rose to 2.5 percent. In 1971, the number of visitors increased but many of them were part of groups who spent less than independent travelers.

The Ministry of Tourism of the Baha-

mas has computed the total cost of attracting a visitor to the Bahamas during the period 1961-1971. The cost per visitor—the budget of the Ministry of Tourism divided by the number of visitors—was $7.01 in 1961. By 1971, the figure had dropped to $4.70.[1] (The figures are in Bahamian dollars which are usually close to parity with the U. S. Dollar). The chart above shows the decline in cost for each of the years 1961 through 1971. The Bahamas budget for tourism in 1961 was $2.582 million. In 1971, it had increased to $6.88 million, probably the largest tourism budget per capita of any government.

For those interested in the organization of a government tourist organization, the Bahamas Ministry of Tourism organization is shown on the facing page. Some 70 persons are employed in the office in Nassau.[2]

The U. S. Virgins

The Virgin Islands are an example, par excellence, of what tourism can do economically for an area. Given an ideal climate, relatively inexpensive and fast access to a

[1]*1971 Annual Report of Tourism,* Commonwealth of the Bahama Islands, Nassau, 1972.
[2]*Ibid.*

ORGANIZATION OF
BAHAMAS MINISTRY OF TOURISM
1971

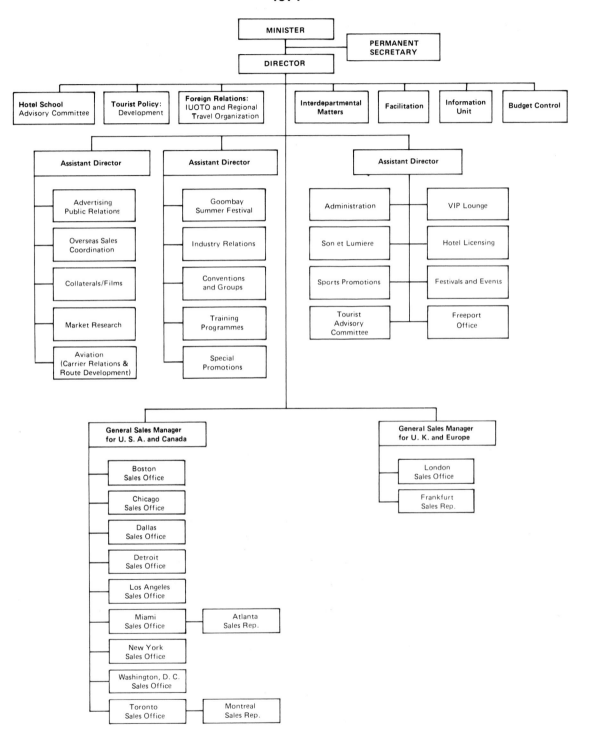

VIRGIN ISLANDS' TOURIST BOOM SPURS ECONOMIC GROWTH

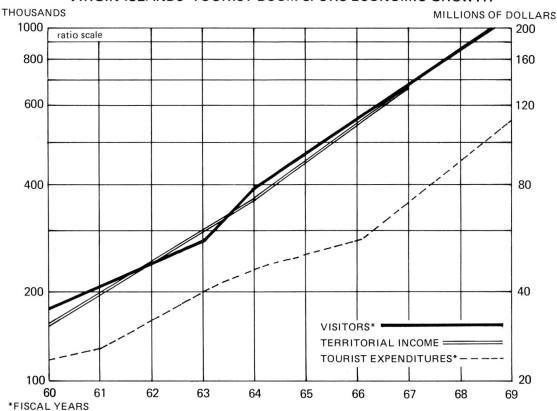

THOUSANDS   MILLIONS OF DOLLARS

ratio scale

VISITORS* ━━━━━
TERRITORIAL INCOME ═══════
TOURIST EXPENDITURES* ─ ─ ─ ─ ─

*FISCAL YEARS

Source: "The U. S. Virgin Islands," *World Business,* No. 11, April, 1968.

major tourist market, plus special privileges granted by a national government, the islands represent a microcosm for the study of tourism. They also represent a case study of the effects of such rapid growth upon the psychology of the residents.

Following World War II, the U. S. Virgin Islands were a sleepy group of Caribbean Islands not dissimilar to dozens of other such islands in the West Indies The growth of sugar cane, once the island's economic mainstay, had almost vanished because it could not compete with the sugar cane grown on level lands. The people lacked skills, resources and enterprise.

In the period around 1950, tourism began growing at a remarkable rate and has continued to do so year after year. In 1950, seven cruise ships stopped at the island bringing some 3124 passengers, sightseers and shoppers for the town of Charlotte Amalie, St. Thomas. By 1962, 163 ships anchored, bringing 64,239 passengers. In 1971, some 600 cruise ship calls were

registered at Charlotte Amalie, bringing 364,645 passengers and making Charlotte Amalie the largest cruise-ship stopping point in the world.

Air traffic to the Virgin Islands grew in similar dramatic fashion, from 12,650 passengers in 1949-50 to 215,809 in 1962-63. In 1969, 908,776 visitors arrived by plane.

Tourist expenditures, which in the year 1950-51 were estimated at $2.3 million, grew to $25.8 million in 1960-61. By 1969, expenditures were estimated at $112.3 million.[1]

The chart above shows the rapid growth of tourism for the years 1960-67.

───────

[1]Statistics from: "A Study of the Tourist Industry in the U. S. Virgin Islands," *Small Business Management Research Reports,* Washington, D. C., Feb., 1964; 1969 *Annual Report, Virgin Islands to the Secretary of Interior* (Washington, D. C.: Government Printing Office) 1970; "Social and Economic Indicators, U. S. Virgin Islands, 1960-1965-1969," Bureau of Statistics and Economic Studies, Govt, of the Virgin Islands, Sept. 1970. Also *Travel Trade, Sales Guide,* Aug. 21, 1972.

The economic impact on the island residents has been considerable. In 1960, per capita income was about $950. By 1967, it had grown to $2100; it jumped to $2700 in 1969,[1] and was estimated at $3000 in 1970.[2] Not all of the economic growth can be attributed to tourism. The island manufactures rum from sugar cane and has a sizable watch-assembly industry made possible by the elimination of duty on watches exported to the continental U. S. There are also oil and aluminum processing plants, again made possible by preferential tax advantages. Tourism, however, remains the prime mover of the economy.

Basis of Growth

Reasons for the remarkable growth in tourism are several:

1. Preferential treatment, under U. S. Customs regulations, which permits the purchase of imported luxury goods at virtually free port prices has been a major factor in attracting visitors to the Virgin Islands. Visitors from the mainland are allowed to bring back $200 worth of goods, tax exempt. This exemption is double that for any other region, except Guam and American Samoa. The exemption is not dependent upon the 48-hour stay generally required for visitors returning from other areas.

2. U. S. citizens, including Puerto Ricans, are allowed one gallon of alcoholic beverages, duty free.

3. The close-down of Castro Cuba to American visitors in the late 1950's diverted tourists to Puerto Rico and to the Virgin Islands. (It helped tourism in the Bahamas and Jamaica even more.)

Much of the tourism in the Virgin Islands piggybacks on that of Puerto Rico. St. Thomas lies only about 70 air miles from San Juan, Puerto Rico. A large number of visitors to Puerto Rico fly over to St. Thomas for the day or for a short stay in the Virgin Islands to sight-see and take advantage of the free port privileges.

4. The trip from New York to the Virgin Islands is relatively fast, convenient and inexpensive. Although the Virgin Islands are some 1400 miles southeast of New York City and about 1000 miles from Miami, the coming of the jet engine made the flight from New York to St. Thomas relatively quick and easy. Flying time from New York City is 3½ hours. The market for the Virgin Islands is largely focused in New York State and the Northeastern United States. All but five percent of the visitors come from the U. S. or Puerto Rico; almost a third reside in New York State; two-thirds in the Northeast.[3]

5. The tremendous natural beauty and ideal climate of the Virgin Islands is a further drawing card. Average temperature is 78°, with seasonal variations. Excellent swimming and snorkeling beaches are scattered among the three islands of St. Thomas, St. John and St. Croix.

6. Investment incentives have encouraged the construction of hotels and guest houses. By June 1967, 41 hotels and guest houses held certificates of Tax Exemption and Subsidies. Since then the Industrial Incentive Act has been changed to include condominiums, and other hotels have been granted tax benefits.

A feature of tourism in the Virgin Islands not conducive to creating hotel demand is the very short period of time most visitors stay there. Average stay of air visitors is estimated to be 2½ to 3½ days, compared with nine days in Jamaica and seven days in Puerto Rico. About 20 percent of the visitors are cruise ship passengers whose spending is generally limited to purchases in shops. The short stay accounts for the fact that, even though there are more than a million visitors to the islands each year, total guest rooms in 1970 numbered only 4012.

Because of what amounts to "over-employment," the native islanders pick and choose what work they will do. Almost none work in the hotels and restaurants, feeling that such work carries implications of low status. About half of the total labor force (estimated to be in excess of 32,000) are from "off" the islands, "aliens" who come in originally to the islands on a one-

[1] "The U. S. Virgin Islands," *World Business,* No. 11, Apr. 1968, *Chase National Bank,* N. A.
[2] Interview with James A. O'Bryan, Dept. of Commerce, Trade & Industry Division, U. S. Virgin Islands, 1971. As a comparison, gross national product per person for Puerto Rico in 1970 was $1340; $460 for Jamaica; $70 for Haiti. (Figures from World Bank Atlas).
[3] *The U. S. Virgin Islands, op. cit.*

year visa, mostly from the down islands, islands such as Anguilla, Montserrat, St. Lucia, Nevis and other formerly English-dominated islands where wages are much lower.[1]

Until 1971, aliens were treated almost as indentured servants. They were "bonded" to an employer and could remain in the Virgin Islands only as long as they stayed with a particular employer. Alien children were not allowed to attend public schools; aliens did not qualify for public housing and few received the usual fringe benefits such as paid holidays, retirement benefits and health insurance. Aliens, in the words of a consulting firm that conducted a major study of the problem in 1969, were "nonpersons."

In May 1970, the U. S. Dept. of Labor dropped the bonding system and aliens that were on the islands could send their children to public schools. At the same time, virtually no new aliens were allowed to enter. Aliens who had arrived illegally were deported to their native islands.

Because the labor force is relatively untrained and unmotivated, hotel men of the area estimate that from 2 to 2½ employees are needed to do the same job in the Virgin Islands as would be needed on the mainland. The fact that 24 holidays are officially recognized does not help productivity.[2]

Status Structure Creates Problems

Part of the personnel problem in the tourist business of the Virgin Islands develops around the status structure. When the Danes held the islands, a rigid hierarchical system was developed, with government officials at the top of the social scale, laborers at the bottom. A government job is prized; manual work, including most hotel and restaurant employment, is avoided. The government has made such jobs available in numbers. Under Ralph Paiewonsky, Governor from 1961 until 1969, the government payroll rose to 7500, one-tenth of the estimated population.[3]

The continental hotelier is non-plused by the lack of motivation among the natives to seek well-paying positions within the hotel, not realizing that in the Virgin Islands prestige of position is more important than financial reward. The North American educator wonders why so few natives[4] in Bermuda, Bahamas, Puerto Rico and the Virgin Islands attend vocationally oriented educational programs, not realizing that any work done with the hands is loaded with a stigma hanging over from the days of field work and slavery. It is quite all right to work as a front desk clerk even though the pay may be less than that of the bellman or the cook. The tourist may wonder at the disdain with which the front desk clerk treats the rest of the "help" but this would not surprise him if he was aware of the local hierarchy of social status. It is honorific to be a gift shop clerk, a hotel receptionist or an airline hostess. The taxicab driver enjoys a particular status because he is in business for himself. Few people will work as electricians, plumbers, cooks or bakers, regardless of wage. The chambermaid takes the job only from economic necessity.

Another area of misunderstanding between the continental hotelier and local employees in the U. S. Virgin Islands revolves around the relationship between the supervisor and employee. A local resident is much more concerned with style and grace on the job, the nature of the relationship, than he is with efficiency. It is important that he be treated with dignity at all times. According to G. K. Lewis, author of a treatise on the Virgin Islands, there is a paranoic obsession with the outward insignia of well being.

Lewis declares that dress remains the emulative device for all classes who resist the habit of informality affected by the continentals (those from the U. S.).[5] Formal titles of Mr. and Mrs. and Miss are a must in Government departments because of the pathological need for respect. To seek com-

[1]*The 1969 Annual Report, Virgin Islands* (Washington, D. C.: Supt. of Documents, 1970), p. 65.

[2]Estimates of productivity vary. The Checchi Company in their Bahamas study, quoted elsewhere in this book, put the number of hotel workers per hotel room as 1.15 in Southern Florida; 1.2 in Bermuda; 1.2-1.3 in the Bahamas; 1.68 in Puerto Rico.

[3]Anthony Luckas, "We Have Been Encroached On, Invaded, Engulfed," *The New York Times Magazine*, April 18, 1971, p. 102.

[4]The term "native" is preferred by the Creole group in the Virgin Islands, may be resented by other West Indian islanders.

[5]Gordon K. Lewis, *The Virgin Islands, A Caribbean Lilliput* (Evanston: Northwestern University Press, 1972).

pensation from a feeling of inferiority as related to the continental, the middle class Creole demands exaggerated deference from his social inferiors and enforces it by an elaborate art of social bullying. According to Lewis, there is little sense of humor about self and a marked deficiency of community spirit and social obligation.

Class hostility runs throughout the culture, suspiciousness being the norm. It is not that the native is not a hard worker but in his society form is more important than productivity. Living by one's wits is esteemed as much or more than real achievement. The lower class, colored native envies and suspects the lighter-skinned upper class. While the machinery of government is controlled by the Creole, commerce and tourism is dominated by the continental, which tends to heighten the schism between classes.

Sociologically, the Virgin Islands represent a destination area which has, to some extent, been overwhelmed by tourism and the influx of "aliens" brought on by tourism. More than a million tourists each year pour into the group of islands whose total population is less than 80,000.

Native Population Loses Ground

What is more important is that the native population now constitutes less than one-fourth of the total population. Those born in Puerto Rico comprise about 15 percent; continentals, those born on the American mainland, about 10 percent; those born in Europe about 5 percent, and down-island aliens—legal and illegal—about 30 percent. The native Virgin Islanders quite naturally resent the fact that they find themselves a minority; they feel that they are going to lose their identity as Island people. Tensions between different groups of aliens and native residents have been considerable.[1]

Quite naturally, residents resent the fact that most of the better beaches are being preempted by resort developments. Of the 40 beaches on St. Thomas, only two are publicly owned and the situation is comparable on St. Croix. To use a hotel beach, the average price is $2.00 per adult, $1.00 per child; some hotels charge considerably more.

In 1970-71, a sharp drop in occupancy occurred throughout the islands. The number of visitors that traveled by air dropped from 908,776 in 1969-69 to 639,507 in 1969-70. Though cruise ship visitors increased, total visitors to the three U. S. Virgins declined by over 200,000. The total number of visitors declined further in 1970-71.[2] A number of hotels closed or changed hands. The president of the Virgin Islands Hotel Association, Richard L. Erb, stated that a number of factors made hotel profits almost impossible:

1. Wages, two to three times those in the other West Indian Islands.
2. Necessity to import almost all food consumed in hotels.
3. Electricity costs of 50 percent or higher than on the mainland. Costs caused by outages and surges which burned out equipment.
4. Dismal phone service.
5. Water costs in excess of 1¢ per gallon.
6. Employee fringe benefits of up to 89¢ per hour.
7. Low productivity of employees. (Maids clean 9 rooms as compared with 12 to 16 on the mainland.)

In 1971, the combined net loss of hotels in the U. S. Virgins approximated $5 million.[3] Part of the dropoff was attributed to the economic recession taking place on the mainland. But there were other reasons.

As previously noted, a major reason why tourism has fallen in the Caribbean generally has been the lack of courtesy, particularly in Puerto Rico. Fear created by a series of bomb threats in Puerto Rican hotels has added to the tension. A bomb exploded in the Hotel Conquistador was reported to have caused some $200,000 in damages. News of such bombings does not endear a particular destination to the tourist. The results are felt directly in the Virgin Islands since about 75 percent of all tourists visiting Puerto Rico also junket to the Virgin Islands.[4]

[1]*The New York Times Magazine,* Apr. 19, 1971, p. 110.
[2]*Tourist Travel to the Caribbean, 1971,* Caribbean Travel Assn., New York City, 1972.
[3]Richard L. Erb, report to the Caribbean Hotel Association, June 14, 1972.
[4]The U. S. Virgin Islands, *op. cit.*

Anti-white feeling has built up in the Virgin Islands and is being seen in the treatment of tourists. Many white residents are fearful. According to *The Wall Street Journal,* a number of rapes of white women took place on St. Croix in 1970 and the islands had their first armed bank robbery.[1] Purse snatchings, assaults, and burglaries of hotel rooms, homes and businesses are on the rise.

The kind of news reported below accounts for some of the decline in Virgin Island tourism:[2]

"Last Sunday night a terrible incident occurred at the Yacht Haven Hotel, which may very well have far reaching effects on the overall economy and on the lives of the people of these islands. Even though it is still not too clear who started the fracas, the results are clear. It was reported that a man was held in the pool for over a half an hour and every time he would try to get out he was pushed back; a woman was thrown into the water, and even though in agony from a sprained ankle, was not allowed any assistance; another guest was badly beaten and a large number of hotel guests had to seek refuge in a large storeroom on the premises.

"In fact, even the Commissioner of Public Safety, our number one police officer, was assaulted and cuffed around.

"All this was master-minded and achieved by a band of local youngsters who had unlawfully climbed the walls and begun mingling with the guests, asking for cigarettes and generally making insulting and racist remarks. As the insults began to turn to violence and personal injuries began to become more intense, the police were called and eventually the matter came under control."

From a touristic viewpoint one of the worst things that could happen to a resort destination happened in 1972 on St. Croix when five masked bandits engaged in robbery shot and killed eight people, four of them tourists, at the Fountain Valley Golf Course.[3]

The Virgin Islands, with a population of less than 80,000, has about 170 uniformed police but private security guards on the islands number more than the official police. Incidents where black policemen looked the other way when tourists were assaulted have been noted. Numbers of visitors say they will never return to the Islands. The Blacks are resentful, saying that they can't buy land in their own realm because speculation has driven property values sky-high. They also resent being employed only as waiters, bus-boys, maids and bartenders.

Visitors Misunderstand Islanders

Hotel managers and others in the Virgin Islands are quick to point out that the islands are no more dangerous than the streets of any American city. They also claim that the attitude of the native is often mistakenly interpreted by the visitor. The native Black, proud of his new economic independence and caught up to a certain extent with the black militancy expressed in the U. S. and elsewhere, may overact in his new role as a "dignified, independent human being."

The Islander, according to some observers, has inherited a cultural habit of being fairly non-committal in his reactions to Whites. He may limit his conversation to what might be interpreted as a brusk response to questions. What is also disturbing to many is that some Blacks have a tendency to "not see" a White, even though they are vis-a-vis. The Black simply looks through the White or looks as though no one were there. For him, the White does not exist, at least openly.

While tourism has stimulated the economy and brought relatively high income to the residents, there are also dislocations.

The economic consequences of rapid tourist growth has been an over-heated economy with rapidly increasing wage and other costs. Because there is almost no unemployment, wage costs have increased so that they are as high or higher than on the mainland for equivalent jobs. In some residential areas, land values have doubled every four to five years.[4]

[1]"The Uneasy Islands," *The Wall Street Journal,* Dec. 22, 1970.
[2]"The Maduro Report," *The Home Journal,* St. Thomas, Dec. 13, 1971.
[3]Horace Sutton, "The Sun-Filled Islands: Are They Safe?" *Harper's Bazaar,* Dec., 1972.
[4]The U. S. Virgin Islands, *op. cit.*

Shipping delays in getting spare parts or in ordering new materials from off the island can be exasperating. At one famous hotel, candles which were ordered for Christmas arrived a year and a half late. Electrical breakdowns, water-shortages and numerous paid holidays also frustrate and add to the cost of business. High costs mean high rates for hotel rooms and high prices for restaurant meals.

Population has also increased rapidly, rising from 32,099 in 1960 to an estimated 71,000 in 1970.[1] Such rapid growth in population and visitors has placed strains on the infrastructure. Roads on St. Thomas are congested; those in Charlotte Amalie, jammed at times. Even though desalting plants produce close to 5 million gallons of water per day, much water must be barged in from Puerto Rico. The electrical supply and phone system leave something to be desired.

Having pointed out many of the problems of the U. S. Virgin Islands, the observer is faced with evaluating the impact of tourism on the people and the economy, balancing benefits with costs. Certainly, tourism and Federal largesse have brought prosperity to the residents, wealth to a number of them. It has also brought social unrest and tensions between residents and newly-arrived workers. The crime rate is up, the visitor rate down. The U. S. Virgins are no longer a "tropical paradise." Hotel investors have lost money. The problems of hotelkeeping are many and perplexing, the natural beauty remains. It will be up to the people of the Virgins to work out the dislocations which have been brought on by the rapid development of tourism.

The Bermuda Experience

Bermuda is an example of phased growth, balanced with an orderly rise in the number of tourists. Tourism, the all-important industry in Bermuda, sees some 400,000 visitors come each year and leave upwards of $65 million, which accounts for three-fourths of the island's income. With a permanent population of only 52,000, per capita income from tourism exceeds $1200 a year.

The government does not want to see more tourists than can be accommodated comfortably nor are more visitors wanted than can be handled by the available labor force. To limit the number of tourists on the island at any one time, only four cruise ships are allowed in at once; two can be tied up at the piers and two at anchor so that not more than 2500 or 3000 cruise passengers are on the island at any given moment. No high-rise structures are allowed; the tallest building now is the seven-story bank in Hamilton, the principal town. Only 562 cabs have been licensed.

By 1970, there was a considerable labor shortage with the Government Labor Office listing twice as many jobs available as applicants. Only about 64 percent of the 4000 people employed in the island's 115 licensed hotels, cottage colonies and guest houses were natives. The others, allowed in on special work permits, were largely from Canada, the Azores, Europe and the Caribbean.

By phasing growth, Bermuda hopes to avoid some of the tensions characteristic of the Caribbean islands. Even so, there are tensions. Although 60 percent of the island's permanent population of 52,000 is Black (or colored, as they are called there), not one Black is a hotel manager. Only one Bermudian holds a position as high as assistant manager. Forty percent of all waiters and bartenders are imported Whites.

To qualify Blacks for better jobs, a hotel and catering college was launched in 1962. By 1970, it had graduated only 200, even though the tuition is a nominal $75 a year, which is waived if the applicant feels he cannot afford it. Pre-vocational hotel training courses are being introduced into Bermuda's secondary schools to train housekeepers, waiters, cooks and applicants for office positions.

In 1970, Caribbean resorts generally reported a serious decline in the tourist trade but Bermuda showed a 5 percent increase over 1969.

---

[1] *Ibid.*

The Barbados Experience*

Barbados, the most eastern of the Caribbean Islands, has also moved into the U. S.-Canada tourist orbit with some 276,000 tourists visiting the island each year. Although about 93,000 of the visitors in 1971 were from cruise ships, the economic impact on the island was considerable. The Barbados Tourist Board estimated that in 1970 the visitors spent about $63.5 million. With a population of 250,000, the impact per capita, about $260, was small relative to some of the other Caribbean islands, but in a country whose total per capita income is only $500 that amount is considerable.

Tourism in Barbados has grown rapidly since 1958 when the government established a Barbados Tourist Board. An annual growth rate of 16 percent was experienced during the period 1961-1970. Since 1958, the number of hotel rooms increased from about 700 to 3500. The number of rooms may appear small, as compared with the 11,000 rooms in the Bahamas, but on an island which is only 20 miles long and 14 miles at its widest the tourist business is highly visible. Add to this the fact that almost all of the hotels are low rise and occupy relatively large land spaces and it can be seen that most of the island's 33 beaches have hotels nearby.

Beaches of Exceptional Beauty

The island contains some of the most beautiful beaches in the world; the west coast, facing on the Caribbean, is placid, the east coast has the rolling surf of the Atlantic. The beaches of Sandy Lane and Discovery Bay rank in beauty with those on Maui and the Virgin Islands.

Predictable tropical climate, constantly cooled by the trade winds, is an added attraction, especially during the winter season. Generally, the country is outside the Caribbean hurricane belt, although disastrous hurricanes hit the island in 1780 and 1831.

Though most Barbadian resorts are lackluster in design, a few are strikingly beautiful. Sandy Lane, operated by Trust Houses Forte of England, is one of the fine tropical resorts of the world. The Barbados Hilton, government-owned, is imaginatively designed around an inner court filled with tropical plants. Some of the buildings have been built to appear as if they are part of an old fort. The convention business is limited because of the absence of large hotels or a convention hall.

Several of the smaller hotels were originally plantation houses, heavy-walled of coral stone. A restaurant, The Bagatelle, is one of the original plantation homes, built in 1636. The Sugar Cane Club, a small resort and restaurant is a work of art, sitting on a land platform looking over sugar cane fields and, in the distance, the sea.

A major asset for tourism in Barbados is the people—friendly, literate, healthy and ambitious. Unlike many other Caribbean islanders, the "Bajans," despite their poverty, seem eager to work and optimistic about the future. Politeness to strangers is a part of the island's tradition. Even so, since independence in 1964, thievery has increased. Cars are stripped if left unattended. Windows and doors are barred for protection against would-be robbers.

The question of whether or not to have tourists in Barbados is academic. Throughout the foreseeable future, sugar will be an important crop but not to the extent it has been since the island was settled over 300 years ago. Much of the topography is hilly, making it impractical to mechanize all sugar cane production and so far only a little mechanization has taken place. This condition will have to change because the native Bajan is not willing to cut cane by hand.

In 1970, 600 natives of St. Vincent and St. Lucia had to be brought in as bonded workers to harvest the cane. The island is not well suited for large-scale production of other crops either, at least as far as is known.

Each Caribbean island is limited by topography, prevailing winds, soil conditions and rainfall to the production of only a few crops. Papayas grow readily in Barbados, and could be marketed in the United States. Limes do well. Vegetable crops are a possibility. Tourism, however, seems to hold the best possibility for economic development.

*Much of the material for this section was gathered by the author. Statistics came from the *Eleventh Annual Report-Barbados Tourist Board,* 1969, and from an interview with F. J. Odle, Manager of the Board.

The Latin-American Rim Countries

Of the nations that comprise the land boundaries of the Caribbean on the west and south, Mexico, Colombia and Venezuela seem to have the most promise for tourism growth. Tropical climate and white sand beaches backed with suitable infrastructure provide the essentials for turning winter into summer. The Latin cultures if presented as safe exotica, backed by good accommodations and courtesy, are appealing.

Another considerable advantage held by these Latin/Caribbean countries is price. Hotel rates and food are considerably less expensive there than on most of the islands. Group inclusive tours to Venezuela and Colombia have been travel bargains since about 1970. Fares to the Yucatan peninsula compete favorably with those to the Bahamas, Jamaica, Puerto Rico and the Virgin Islands.

The Mexican Caribbean

Technically, the Mexican Caribbean is limited to the southern part of the Yucatan peninsula which borders on the Caribbean. Most of the tourism there is centered on the island of Cozumel and the other offshore islands. The island of Cancun is being developed into a sizable resort destination.

Mexico has experienced one of the fastest growth rates in tourism in the world, increasing from 408,000 visitors in 1955 to more than 2 million in 1970 (excluding border crossings).

The growth rates in visitors and in tourist expenditures are seen in the table below:

TABLE XXIII—TOURISM TO THE INTERIOR OF MEXICO

	Number of Persons (Thousands)	Expenditure (U. S. Millions of Dollars)
1950	408	111
1960	761	155
1965	1350	275
1970	2250	562
Yearly Rate of Increase Percent		
1950-1960	6.4	3.4
1960-1970	11.5	13.7

Mexican Bureau of Statistics and Bank of Mexico.*

Though the growth rate is high, the question may be raised as to why it is not higher. Being contiguous to the Southwest U. S., it might be expected that Mexico would attract as many or more U. S. tourists than Canada.

Mexico offers a range of climate and scenery. Prices for visitors are relatively inexpensive. There are beach resorts like Acapulco, Puerto Vallarte and Cozumel; museum cities like Taxco and San Miguel Allerde; antiquities as found in Yucatan; sports fishing as found in Baja, Calif., and the metropolitan life of Mexico City.

In 1970, there were 4765 lodging establishments in the country with 132,701 rentable units. Direct income from tourists in 1967 totaled almost $1 billion and constituted the second most important source of income in Mexico's balance of payment. About half of the travelers to Mexico fly; the other half come by auto.[1]

The economic recession of 1970-1971 in the United States left its impact on tourism in Mexico. Room occupancies fell from 80 percent in 1970 to 63 percent in 1971, and the average room rate dropped 15 percent, to $18.44.

Retarding tourist growth are some obvious factors: a low level of food sanitation prevails. Montezuma's Revenge and The Aztec Two Step are black humour labels given attacks of food poisoning often experienced and unappreciated by travelers in the country. Reports of unreasonable treatment by police and courts do not encourage tourism. Tourists involved in an accident have been known to suffer unusually severe financial costs and sometimes unnecessary imprisonment.

The Mexican Government would do well to emphasize food sanitation standards in all public eating places but especially in those catering to tourists. Public health courses for food handling personnel, food sanitation inspections and publicly dis-

*Antonio Enriquez Savignac, "The Computer Planning and Coordination of Cancun Island, Mexico: A New Resort Complex," *Third Annual Conference Proceedings,* The Travel Research Assn., Salt Lake City, 1973.
[1]Diez Anos de Turismo Receptivo en Cifras, 1959-1969 (Mexico City: Instituto Mexicana de Investigaciones Turisticas, 1970).

played sanitation ratings would probably do more for tourism in Mexico than hundreds of thousands of dollars spent in advertising and promotion. The Government might also offer all-inclusive auto insurance policies which would eliminate ambulance-chasing attorneys and fear of imprisonment and severe financial loss through auto accidents.

Mexico's market is clearly defined at the moment, more than 87 percent of the visitors to the country are from the U. S., and of these almost one-half come from Texas and California. The table[1] below shows the origin of tourists to Mexico in 1970:

Source	Number of Tourists	Percentages
Canada	63,299	3.19%
Central America	54,568	2.75
Cuba and Antilles	3,373	.17
U. S. A.	1,730,900	87.23
Europe	77,983	3.93
South America	40,479	2.04
Others	13,694	.69
	1,984,296	100.00%

Foreign travelers to Mexico go in the greatest numbers to Mexico City. The Northern states of Nuevo Leon and Sonora, which border the U. S., also attract large numbers of visitors. In 1971, Cozumel and Isla Mujeres were visited by about 55,000 foreign tourists—but the number is expected to increase rapidly in the next several years. In 1969, the Mexican government established as part of the National Bank of Mexico a trust fund organization, INFRATOR, responsible for developing tourism.

The growth of tourist facilities in Mexico has been retarded by legal ambiguities concerning ownership of land by foreigners. The Mexican Constitution prohibits ownership by foreign nationals of land located within 30 miles of the coast. This did not preclude foreign participation in one form or another and, in 1971, the government authorized the purchase of coastal lands by banking institutions which, in turn, can lease them to foreigners for 30 years. The financial institution owns the land, the lessee receives a non-ownership real estate certificate limited to 30 years. At the end of the period, the trust is dissolved and the owning institution may sell the land to qualifying persons.[2]

Continued tourist growth can be expected, especially as the Mexican government and foreign investors continue to build first class facilities. Proximity to markets is a favorable factor. The Yucatan peninsula, for example, is only about two hours jet time from Miami or Dallas; three hours from New York or Chicago.

Large developments are planned on the island of Cancun, off Yucatan. The Interamerican Development Bank has provided a loan of $21.5 million for basic infrastructure (international airport, drinking water supply, sewage, electric power, insect control, housing for hotel employees, telephone service, two golf courses, etc.). Mexican government and private investment bring the total investment to $67 million planned for 1972-1974.[3]

The Venezuelan Caribbean

Tourism in Venezuela is a relatively new phenomenon; one which has much potential for growth. Rapid growth has taken place since 1967. Venezuela has some 1750 miles of land edging the Caribbean, the largest beach area of any Caribbean country. Much of it, however, is not suitable for resort development. In the early 1950's, there was but one first-class hotel in Caracas. The Hotel Tamanaco, now owned by Inter-Continental Hotels Corporation, set the pace for hotel building and the government in the 1950's built ten first class hotels now operated by the Government Tourist Corporation under the acronym Conahotu. Growth of visitors to the country more than tripled in the period 1965 to 1972, increasing from 54,175 to 171,000.[4] The single factor most responsible for the growth of tourism after 1967 was the group inclusive tours (GIT's) promoted by Viasa, the national airline; Conahotu, the Government

[1]"The Tourist Industry in Mexico," *The Lodging Industry, 1972 edition,* LKH&H, Philadelphia, 1972.
[2]William E. Gilbert, *Investor's Guide to the Coming Land Boom in the Caribbean-Latin American Waters,* (New York: Frederick Fell, 1973).
[3]Antonio Enriquez Savignac, "The Computer Planning and Coordination of Cancun Island, Mexico: A New Resort Complex," *Third Annual Conference Proceedings,* The Travel Research Assn., Salt Lake City, 1973.
[4]*Venezuela Plan Nacionale de Turismo,* Corporacion Nacionale de Turismo Caracas, (undated) and Venezuela, Venice With Mountains," *Travel Trade, Section Z,* April 2, 1973.

tourist bureau, and by Pan American World Airlines.

Comparatively low rates are in part responsible for the rapid growth in visitors, rates as low as $5.00 and package plan prices, which include plane fare, hotel rooms and meals, that are relatively inexpensive for the Caribbean.

Two hotels in Venezuela—the Humbolt and the Macuto Sheraton—have the distinction of having been the most costly to construct anywhere in the world. The Humbolt hotel, located on top of a mountain which is part of the rim of mountains surrounding Caracas, was built at a cost exceeding $100,000 a room. It has never been remotely profitable. The Macuto Sheraton, located on the ocean front near the Caracas airport, was originally built as an officers' club with marble imported from 22 different places, huge public spaces, 500 rooms. The price tag of $60 million places the cost per room at $120,000, hard to believe. A 1967 earthquake brought a tidal wave which wrecked the breakwater protecting the hotel's beach and much of the building. The building was closed for two years. The top floor, originally given over to restaurants, was made into guest rooms. The hotel has a 650-seat theatre equipped for Cinerama which is open to the general public as well as to hotel guests. Since the entire cost of the building was written off, the place now makes money. Sheraton has a management contract which gives the company a percentage of the gross sales.

The Venezuelan Government is into tourism in a big way. It owns and operates most of the first-class hotels in the nation. Two of the largest, The Macuto Sheraton and the Caracas Hilton are under management contract, owned by the Government. The Spanish hotel and apartment chain, Melia, is building a 1000-room property in Caracas, a 600-room hotel at Macuto and a 600-room resort at Puerto La Cruz.

The islands of Margarita (two islands joined by one isthmus) have considerable appeal for the North American because of climate, beaches and relatively low prices. A World Bank loan will finance additional hotels on the mainland. The promotion of package tours by the government and Viasa

(the national airline) can ensure visitors.

Venezuela, with the rest of the Caribbean, shares a forecast made by the World Bank for a doubling of tourism and of visitors in the 1970-1980 decade.[1]

Colombian Tourism

Like Venezuela, Colombia faces on the Caribbean and has sections of the coast which are highly desirable. In 1970, Colombia received 143,000 foreign visitors, up 180 percent over 1965. Like Venezuela, the factor most responsible for the growth has been the group inclusive tours which in Colombia are packaged by Avianca, a privately owned airline but, in effect, the national airline of the country. Tourism is centered in the capital, Bogota, and on the coast at Cartagena, Barranquilla and Santa Marta. Colombia also has the Caribbean island of San Andres, off Nicaragua, largely patronized by Colombians because of its beautiful beaches and the fact that the government has declared it a free port.

Since 62 percent of Colombia's exports are coffee, the country is overly dependent upon the price of coffee. To overcome this, the government is making efforts to encourage industry and tourism. The National Tourist Corporation, founded in 1968, oversees development as well as promotes tourism. The Government offers tax exemptions, improves sites which are potentially attractive to tourists and provides advisory services for the study of plans for projects.

The rim countries of the Caribbean, especially Venezuela, Colombia and Mexico, are not burdened by the Black/White tensions faced on many of the Caribbean islands. Some of the problems centering around tourism as expressed in Puerto Rico, however, will probably eventually appear in the Latin rim countries as well.

Some Observations

While the Caribbean is likely to be viewed as a totality which reflects to a large extent the climate and a stereotyped view of the Caribbean, the area is more accurately pictured as a collage of cultures broadly divided into Hispanic/Black, British/Black,

---

[1] *Tourism, Sector Working Paper,* World Bank, Washington, D. C., 1972.

French/Black, and Dutch/Black. While some of the larger islands such as Cuba, Dominican Republic, Puerto Rico and the rim countries have, or can expect, a balanced economy, many of the rest of the islands will be dependent upon tourism and/or subsidies from other governments for at least the next decade or so.

Some of the island people are wholeheartedly in favor of tourism; others oppose it; still others have mixed feelings about it.

The shift of political power from colonial dependency status to independent or relatively independent status has brought expected social dislocation and concern about identity. Tourism as a major economic force brings together people of markedly different economic and psychological states; this has created tensions. These can be accommodated provided leadership is committed to and has the ability to achieve such accommodation.

More Dominant Role for Government

It seems probable that on some of the islands and elsewhere the governments will have to play a much more dominant role in planning and developing tourism if it is to be of economic benefit to the people as a whole and if desirable ecological equilibrium is to be maintained. Strong personal leadership will need to be exerted to polarize feelings in favor of tourism.

Tourist markets for the Caribbean have changed to include the mass markets made up of middle income groups, groups served by group inclusive tours as well as independent travelers. Present hotels, however, are largely of the type serving the luxury market.

Accommodation pricing is probably in line with costs but is too high to compete with European hotel and food prices. Moderately priced hotels and cottages should be developed to satisfy the new markets and to compete with European facilities.

Camping is a neglected opportunity. Camping is presently encouraged only in a small area, Cinnamon Bay on St. John, and at one location in Jamaica. Venezuela also permits, but does little to encourage, camping. On some islands and in littoral countries provision for campers would be a means of developing tourism and would benefit the countries concerned if appropriate taxes were levied on transport, food and facilities.

Governments will have to prevent rampant land speculation by controlling land prices. This can be accomplished by government ownership and leasing or selling land desirable for tourism development at controlled prices. Governments may wish to sponsor sizable tourist developments or they may wish to go into partnership with corporations or consortiums for the same purpose. Governments should insist on fair wages for employees connected with tourist development and should also see to it, by means of taxes (income, excise and other taxes) that the government and the people as a whole benefit from tourism.

Once government has provided or participated in overall planning and if needed, financing, it is probably wiser to contract the operation of the facilities to private enterprise. Government operation of anything is likely to be colored by politics. What is a good political decision may be a poor business one. Bureaucracy flourishes in government enterprise even more than in private business. Sick leaves, bonuses, pensions, holidays, leave to attend funerals, automatic pay increases reduce incentive to produce, increase the incentive to extract the maximum from the bureaucratic system.

The Caribe-Hilton in San Juan, Puerto Rico, is an example of a government-sponsored tourist facility, operated by private enterprise, which has paid off handsomely for Puerto Rico and for Hilton International, the operating company.

It may be desirable, at least in beginning phases, to build tourist facilities as enclaves, well separated from the rest of the community. (The Clubs Mediterranee in Guadeloupe, Martinique and Mexico are examples.) The problem arises if the enclaves are seen as depriving the residents of beach. Governments can set aside blocks of land not now used for such purposes and by means of taxes and controls insure that benefits from tourism accrue to the economy as a whole. With the exception of Puerto Rico, there has been minimal government planning or participation in planned tourism development in the Caribbean.

TRAVEL CHARACTERISTICS OF PSYCHOGRAPHIC TYPES

PSYCHOCENTRICS

Prefer the familiar in travel destinations.

Like commonplace activities at travel destinations.

Prefer sun 'n' fun spots, including considerable relaxation.

Low activity level.

Prefer destinations they can drive to.

Prefer heavy tourist accommodations, as heavy hotel development, family type restaurants, and tourist shops.

Prefer familiar atmosphere (hamburger stands), familiar type entertainment, absence of foreign atmosphere.

Complete tour packaging appropriate, with heavy scheduling of activities.

ALLOCENTRICS

Prefer non-touristy areas.

Enjoy sense of discovery and delight in new experiences, before others have visited the area.

Prefer novel and different destinations.

High activity level.

Prefer flying to destinations.

Tour accommodations should include adequate to good hotels and food, not necessarily modern or chain type hotels, and few "tourist" type attractions.

Enjoy meeting and dealing with people from a strange or foreign culture.

Tour arrangements should include basics (transportation and hotels) and allow considerable freedom and flexibility.

Which North Americans Constitute the Caribbean Market?

As previously stated the big market for the Caribbean is the U. S. and Canada, particularly the Eastern Seaboard of the U. S. Various studies have been made of the market emphasizing the demographics—age, occupation, income level, place of residence. For example, the Ministry of Tourism of the Bahamas has conducted several analyses of its visitors and found that about 43 percent of the visitors are engaged in business or industry, 9 percent are professionals, about 5 percent are retired. Only about 2 percent are in government, 4 percent in the academic world; 10 percent are students. It may be more important to identify the markets by personality types.

The so-called behavioral studies have looked into life styles of travelers as compared with non-travelers and found that indeed there are personality differences. The Behavior Science Corporation has done several psychographic studies and found that people arrange themselves on a normal curve

from "psychocentric" to "allocentric." The psychocentrics are concerned with little problems, with themselves, are generally anxious and non-adventuresome. At the other end of the continuum, the allocentrics are characterized by a considerable degree of adventurousness, self-confidence and curiosity. They are eager to reach out and experiment with life. Travel is one way of doing this.[1]

According to Stanley C. Plog, President of Behavior Science Corporation who did the research, the table above distinguishes between psychocentrics and allocentrics as regards travel characteristics.

As a destination becomes more commercialized, it loses its authentic qualities and those qualities which attracted the allocentrics. It moves down the scale and becomes more mundane, appealing to the less adventuresome. Because of the distances involved and the differences in culture pre-

[1]Stanley C. Plog, "Why Destination Areas Rise and Fall in Popularity," paper presented to Southern California Chapter of the Travel Research Assn., Oct. 10, 1972.

sented between the Caribbean and North America, it would seem that the Caribbean has a long time to go before it approaches the status of a Miami Beach. Parts of Puerto Rico, however, are probably already "old hat" to the much-traveled, sophisticated New Yorker. As travel becomes easier and relatively less expensive, the Caribbean may not appeal to the allocentric but will have added appeal for the great mass of travelers classified in the mid-centric group.

The notion of psychographics, arranging people from psychocentric to allocentric and predicting their travel behavior, is an interesting one for the Caribbean. Certainly, as new destination areas open up, they will appeal primarily to the adventuresome, the curious, the energetic and the outgoing. Most of the Caribbean is in a developmental stage; many new destination areas will be developed in the next few years. Such destinations will appeal to the allocentric. As they mature, add attractions and facilities, their appeal will shift to the great mass-travel market.

It is worth noting that, as the market shifts to the mid-centric, that market will be more sensitive to rumors, true or not, of

rudeness and violence. The Caribbean can be effectively cut off from the mass market if the tourist is made to feel unwelcome or apprehensive in any way.

According to Plog, the Caribbean is now attracting people classified as "mid-centric," people who are in between the extremes, neither really adventuresome nor fearful of travel, the kind of person who constitutes the bulk of the population. The allocentrics are seeking out the exotic, places like the South Pacific, Africa and the Orient. The home-bodies go to Coney Island and those who are "near-psychocentric" to Miami Beach or stay in the U. S. for their travel. If they become more adventuresome, they may go to Honolulu, the Caribbean, Europe, Mexico and Southern Europe. The chart below shows the distribution of the various types.

The Future?

The Caribbean holds tremendous promise as a tourism destination, especially during the winter months. As in Florida, summer tourism in the Caribbean can also be of considerable importance in catering to a less-moneyed market. The promise of tour-

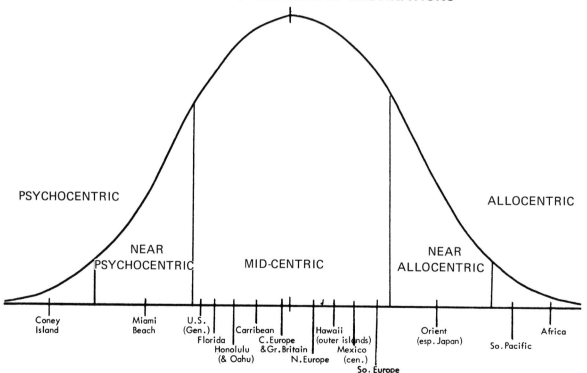
PSYCHOGRAPHIC POSITIONS OF DESTINATIONS

ism was greatest during the period 1950-1969 when dozens of first class hotels were constructed and in many of the islands rapid development of supporting infrastructure was accomplished. Tourism, indeed, seemed to be the Golden Goose. Occupancies and rates were high, especially in the Bahamas, the Virgin Islands and Puerto Rico—but storm clouds were gathering. Hotel rates, in many cases, only reflected high land costs, high construction costs and high operating costs.

In the late sixties the tide turned. Residents of many of the islands—Jamaica, Puerto Rico, the U.S. Virgins, the Bahamas, Trinidad/Tobago, Antigua—felt put upon by tourists and tourism. Many potential visitors were turned off by the threat of danger, real or imagined. Black/White tensions served to exacerbate relations between many natives and tourists. Rudeness and indifference, sometimes hostility, appeared endemic to particular islands. In Puerto Rico, politics (Independencias vs. Conservatives) got injected into the tourism picture and at least two hotels were bombed. The unfavorable image created by such acts unfortunately spilled over to color tourism on other islands where visitors are welcomed.

In the Caribbean, psycho/sociological currents seem to mix more turbulently with economics and politics than elsewhere. Historical influences surface to disrupt tourism. On many of the Caribbean Islands the whole society will necessarily be involved in changes which will have to be made if tourism is to flourish. The Caribbean rim countries—especially Venezuela, Colombia and Mexico—have the opportunity of planning tourism development so that it brings benefits to the community as a whole.

The fact that the World Bank is lending many millions of dollars to Venezuela, Mexico and the Dominican Republic to develop tourism supports the bank administrator's belief that tourism will grow in these areas. The World Bank projects an additional three to four million tourists, or almost a doubling of the number to the Caribbean Basin in the next decade.[1] That development, a bank report points out, should be done in large pieces, to serve relatively large concentrations of visitors. Such concentrations reduce the per unit cost of constructing the infrastructure and provide areas with a diversity of services, entertainment and activity.

Should the image of much of the Caribbean remain negative, those islands and rim countries that project a warm welcome for visitors will benefit. North Americans will continue to travel to the sun and sand, selecting those destinations which are safe, relatively convenient and inexpensive.

---

[1] *Tourism, Sector Working Paper,* World Bank, Washington, D. C., 1972, p. 6.

An aerial view of Waikiki, Honolulu, looking toward the famous Diamond Head. The aerial photograph taken about 1949 by William B. *Tabler indicates that hotels and other tourism facilities were almost nonexistent in Hawaii at that time.*

The same view of Waikiki, Honolulu taken in 1972, also by William B. Tabler, and used by permission. These "before and after" shots offer dramatic evidence of the spectacular growth of tourism in the Waikiki area of Hawaii.

TRAVEL RESEARCH AND MARKETING

Who is the tourist? Why does he travel? Which destination does he select and for what reasons? Answers to these questions are constantly being sought by governments, land developers, public carriers and resort owners. Some of the answers are available; others must be secured through research. Armed with such information, people who sell travel and tourism then set about trying to communicate with their "market" by advertising, promotion and other means. With "markets" identified, investors can make a decision whether to buy or build tourist-related businesses.

Marketing is the broad effort or social process of determining what products and services are needed, then taking the necessary steps to provide and sell these products and services to particular groups of people. Marketing includes the determination of what people want, the planning and production of products and services to meet those wants. Marketing goes hand in hand with research. It also includes promoting these products and services in the broad sense. Part of the function of promotion is to select the most effective ways of communicating with potential buyers.

Marketing also includes pricing products and services so that they are competitive and yet produce a profit for the entrepreneur. As related to travel, marketing includes research as to why and where people are now traveling, ways of inducing persons, first, to travel and then to travel to a particular destination or resort.

Who Will Come to the Area?

In marketing a destination area, a government or firm collects information as to what persons and how many are likely to come to the area or can be induced to come there. Nearly every national government is interested in marketing its country or parts of it. Smaller governmental units—states and smaller areas—are similarly engaged in determining their "market" and "promoting" travel to those areas. Corporations and individuals who own hotels, restaurants, tour companies, airlines and other travel-related businesses are also interested in increasing the use of their products and services. Marketing relies on research, judgment, intuition and effort to achieve the goals of greater use of products and services and increasing profits.

A first step in planning any tourist facility attraction or service is to determine if the product is really needed and can be sold. Market research is conducted to identify the people who will use the product or service or to find out if certain groups can be influenced to use a product or service. Too many hotels and other tourist facilities have been built on optimism or blind faith that a market exists for them. Many an entrepreneur has built a facility in an active destination area believing that his facility will attract a new market or that he will get a "share" of the existing market.

The basic figure in any tourist market research and feasibility study is the number of people that can be expected to use the facility at a certain price. If this forecast is wrong, the rest of the study may be of little value. Market research is seen to be a broad term designed to determine markets (potential buyers of the product or service) and factors which influence the use of a product or service.

Tourism research may require highly sophisticated concepts and techniques. An example is the Market Potential Index being developed by the United States Travel Service.[1] The Index will rank countries in terms of their potential for providing travelers to the U. S. Knowing this information, money for promoting travel to this country can be directed to reaching the best candi-

[1]William Dircks, *Types of Statistics Needed Most from Tourism Research,* U. S. Travel Service, Washington, D. C., 1971.

dates for travel and influencing them to visit the U. S.

The pilot study for the Market Potential Index centered on the Mexican market. Information was obtained through a probability sample of 4000 adults residing in Mexican cities of 10,000 or more population. From the study, it was learned which segments of the population travel here and which do not. Income and place of residence were found to be the important variables in the Mexican market for travel to the U. S.

The Market Potential Index is thought of as a model which can digest information from eleven variables and produce suggestions as to where promotional dollars can best be spent.

What Are the Variables?

Variables which affect travel to the U. S. were found to include:

1. The financial ability of individuals in a country to travel.

2. The authority of individuals to choose to travel to the U. S.

3. The political and economic relationships between the U. S. and a country.

4. The cost and ease of travel between a country and the U. S.

5. The social/cultural relationships existing between a country and the U. S.

Work with the Market Potential Index has shown that there is no simple one-to-one relationship between advertising and promotional expenditures and the number of visitors and their expenditures at a destination. Observers of tourism marketing have long known this but there has been a tendency for some agencies that promote travel to imply that for each dollar of advertising spent on tourism so many dollars of visitor expenditure will result. As pointed out by William Dircks, Director of Research and Analysis for the U.S.T.S., numerous factors, in addition to the effect of advertising and promotion, affect tourist expenditures. The travel promoter needs to view the entire travel environment of the prospective traveler in terms of his alternatives in choosing a travel destination. Why does he select a given destination over other choices?

Undoubtedly, for many markets, advertising done by competitive destination areas constitutes an intercorrelation with advertising expenditure and travel to another area. The availability of cheap charter flights may be an important variable in the equation and in many markets charter flights are growing in importance. Economic recession or expansion in a tourist-generating country may be highly important for a particular destination area, a factor which must be intercorrelated with the effect produced by advertising.

Travel statistics must be carefully interpreted to have meaning for decision makers. For example, the statistic that the Bahamas ranks fourth as a tourist generating country to the United States may mean nothing more than the fact that a relatively few Bahamians take a number of shopping trips to Miami. The fact that numerous people cross the Canadian or other borders for one-day visits or for shopping purposes also inflates the travel statistics.

Broadly speaking, travel market research can be divided between the demographic and the behavioristic. Demographic research is counting and classifying; the behavioristic approach tries to get at the motivation and values of the individual. Most research done by governments emphasizes demographics, counting visitors and classifying them in various ways. The behavioristic approach emphasizes finding out why people travel or what can be done to induce them to travel to a particular place.

With the demographic approach, there is usually concern with selecting a representative sample from a universe of people, counting and analyzing the example. If the sample is indeed representative, the larger universe is also delineated. For example, the question may be asked, how many people go to Cape Cod during a summer season? It is not practical to count each and every visitor to Cape Cod because of the cost and time that would be required. However, it may be practicable to collect data on every tenth person on a given day. If every tenth person is representative of the other nine, for example, we have a good sample. Describing the sample also describes the universe.

For some destinations, it is possible to count and describe every visitor because every visitor is required to complete a questionnaire before entering. The Bahamas is an example. Hawaii accomplishes almost the same result by asking visitors to complete a questionnaire while enroute in a plane.

One way of collecting data on visitors traveling by automobile to a state is to photograph license plates of the automobiles as they pass under an automatically operated camera. Another way is to invite visitors to stop at a welcome station to get a glass of free orange juice. Vermont provides information centers; those who stop are requested to complete a questionnaire.

Getting Answers by Mail

Probably the most common method of conducting demographic research is to send questionnaires by mail to selected persons. The sample selected, however, is likely to be biased. Ordinarily, perhaps less than 10 percent of those who receive the questionnaire respond. To overcome this defect, some research firms enclose a quarter, fifty-cent piece, or dollar bill, asking the recipient to "sell a small bit of his time." In this way, more people respond, the "sample" is broadened and made more representative of the universe being studied.

"Origin and destination studies" are often conducted by state governments at entry points into a state. With the help of a road block set up by the state police, a sample of visitors is asked to complete a questionnaire. As implied by the term, origin and destination studies are for the purpose of determining the place where the visitor started his trip (usually his home town) and his destination (where he is going). Such studies often record an estimate of what the traveler thinks he will spend, or has spent, each day and how he will spend it. The studies may include reactions of the visitor to a particular place, what he liked or disliked, how he spent his time, etc.

Hundreds of surveys have been made of travelers; many of these classify travelers by income group, educational level, number of persons traveling in the party, purposes of trip, etc. As previously stated in this book, it has been found that travel is highly correlated with income and educational level. It is also correlated with where a person lives. Urbanites are more likely to travel than rural dwellers. Persons from some states travel more than people from others.

Every marketing man is well aware that international travel is highly correlated with income. Income, of course, reflects many other factors—education, energy level, confidence, social position, readiness for change, etc. Pan American has produced some rather startling statistics relating income to foreign travel:

Income	Transatlantic Trips Per Thousand Families
Under $5000	4
$5000 to $10,000	9
$10,000 to $15,000	20
$15,000 to $20,000	47
$20,000 to $25,000	108
$25,000 to $50,000	253
Over $50,000	753

The chart presents what everyone can guess, the poor don't travel abroad; the rich do. The very rich do, and go not once but many times.

Travel-related business firms are constantly sampling travel markets and attempting to project changes in their market. Some magazine publishers want to know how many of their readers want to read travel-related articles. State governments need to know the extent and value of tourism within their states.

The airlines and the airplane manufacturers have a large stake in travel research and several of them actively engage in it. Quite naturally, they are interested in projecting the growth of air travel and estimating the number of travelers to particular destination areas. Some of the studies are done "in house" by state or company employees; others are done by consulting firms.

Demographic researchers are constantly looking for methods of improving their samples while avoiding the expense of surveying an entire universe of people.

An example of the results of such market research is a breakdown of visitors to Hawaii into 36 groups or "cells." The research was done by a consulting firm, Mathematica of Princeton, New Jersey. Using survey data collected from visitors who arrived by plane, as well as available data, the researchers classified the visitors into 36 groups. Within each group the visitors were further classified by age, income, length of stay and size of party. The amount each class of visitors spent each day and per visit was calculated. The percentage of the total number of visitors to Hawaii represented by each group was also computed.[1]

The tables on pages 264 and 265 display this information. From the tables, it is seen that certain groups tend to stay considerably longer in Hawaii than others. Group number 15, those from the North Central area in the age group 31-49 having incomes of over $15,000, stayed an average of 18.8 days. At the other extreme, are low income visitors from the South who spend less than 9 days in Hawaii.

What may be most important to the tourist operator is the amount of money spent per day by various tourist groups, presumably the high spenders represent the more desirable market. In column 7 of the table, it is seen that expenditures varied widely between groups, starting with a low of $27.80, spent by those persons with incomes of $7500 and less coming from North Central United States. This group also remained a relatively long period of time, 18.8 days on the average.

At the other extreme is the group in the age bracket 31-49, from the Northeast, who have incomes of over $15,000. They spent almost $82 a day. In other words, some tourists, while in Hawaii, spent almost three times as much per day as others.

If one were interested in attracting the quality market to Hawaii, he would be going after tourists from the West, with $15,000 incomes, who are 50 years and older. Each party spent well over $1000 per visit. At the other extreme were the fast-trippers, coming in small parties, under the age of 30, whose incomes are less than $7500. These parties spent about $293 per visit. The tables tell us that California offers an excellent market for Hawaii but the market mix is considerable. A number of other observations could be made, basing interpretation upon information in the tables.

In the late 60's Japan became a major source of tourists to Hawaii. By 1972 about one quarter million Japanese tourists came to Hawaii, usually in groups. Japanese investors began buying and building hotels and restaurants and condominiums.[2]

The Canadian Government Travel Bureau is another example of a government agency which sponsors or conducts regular research with a view to identifying markets from which tourists come to visit Canada. Quite naturally, the U. S. is the major source of travelers to Canada; more U. S. residents travel "abroad" to Canada than to any other country. Some 26 percent of U. S. expenditures on travel outside the U. S. goes to Canada. Who goes and how much do they spend?

The answers provide information as to where Canadian travel advertising should be concentrated. The map (facing page) shows percentages of visitors to Canada from various census regions of the U. S. It also shows the amount of money spent by each visitor from a region. From the map we see that those people who travel longer distances to visit Canada spend more money when they arrive. The Great Lakes states and the Northeast provide 81 percent of the U. S. visitors to Canada; combined, they are Canada's greatest "travel market." The South represents a very poor "market," less than 5 percent of the total.

Behavioristic Approach to Travel Research

Research concerning tourists' likes and dislikes has been done on a surface level, with little attempt being made to reach into the more subtle feelings, or the reason for them, which the tourist has about a particular area. An example of the kind of research which can be done is that conducted by John E. Barclay and Professor Herbert B. Weaver of the University of Hawaii.[3] Their study compared two methods of developing questionnaires which can be used to probe tourist attitudes. Here is one of the scales for measuring tourist attitudes as developed by them:

---

[1]*The Visitor Industry and Hawaii's Economy: a Cost-Benefit Analysis,* Mathematica, Princeton, 1970, pp. 94-95.
[2]*Travel News,* Dec. 11, 1972.
[3]"Comparative Reliabilities and Ease of Construction of Thurstone and Likert Attitude Scales," *The Journal of Social Psychology,* 1962, pp. 58, 109-120.

CHARACTERISTICS OF HAWAII VISITORS, 1968[1]

(1) Cell Number	(2) Region	(3) Age	(4) Income
1	West	30	7500
2	West	30	7501-14999
3	West	30	15000
4	West	31-49	7500
5	West	31-49	7501-14999
6	West	31-49	15000
7	West	50	7500
8	West	50	7501-14999
9	West	50	15000
10	North Central	30	7500
11	North Central	30	7501-14999
12	North Central	30	15000
13	North Central	31-49	7500
14	North Central	31-49	7501-14999
15	North Central	31-49	15000
16	North Central	50	7500
17	North Central	50	7501-14999
18	North Central	50	15000
19	North East	30	7500
20	North East	30	7501-14999
21	North East	30	15000
22	North East	31-49	7500
23	North East	31-49	7501-14999
24	North East	31-49	15000
25	North East	50	7500
26	North East	50	7501-14999
27	North East	50	15000
28	South	30	7500
29	South	30	7501-14999
30	South	30	15000
31	South	31-49	7500
32	South	31-49	7501-14999
33	South	31-49	15000
34	South	50	7500
35	South	50	7501-14999
36	South	50	15000

---

[1]*The Visitor Industry and Hawaii's Economy: a Cost-Benefit Analysys,* Mathematica, Princeton, New Jersey, 1970.

(5) Length of Stay	(6) Size of Party	(7) Daily Expenditures Per Party	(8) Total Expenditures Per Visit	(9) Visitor Mix (%)
10.4	1.2	28.19	293.18	7.3
10.7	1.3	40.40	432.30	5.4
13.4	1.3	39.32	526.92	2.2
9.9	1.3	34.45	341.03	1.8
11.2	1.7	49.95	553.84	6.4
11.6	2.2	66.34	769.49	6.3
13.2	1.4	31.42	414.80	2.9
13.7	1.8	51.61	707.00	3.7
14.8	2.0	75.10	1111.48	3.7
10.3	1.1	34.20	352.70	6.1
9.7	1.3	46.38	449.90	3.3
12.6	1.5	54.53	687.02	1.1
11.1	1.4	35.14	390.04	1.1
11.3	1.7	53.93	609.39	2.3
12.5	1.9	78.55	981.83	3.3
18.8	1.6	27.80	522.64	2.0
13.2	1.7	47.67	629.26	2.4
14.5	2.0	65.39	948.11	3.1
10.0	1.1	35.96	359.57	4.5
10.2	1.3	45.82	467.34	2.4
11.8	1.4	59.09	697.24	0.7
10.7	1.5	38.42	411.09	1.0
11.5	1.6	50.61	581.99	1.6
10.2	1.8	81.99	836.34	1.3
12.2	1.5	34.31	418.55	1.6
12.1	1.6	44.41	537.41	1.6
14.3	2.0	66.92	956.96	2.2
8.9	1.1	45.54	405.28	5.8
8.9	1.1	51.76	460.64	4.5
9.8	1.3	47.68	467.22	0.6
9.1	1.2	55.16	502.00	0.6
9.0	1.3	56.15	505.37	2.6
10.8	1.6	73.55	794.33	1.5
11.6	1.6	43.60	505.74	0.9
12.3	1.7	47.19	580.38	0.9
12.8	1.9	72.20	924.12	1.5
				————
				100.0

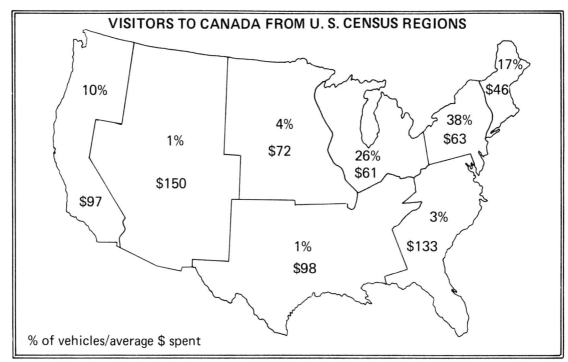

VISITORS TO CANADA FROM U. S. CENSUS REGIONS

10%

17%
$46

1%
$150

4%
$72

38%
$63

$97

26%
$61

3%
$133

1%
$98

% of vehicles/average $ spent

Source: *The Changing World of Travel Marketing,* Canadian Government Travel Bureau, 1971.

"This is a study of attitudes of tourists toward their vacation in Hawaii. Below you will find twenty-one statements expressing different attitudes toward vacationing in Hawaii. Please circle the response which most closely represents your attitude toward each statement.

SA   Strongly agree
A   Agree
U   Undecided
D   Disagree
SD   Strongly disagree

SA A U D SD   I must return to Hawaii soon.

SA A U D SD   No other place but Hawaii has such a friendly spirit.

SA A U D SD   I guess Hawaii is all right as a place to live, but there are many other places I would choose first.

SA A U D SD   The scenery alone in Hawaii is worth every penny I spent for this trip.

SA A U D SD   Vacationing in Hawaii is like being in Paradise.

SA A U D SD   This is the most wonderful vacation I have ever had.

SA A U D SD   Hawaii is a nice place, but no better than many other vacation spots.

SA A U D SD   I just can't praise Hawaii enough.

SA A U D SD   I'll tell everybody I meet that they should visit Hawaii.

SA A U D SD   I found Hawaii to be far more wonderful than I expected.

SA A U D SD   Hawaii is no Island Paradise to me.

SA A U D SD   I can get plenty of satisfaction out of life without ever visiting Hawaii again.

SA A U D SD   I never would believe that a vacation in Hawaii could be so wonderful.

SA A U D SD   Hawaii is over-rated as a vacation spot.

SA A U D SD   I'm quite convinced that Hawaii is the greatest vacation spot there is.

SA A U D SD   I'd like to visit Hawaii again soon.

SA A U D SD   I will not be sorry to leave Hawaii.

SA A U D SD   I think Hawaii is grand.

SA A U D SD   There's never a dull moment in Hawaii.

SA A U D SD   It must be nice to live in Hawaii.

SA A U D SD   I wish I could stay in Hawaii longer.

It can be seen that by including a number of items about attitudes toward a tourist destination, the researcher can arrive at a general feeling toward the area, in this case the amount of enthusiasm, small or large, that the visitor has for Hawaii

By inserting questions about special aspects of a destination, the researcher can learn how the tourist reacts to them. The information can be used to make necessary changes or to add attractions which are favored by the tourists.

People interested in the tourism of a particular destination may be misled by statistics concerning the number of tourists. It is quite possible that even though tourism may show a 5 percent, 10 percent or 15 percent growth each year over a period of years, the basic attitudes of the tourists toward the destination are such that they would not return. The area may be relying completely on one-time trippers, without knowing it. Perhaps the tourist operators don't care. At least, they should know the nature of their market. Most tourist areas that have a solid growth over a number of years build upon repeat visitors and favorable recommendations.

Analysis of the subjects who complete a questionnaire can also be enlightening. It tination area for one week to be highly enthusiastic about the area. If they remain for two or three weeks, the glamour begins to pale. Some resort operators do not want guests to stay more than a week or so; these operators realize that long-stay guests inevitably become bored and do not hesitate to denigrate the resort to their friends. Long term guests may also be a source of irritation to newly arrived guests. Visitors to the neighboring Islands of Hawaii often become bored after a two- or three-day stay and return to Honolulu.

By seriously probing tourist attitudes, the researcher can learn what really pleases and displeases the traveler. Too little of such research has been done. Too much reliance has been placed on hunches that come to advertising agencies responsible for selling an area.

An even more indirect method of reaching into the feelings of a visitor to discover his real likes and dislikes is the use of vari-

ous projective techniques. When such techniques are used, the potential, or the already-arrived, visitor is asked in such a way to react to various stimuli that usually he is not aware that in his answers he is actually displaying (projecting) his own attitudes.

Example of Projective Technique

In one example developed by Professor Weaver, of the University of Hawaii, of the use of such techniques, subjects were asked to describe or to react to various full color pictures or photographs. One, a photo, was of a man and wife in a living room of their home. The man asks the question, "Why do you want us to go to Hawaii for our vacation this year?" A balloon above the head of the wife gives the subject the opportunity of filling in a reply. The answer, of course, is intended to reflect the feelings of the subject.

Another photograph shows a man and a wife leaving a jet plane and being met by a group of hula dancers. The wife asks, "Now that we are finally here, what are you looking forward to most?"

The husband is supposed to reply.

Another photograph, obviously of Waikiki Beach, has the husband asking, "Why do you want to come back to Hawaii again next year?'

A number of photographs are presented and the subject is asked to tell what each one makes him think of and how it makes him feel. Photographs of a ship, the Royal Hawaiian Hotel, a beautiful mountain and beach scene and other similar photos follow.

Barclay and Weaver also presented pictures to subjects who were asked to make up a dramatic story to fit the picture. The stories were to include or lead up to the scene shown, then tell: what is happening at the moment, what the people are thinking and feeling and what will be the outcome of the story. The photographs included a beach scene in which a beachboy has speared a fish; a solitary man walking alongside a broad expanse of bay; a swimmer who has just speared a fish and is visibly pleased at displaying his capture to two attractive, young women in an outrigger canoe.

In each case, the visitor "projects" his

feelings about the subject while making up a story to fit the pictures. He is not necessarily aware that in constructing the story he is really displaying his own feelings toward the subject.

The question may be raised, "Why not ask the tourist directly what he likes and dislikes about Hawaii?" The answer is that many times people cannot or will not express their true feelings about places and things. They are too polite, are blocked or, perhaps, are not skilled in verbalizing their feelings.

If a person is asked outright, "Do you like Hawaii?" he may consider why the question is asked, who is going to use the answer and for what purpose? Most travelers to Hawaii are fairly sophisticated. Their answers may be framed in terms of a particular recent incident, pleasurable or unpleasant. Projective techniques are more impersonal and less threatening to the respondent. In a sense, they are also more devious, since the subject is not supposed to be aware that his own feelings are being measured.

Professor Weaver suggests being even more explicit in research as regards likes and dislikes of tourists as they experience a particular attraction. He suggests that still photographs of the facial expressions and postures of tourists be taken as they visit the Polynesian Village, a luau or other attractions. Motion pictures can also be used to ascertain, by analysis of gestures and other movements, the degree of tension and excitement and, perhaps, pleasure being experienced.

A camera is hardly needed to catch the picture of frustration apparent in the long waiting lines of tourists checking in or out of a tourist hotel. A sense of dismay might be recorded for posterity when the tourist is presented with a check from some of the fancier eating establishments. Or what about a picture of the tourist who after gambling for hours is down to his last $5?

Family Background as Travel Influence

Using depth interviewing, (open-ended, relatively unstructured interviews) and group sessions, some researchers start with the usual demographic and socio-economic information but also include parental background and childhood development history.[1] It was found that children of college-educated parents are likely to take more vacations than persons whose parents are not college trained. Having been a Boy or Girl Scout also was an indicator. As adults, the subjects travel a good deal and are more likely to take a chance on a resort where they have never been before.

The group of people who like to do-it-yourself are likely to spend less money on a vacation and to travel by auto rather than by plane. Persons who go to the movies, the theatre and to concerts travel greater distances than those who stay home most of the time. Being active in civic and fraternal organizations is associated with frequent travel.

Persons with greater expectations in the way of salary traveled more than those who expected less.

The researchers divided their subjects into "passives" and "creatives." Creatives tended to play golf while the passives tended to go hunting and fishing. Creatives flew to their vacation spot; passives tended to travel in their own car.

In traveling, the creatives were more likely to use a travel agent, stay at a city hotel, or a resort hotel. Once back from a vacation, creatives were likely to start planning their next one. The creatives were likely to own a sailboat, take sports instruction, and favor American, United or Pan-American as airlines.

Magazines that attract travel advertisers conduct a number of travel research studies. *Better Homes and Gardens* carries a travel section in each issue and has sponsored a number of research studies aimed at determination of the family travel market. Their studies indicate that parents are much concerned with tieing education and travel together. Perhaps this ia a rationalization in that the parents can justify a trip to Disney World or to the Statue of Liberty for the good of their children. The parents may enjoy the trip as much or more than the children. Motivation for travel is often the result of a matrix of motives.

[1]Emanuel N. Denley, "Travel's Not So Far Away," *Proceedings of 1969, 1970 Conference,* Eastern Council for Travel Research, 1971, pp. 46-54.

What triggers a travel experience may be just one of a number of factors which have gone into the motive mix. The figure below gives some idea of the importance of various motivators which play on the family travel decision [1]

Changing social values affect travel and are being studied by some researchers. Philip N. Robertson listed several social changes which he and his company have identified as being relevant to travel.[2] Some of the changing social values and their relation to travel behavior were as follows:

1. Personalization. A trend among young people to want a personalized vacation, to avoid the standard tour, to do the thing which fits their personality. This might include hitchhiking through Europe or spending a week on a chartered sailboat.

2. Return to nature. The desire for spiritual values and communing with nature. Hiking and camping would be preferred over stopping in hotels.

3. Greater sexual freedom and familism. Apparently, this would be reflected in travel as a family or in mixed sex groups.

4. Decreasing respect for authority. The regimented tour led by an authority would be avoided. It may also mean that there will be a great increase in the F.I.T.'s (Foreign Independent Travelers).

5. Greater tolerance for chaos and disorder. Apparently, younger people don't mind, perhaps even want, less structure in their travel program. They want to "stay loose." Mystery tours might be popular.

6. Hedonism, pleasure for its own sake, the idea that the individual deserves pleasure and that he should do as he wants, even though it may be contrary to established routines and ethics.

7. Sensuousness. Members of the younger generation supposedly take economic security for granted and are more likely to spend money for travel than for possessions. They may fly to visit a friend rather than replace a worn out suit, dress or sofa.

Another motivational travel researcher, Dr. Gilman, has found that people who travel can be classified into two groups, the vacationer and the traveler. The vacationer, he says, is seeking relaxation; the traveler seeks excitement in new experiences. The vacationer wants to escape routine and repetition; the traveler has a more sophisticated view of the travel experience.[3]

Research done for the Canadian Government Bureau revealed that when people take a vacation, they go through three phases. The first, a dream phase, is when people speculate about the ideal vacation. The second phase is concerned with gathering information and help in exploring the possibilities of realizing their dream vacation. The last phase is when dreams face realities and practical travel decisions are made. To be effective, the advertising for each phase must be different. The dream phase calls for "image" advertising; the second phase for "inquiry" ads, those which offer information; the third phase is "hard sell" advertising, such as "Fly to Montreal" or "Capture Canada."[4]

Image of Destination

Motivation research is used to get at the image cast by a tourist-receiving area. In the case of Canada, the image of the country was a limited one and prospects were somewhat misinformed.[5] Motivation research disclosed that Canada, as perceived by potential tourists to the country, was not the friendly, rapidly growing country perceived by the Government Travel Bureau. The potential traveler's image of Canadians was of a somewhat staid and conservative people, an image that tended to attract older people. Canada was seen as remote and lacking in excitement. As a whole, the image was weak and not well identified. Knowing the image, marketing efforts can be changed to sharpen the image or change it as deemed desirable.

Another example of "image" research was conducted by Marketscope Research Company and sponsored by American, East-

[1]Taken from "Developing the Family Travel Market," Stanley C. Plog, *Third Annual Conference Proceedings,* The Travel Research Assn., 1972, p. 215.
[2]Philip N. Robertson, *The Effect of Changing Social Values on the Travel Industry,* Eastern Council for Travel Research, 1970, pp. 46-54.
[3]*The Changing World of Travel Marketing,* Canadian Government Travel Bureau, 1971.
[4]*Ibid.*
[5]*Ibid.*

RATINGS OF THE IMPORTANCE OF FAMILY TRAVEL MOTIVATORS

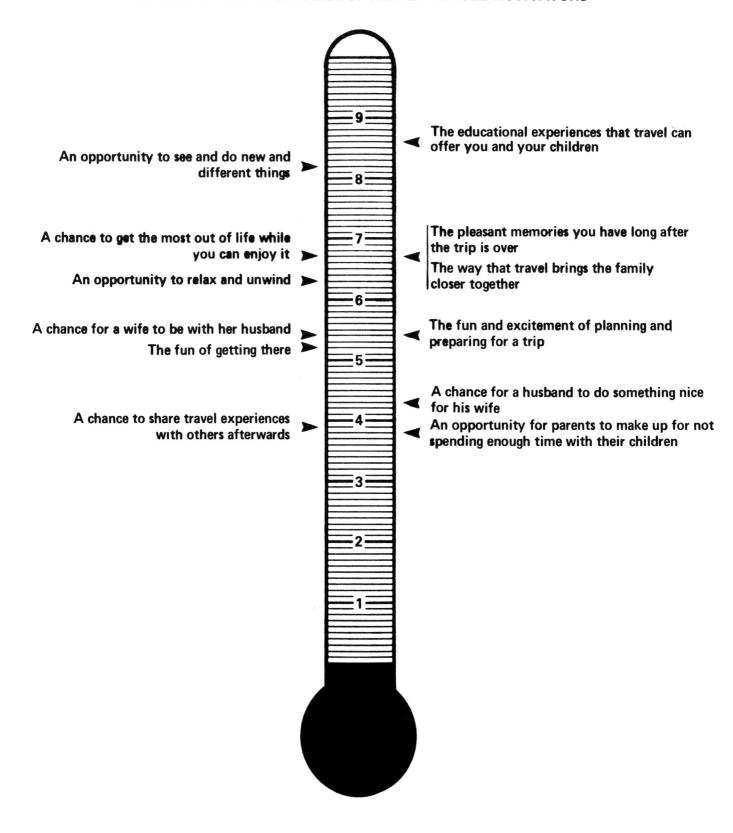

ern, TWA and United Airlines, together with the Port of New York Authority.[1] The airlines and the Port Authority were concerned that New York City had experienced a lower rate of economic growth than the rest of the nation and that domestic air traffic at New York City had declined as a percent of the nation's total since at least 1950.

The research company conducted 3500 telephone interviews in 17 cities throughout the U. S. to determine attitudes toward New York and other destinations. It was learned that, indeed, the image of New York City had declined relative to other major American cities. New York City was ranked worst in social unrest, air traffic congestion and in cost of hotels and restaurants. Interest in going to New York on pleasure trips had declined.

Although New York was considered the leading city as a center for art, culture and entertainment and as a place for sightseeing, it had developed a poor reputation for delays at the airports and inconvenience in ground transportation. It was also considered one of the most dangerous places to visit because of crime, tension and student unrest and there was some reaction against the size, density and congestion of the city. Overall appeal to both pleasure and business travelers had declined.

Such image studies provide information as to how particular groups or markets actually feel about a destination, information which can be compared with what the promoters think is true. If the area is viewed as a place for fun and frolic, promoters can aim their advertising at groups who want that kind of entertainment. Areas which project images of "rest and relaxation" can be promoted among other markets.

Ill-defined images can be sharpened by advertising. Unfavorable atttudes toward an area can be changed by offering something different, correcting problems and through advertising.

Lifestyle Studies

Lifestyle studies are an interesting approach to learning who travels and for what reasons. Apparently, people who do considerable traveling live differently from those who do not. The problem is to identify lifestyles associated with travel. Which lifestyles are conducive to travel; which are not? The Harper's/Atlantic Company has sponsored research to learn the lifestyles of their subscribers as compared with the people who live next door to their subscribers.[2] In the process, lifestyles of travelers versus non-travelers were identified.

It's perfectly possible for families who live side by side and who are of the same social-economic-educational group to have quite different lifestyles. Apparently, the factors which make up lifestyle are good indicators of whether a family will subscribe to a particular magazine, as well as whether they take off-season vacations, or engage in foreign travel.

The lifestyle studies found clusters of behavior and other factors which were used to classify those who responded to the study into four groups. These were named "the movers and the shakers," "the homebodies," the "older folk," and "the established." The "movers and the shakers" were the highly visible doers in our society, active in sports and travel. They were the ones who attended concerts, wrote articles for publication and were involved politically and socially—professional people. They were well educated, mobile, young. They placed more value on "experience" as compared with possessions than did the other three groups. They were more likely to take wine with their meals and to buy an original painting or sculpture.

The homebodies were "nest-oriented," people who liked to putter around the house, work with their cwn power tools, and do such home repair jobs as laying wall-to-wall carpeting. They were strong on watching TV.

Lifestyle three, "older folk," were in the lowest income group, having incomes of less than $10,000. Their lifestyle emphasized watching TV. A surprisingly large percentage, 66 percent, read Reader's Digest.

Lifestyle four, "the established," were

[1]Address before the Eastern Council for Travel Research by Dr. Morton Ehrlich, Eastern Airlines, Mar. 16, 1971, New York City.
[2]*The People Next Door Revisited*, Vol. 2, "Movers and Shakers," Harper's/Atlantic, New York, N. Y., 1970.

dominated by businessmen. This group was the most affluent; 50 percent had incomes of $25,000 and more. The "established" played a lot of golf and belonged to country clubs. Like the "movers and shakers," they liked cocktails and wine, were likely to buy an original painting or sculpture, and did a lot of air travel. They differed from the "movers and shakers" in that they were less involved in political and civic affairs.

Studies to determine what people constitute a market for flying, as compared with those who do not fly, have investigated lifestyle, or the psychographic approach. Studies done for Air Canada by the Behavior Science Corporation differentiated between the heavy flier, the light flier, and the non-flier. As might be expected, the heavy flier is more affluent, better educated and more self-confident. He tends to be adventuresome, optimistic, and liberal. He is more imaginative and likely to try new brands.

Also as might be expected the non-flier is more apt to be a worrier, afraid of the future and of change. He is more conservative, price conscious, and tends to drop out of life as regards sex and liquor. Psychographs or profiles of various consumer markets can be drawn which suggest the kind of media which will be most effective in reaching a particular market as well as appeals that should be used for each market.[1]

Off-Season Vacationers

Factors found to correlate highly with taking an off-season winter vacation were:

1. Bought and/or sold stock in the past year;
2. Income of $12,000 and over;
3. Had been asked for advice about investing in stock.

Other variables which were correlated with taking a winter vacation included having rented a car in the past year, traveled to the continent in the past year, spent more than $500 on jewelry during the past three years.

People who took off-season vacations were likely to be members of a cultural organization and active politically to the extent that they had met a U. S. Congressman, senator or state legislator.

One of the important correlates with foreign travel turned out to be the purchase of an original painting or sculpture during the past three years. A leading correlate with air travel was attendance at a concert during the previous month and the consumption of wine at home.

The lifestyle studies were conducted by questionnaire; these were mailed to subscribers to Harper's or the Atlantic and to their next door neighbors. The studies found that families of the same socio-economic groups can be further differentiated by their lifestyle.

Market Identification and Advertising

Decision makers in the travel business are constantly confronted with the question of where and how to advertise and promote their businesses. Oddly enough, millions of dollars in advertising are spent each year in travel related businesses without the spender knowing much about the sales generated from such investment. The problem is to identify the market or potential market clearly and aim the advertising at these well-identified groups of people. This is easier said than done. The advertiser may have a good fix on his present consumer but be unaware of trends which are changing his market. And markets do change.

Some advertisers concentrate on developing new markets; others concentrate on established markets. An airline may have been granted a new route; consequently, a disproportionate piece of the advertising budget is allocated to penetration of the market for that route.

The big spenders in tourist promotion are the airlines. In 1970, domestic and international airlines spent $159.3 million on advertising in U. S. major media (newspapers, magazines, T.V., radio, outdoor).[1] In the same year, the 50 states spent just over $10 million on travel and tourism advertising within the U. S. What is perhaps

---

[1]*An Overview of Airline Marketing and Lifestyles of Airline Consumers,* Walter A. Garrett, Proceedings of the Third Annual Travel Research Assn., 1972.

[2]Travel and Tourism Expenditures in the United States, Robert A. Peattie, Transcript, Harris, Kerr, Forster Co., New York, Jan., 1973.

most interesting is the expenditure on advertising made for each traveler. Foreign countries spent $15,317,000 in tourism advertising in the U. S. in 1970 to reach the approximate 2.5 million U. S. residents who go overseas in any given year. If the approximately $6 million spent by Canada in the U. S. for advertising is subtracted, the total, something like $9 million, would be spent by foreign countries to reach the 2.5 million U. S. residents who travel overseas each year. Since more than half of these persons travel on U. S. airlines, the foreign airline advertising cost per U. S. traveler to an overseas country is on the order of $6.

Domestic airlines spent almost $118 million in advertising in the U. S. in 1970. Their advertising must be directed largely to the 6 percent of U. S. adults who account for almost three-fourths of the domestic airline revenue. These persons are likely to be businessmen who fly a lot.

The effect of airline advertising is fairly immediate: airplane seats are filled or not filled. Knowing that the breakeven load factor for a particular airline may be 52 percent, the decision makers have a clear target as to what they are trying to do; raise the load factor. Each airline has presumably studied its market and knows its customer by age group, income bracket, educational level and place of residence. Presumably, the media which best reaches the market is also known, be it television, magazine, newspaper or some other.

Airline policy regarding percentage of income devoted to advertising varies between airlines and with time. Probably the persuasiveness of the advertising agency which handles the airline account influences the advertising budget. So, too, does the personality of the principal executive, and maybe his wife as well.

How They Advertise

Allocation of advertising budget to various media is an inexact science, as witnessed by the wide variation in how the advertising dollar is spent by individual states in promoting tourism. It is difficult to determine the relative effectiveness of various media in attracting tourists.

National promotional budgets vary widely, as might be expected. The 67 National Tourist Offices that belong to the International Union of Official Travel Organizations spent $95 million in promotional efforts in 1970. Canada headed the list, spending $5.9 million on promotion. The Bahamas spent $5 million. The U. K. and Greece both spent more than $4 million. Spain, Switzerland and Italy spent more than $3 million each. The airlines spent more money on newspapers than any other media. T.V. was next in importance and gaining rapidly in favor. State tourist offices spent 67 percent of their advertising money in magazines in 1970; 24 percent was spent in newspapers.

In 1969, Florida spent $232,000 for advertising via television. Only one other state, Michigan, spent anything for T.V. advertising; Oregon ($55,000) and Florida ($17,000). Florida's winter tourist market is well centered around the New York Metropolitan area and perhaps T.V. was a wise choice of media since it could be concentrated in the New York Metropolitan area.

Florida led all states in major media advertising in 1969, spending $596,000. New York State was number two spending $574,000 for the same purpose.

Some decision makers in state governments apparently felt that radio advertising was effective; most did not. In 1969, the State of Pennsylvania spent $53,000 for radio advertising to attract tourists; Oregon spent $34,000; Utah, $24,000 and Georgia, $23,000. Most of the other states did not use radio at all for such purposes.

Some destination areas devote a large part of their promotion budgets to interesting travel agents in a particular destination. Familiarization tours are arranged by airlines and destination governments. Large numbers of agents are transported, accommodated, wined and dined at the destination at little or no expense to themselves.

Some destination decision-makers believe strongly in printed material and distribute literally millions of maps and pieces of descriptive literature. Other destination areas spend relatively little on such effort. Direct mail is used massively by the Canadian Travel Bureau: some 8½ million letters were sent in 1970. Between 1968 and

1970, about 2.5 million inquiries were answered. Analysis showed that 40 percent of the people who inquired actually traveled to Canada and on the average spent $200 per party.[1]

The individual resort is hard-pressed to promote and advertise alone. The operator can build a guest list based on guest histories developed from registration and other information. Periodic mailings are made to a guest list. The operator can hold cocktail parties in a community where he has a concentration of market. He lacks the budget, however, to do much newspaper or magazine advertising. T.V. advertising is probably precluded completely because of cost.

The independent may join one of the promotional groups that advertise a certain class of hotel; he may join his local Chamber of Commerce and be included in the Chamber's advertising efforts. He may prevail upon the local government to advertise his area and benefit in that way.

If he is relatively small and isolated, he must appeal to a relatively small group of people who like to be away from it all. As part of a resort complex such as Las Vegas or Miami Beach, he benefits from the advertising done by the airlines. Perhaps, he need do no advertising but can ride on the area or airline advertising.

State Advertising and Promotion

In the period 1969-1973, the demand was made of several state tourist divisions to justify their advertising and promotion expenditures and, in some cases, their very existence. Some of the states involved were Massachusetts, Maryland, Pennsylvania, Oregon and California. In Maryland, for example, an Arthur D. Little study was commissioned to ascertain the economic impact of tourism on the state. The study, costing $60,000, changed the climate of acceptance for tourism, advertising, promotion and development, stating that tourism was worth $300 to $500 million to Maryland.

As a result of the study, a law was passed which added a tax to all transient rooms sold (1 percent the first year, 2 percent the second, and 3 percent the third year of its existence). The study increased

the budget available for advertising promotion and recommended that seed money be made available to investors for building tourist facilities in certain areas. It was also recommended that the state provide a mortgage guarantee program for tourist development.[2]

While people in advertising feel that anyone who does not value advertising and promotion for tourism is completely naive, some skeptics want hard data in the form of cost benefit studies to justify any expenditure for travel and tourism. In reply to statements that tourism expenditures within a state have increased by a certain percentage as the result of advertising, critics suggest that such growth in expenditures would have occurred anyway, advertising or no advertising.

Such skepticism is hard to overcome because of the difficulty in getting really hard data concerning traveler motivation. It is relatively easy to place an ad in the *New York Times* travel section and include a coupon which a respondent may send in requesting a state brochure. Follow-up study will show that a certain percentage of those who requested the brochure actually visit the destination advertised. A cost/per/inquiry study or a cost/per/visitor study shows that it may cost anywhere from a few cents to many dollars to attract a visitor, if indeed the advertising was the direct agent of the decision to visit a state.

Cost/per/inquiry studies are commonly done to justify advertising and promotion expenditures but, of course, do not get at the matrix of motivation existing in the mind of the traveler. A person may have been interested in visiting Mexico as a result of seeing a particular movie, reading a number of books on the subject, taking a Spanish class, and hearing his neighbor talking about a similar visit. The fact that he wrote for a brochure and later took a trip may be incidental to the forces which formed his decision to travel to Mexico.

Another means of justifying advertising

[1]*The Changing World of Travel Marketing,* Canadian Government Travel Bureau, Ottawa, 1971.
[2]Conversation with Arthur D. Crandall, Director Division of Tourism, Maryland, 1973.

expenditure has come in readership surveys in which a researcher records how well or over how widespread an area a particular ad is read. According to Victor B. Fryer, Travel Information Director for Oregon, the only answer to skeptics of the kind mentioned is a very comprehensive and expensive in-depth survey of vacationers who have been to a particular place to find out why they went there. It might take a psychoanalyst's couch to arrive at the real reason.

Regardless of the vagueness associated with the conversion of advertising into effective action, advertising and promotion is generally accepted as being effective and advertising and similar expenditures for tourism increase year after year. Particular states or other destinations may shift their advertising from one agency to another and shift their media from magazine to T.V. or back again without any real facts to justify such shifting. This too is likely to continue because of the cost in time and money of getting more exact information.

The travel researcher is interested in identifying a market and measuring its size but also he wants to know the changes that are taking place within it. Is the market growing in size; who is leaving the market; who is entering it?

Market Trends

For basic economic data, the researcher usually turns to government or local bank statistics already available for a destination. In some cases, the information would be impossible to collect other than by a government unit or with the cooperation of such a unit.

The information in the table below is illustrative of the type that is based upon government statistics, in this case the U.S. Dept. of State and the U.S. Census Bureau.

Such information is highly significant

TRIPS TO EUROPE*
PERCENT OF U.S. POPULATION

1965	0.7%
1966	0.8%
1967	0.8%
1968	0.9%
1969	1.0%
1970	1.3%

to anyone engaged in international travel. It shows that in a five-year period the percentage of U.S. population traveling to Europe almost doubled.

The researcher is not only interested in actual numbers but in noting how the "mix" changes with time. Suppose a travel-oriented company is interested in how the travel "mix" is changing. The table[1] top of facing page shows how some selected occupational groups have changed in the period 1962-69 as percentage of total passport recipients. The information is valuable for such diverse companies as airlines, travel agencies and international hotel chains.

Americans are said to be the most widely traveled and the biggest spenders among tourists. In 1970, about 21.9 million U.S. citizens departed for countries abroad; 6.1 million of them for overseas countries. The dominance of the U.S. traveler is seen in the fact that in Japan over half the foreign visitors (207,000) were U.S. citizens. A rather amazing fact: of the $17 billion estimated as being spent in international travel in 1970, some $5 billion of the total was spent by U.S. travelers.

European Destinations

Major destinations for U.S. travelers to Europe in 1968 were:

United Kingdom	944,000 (1,317,621 in 1969)
Germany	712,000
Italy	632,000
France	580,000
Switzerland	554,000
Netherlands	397,000

Per capita travel in Europe is high. A much larger percentage of West Germans, Danes and Swedes travel abroad than U.S. citizens. Canadians spend more per capita than any other national group.[2] In 1970, about 2 million West Germans traveled outside of Germany and 1.6 million Swedes

Proceedings' First Annual Conference, "Emerging Life Styles and Their Effect on the Travel Market," Travel Research Assn., Salt Lake City, 1970.
[1]*Proceedings' First Annual Conference,* "Emerging Life Styles and Their Effect on the Travel Market," Travel Research Assn., Salt Lake City, 1970.
[2]*The Changing World of Travel Marketing,* Canadian Government Travel Bureau, Ottawa, 1971.

TABLE XXIV –OCCUPATION
OF PASSPORT RECIPIENTS

	1962	1965	1969
Student	11%	17%	21%
Independent Business or Professions	29%	32%	33%
Housewife	24%	20%	16%
Teacher	5%	4%	6%
Clerk-Secretary	4%	4%	4%
Skilled, Technical, Sales	8%	4%	3%
Retired	6%	6%	5%
All Other	8%	8%	8%
None	5%	5%	4%
	100%	100%	100%

left their countries for travel abroad. In the United Kingdom, over 8 million persons were outbound tourists in the same year. These countries show a higher "travel propensity" for travel abroad than the U. S. As said before, it must be realized that moving from one European country to another is relatively simple, as compared with the time and expense involved for travel abroad by the average U. S. citizen.

The researcher and market decision maker wants to know what the geographic origin is of the market for a particular destination area and how that market is changing. With such information, advertising budgets may be allocated to reach a present market or to develop new markets. One way to delineate the markets for a destination area is to use maps showing the source of visitors to a destination. The three maps, p. 277, compiled by the Market Research Department of Douglas Aircraft Company show the percent of total U. S. visitors to Hawaii by geographic regions of the Continental United States.[1] California is seen to be the largest source of visitors from the mainland, followed by the Midwest and the Eastern states.

The three charts—for 1965, for 1969, and a projection to 1975—show how the Hawaiian market has changed and is projected to change in the future. The number of travelers from the Midwest and Eastern states rose during the 1965-69 period and is expected to continue to rise through 1975. Travelers from the South more than doubled while the percentage of Californians

decreased. The fact that direct flights have been introduced to Hawaii from a number of cities helps to account for the shift in market. Another factor has been the increase in airlines serving Hawaii, from eight airlines in 1960 to 29 in 1971.

Collecting data for making the kinds of forecasts shown in the charts is costly and time-consuming. Information for the Douglas study was drawn from the local airlines, several state offices, banks, the Hawaiian Visitors Bureau and from reports on work done by a consulting firm. The study concluded that the jet aircraft was largely responsible for turning the infant tourist industry of Hawaii from only 15,000 visitors in 1946, who spent $6.3 million, into a highly complex recreational structure which, in 1970, served close to 1.6 million visitors who spent over $500 million. Visitors to Hawaii were projected to exceed three million in 1975.

Input-Output Analysis and Econometric Models

Another area of travel research involves the use of mathematical models and computers. Factors important to an economy or business are expressed mathematically. Each factor or variable is identified and the relationships between factors expressed as part of an equation. One variable may affect all others in varying degrees. By using a computer, calculations of these effects can be made in a few minutes.

Input-output analysis is the broad term for a method of analyzing a problem or system. A system is designed showing inputs and outputs. The economic system of a destination area can be so described. An economic model would be part of the input-output method of analysis.

Union Carbide, and dozens of other companies, are using input-output analysis to determine what will happen to the demand for their products as changes occur in the total economy or in parts of the economy.

How much of a reduction in demand will there be for a windshield sealant if the

---

[1]*Hawaii—Crossroads of the Pacific,* McDonnell-Douglas, Long Beach, 1971.

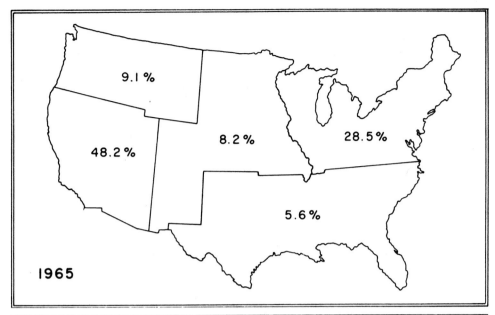

1965

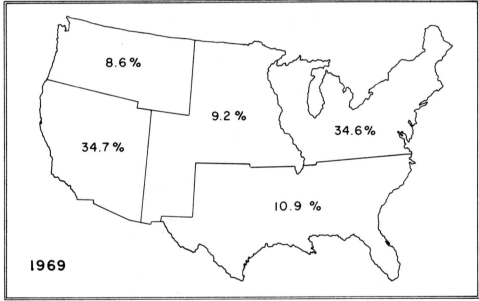

1969

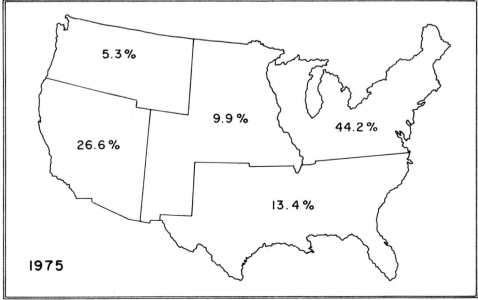

1975

SOURCE: <u>HAWAII-CROSSROADS OF THE PACIFIC</u>, McDONNELL DOUGLAS, LONG BEACH, 1971

production of automobiles is reduced 20 percent?

The same sort of analysis can be done for a destination area by asking the question: how much of a reduction in the number of visitors will take place if the national economy does not rise in a particular year? Will reduced roomrates increase the number of tourists to an area? What will be the effect of reducing air fares to a destination? What increase in tourism can be expected for a destination area as per capita income increases in California or New York City or Chicago?

Input-output analysis can help to provide such answers. The problem in devising models for input-output analysis is to come up with relevant inputs and an accurate measure of them as they affect the outputs important to the researcher. These are expressed in the form of an econometric (or economic) model.

Econometric models are used as a tool for planning, as a learning device and as a device for testing hypotheses concerning an economy. In the construction of a model, factors important for an economy are identified and their interrelationships explored. It is necessary to focus on the important factors which influence an economy and upon the significant relationships existing between them. The model enables the planner to organize, interrelate and analyze large quantities of statistical data. It also permits the planner to examine various hypotheses as to why a particular economy is growing or will grow in the future and the directions which the growth will take.

With Model, Planner Can Predict

The mathematics of developing the interrelationships are so time consuming that without the use of a computer even the simplest of models would be impossible to construct or use. Planning models are expressed in mathematical symbols. They are abstractions of what is thought to be going on in the real economic world which the model represents. Necessarily, the model is a simplification of the real world; a simplification in the sense that only the primary factors (and their relationships) which affect the growth and well being of an area

are considered.

The model, if well done, permits the planner to predict what will happen if various inputs into an economy are changed. With a model, the planner can consider the economic impact of various changes in the economy without the necessity of bearing the costs of trying out a hypothesis in a real life situation.

Econometric models need not be built for an entire economy or an area but can be built for the "economy" of a hotel or restaurant. Professor Norman Cournoyer of the Dept. of Hotel and Restaurant Administration at the University of Massachusetts has developed a model for a hotel in the Pioneer Valley of Massachusetts. Professor Francis Cella of the University of Oklahoma has developed models for various types of restaurants. With his models, he is able to predict the volume of sales for an existing or proposed restaurant.

Information needed for his models covers such factors as the calibre of management, the traffic flow past the location, the design of the restaurant building, the population upon which the restaurant will draw and the income of the population. Professor Cella has made over 1000 "site evaluations," using his models to determine the kind of restaurant most suitable for a location and whether or not that particular restaurant will succeed on a particular site.

Model of U. S. Economy Being Developed

A gigantic undertaking, the construction of a model of the U. S. economy, is under way, the work of a team made up of academic economists and staff members from the Federal Reserve System. One purpose is to measure the influence on the national economy and the stock market of the rate at which money is created and extinguished.

The Dept. of Planning and Economic Development of the State of Hawaii has made an economic model of Hawaii.[1] It offers an example of what can be done with mathematics and the use of a computer to pinpoint the factors and the interrelation-

[1]*State of Hawaii, General Plan Revision Plan, Part 3,* "Patterns of Economic Growth, The State Economic Model," Dept. of Planning and Economic Development, Honolulu, 1967.

ships of those factors which bear on the operation of a particular economy.

The more important vectors (factors affecting the economy) in the Hawaiian system turned out to be government expenditures, visitor expenditures and the incomes realized from contract construction, wholesale warehousing and trucking, banking and finance, other transportation, utilities and communications, eating, drinking and recreation.

Similar studies could be made of any tourist community such as Cape Cod, Las Vegas or any large area such as Puerto Rico, Florida or of a small nation. Such models could provide information as to which alternatives in expenditures should be made, depending on the social goods desired. A good model will enable planners to anticipate the effect of increasing numbers of tourists upon the overall economy. Trend lines can be developed for various industries and the results of these trends fed into the model to show the effect upon the total economy.

With the use of an economic model, planners can see what will happen to an economy if one or several of the inputs important to the economy change. A planner may need to know what will happen to the per capita income of each resident if tourists increase from one million to two million. What will be the effect of government income of such an increase? How much money must be spent to increase the number of tourists by ten percent? What happens to per capita and governmental income if the average tourist stays three fewer days or spends fifty fewer dollars in the economy?

An input-output study showing how various sectors of a regional economy are interlinked was done for the area of Anglesey, Wales. Tables were drawn up showing the effect of an increase of 10,000 pounds in tourist spending on 31 sectors of the economy. Tourist groups were broken down into those who stayed in hotels, those who stopped at farm houses, and those who stayed in their own trailers or in tents.[1]

As might be guessed, each class of tourist had a different impact on such things as insurance, banking and finance, education, grocery stores and construction. The input-output analysis enabled decision makers to see what changes would occur in the various sectors as more tourists of a particular type came to the area. For example, the tourist traveling by trailer needed less than half the amount of water used by the tourist staying in a hotel. The visitor staying in a tent purchased considerable food from a grocery store, while the visitor traveling in a trailer apparently brought much of his food with him. Such studies permit a more precise analysis of the impact of various types of tourism, their total impact and their impact on various parts of the economy.

Economic models using computers permit quick answers to such questions, provided, of course, the model accurately reflects reality.

Travel Data Resources

Anyone interested in travel research should acquire a copy of the Travel Research Bulletin, Volume IX, No. 3, Winter 1970-71 published by the Travel Research Association, Business Research Division, University of Colorado, Boulder. That issue contains an article, "Where to Find Travel Research Facts," which lists Indexing Services, Bibliographies and Finding Guides to Travel Periodicals and Travel Trade Associations. It also names government publications of interest and points out that there are some 89 programs in ten executive departments plus 47 programs in 36 independent agencies that are active in the development of recreation travel and tourism in the United States. All of these agencies are involved in collecting travel information.

The article lists various yearbooks which contain travel information: Yearbook of Railroad Facts, Air Transport Facts and Figures, Automobile Facts and Figures, Handbook of Airline Statistics and World Air Transport Statistics. Other sources of information are noted.

[1]*The Uses and Abuses of Multipliers,* Brian H. Archer, Proceedings of the Fourth Conference of the Travel Research Association.
*The Salt Lake City address is Western Council for Travel Research, P. O. Box 8066, Foot Hill Station, Salt Lake City, Utah 84108.
The Eastern office address is Eastern Council for Travel Research, 1828 L St., N.W., Washington, D. C. 20036.

The travel researcher will want to join the Travel Research Association which has offices in Salt Lake City and Washington, D. C.*

Travel Research and Marketing Is Multi-Disciplinary

It is seen that to identify and develop markets for travel is a multi-disciplinary effort. In the past, market research has been done by marketing experts who have come out of business schools, by economic analysts, statisticians and accountants. More recently, the behavioral sciences have become involved in travel research, including psychologists, social psychologists, and sociologists. Political scientists are needed to identify political changes which will affect the viability of an economy. In many destination areas, political considerations are overriding factors in determining if the area will be attractive to a particular market.

Changing lifestyles and other social changes may alter the travel mix drastically in the next few years which, in turn, will change the type of tourist facilities needed. Travel research in the broad sense is a prerequisite to construction of a facility and to marketing it once it is built. It is needed as a barometer and sensing device to take regular readings of what is happening in the travel world.

APPENDIX

TRAVEL BUSINESS ABBREVIATIONS

The travel agency and transportation business has its own alphabetese; abbreviations abound and are not likely to be known except by the initiated. A number of the abbreviations were carried in *Travel Agency Magazine* and are listed below.[1] The list is not inclusive; new organizations and their abbreviations can be expected to appear with time.

AAA	American Automobile Association
ABTB	Association of Bank Travel Bureaus
ACTO	Association of Caribbean Tour Operators
AGTE	Association of Group Travel Executives
AP	American Plan (three meals daily)
ARTA	Association of Retail Travel Agents
ASTA	American Society of Travel Agents
ATA	Air Transport Association
ATBEC	Association of Tourist Boards of the Eastern Caribbean
ATC	Air Traffic Conference
ATARS	Automated Travel Agents Reservation System
AWTA	Association of Westchester Travel Agents
BAATA	Brooklyn Association of Authorized Travel Agents
BHA	Bahamas Hotel Association
BP	Bermuda Plan (breakfast only)
CAB	Civil Aeronautics Board
CATM	Consolidated Air Tour Manual
CBIT	Contract Bulk Inclusive Tour
CHA	Caribbean Hotel Association
CTC	Certified Travel Counselor
CTO	City Ticket Office
CTOA	Creative Tour Operators of America
DATO	Discover America Travel Organization

DIT	Domestic Inclusive Tour
DSM	District Sales Manager
EP	European Plan (no meals)
ETC	European Travel Commission; Eastern Travel Club
FAA	Federal Aviation Administration
FIT	Foreign Independent Tour
FMC	Federal Maritime Commission
GIANTS	Greater Independent Association of National Travel Services
GIT	Group Inclusive Tour, 15 or more
HVB	Hawaiian Visitors Bureau
IATA	International Air Transport Association
ICTA	Institute of Certified Travel Agents
ISTA	International Sightseeing & Tours Association
IT	Inclusive Tour
ITC	Inclusive Tour Charter
ITX	Inclusive Tour-Basing Fare
IUOTO	International Union of Official Travel Organizations
JTO	Joint Tour Operators
MAP	Modified American Plan (breakfast and lunch or dinner)
MCO	Miscellaneous Charge Order
NACA	National Air Carriers Association
NSF	Not Sufficient Funds
NTBA	National Tour Brokers Association
PAC	Passenger Agency Committee (IATA)
PATA	Pacific Area Travel Association
RTPA	Rail Travel Promotion Agency
SARC	Systems Analysis and Research Corp.
SATO	South American Travel Organization

(cont.)

[1] *Travel Weekly,* March 17, 1970, p. 34.

SATW	Society of American Travel Writers		Environment
SKAL	Honorary world-wide social groups	TGC	Tour Group Charter (90 days advanced booking required)
SPATA	Society of Polish American Travel Agents	TPPC	Trans-Pacific Passenger Conference
TAC	Travel Advisory Committee	UATP	Universal Air Travel Plan
TAPSC	Trans-Atlantic Passenger Steamship Conference	UFTAA	Universal Federation of Travel Agents Associations
TIE	Transportation Industry Employees Union Travel Industry for the	USTS	United States Travel Service
		WATA	World Association of Travel Agencies

TRAVEL PERIODICALS FOR THE AGENT

ASTA Travel News

New York: American Society of Travel Agents, Inc., monthly, $5.00 a year, single copy 50¢.

Discover America Magazine

New York: Travel Trade Publishing Corp., weekly, $3.00 a year in U. S., $5.00 in Canada, $10.00 elsewhere.

Pacific Travel News

Western Business Publications
274 Brannan Street
San Francisco, California 94107

Service World International

Institutions Magazine and Practical Press
205 E. 42nd Street
Suite 1501
New York, New York 10017

The Travel Agent Personnel Directory

No travel office is complete without this book. It is the key to the industry, providing a complete listing of offices and officers of airlines, steamship companies, foreign governments, transportation conferences, etc.
    The Travel Agent
    2 West 46th Street
    New York, New York 10036

The Travel Agent Magazine

A semi-weekly magazine providing an interesting cross-section of activities in the industry.   A news type of periodical aimed at travel agents.
    American Traveler, Inc.

2 West 46th Street
New York, New York 10036

Travel Data Newsletter

Orange, California: Travel Marketing Newsletters, monthly, $10.00 per year.

Travel Printout

Washington, D. C.:   Discover America Travel Organization, Inc., monthly, free.

Travel Trade Publications

A weekly newspaper, a weekly sales package, a monthly feature magazine, a monthly Discover America magazine and other travel related materials.
    Travel Trade
    605 Fifth Avenue
    New York, New York 10017

Travel Scene

Travelage East

Travelage West

Travel Management Daily

Travel Management Newsletter

    Reuben H. Donnelly Corp.
    888 Seventh Avenue
    New York, New York 10019

Travel Weekly

A semi-weekly newspaper-type publication covering the industry, its activities and problems.
    Ziff Davis Publishing Company
    1 Park Avenue
    New York, New York 10016

TRADE ASSOCIATIONS

Air Traffic Conference (ATC)
MAIN U. S. OFFICE
1000 Conn. Ave., N.W.
Washington, D. C. 20036

Alpine Tourist Commission
Representing Austria, France, Italy, Monaco,
Switzerland, West Germany, Yugoslavia
MAIN U. S. OFFICE
P. O. Box 91
New York, N. Y. 10010

American Hotel & Motel Association
MAIN U. S. OFFICE
888 Seventh Ave.
New York, N. Y. 10019

American Sightseeing Association
MAIN U. S. OFFICE
1576 Broadway
New York, N. Y. 10036

American Society of Travel Agents (ASTA)
MAIN U. S. OFFICE
360 Lexington Ave.
New York, N. Y. 10017

Association of Bank Travel Bureaus, Inc.
MAIN U. S. OFFICE
c/o James J. Glover, Executive Secretary
8265 Washington Blvd.
Indianapolis, Ind. 46240

Association of Caribbean Tour Operators, Inc.
MAIN U. S. OFFICE
c/o United Tours, Inc.
59 S.E. 8th St.
Miami, Fla. 33131

Association of Group Travel Executives (AGTE)
MAIN U. S. OFFICE
c/o New Dimensions, Inc.
320 East 58th St.
New York, N. Y. 10022

Association of Local TRansport Airlines (ALTA)
MAIN OFFICE
242 Wyatt Bldg.
Washington, D. C. 20005

Association of Retail Travel Agents (ARTA)
MAIN U. S. OFFICE
8 Maple Street
Croton-on-Hudson, New York

**Association of Tourist Boards of the
Eastern Caribbean**
20 E. 46th Street
New York, N. Y. 10017

Caribbean Cruise Association
MAIN U. S. OFFICE
17 Battery Pl.
New York, N. Y. 10004

Caribbean Hotel Association
MAIN OFFICE
1120 Ashford Ave.
Santurce, Puerto Rico 00907

Caribbean Travel Assn.
MAIN U. S. OFFICE
20 E. 46th St.
New York, N. Y. 10017

**Conference of European
Railroad Representatives**
MAIN U. S. OFFICE
630 Fifth Ave.
New York, N. Y. 10020

**Discover America Travel
Organization, Inc.**
MAIN U. S. OFFICE
1100 Connecticut Ave., N.W.
Washington, D. C. 20036

Grand Order of European Tour Operators
MAIN OFFICE Southwestern Division
Boite Postale, 177 06
Cannes, France

**Gray Line Sightseeing Companies
Associated, Inc.**
MAIN U. S. OFFICE
1 Rockefeller Plaza
New York, N. Y. 10020

Hotel Sales Management Assn. Int'l.
MAIN OFFICE
358 Fifth Avenue, Suite 1407
New York, N. Y. 10001

Inter-American Travel Congresses (O.A.S.)
PERMANENT SECRETARIAT
Pan American Union,
Organization of American States,
Washington, D. C.

International Air Transport Association (IATA)
HEAD OFFICE
1155 Mansfield St.
Montreal, 113., Que.,
TRAFFIC SERVICE OFFICE
500 Fifth Ave.
New York, N. Y. 10036
Phone: OX 5-0862   Cable: Iataiata

International Association of Skal Clubs
MAIN OFFICE
Centre Intl. Rogier
Brussels, Belgium

International Hotel Assn.
MAIN OFFICE
89 Rue du Faubourg Saint Honore
F75 Paris 08, France

International Sightseeing and Tours Assn.
109 Via Due Macelli
Rome, Italy

International Union of Official Travel Organizations
MAIN OFFICE
Centre International, Case Postale 7
1211 Geneve 20, Switzerland

National Air Carrier Assn., Inc.
MAIN U. S. OFFICE
Suite 710, 1730 M. St., N.W.
Washington, D. C. 20036

National Air Transport Conferences (NATC)
1156 15th St., N.W. (Suite 510)
Washington, D. C. 20005

National Tour Brokers Assn.
MAIN U. S. OFFICE
c/o Mary Lee Travel Agency
209 Depot St.
Latrobe, Pa. 15650

Pacific Area Travel Assn. (PATA)
MAIN U. S. OFFICE
228 Grant Ave.
San Francisco, Calif. 94108

Rail Travel Promotion Agency
MAIN U. S. OFFICE
516 W. Jackson Blvd.
Chicago, Ill. 60606

Society of American Travel Writers
MAIN U. S. OFFICE
1146 16th St.
Washington, D. C. 20036

South American Travel Organization
MAIN U. S. OFFICE
100 Biscayne Blvd. North
Miami, Fla. 33132

Trans-Atlantic Passenger Steamship Conference
MAIN U. S. OFFICE
17 Battery Pl.
New York, N. Y. 10004

Trans-Pacific Passenger Conference
HEADQUARTERS OFFICE
2 Pine St.
San Francisco, Calif. 94111

Travel Committee, Inc.
271 Madison Ave.
New York, N. Y. 10016

Travel Research Association
P. O. Box 8066 Foothill Station
Salt Lake City, Utah 84108

Universal Federation of Travel Agents' Assn. (U.F.T.A.A.)
MAIN OFFICE
30, Avenue Marnix
Brussels 5, Belgium

World Association of Travel Agencies (WATA)
MAIN OFFICE
37 Quai Wilson
Geneva, Switzerland

INFORMATION CHECKLIST
FOR LARGE-SCALE LAND DEVELOPMENT PROJECTS[1]

I. General Information
   A. Name of Project
   B. Ownership
   C. Location
   D. Development History
   E Present Scope:
     1. Size of Holdings
     2. Type Uses

II. Land
   A. Acreage Controlled
     1. Owned
     2. Optional
     3. Leased
     4. Total
     5. Zoned for Development
     6. Type of Zoning
   B. Initial Cost/Value
     1. If Purchased, Agreement of Sale
     2. Special Terms and Conditions
     3. If Owned, Estimated or Appraised Value
   C. Final Value
     1. Fully Developed
     2. Appreciation of Surrounding Lands
   D. "Wholesale" Dispositions
     1. Within Project Area
     2. Outside Project Area

III. Feasibility
   A. Was Economic Study Conducted? By Whom? Copies?
   B. Was Market Research Included? Copy?
   C. Has Actual Buyer Profile Been Compiled? What Is It?
   D. Comparison Between Study Projection and Actual Performance?

IV. Planning
   A. Is Master Plan Available? Being Followed?
   B. Have Civil Engineering Studies Been Made?
     1. Roads
     2. Water
     3. Sewage

   C. Is Development Area Accessible?
     1. By Auto, Travel Times?
     2. By Plane, Travel Times?
     3. Nearest Urban Location?
   D. Amenities Planned/Offered
     1. Within Project Area
       a. Golf Course
       b. Country Club
       c. Riding Club
       d. Beach Club
       e. Marina
       f. Tennis Club
       g. Hunting Facilities
       h. Camping Facilities
       i. Fishing
       j. Other
     2. Outside Project Area (But Near)
       a.
       b.
       c.
       d.
     3. Which Amenities Are Available to Early Buyers/Guests?

V. Architecture
   A. Have Architectural Controls Been Established? How?
   B. Is Effect Pleasing?
   C. Has Developer Initiated Design Studies for Major Uses?
   D. Obtain Pictures/Renderings of Typical Architecture!

VI. Legal
   A. How Is the Land Holding and/or Development Company Structured?
   B. Joint Venture Agreements?
   C. Special Tax Considerations?

VII. Marketing
   A. Hotels
     1. Number of Sites? Size?
     2. Number of Hotels?

---

[1]Developed and used with the permission of Sanford I. Gadient and Mark Cockrill, Pacific Area Management Consultants, Honolulu.

3. Number of Rooms? Density?
4. Price of Rooms? Quality? Design?
5. Operators There/Committed?
6. Land Leased (Rate)/Fee (Price)?
7. If Operating Agreement, Terms?
8. Get Brochure, Rate Schedule, Services Description!
9. Guest Profile (Origin, Length of Stay, etc.).

B. Apartments (Condominiums, etc.)
1. Number of Areas? Projects? Units?
2. Size and Price of Offerings?
3. Project/Outside Developers?
4. Land Leased (Rate)/ Fee (Price)?
5. Operating Agreement with Hotel?
6. Project Sponsored or Developer(s) Initiated?
7. Quality of Design and Construction? Cost?
8. Owners Association?
9. Buyer Profile

C. Vacation Estates (Free Standing Residences)
1. Number of Areas? Projects? Units?
2. Size and Price of Offerings?
3. Project/Outside Developers
4. Land Leased (Rate)/ Fee (Price)?
5. Operating Agreement with Hotel?
6. Project Sponsored or Developer(s) Initiated?
7. Exterior Maintenance Agreement with Project?
8. Services Available from Hotel(s)?
9. Buyer Profile

D. Worker Housing
1. Number of Areas? Projects? Units?
2. Size and Price of Offerings?
3. Project/Outside Developers
4. Land Leased (Rate)/ Fee (Price)?
5. Project Sponsored or Developer(s) Initiated?

6. Quality of Design and Construction? Cost?
7. Buyer Profile.

E. Residential Lots
1. Number of Areas? Projects? Units?
2. Size and Price of Offerings?
3. Project/Outside Developers?
4. Land Leased (Rate)/ Fee (Price)?
5. Project Sponsored or Developer(s) Initiated?
6. Buyer Profile.

F. Amenities Provided/Private Clubs Offered (As Related to Each of Above)

G. Public Relations/Advertising Concept (for Each)

H. Marketing Methods/Organization (for Each)

VIII. Project Coordination
A. Financial and Operating Statistics from Inception of Project to Date Including:
1. Income and Expense Statement by Year and by Profit Center (i.e. hotels).
2. Total Sources and Uses of Cash and Net Cash Committed by Category.
3. Total Assets and Liabilities as of Each Year and by Category (as Appropriate)
4. Discounted Returns (If Available).

B. Future Projections (Up to Five Years) of Each of Above (VIII. A. 1., 2., 3., and 4.) and Physical Operating Plans as Available.

C. Management Organization
1. Top Management
2. Functional Management
3. Organization Chart
4. Position Descriptions
5. Financial Controls
6. Compensation Methods
7. Performance Incentives
8. Turnover
9. Overhead Budget
10. Policy Regarding Use of Consultants Versus Staffing

D. Project Scheduling
 1. Phasing of Development
 2. Use of Critical Path Scheduling
E. Is Development Partner Involved?
 1. Operating Agreement?
 2. Financial Arrangements?
 3. Equity Committed?
 4. Performance Record?

IX. Construction
 A. Typical Costs
  1. Structure
  2. Per Square Foot
  3. Per Hotel Room, etc.
 B. Completion Time Schedules
 C. Negotiated or Bid
 D. One of Several Builders
 E. Does Contractor Participate in Development? How?
 F. Estimated Volume of Construction and Contractor's Profit Over Development Term?
 G. Unique Building Methods/Techniques/Materials

X. Financing
 A. Amount of Mortgage Financing Required, by Type of Use?
 B. Suppliers of Mortgage Money
 C. Rates and Terms
 D. Participation/Kickers, If Any
 E. Subordination Provisions
 F. Is Financing Agent Partner in Development? Form of Agreement?
 G. Special Financing Methods
  1. Improvement Districts
  2. Borrowing on Land Contracts
  3. Other

XI. Property Management
 A. Methods and Techniques
 B. Central Versus Decentral by Area
 C. Role of Homeowners Association
 D. Cost and Quality
 E. Direct or Subcontracted

TRAVEL INDUSTRY DIRECTORIES

A valuable reference tool for anyone interested in the travel business is the *Travel Industry Personnel Directory*, published each year by *Travel Agent Magazine*, 2 West 46th St., New York, New York, 10036. A similar directory, *The Travel Trade Personnel Sales Guide*, is available from *Travel Trade*, 605 Fifth Ave., New York, 10017. Both directories constitute a comprehensive reference for the travel industry and include a listing with addresses of airlines, ship lines, railroads, tour operators, car purchases, rental coaches and sight-seeing, travel organizations, passenger conferences, state travel bureaus and travel services. The directories also include a listing of hotel representatives in the major cities of the United States and Canada.

THE SERVICE WORLD INTERNATIONAL "100"

Rank	Chain	No. Rms.	No. Hotels	No. Food Units	Comments
1	Holiday Inns, Inc. 3442 Lamar Ave. Memphis, Tenn. U. S. A.	222,700	1474	2015	Biggest in world added 20,813 rooms in '72, 97 hotels. No stopping HI; they now report more rooms under construction than at any other time in their history! Sales were $1.9 *billion*. Building in S. America, Africa, Mid-East, Far-East, Pacific—EVERYWHERE.
2	Best Western Motels, Inc.** 2910 Sky Harbor Blvd. Phoenix, Ariz. U. S. A.	80,000	1240	775	World's largest referral association (independent motel operations) planning addition of 200 new properties. Big efforts to add members on U. S.'s Atlantic Seaboard and East Coast, as well as Canada. Associate membership in other countries.
3	ITT Sheraton Corp. of America 470 Atlantic Ave. Boston, Mass. U. S. A.	71,546	263	885	Number 2 chain in world continues growth: over 91 properties scheduled in U. S. 13 properties going up worldwide, adding 6484 rooms. Expansion overseas primarily through management contracts and franchising. 1018-rm. hotel going up in Rome. Formidable competition.
4	Ramada Inns, Inc. P. O. Box 590 Phoenix, Ariz. U. S. A.	60,040	455	406*	Incredible upsurge for growth chain; built over 14,000 rooms in 1972 in 88 hotels! Sales increased 22%. Presently in U. S., Canada, Mexico, Singapore, New Zealand. Hotels in Belgium and Germany to open soon. Will build 10 in Japan.
5	Friendship Inns International** 245 W. on Temple St. Salt Lake City, Utah U. S. A.	52,000	1000	400	Referral group recently changed its name (from Friendship Inns of America) and went international. Now have 32 units in Canada, 9 in Mexico, 3 in Europe. Diversifies into complete motor inn supply company and a travel agency.
6	Hilton Hotels Corp 720 S. Michigan Chicago, Ill. U. S. A.	47,746	103	287	Sixteen new Hilton hotels and motor inns will open this year. 20 more in 1974. Project 60-75 new properties by 1978. Sales in '72: $525.5 million. Big banquet business—10.5 million covers served, with 41% of F/B sales derived from banquet sales.
7	Howard Johnson Co. 222 Forbes Rd. Braintree, Mass. U. S. A.	46,790	460	926	Watch for more growth from HJ—35 new properties will open in '73, 45 in '74, and 265 are expected to open in the next 5 years. Presently operating in U. S., Canada and Mexico. Diversification: supply and equipment co., grocery products; vending.
8	Balkantourist 1 Lenin Square Sofia Bulgaria	32,800	400	320	High hopes for big tourism increase. State-owned hotel, restaurant, travel group is concentrating on new investments, new pricing policies and intensified cooperation with foreign groups. Charter groups are expected to help: 1975 goal is 175,000 rooms.

THE SERVICE WORLD INTERNATIONAL "100"

Rank	Chain	No. Rms.	No. Hotels	No. Food Units	Comments
9	Master Hosts Inns/ Red Carpet Inns P. O. Box 2510 Daytona Beach, Fla. U. S. A.	32,000	260	260	Combined franchise companies now operating in U. S., Canada, Mexico and Australia. Plan 40 new inns this year, 110 next year. Room sales are 59.7% of sales, food/beverage is 40.3%. Room sales: $126 million; F/B sales: $85 million. Employees number 21,000.
10	Quality Inns 10750 Columbia Pike Silver Springs, Md. U. S. A.	31,852	361	300	Changed its name (from Quality Courts Motels) for new, upgraded image. First international move last September: groundbreaking for first Quality Inn in Europe in Dusseldorf. Other inns will soon open in Bremen and Antwerp. Moving into France as well.
11	TraveLodge International P. O. Box 308 El Cajon, Calif. U. S. A.	28,250	459	23*	Looking for more international franchisees! Now operating 27 in Canada, 1 in Mexico, remainder in U. S. Of total properties, 296 are joint ventures, 133 are franchised, 30 wholly-owned. Sales (excluding franchises) were $73.1 million in 1972.
12	Trust Houses Forte Ltd. 166 High Holborn London England	24,400	250	313	THF added 3400 rooms, 43 restaurants to empire. Sales were $596.4 million. Hotels located in 16 countries. Will open in Belgium, Germany, Denmark, Jamaica. Highly diversified, very international.
13	Inter-Continental Hotels 200 Park Avenue New York, N. Y. U. S. A.	20,550	64	142	Latest news from worldly chain: first move into U. S. with purchase of San Francisco's 550-rm. Mark Hopkins Hotel! Planning to build major hotels in U. S. gateways served by Pan Am. Sales in 1972: $210 million. Overall '72 occupancy was up—69.4%.
14	Hilton International 301 Park Avenue New York, N. Y. U. S. A.	20,437	60	247	Worldwide chain has 4 less hotels than last year, but added 2304 rooms. Thirteen hotels are now under construction, with 3 hotels getting additional rooms: total of 6122. Total sales were $250 million. Food sales: $77 million, beverage sales were $38.8 million.
15	Club Mediterranee Place de la Bourse 75 Paris France	18,150	57	130	Innovation in the hotel industry earned CM a $2.7 million net profit in 1972. Opened Paris hotel—first operation run not as a club—as well as first resort on West African Coast. Opening 2 Mexican Villages (600 rms.) in 1974, and will add 220 rooms to Tahitian CM.
16	Intourist 16 Marx Ave. Moscow U.S.S.R.	17,100*	70*	125*	Huge, governmental hotel/tourism organization beginning to give more information: plans for 35,000 new beds, plus additions to existing Soviet hotels. Beginning to build "super-deluxe" hotels, adding 11,000 beds. Total by 1975: 48,000 new beds.

THE SERVICE WORLD INTERNATIONAL "100'

Rank	Chain	No. Rms.	No. Hotels	No. Food Units	Comments
17	Western International Hotels The Olympic Seattle, Washington U. S. A.	17,000	56	200	The "hoteliers' hotel company" added 1500 new rooms in '72; 2000 new rooms (7 new hotels, 2 additions) planned for 1973. Sales were $136 million, with $62 million in food/beverage. New hotels by 1976: Canada (2), U. S. (4), and Copenhagen (1).
18	Hyatt Corp. 1338 Bayshore Hwy. Burlingame, Calif. U. S. A.	13,564	64	93*	The key words at Hyatt: build, build, build. Outstanding architecture and new openings throughout U. S. Recent new success: 1000+ room Houston hotel. Expect 20-30 new properties in next 5 years.
19	Rodeway Inns of America P. O. Box 34736 Dallas, Texas U. S. A.	12,230	116	73	Lively motor hotel chain will see BIG growth: over 22 units (3181 rms.) now under construction, all but one are franchised. Have 44 franchises sold and under development. New development division will add major construction company for diversification.
20	Grand Metropolitan Hotels 7 Stratford Place London England	12,036	92	11,726	With 1972 takeover of Watney-Mann Breweries, GM is now one of world's largest catering/hotel empires. Group sales were $1.8 billion, including diversified companies. Hotel, entertainment, catering sales $300.3 million. Operates in 8 countries, including U. S.
21	Cedok Prikopy 18 Prague Czechoslovakia	10,691	198	225	Increased tourism, new restaurant venture in Japan, and opening of striking Inter-Continental Hotel in Prague makes this government travel/hotel group an exciting one. Watch expanding hotel and catering ventures take shape in the next 2 years.
22	The Downtowner Corp. 162 Union Ave. Memphis, Tenn. U. S. A.	10,500	76	125	U. S. motor hotel chain is selling off more franchises, while opening new, company-owned properties. Fifteen Downtowners are now under construction. Sold 14 in 1972, totaling 1562 rooms.
23	Motel 6, Inc. 51 Hitchcock Way Santa Barbara, Calif. U. S. A.	10,039	110	—	Average room rate for budget hotel chain is $8.25. Sales in 1972 totalled $18.7 million. No restaurants in motels are owned by corporation, but leased. Will open 75 hotels this year, 100 next year, and 550 by 1978.
24	Gotham Hotels Ltd. 405 Lexington Ave. New York, N. Y. U. S. A.	9668	28	62*	Six big New York hotels include the 1400-rm. McAlpin in prime, central Manhattan area. One property in Toronto, Canada: the Ford Hotel (588 rooms).
25	Inter Hotel Chaine** 14 Allee des Zephirs Ramonville-St.-Agne France	9122	240	206	International referral organization now in four countries, with main customers being the traveling businessman. Presently regrouping 2 and 3 star hotels. Project under development: creation of a hotel and club in Paris.

THE SERVICE WORLD INTERNATIONAL "100"

Rank	Chain	No. Rms.	No. Hotels	No. Food Units	Comments
26	Marriott Corp. 5161 River Rd. Washington, D. C. U. S. A.	8403	19	1246	In 1972, the hotel division of diversified company accounted for 35% of corporate sales and profits. Plans to build 394 rooms in Amsterdam with Watney-Mann Breweries, opening in 1975. By '75, Marriott will add 7 hotels, 3 additions: total, 3257 rooms.
27	Americana Hotels, Inc. 605 Third Ave. New York, N. Y. U. S. A.	8300	14	63	Major reorganization of American Airlines subsidiary. (Formerly Flagship Hotels.) Added 3700 rms. by leasing 3 major properties from Loews Hotels. Theme "Fly American—stay Americana" to highlight promotion, tying in reservations. Building boom in U. S. expected.
28	ETAP Hotel/Euromotel 69 Blvd. Haussmann Paris France	8182	98	154	Last November, ETAP signed agreement with British Transport Hotels to promote an international sales force between the two firms. Will build 4 hotels in '73-'74, 1 in '75. Projects include 14 more hotels throughout Europe and Middle East. Doubled size in 1972!
29	Interhotel Association Simplonstrasse 52-56 1035 East Berlin G.D.R.	8169	26	65*	Government owned hotel chain has new, modern facilities throughout East Germany. Maintains own architectural, interior design department. Newer hotels are built to appeal to Western tourists. Stadt Berlin Hotel still tallest in Europe (50 stories).
30	Royal Inns of America 4855 N. Harbor Dr. San Diego, Calif. U. S. A.	8057	66	32	Company operates on a partnership basis, with 63 properties under joint venture, 3 franchise. Royal Inns built 11 hotels and 1863 rooms last year, but recent financial troubles have been reported.
31	Commonwealth Holiday Inns of Canada Ltd. 304 York St. London, Ont. Canada	7825	40	81	Boom for this active company: opened 2071 rms. and world's largest Holiday Inn (750-rms.) in Toronto. Room sales up $6.8 million, F/B sales up $5.7 million. Will open 11 new HI's in '73 (2878 rms.) in Canada, U. S., U. K. and Caribbean.
32	Montenegroturist Hotel Enterprise** 81310 Buvda Yugoslavia	7270	48	100	Tourist and hotel services are provided by this huge referral organization, one of the largest in Yugoslavia. Member hotels are all in the Republic of Montenegro.
33	Pick Hotels Corp. 20 N. Wacker Dr. Chicago, Ill. U. S. A.	7000	26	55	Privately-owned company operates only in U. S. Sold off 2 hotels last year, but added to existing properties. Sales in 1972: $32 million. Operate 16 restaurants outside their hotels. No expansion plans set. Employees number 5000.

THE SERVICE WORLD INTERNATIONAL "100"

Rank	Chain	No. Rms.	No. Hotels	No. Food Units	Comments
34	United Inns, Inc. 555 S. Perkins Extended Memphis, Tenn. U. S. A.	6693	31	48	Holiday Inn franchisor is now international with 2 HI's opening in Germany this June. Expansion this year: 6 hotels will add 1118 rooms. Four will open in 1974. Sales were $44 million, with impressive occupancy of 78.3%, projected to 80.5% in 1973!
35	Crest Hotels Ltd. 26 Bridge St. Banbury England	6666	89	130*	Subsidiary of giant Bass Charrington Breweries bought 17 Esso Motor Hotels for $60 million. Now operating in U. K., Australia, Belgium, Germany, Holland and Italy. Will build 3 more in U. K., in Europe (including one new market: France). Sales: $24.5 million.
36	Relais de Campagne** Domaine de la Tortiniere Montbazon France	6500	180	178	This referral organization is somewhat unique: hotels offer fine dining as a promotion, with a special group, Les Relais Gourmands, for dining of "grand prestige."
37	American Motor Inns, Inc. 103 Campbell Ave., S. W. Roanoke, Va. U. S. A.	6422	48	56	Sales up $10 million for lively, diversified Holiday Inn franchisee. 7 motels (1056 rms.) under construction in U. S. Puerto Rico; opening in Virgin Islands. Healthy banquet business: 17% of food/beverage sales. Established new training division.
38	Strand Hotels Ltd. Cadby Hall London England	6295	27	32	Subsidiary of giant catering conglomerate, J. Lyons & Co., operates in England, Ireland and owns 1 property in Holland. Combined with sister company Falcon Inns. Strand opened or acquired 6 hotels in 1972. In '73, opening of 830-rm. London's Tower Hotel.
39	Hungarhotels V. Petofi, U. 14 Budapest Hungary	6200	34	158	Impressive management in East Europe—company is profit-oriented. Sales totaled $36 million, with $21 million in food/beverage sales. 34,500 meals per day are served: 9655 employees. Occupancy rate: 69.5%. Operates restaurants outside Hungary.
40	S.E.M.I. Piazzale E. Mattei, 1 00144 Rome Italy	6100	61	118	Subsidiary of AGIP Oil Co., this ubiquitous chain operates throughout Italy, with 6 units in Africa, 1 in Svizzera. Built 3 motels last year, will add 5 more in 1973. Has holiday resorts, hunting reserve.
41	Canadian Pacific Hotels, Ltd. 100 Front St. Toronto, Ont. Canada	5897	14	45	CP Hotels made its first international move in March by taking over its first hotel property outside Canada: the 384-rm. Chateau Royal in Mexico City. Another hotel in Acapulco planned. CP is looking for more expansion outside Canada. Watch their growth!

THE SERVICE WORLD INTERNATIONAL "100"

Rank	Chain	No. Rms.	No Hotels	No. Food Units	Comments
42	Dunfey Family Corp· 490 Lafayette Rd. Hampton, N. H. U. S. A.	5508	21	25	Successful chain in New England increased sales by $8.6 million last year: total sales were $45.6 million. Four new hotels were added in '72, and 4 more will open in '73 (806 rooms). 903,000 banquet covers were served. Owned by Aetna Life Insurance Group.
43	TraveLodge Australia Ltd. 110 Bayswater Rd. Ruchsutters Bay, N.S.W. Australia	5346	75	70*	Ubiquitous, energetic firm continues to diversify, branch out and grow! Largest in Australasia, TLA building 7 new hotels in Australia, Tahiti and Japan (Narita) while adding to 2 hotels in Australia and Fiji. Total by end of '74: 1487 new rooms.
44	Italhotels** Via P. Sacchi 8 Turin Italy	5240	60	60	Referral organization bands Italian hotels together (averaging 100 rms.). Group began only 5 years ago, has grown from 20 member hotels to 60. Expansion expected.
45	Plava Laguna 52360 Porec Yugoslavia	5220	23	21	Largest private hotel and catering company in Yugoslavia added a 220-rm. hotel in Zagreb. Opening 2 new hotels: a 200-rm. property in Ljubljana and a 500-rm. hotel in Porec. Large tourist resorts on Adriatic Coast.
46	Inter Hotel (Great Britain and Ireland)** 29 Harrington Gardens London England	5206	88	100	Consortium of privately-owned, medium-priced hotels. Offer group purchasing, joint marketing, central reservations to members. Associate members in France, Italy, Switzerland and Netherlands. Links with U. S. chain.
47	France Mapotel** 31, rue de Metz Toulouse Cedex France	5100	90	77	Family-owned referral chain is unusual in that it offers central purchasing, selection of supplies to members. Other benefits: reservations, sales, public relations. Projects under development: hotels in Spain, Portugal, England, Germany, Italy—Europe!
48	Hoteles Mallorquines c/Massanet, 14 Palma De Mallorca Spain	5000	23	34	The Balearic Islands bring big business to Spain's largest hotel chain. All resorts are located in Mallorca, with an occupancy rate of 76%. Another hotel in Palma (400-rms.) will open in March, 1974. 27,500 meals per day are served. Employees total 2850.
49	Husa Hotels Reina 17 Madrid Spain	5000	16	45	Big expansion plans in Barcelona, Lisbon, Tenerife, Costa del Sol still well under way (total: 1800 rooms). No new hotels, however, were constructed in 1972.
50	France Accueil Hotels** 46 Blvd. Cote Blatue Clermont Ferrand France	4850	99	297	Active French referral organization is projecting an 85% occupancy rate in 1973 (in 1972, occupancy was 79%). Diversification includes travel groups, incentive tours. ("Accueil" means "welcome".)

THE SERVICE WORLD INTERNATIONAL "100"

Rank	Chain	No. Rms.	No. Hotels	No. Food Units	Comments
51	Hyatt International 1338 Bayshore Hwy. Burlingame, Calif. U. S. A.	4774	11	32	International group more than doubled rooms and hotels in 1972! Lush properties in Canada, Australia, Puerto Rico, Thailand, Mexico, Hong Kong, Philippines, Ceylon, Singapore, Panama. Will build in Indonesia, Iran, Israel, Jamaica.
52	Interchange Hotels of Great Britain** 1 Victoria Rd. London England	4772	98	–	A marketing consortium of privately-owned hotels and inns located in England, Scotland and Wales. No expansion plans are indicated, but Interchange doubled in size a few years ago.
53	Sveriges Centrala Box 21048 Stockholm Sweden	4730	54	150	Sweden's giant catering and hotel company had sales of $90 million in 1972, with $75 million in food/beverage. Operate 96 free-standing restaurants, 54 hotel dining rooms. Opening a hotel in Gothenberg in 1974. Government-controlled.
54	Melia Hotels Princesa 25 Madrid Spain	4700	20	80	Four new hotels since last year, but 25 are planned all over the world: 3 in Morocco, 3 in Mexico, 3 in Venezuela, one each in London, Paris, Puerto Rico, Barbados, Aruba, Iraq, Panama, Greece, Germany, Colombia, Portugal—and 4 in Spain.
55	Loews Hotels 666 Fifth Ave. New York, N. Y. U. S. A.	4683	8	45	Recently leased 4 big hotels (3993 rms.) to Flagship, but world growth continues. Just opened in Hamburg; Frankfurt, Monte Carlo, Athens coming up. Opening Washington, D. C. hotel this summer. Canadian acquisition firming up. Expect big things from well-managed corp.
56	Tokyu Hotel Chain Co. 6-6 Kajimachi Chiyoda-Ku Tokyo Japan	4596	21	69	Japan's largest continues dynamic growth and international expansion. Operates 17 hotels in Japan, 1 in Korea, 2 in U. S., 1 in Thailand. By mid-1974, will open 1166 rooms in Sapporo, Kuala Lumpur, Fiji, Nagasaki.
57	Canadian National Hotels P. O. Box 8102 Montreal, Quebec Canada	4462	10	75	Railroad subsidiary building in St. Johns (Newfoundland) in 1975. Added 212-rm. hotel since last year. Two hotels, one the giant Queen Elizabeth in Montreal, operated by Hilton International.
58	C.I.G.A. Ramo dei Fuseri 1812 Venice Italy	4334	19	32	Luxury, resort hotels in Italy recently went international with purchase of 3 deluxe Paris hotels: the Grand, Meurice and Prince De Galles. New director, Mario di Genova, was VP with Inter-Continental Hotels.
59	Southern Sun Hotel Corp. 51 Juta St. P. O. Box 5087 Johannesburg South Africa	4313	29	73	Dynamic growth! Southern Sun has tripled in size in 3 years. Last year, takeover of Cape Hotels made them S. Africa's largest hotel and restaurant chain. In 1974, will build 8 hotels (2790 rms.), and by 1976 will add 7 more hotels (1200 rms.)!

THE SERVICE WORLD INTERNATIONAL "100"

Rank	Chain	No. Rms.	No. Hotels	No. Food Units	Comments
60	Centre Hotels 57 Russell Square London England	4308	27	77	First international move for U. K. chain: Amsterdam hotel to open in spring, '74. Formed marketing and purchasing consortium called "Centrelink" with 5 hotels. Own chain of 41 "Old Kentucky" Restaurants. Sales in '72, $18 million.
61	Bonne Chaine Hotels via Broletto, 46 Milan Italy	4200	73	–	Italy's referral association of medium-sized/priced hotels tied in with Inter-Hotel in Belgium, France, England and Switzerland for reservations.
62	France Ouest Hotels** P. O. Box 51 St. Servan France	4200	87	81	Regional chain in the West of France ties together independent hotels in 28 counties. 2-3 star properties are referred. One of main benefits: central purchasing for all hotels.
63	Italjolly Via Bellini 6 36078 Valdagno Italy	4159	42	82	"Jolly" hotels controlled by Compagnia Italina dei Jolly had 90% occupancy in 1972, and project 96% for next year! 39.6% of sales are in food/beverage, with total sales of $20.7 million. Opening in Bari, Torino, Genoa.
64	Allen & O'Hara, Inc. 3385 Airways Blvd. Memphis, Tenn. U. S. A.	4041	23	36	Holiday Inn franchise also is big in student housing, with 15,112 rooms in 20 facilities. Increase in food/beverage volume, due to new, appealing decor in the restaurants. Diversification in construction, management, development. New acquisition possible in '73.
65	Barshop Motel Enterprises 1710 N. Main St. San Antonio, Texas U. S. A.	4000	34	7	Franchisee of Ramada & Rodeway Inns (also La Quinta Motor Inns) opening 13 motels by January, 1974. Future market areas: Northwest, Midwest, Southern U.S.
66	Scottish & Newcastle Breweries Ltd. 111, Holyrod Rd. Edinburgh Scotland	4000	102	–	Hotel subsidiary of one of top five breweries in England added 7 hotels in 1972. Three new hotels to open spring of '73 in Liverpool, Luton, Edinburgh (581 rms.). Major unit expansion plans throughout U. K. Breweries operate 1500 pubs.
67	British Transport Hotels Ltd. St. Pancras Chambers London England	3922	31	1290	In 1972, set up joint marketing operation with Etap/Euromotel giant in France. Company also responsible for British Rail Catering (900 on-train catering units) and 320 station restaurants. Sales in 1972: $94.2 million.
68	Knott Hotels Corp. 575 Madison Ave. New York, N. Y. U. S. A.	3900	11	10	Chain operates in U. S., Canada, England and Belgium. Opening one property in Chicago in 1973. Sales in 1972: $27.4 million. Room sales are 59%, food/beverage 33%. More than 200,000 banquet covers were served in 1972, accounting for 21% of F/B sales.

THE SERVICE WORLD INTERNATIONAL "100"

Rank	Chain	No. Rms	No. Hotels	No. Food Units	Comments
69	Orbis 16, Bracka St. Warszawa Poland	3740	23	83	Cooperative hotel and travel organization added more restaurants last year. Plans 3 new hotels in 1973, 7 in 1974, 10 by 1978. Emphasis on food units; restaurant sales are double room sales. Employees, including the tourism company, number 9162.
70	Lansburgh Hotels Eden Rock Hotel 4525 Collins Ave. Miami Beach, Fla. U. S. A.	3663	9	27	BIG properties in Miami Beach owned by Morris Lansburgh, usually close-mouthed about his hotel operations. Also owns two hotels in Freeport, Grand Bahamas (total: 1200 rooms).
71	Steigenberger Hotels P. O. B. 16440 Frankfurt Germany	3600	20	40	1972 a big year for Steigenberger: added to separate restaurant chain with 11 units at Frankfurt airport; opened hotel in W. Indies; bought a hotel school; increased reservation service (SRS) to include 100 hotels in 31 countries! Watch for more in 1973.
72	Liburnia Hotel Enterprises** 65, M. Tita Opatija Yugoslavia	3456	30	48	The Opatija "Riviera" hotel resorts are government-controlled and profit-conscious. Average room rate is $10. Recently expanded 1 hotel, and built 3 new hotels which opened early January, 1973.
73	Hotel & Tourist Enterprise "Dubrovnik" Mise Simoni 2 Dubrovnik Yugoslavia	3420	26	63	A publicly-held enterprise helps the hotel and tourism business flourish in Yugoslavia. 39.9% of sales are from food: the hotels operate 27 dining rooms, 30 coffee shops, and 6 specialty restaurants.
74	Western International Hotels de Mexico Hotel Camino Real Leibnitz No. 100 Mexico City, D.F.	3319	22	39	Affiliated with Western International (U. S.), this chain has luxury hotels in big cities and resorts in Mexico. Eight of properties carry name of the company's flagship hotel in Mexico City: Camino Real.
75	Stouffer Restaurant & Inn Corp. 1375 Euclid Ave. Cleveland, Ohio U. S. A.	3310	12	52	New international takeover bid: Swiss-based Nestle recently made offer to Stouffer's parent, Litton Industries, to buy network of restaurant, motor inns and retail frozen prepared food line. Food/beverage sales: $62 million.
76	Organization Eurotel Ltd. Steffisburgstrasse 1 Thun Switzerland	3117	23	30	Dynamic growth expected by aggressive chain: 10,000 beds expected by 1977. Opening new hotels in Antwerp, Neuchatel and Lugano by January, '74. The company has investments of $210 million and will expand into Madrid, Monte Carlo, Vienna and Germany in next 3 years.
77	Reso Klara N. Kyrkogata 31 105 24 Stockholm Sweden	3045	18	18	Chain operates in 12 Swedish cities, with over 1000 rooms in Stockholm alone (in 5 hotels). Food/beverage sales account for 57.8% of total sales, with over 9000 meals served per day. Also operates a travel agency and travel groups.

THE SERVICE WORLD INTERNATIONAL "100"

Rank	Chain	No. Rms.	No. Hotels	No. Food Units	Comments
78	Neckermann & Reisen Postfach 119091 6 Frankfurt am Main 2 Germany	3000	7	20*	This German company owns 7 hotels in Spain, France, Italy, Tunisia, Senegal and Kenya. The properties are managed individually, but head N&R office coordinates sales, advertising and administration standardization. Newcomer to "100".
79	Oberoi Hotels Ltd. 7, Alipur Rd. Delhi India	3000	15	60	Pioneering chain opened in Bombay (Oberoi Sheraton) and Colombo, Ceylon for total of 750 new rooms, 15 restaurants. Opening 4 more hotels in India (800 rooms), each with 5 restaurants. Move into international market will be target for more expansion.
80	Fujita Tourist Enterprises 2-10-8 Sekiguchi Bunkyo-ku Tokyo Japan	2867	18	62	Partners with big tourist/travel group (Fujita) added 546 rooms with additions to Nagoya, Guam and Nagano hotels. Operates resort hotels in Hakone and Izu Islands, plus city hotels.
81	Hallway Hotels Overseas 1-5 New Bond St. London England	2690	28	42	Company is interested in expanding into Europe, Pacific, Far East. Now operates hotels, resorts, fishing & wildlife lodges in Africa under management contract. Opening in Jamaica and Zanzibar in 1973.
82	Hotel New Osaka Chain 5-3-chome, Nakanoshima Kita-ku Osaka Japan	2645	12	36	Big hotels appeal not only to tourists, but to the international businessman as well. 750-room annex to famous Osaka Royal Hotel to be completed this October. Chain is planning to increase properties in Western Japan.
83	Interhotel S.A. Avda. Generalisimo 30 Madrid Spain	2625	12	36	Spanish resort chain expanded Costa del Sol hotels Triton and Siroco by 325 rooms. Computerized reservations and administration. One hotel operated under management contract.
84	Hankyu Hotel Chain 38 Kobuka-cho Kita-ku Osaka Japan	2581	9	37	Occupancy rate for Japanese chain runs as high as 97% during summer seasons! Operates airport hotel, mountain resort, and hotels in Japan's major cities. Largest is Tokyo's 700-room business hotel.
85	Petits Nids de France** 73, rue de Dunkerque Paris France	2452	88	55	A change for this strong French referral organization: dropped 1 star hotels from membership and added 3 star properties. Central reservations. Presently under study: new construction, more hotels.
86	Ind Coope Hotels Ltd. Station St. Burton-on-Trent Staffordshire England	2398	45	56	Owned by giant Allied Breweries, Ind-Coope Hotels are continuing a refurbishing and extension plan. Food sales are big and profitable: 73.7% sales from food/beverage. Will build 5 new hotels by 1978.

THE SERVICE WORLD INTERNATIONAL "100"

Rank	Chain	No. Rms.	No. Hotels	No. Food Units	Comments
87	Interisland Resorts Ltd. P. O. Box 8539 Honolulu, Hawaii U. S. A.	2381	7	17	Hawaiian resort chain diversifies into Grayline Tours and U-Drive Car Rentals. Sales in '72: $22.2 million. $12.7 million in room sales; $9.5 million in food/beverage. Occupancy rate in '72 was 62%, but company projects increase to 70% this year.
88	Radisson Hotel Corp. 12820 B 16th Ave., N. Minneapolis, Minn. U. S. A.	2342	9	24	U. S. chain now has 2 hotels in Tobago (W. Indies), just opened 350-rm. property in Tulsa, Oklahoma. Outstanding restaurant operations: food/beverage accounts for 58.8% of sales totalling $21.6 million. Building 5 hotels in 1974, 18 in next 5 years.
89	Chaine Novotel Autoroute A6 Evry France	2321	25	26	New to the "100", this growing chain added 11 hotels (1269 rms.) in 1972, will add 11 more this year and 15 in 1974! About half Novotel properties are franchised. Building all over France, many near airports. Watch this company move!
90	Gooderson Group of Hotels 34 Cato St. Durban South Africa	2290	15	39	Last year, diversified chain opened 2 new hotels: Nelspruit (90-rms.) and Johannesburg (150-rms.). More expansion expected. Other businesses include wine and liquor manufacturing, plus over 20 liquor supermarkets.
91	New Zealand Breweries Ltd. P. O. Box 2718 Wellington New Zealand	2290	78	79	While the beverage business accounts for over 80% of this company's sales, N.Z.B. is still the largest privately-owned chain in New Zealand. Built 4 hotels last year, planning more.
92	Prince Hotel Chain 3-3-1 Shibakoen Minato-ku Tokyo Japan	2284	24	59	Japan's growth chain will open two hotels this year: one in North Japan (Karuisawa Prince) with 72 rooms; one in Toronto (Don Valley Prince) with 400 rooms. The Toronto hotel is Prince's first international move. More building or acquiring outside Japan expected.
93	Xenia Hotels Voukouiestiou 22 Athens Greece	2280*	65*	80*	Very strong through the Greek Isles, this government-owned chain keeps to itself—with no public relations program. Hotels designed (innovative architecture) especially to appeal to tourists.
94	Skyline Hotels Ltd. 655 Dixon Rd. Rexdale, Ont. Canada	2225	7	18	Canadian company now international, with 1972 opening of hotel in London (300-rms.) and another London property opening this May. All other hotels are located in Canada—vie for convention business in Toronto, with 33,000 sq. ft. of convention space.

Copyright 1973, Cahners Publishing Co. *estimated figure; **referral association

THE SERVICE WORLD INTERNATIONAL "100"

Rank	Chain	No. Rms.	No. Hotels	No. Food Units	Comments
95	PLM 86 rue St. Lazare Paris France	2061	12	60	Growing, growing, growing! In 1972, the innovative PLM St. Jacques (812-rms.) opened in Paris. Now developing chain of motels in France and a catering subsidiary (industrial and welfare). Will open hotel in Guadeloupe in June, 1973. Highly diversified.
96	Princess Hotels International 1345 Avenue of the Americas New York, N.Y. U.S.A.	2060	5	22	Youthful chain with innovative architecture paused to catch its breath after big building activities. Didn't expand in 1972, but plans to build in major European cities. Operates in San Francisco, Acapulco, Bermuda (2) and Bahamas.
96	Rockresorts, Inc. 31 Rockefeller Plaza New York, N.Y. U.S.A.	2036	8	20	Partly owned by Eastern Airlines, this sprightly chain operates in Puerto Rico, Virgin Islands, Hawaii, U.S. Newest property: 503-rm. Cerromar Beach Hotel, Puerto Rico. Lodge and cabins in Wyoming. Chairman of company is Laurance S. Rockefeller.
98	Playboy Clubs and Hotels International 919 N. Michigan Ave. Chicago, Ill. U.S.A.	2025	5	23	Hefner's hotel & club empire announced new club openings in England and Montreal. Sales in '72 were $65 million, with $30 million in food/beverage. Diversification: entertainment, gaming, gift shops, resort golf courses, skiing.
99	Chaine des Hotels Concord BP 71-75021 Paris France	2000	13	18	Newcomer to "100" is opening 1000-rm. hotel in Paris next year. Properties located only in France: Paris, Angers, Lille, Marseille, Nancy, Toulouse, Metz, Melun, LeMans, Clermont Ferrand. President is Claude Taittinger. Diversification: real estate, department stores.
100	U.T.H 19, Blvd. Malesherbes Paris France	2000	14	33	Welcome to the "100"! Union Touristique at Hoteliere is sister company of U.T.H. French Airlines. Built 894 rooms in 1972 in Senegal, New Caledonia (2), Djakarta. Other hotels on U.T.H. routes. Look for further growth for this young, aggressive company!

INDEX